DREAM FACTORIES OF A FORMER COLONY

Dream Factories of a Former Colony

American Fantasies, Philippine Cinema

José B. Capino

University of Minnesota Press
Minneapolis
London

Copyright 2010 by the Regents of the University of Minnesota

All rights reserved. No part of this publication may be reproduced, stored in a retrieval system, or transmitted, in any form or by any means, electronic, mechanical, photocopying, recording, or otherwise, without the prior written permission of the publisher.

Published by the University of Minnesota Press
111 Third Avenue South, Suite 290
Minneapolis, MN 55401-2520
http://www.upress.umn.edu

Library of Congress Cataloging-in-Publication Data

Capino, José B.
 Dream factories of a former colony : American fantasies, Philippine cinema / José B. Capino.
  p. cm.
 Includes bibliographical references and index.
 Includes filmography.
 ISBN 978-0-8166-6971-4 (hc : alk. paper) — ISBN 978-0-8166-6972-1 (pb : alk. paper)
 1. Motion pictures—Philippines. 2. Myth in motion pictures. 3. Imperialism in motion pictures. 4. Culture in motion pictures. 5. United States—In motion pictures. 6. National characteristics, American, in motion pictures. 7. Motion pictures and transnationalism. 8. Motion pictures and globalization. 9. Philippines—Civilization—American influences. I. Title.

PN1993.5.P5C37 2010
791.4309599—dc22   2010019918

Printed in the United States of America on acid-free paper

The University of Minnesota is an equal-opportunity educator and employer.

17 16 15 14 13 12 11 10   10 9 8 7 6 5 4 3 2 1

For my mother, Linda

Contents

Note on Translations	ix
Acknowledgments	xi
Introduction: A Tale of Two Sisters	xiii

Part I. Visions of Empire

1. Terror Is a Man: Exploiting the Horrors of Empire	3
2. My Brother Is Not a Pig: American Benevolence and Philippine Sovereignty	33
3. (Not) Searching for My Father: GI Babies and Postcolonial Futures	69

Part II. Transnational Imaginings

4. The Migrant Woman's Tale: On Loving and Leaving Nations	107
5. Filipino American Dreams: The Cultural Politics of Diasporan Films	135

Part III. Global Ambitions

6. Naked Brown Brothers: Exhibitionism and Festival Cinema	171
7. Philippine Cinema's Fatal Attractions: Appropriating Hollywood	199
Coda: A Tale of Two Brothers	235
Notes	241
Filmography	271
Index	273

Note on Translations

When available, I use the English titles of the films given in the Internet Movie Database (imdb.com) or in English-language reviews published outside the Philippines. To the reader highly proficient in Filipino, these titles may appear awkward or stripped of resonance. My recourse to them, however, serves the aim of helping non-Filipino readers identify the films through the online resource. When I first name the films in each chapter, I note in parentheses their original titles. As for the Filipino dialogue quoted throughout this book and rendered in English, I supply my own translations, seeking to undo the semantic losses that subtitling the films' home video releases necessarily incurs.

Acknowledgments

The scuttle of Manila's byways and the idyll of Urbana's cornfields are filled with people to whom I owe a large debt of gratitude. I would like to thank dozens of colleagues at the University of Illinois at Urbana–Champaign (UIUC) but have only enough space here to mention Martin and Sandy Camargo, Ramona Curry, Lauren Goodlad, Gordon Hutner, Susan Koshy, Robert Markley, Bruce Michelson, Lisa Nakamura, Tim and Lori Newcomb, Kent Ono, Robert Dale Parker, Curtis Perry, Sarah Projansky, Junaid Rana, Ricky Rodriguez, Michael Rothberg, and Siobhan Somerville. Without the good cheer and wit of Martin Manalansan IV, Augusto Espiritu, and Anna Gonzales, my life in the prairie would not be as sweet as it has been. My gratitude also goes to the UIUC campus research board for providing research money and a semester off from teaching.

Chuck Kleinhans, my mentor in graduate school, has been my greatest supporter and friend in academia. I extend my gratitude to him as well as to other teachers, friends, and correspondents, including Nerissa Balce, Ari Berman, Salvador Bernal, Anne Ciecko, Rev. Nick Cruz, Scott Curtis, Jojo De Vera, Rolando Dionisio, Jim Erickson, Roger Garcia, Chris Holmlund, Benjamin Kahan, L. S. Kim, John Lent, Gerry Nepomuceno, Soledad Reyes, Benilda Santos, and Alexander Sherman.

At the University of Minnesota Press, Jason Weidemann championed this project from the start and lent it his fine editing skills. I thank him, along with his colleagues at the Press, especially Danielle Kasprzak and Mike Stoffel. Rick Bonus, Chris Berry, and an anonymous reader at another press offered valuable advice on revising my work. My good friend John Labella provided many useful suggestions for improving my prose and sharpening my arguments. This book is much better because of his help. Sarah Breeding and Sara Luttfring meticulously copyedited the manuscript at various stages in its development.

The wonderful Vicky Belarmino lent her expertise and optimism to my search for film stills. She took me to the following librarians and archivists who fielded my requests with patience and generosity: Mercy Servida at the Lopez Memorial Museum and Library, Mary Del Pilar and J. R. Macatangay at the ABS–CBN archive, Alice Esteves at the Cultural Center of the Philippines, Sonia Cenidoza at the Mowelfund Film Institute, and Pol Del Mundo at the Movie and Television Review and Classification Board. I found other pictures through the kind help of Gay Ace Domingo, Nestor De Guzman, Dara Hosillos, Jerry Ohlinger, Estela and Gil Portes, Rod Pulido, Joey and Eddie Romero, Malou Santos, Eric Schaefer, Samuel Sherman, Tito Velasco, and Frank Vrechek. At the Ateneo de Manila University Library, my old friend Merlyn Servañez helped me sort through microfilms and journals during two summers' worth of research.

Last but not least, I wish to express my gratitude to relatives in the United States and the Philippines who offered me shelter and encouragement while I pursued this and other scholarly ventures. Many thanks to Toni Capino and Connie Maileg; John and Madeleine Capino; Tessie and Alfonso Elmido; Elena and Mel Mistica; Minerva Elepaño; Leticia Gan; Danny, Mary, Gianna, and Katelyn Besmonte; Michael, Bernadette, Miguel, Lorenzo, and Javier Dario; and Bernardo, Linda, Joachim, Isabel, Nicole, and Jose Joaquin Capino.

INTRODUCTION

A Tale of Two Sisters

> *What the First World thinks and dreams about the Third can have nothing whatsoever in common, formally or epistemologically, with what the Third World has to know every day about the First.*
>
> —Fredric Jameson, *The Geopolitical Aesthetic*

> *After demonstrating the bloodiness of the Western instruments of vision and visuality, how do we discuss what happens when "the East" uses these instruments to fantasize itself and the world?*
>
> —Rey Chow, *Primitive Passions*

Some of the most impassioned, sensational, confounding American fantasies ever conjured on film are to be found in Philippine cinema. This is hardly surprising. Take for instance *Of Different Races* (*Magkaibang Lahi*, 1947), a romance from the dream factories of America's former colony. Ramon Estella's film is a tale of two Filipina sisters who journey to the United States just as it was shuttering its empire in the newly independent republic. This fine example of studio-era Philippine cinema begins with the ultimate American rescue fantasy. A simulated newsreel depicts MacArthur's fabled return to the Philippines to repulse the Japanese foe. Then, amid the carpet-bombed ruins of postliberation Manila, the dashing GI Charlie (Art Cantrell) "does a MacArthur" by saving the two sisters from the Japanese soldier charging at them with a bayonet.

This affirmation of U.S. might and benevolence swiftly gives way, however, to other American fantasies that are markedly ambivalent. The younger sister Nenita (Rosita Del Cielo) learns that Charlie desires to take her as his war bride. She may have once dreamed of a white man sweeping her off her feet, but after the war, that sort of American fantasy had become cheap. The romance of interracial love had devolved into sexual transactions between starving Filipinas and lonely, opportunistic GIs. Nenita confides to Charlie her worry over the social stigma of being regarded as a "jeep girl," a loose woman who flaunts her luxury, riding in American jeeps as Filipinos straggle about in the postwar mess. Nenita eventually accepts Charlie's offer of marriage after weeks of living on his precious gifts of corned beef tins. Soon after, she hops on a ship bound for the United States, chasing the immigrant's American dream. Since Charlie has yet to conclude his tour of duty in the Philippines, the older sister Cora (Corazon Noble) accompanies Nenita to Seattle, Charlie's hometown. A movie actress prior to the war, Cora is propelled to the United States by an American fantasy of her own. She believes that stateside medical technology magically would restore an arm disfigured by a bayonet wound.

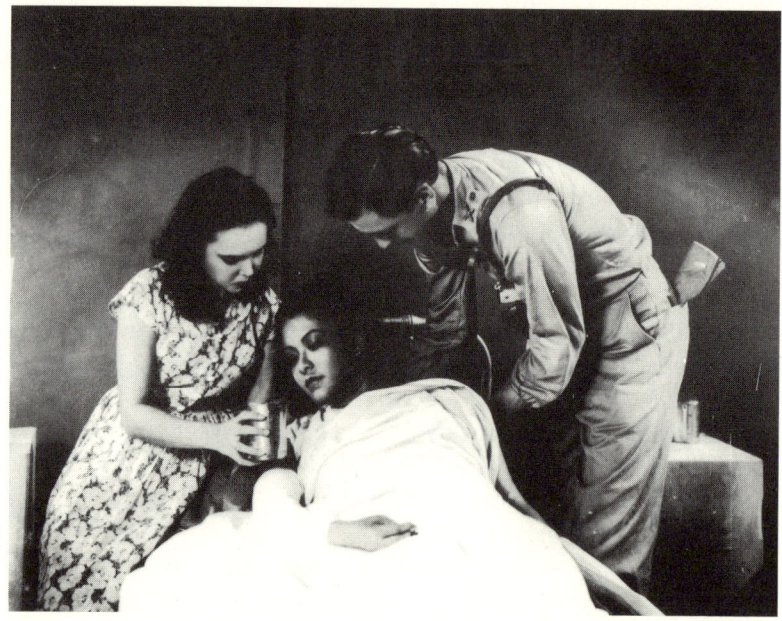

Nenita (Rosita Del Cielo) and Charlie (Art Cantrell) tend to Cora (Corazon Noble) after a Japanese soldier attacks her during the liberation of Manila. Source: Of Different Races. Courtesy of the heirs of Doña Narcisa de Leon, founder of LVN Pictures/The LVN Collection.

Upon reaching Seattle, the Filipinas discover that they are not welcome in America. Charlie's two sisters, Sophie and Nancy, mercilessly deride them when they turn up at the family home. Gripped by miscegenation hysteria, the American sisters worry over the threat posed to the family name by Charlie's interracial marriage, especially in light of Nancy's forthcoming nuptials. "Nancy is engaged to Bob," Sophie tells the Filipinas. "And his family is so particular about breeding. They don't believe in mixed marriage!"

Stunned and disheartened by the wicked sisters-in-law's poor hospitality, Nenita resolves to end her intimacy with Americans. She moves out of her in-laws' house and rejects Charlie when he finally comes for her. "We don't belong to each other anymore," she tells him while releasing herself from his embrace. "I'm not blaming you, Charlie. I'm blaming myself for dreaming of a world that couldn't be mine." Earlier in the film Nenita delivers a tirade against Charlie's sisters, touching on the ungraciousness of Americans like them: "If you were in the Philippines, you would have been given the Filipino hospitality which I've never found in this house!" Nenita's retort exposes the white folks' ingratitude toward Filipinos in whose country Charlie's compatriots had entitled themselves to live for so long.

And yet for Nenita, as for many Filipinos, the American dream dies hard. After divorcing Charlie, she returns to the Philippines with Cora and her fiancé Fidel (Ely Ramos). Unknown to Charlie, Nenita gives birth to his child and raises it with the newlyweds' patronage at Fidel's capacious rural estate. But Nenita continues to long secretly for the American just as he, in turn, longs for her. One night, in a drunken state during an unlucky round of poker, Charlie blurts out to his pals, "I'm going back to the Philippines where I could be with her, where I belong!" He returns to Manila, begging for Nenita's forgiveness and love. Because she has been secretly clinging to the same fantasy of reunification, Nenita takes him back just as soon as he arrives at Fidel and Cora's home.

The perfect ending confirms the allegorical significance of the sisters' tale. Two romantic couples emerge: one native and one interracial. The turbulent formation of the couples dwells on the question of whether—and in what manner—colonial intimacies between Americans and Filipinos might continue after the formal dissolution of empire. The film posits that the American will be welcome in the future ex-colony but only after he expresses contrition and bows to

The rescue scene depicts the devastation of Manila during World War II. Source: Of Different Races. Courtesy of the heirs of Doña Narcisa de Leon, founder of LVN Pictures/The LVN Collection.

the authority of the reinstated Filipino patriarch, represented by Fidel. This postcolonial fairy tale, of course, stood completely at odds with reality. The war left the Philippines in ruins. As historian Nick Cullather recounts, "A month of savage fighting had razed four-fifths of the capital, and with it nearly all of the country's modern industry and cultural, educational, and commercial institutions. Manila, in the words of one resident, 'presented the appearance of some hellish fair or carnival against a background of ravage and ruin.'"[1]

Because of this devastation, the country was utterly dependent on American rehabilitation aid. In the standard textbook of Philippine history, Teodoro Agoncillo recalls how America, in exchange for its aid, took advantage of such dependence by demanding parity rights to exploit the war-torn country's national resources. Agoncillo uses a sexual metaphor to describe the transaction: "The United States, then, played the role of a man who, having been aided by a friend who lost everything in defense of the former, now brashly demanded that he be given the right to live with his friend's wife in exchange for his financial help."[2]

Of Different Races' striking reversal of the historical record, as well as its ability to contain warring sentiments toward the ex-colonizer, points to the uses of American fantasies in the life of a young nation. Apart from repressing the war's intolerable memories and consequences, Estella's film offers a marvelous fantasy of decolonization in which the ex-natives are on a stronger footing with the Americans than ever before. It manages the anxiety generated by the end of colonialism and

Nenita (Rosita Del Cielo) takes Charlie (Art Cantrell) back after he returns to the Philippines for good. Source: Of Different Races. *Courtesy of the heirs of Doña Narcisa de Leon, founder of LVN Pictures/The LVN Collection.*

rationalizes the young nation's justifiable desire to keep itself tied to the apron strings of the former mother country. It counsels the Philippines' grieving citizens to put their tragedies behind them and expect a better life ahead. It is difficult to imagine the nation's psychic survival without such hopeful fantasies. With little basis for hope, the film dares to dream of transcendence while the capital lies in ashes.

American Fantasies

In both the most extravagant and the most mundane of Filipino national daydreams, the American presence looms large. *Of Different Races* is by no means unique in its recourse to what I have been calling here "American fantasies." Simply put, American fantasies are transcultural imaginings defined by an American presence.[3] One of the central tropes of Philippine cinema in the last six decades, the American fantasy occurs in the plots, figures, and settings of commercial and art pictures. In Philippine melodramas, one finds bar girls seeking GIs, young women raped by GIs, and GI babies who dream of reclaiming their white fathers' lost affections. Filipino science-fiction movies teem with American nuclear experts, cold war figures, and monsters of U.S. origins. Cowboys populate Filipino comedies, along with imitation Tarzans, Supergirls, and Maria von Trapps. The American landscape and its built environment—Central Park and the Golden Gate Bridge— furnish the setting for the triumphs and tragedies of Filipino nurses and migrant laborers. While the former subjects of U.S. colonialism remain practically invisible in Hollywood pictures, Americans and the states have kept their place as the primary others and elsewheres in Philippine cinema.

This pervasive American presence is found not only in the diegesis of the films but also in aspects that are less visible or remain entirely offscreen. The desire of Filipino filmmakers to play to U.S. audiences is one example of less conspicuous American fantasies. So are the American-inflected consumerist daydreams embodied by a film's characters or its mise-en-scène. The stylistic and ideological features of Hollywood films that are present in Filipino movies constitute yet another example of such American fantasies.

While some of these daydreams originate in the United States, courtesy of the powerful culture industry and geopolitical influence of that country, most of the American fantasies discussed in this book are kinds of transculturation. Through processes of appropriation and cultural translation, these fantasies are rewritten, indelibly marked, recirculated, or conjured by Filipinos. These screen fantasies belong to a larger repertoire of American fantasies that compose the Philippines' postcolonial imaginary of the United States. They also form part of an even larger assemblage of other nations' fantasies of America.

In Philippine cinema's postcolonial daydreams, the United States and the American function not only as the center and face of empire but also as the theater and figure of the global. At times, the American figures and images in these tales additionally function as substitutes for others. In some of these imaginings, America is either a stand-in for a powerful national figure (such as a Philippine dictator) or, to use Albert Memmi's phrase, a signifier of the very "quintessence of the West."[4] Here the Greek meaning of "fantasy" as "phantom" or "spectral apparition" is especially useful.[5] American fantasies haunt cinemas and nations in many different guises.

What, then, is the value of sorting out the American fantasies that haunt marginal cinemas and Third World countries? Why this critical turn to Filipino daydreams about America? Responding to the work of Fredric Jameson, Colin McCabe writes, "Every text at its most fundamental level is a political fantasy which in contradictory fashion articulates both the actual and potential social relations which constitute individuals within a specific political economy."[6] I am in accord with the idea that politics fantasizes. If fantasies unravel both the social relations already in existence and those yet to be, then it is important to examine what the ubiquitous American presence in fantasies might tell us about the nation invested in them. For instance, elsewhere in this book I ask why, only in the movies, Filipinos who immigrate to the states inevitably choose to come home for good. This compulsory rejection of the American dream is quite telling of the stuff that Filipino nationalism is made of.

It is important to ask what American fantasies say about the relations between the Philippines and America: the bonds between the ex-colony and empire, between a Third World country and the world's leading superpower, and between a marginal national cinema and the dominant global cinema. My earlier discussion of the film *Of Different Races* shows that by tracking the American specters lurking within this Philippine movie, one could begin to sketch a cultural history of decolonization as well as to trace a specific postcolonial cinema's development. One could, moreover, extend the coverage of such an account to this cinema's work in the current moment of globalization. After all, the persistence of American fantasies well into the postindependence era suggests their significance as Philippine figurations of geopolitics.

In case studies of Filipino films made after the end of U.S. colonialism in 1946, I will illuminate the uses of these daydreams. This book discusses the ways in which, marked by an American presence, Filipino pictures undertake diverse—even, at times, antinomial—forms of cultural work. I show how the recurring and constantly transforming American figures, plots, tropes, and elements in postwar Philippine movies are implicated in the projects of decolonization and globalization. Among other things, these fantasies have articulated empire and mobilized against it, provided imaginary maps and fables of identity for Filipino migrants in the West, posed challenges to the alibis of patriarchy and nationalism, and opened up paths for Filipino participation in global culture. One finds these American fantasies at the heart of Philippine cinema's most successful transnational exports (e.g., horror films, gay movies about male strippers) and domestic sensations (e.g., a Filipino knockoff of an American sex drama about New York yuppies), making them conventional vehicles of national introspection, transnational commerce, and intercultural dialogue.

These fantasies, in my view, have no single author, and there is no quintessential or ideal aesthetic form for their expression. What accounts for their recurrence across genres and decades is not always the deliberate work of artists. Rather, these fantasies erupt from the banal political unconscious that holds in reserve the history of anti-imperialist struggle.[7] The imaginings produced through the ex-colonials' obsessive engagement with the predicaments of imperialism and globalization are useful insofar as they produce a critique of empire, generate allegories of the ex-colonials' situation, and devise audacious schemes for winning the struggle against the titans of geopolitics and those local agents who subtend their oblique powers.[8] More specifically, American fantasies provide scenarios for working out some of the most persistent issues of national and geopolitical import—such issues as sovereignty, social justice, gender equality, hospitality, national culture and pedagogy, and the well-being of Filipino citizens abroad. The broad cultural work of these films is accountable not only to the annals of Philippine cinema but also to the larger story of postcolonial and transnational film. Elucidating that work is the project of this book.

In her gloss on social fantasy, Neferti Tadiar proposes that national imaginaries secure the state's hegemonic control over citizens while also sponsoring the interests of "an international order of production" alternately called the "Free World" and "multinational capitalism."[9] While a nation's "fantasy-production practices"[10] also seek to invent "alternative imaginaries"[11] and "unorthodox possibilities for historical change,"[12] they must work both within and against the world system's limited repertoire of imaginable possibilities. For Tadiar, the postcolonial nation's fantasies subscribe to "the codes of international fantasy"[13] and are reined in by the "imaginary of the international capitalist system."[14] Using this model of the imaginary, Tadiar analyzes tropes of the social, political, and economic developments in the Philippines during and beyond the Marcos regime. While *Dream Factories of a Former Colony* also studies the imaginings of Filipinos in relation to the domain of national and world politics, the intricacy of cinematic fantasies leads me to the work of another scholar besides Tadiar—one who duly recognizes fantasy's confounding play.

Jacqueline Rose offers a model of social fantasy that I find most useful. Her study illumines the literary and cultural productions of Israeli and South African nation making. Rose acknowledges that fantasies, such as Israel's dreams of national becoming, could be shared collectively and historically, and yet these national daydreams can also take on surprisingly different and unpredictable shapes in the minds of individuals and at certain historical junctures. Drawing on the unconscious, fantasies are wracked with contradictions and erratic desires. One of the keys to understanding fantasy, Rose tells us, is having the expectation that there is "something coerced and coercive, but also wild and unpredictable, about it."[15] At times, a fantasy is as fierce as can be, as when the dream of nationhood underwrites the deadly violence of revolution. But the same fantasy is not always quite as inexorable. It may propose, at one moment, the antagonist's obliteration, but "unequal to its own injunctions, lets slip just a little," yielding to a possible truce.[16] It happens that "fantasy's supreme characteristic," Rose tells us, "is that of running ahead of itself."[17] This account of fantasy's inconstant aims and energies is useful in thinking about the astounding twists and turns of American fantasy narratives, the unexpected figurations and workings of decolonization and globalization, and the erratic intensity and indirection of feelings engendered by such daydreams. The unpredictability of fantasies calls for nothing less than an imaginative critique.

In the succeeding sections I will offer a definition of key terms and a preview of the book's various chapters.

Decolonization and Globalization

It is useful to think of "decolonization" beyond its customary political significance as the termination of colonial rule or as the removal of the natives' legal subject status. The editors of an anthology on "the decolonization of the imagination" usefully note that there are "many different modes of decolonization." One such mode historically entailed a cultural liquidation of colonialism that "anticipated and paved the way for political decolonization, accompanied it, and follows independence."[18] The diversity of decolonizing processes is due to the diffuse character of the colonial enterprise they seek to bring to closure. As the editors contend, "Since colonization was a highly complex process, decolonization lacks a clear focus and target."[19] This broad and intricate affair of decolonization is an unfinished project and one that plays out in the everyday. For the formerly colonized and their descendants, Albert Memmi writes, everyday life is an "interminable convalescence from the consequences of colonization."[20] Mundane efforts of dealing with empire help significantly in accomplishing the work of decolonization, although for some ex-natives the utopian dream of the absolute "liquidation of colonization" remains as the necessary precondition to their "complete liberation . . . [and] to self-recovery."[21]

Reflecting this diverse conception of decolonization, scholars of culture and cinema offer varying accounts of films' engagement in the work of overcoming empire. It is worth mentioning here the four most commonly identified contributions of cinema to the decolonizing process.

First, films of decolonization proffer a remembrance of the past. They reckon with history, returning to the scene of colonial encounters to exorcise a traumatic past or to mourn colonialism's painful legacies. History returns in several of the films discussed here, as flashbacks of

World War II alliances between Filipinos and Americans, as memories of confrontations between Filipino civilians and American soldiers, and as anecdotes about fallen American leaders betrayed by their nation's ideals. One finds variety in such discourses about the colonial past and in the stylistic representations of these haunting memories.

Related to the first, the second function of these films is to critique the unfinished business of colonialism.[22] "Documenting the abuses of the colonial past" is only one part of a "double approach" in films about imperialism that, according to Roy Armes, often scrutinize colonialism's ongoing impact on contemporary society as well.[23] Films play a part in unmasking new forms of imperial power through a regime most popularly called "neocolonialism" or, in more recent accounts, "new imperialism" and the global capitalist regime of "Empire."[24] Some of Philippine cinema's American fantasies juxtapose current issues with their historical antecedents as when, in films about the U.S. bases, the present-day suffering of Filipinos under American militarism is traced to the lingering effects of colonial domination.

Third, movies that belong to the period of decolonization supply fables of identity. The shedding of a people's subject status or their changing relationship to empire necessitates the fashioning of new identities. Anticolonial or anti-imperialist nationalism has often provided the scripts for such fables of the self.[25] As we shall see in certain of the films discussed in this book, however, identity formation also takes place through a refusal of the scripts given by nation and culture. In films of the Filipino diaspora, one finds characters who do just that.

Fourth, the films of decolonization propose fantasy solutions and visions of the future. They dream up utopian possibilities, including imaginary cures to the problems of colonialism and other "unresolvable social contradictions" of contemporary life.[26] Moreover, as we have seen in the fantasy of the sisters in *Of Different Races*, these envisioned solutions add up to resplendent images of a future in which decolonization—an impossible dream, by Gayatri Spivak's reckoning—is finally achieved.[27] As the example of the two sisters demonstrates, some of Philippine cinema's most hopeful fantasies not only imagine the ex-natives' transcendence of the colonial encounter but also propose new ways of living with America or even empire in its current guises.

The event of globalization overlaps the unfinished, utopian decolonization project in many ways and at different moments. On the surface, decolonization enacts a repudiation of the West, whereas globalization tends toward rapprochement. Both of these processes, however, sustain a dialectical play of relations between the ex-colony and its former ruler. Such relays call for examination and engagement. It is easy enough to make the distinction on the basis of historical periodizations: decolonization refers to "a precise event: the end of colonial rule and the coming into being of independent nation-states" around the mid-twentieth century, while contemporary globalization—in the popular sense of an "accelerated movement across national and regional barriers of . . . people, products, capital"—ostensibly took off much later, in the 1970s.[28] Studying the cultural dimension of globalization, John Tomlinson maintains that "what replaces 'imperialism' is 'globalisation.'"[29] In this view, what we attribute to the latter phase of the decolonization process (i.e., since the 1960s) could be subsumed into—or deemed interchangeable with—globalization. For Roland Robertson, however, "the crucial take-off period of globalization itself . . . [was] 1880–1925," thus preceding not only decolonization but also the very founding of the transcontinental American imperium.[30]

For the modest purposes of this study, I stress the continuity rather than the disjunction of these processes, even as I tentatively draw a distinction between decolonization's overriding preoccupation with a country's relation to one Western entity (namely, the ex-colonizer) and globalization's variable engagement with a more plural conception of the West and East. Decolonization entails an ongoing struggle to break the colonial dyad: "The relentless reciprocity," as Sartre puts it, "[that] binds the colonizer to the colonized."[31] In globalization, even abjected citizens—like factory workers at export-processing zones or tribal peoples aided by transnational environmental groups—are called to think in planetary terms. It may also be useful at times to make this distinction on the national level, where decolonization is largely concerned with nation making, while globalization moves us to seek alternatives to the singularity of nation by exploring other forms of collective belonging, such as transnationalism. This is not to discount the fact that the condition of global visibility sometimes heightens the old desire for national definition—it does, but differently, as I will explain in the succeeding paragraph. In thinking about the role of cultural production beyond decolonization, it is useful to consider one of Rey Chow's questions in her justly celebrated study of Chinese film.

She invites us to consider what else animates Third World cultures apart from "the struggle against the West." She asks, "What if the primary interest of a 'third world culture' is not that of resistance against Western domination?"[32] I respond to these questions by discussing, for instance, Philippine cinema's global exports and showing what it means to collude with the West in nonconflicting and productive ways.

In addition to film's "decolonizing" work, cinema abets and figures globalization in at least two ways. First, films cultivate an awareness of global relations. Fredric Jameson observes that movies help us think (often subconsciously) about our place in the "now global social totality," our role in the unimaginably vast and complex "new multinational world system" of late capitalism.[33] Like other cultural objects, films help us sketch a "cognitive map" of the unimaginably complex workings of a transnational capitalism that shapes our lives in many conspicuous and unseen ways.[34] Impacted by these global operations on all levels, cinema's fantasies register mundane geopolitical relations (i.e., the sexual and material economies linking migrant Filipina nurses and their American patients) as well as less visible relations and processes (i.e., how global finance capital impacts local economies).

Second, films serve the purpose of what I call, for lack of a better term, "global projection." What is projected to the "world"—which may or may not be watching—are the individually and collectively authored images and acts of persons, localities, and nations. Projections are self-conscious and hopeful ways of managing immense and largely uncontrollable aspects of globalization. They entail launching into the vast regions of cosmopolitan fantasies, magnifying the Third World's inconspicuous and marginalized gestures. Because filmmakers negotiate this desired global agency and presence in the realm of the visual, they must wrestle with what Rey Chow terms the "menace" of visuality.[35] Participating in a game of power where images define, enable, and chain all of us, filmmakers bear the burden of projecting visions seductive enough to draw the world's attention and yet plausible enough so that they might claim a relationship to reality. The possibility of failure and unintended outcomes pervades this attempt to act globally and to negotiate how one is seen by the world. Invisibility, however, has become impossible, and impotence, an unacceptable fate. For a small nation to project itself and draw attention to itself in the global system's busy visual field, the country needs to marshal its cultural resources, tap into its familiarity with Western audiences and their desires, and learn to work those venues where the Third World typically commands attention. Filipino remakes of Hollywood films are intriguing examples of global projection, as I will demonstrate in one of this book's chapters.

Philippine Cinema

In this book I will use the term "Philippine cinema" in a broad cultural sense, referring not only to films made in that country but also to diasporan and transnational productions financed or made elsewhere by those who identify themselves as Filipinos. My inclusion of films from all three spheres of cinematic location—the national, the diasporan, and the transnational—represents an attempt to move beyond the delimited province of national cinema historiography in order to do justice to the geographic spread and ambitions of both Philippine cinema and the Filipino experience. That said, I am unable to give equal prominence to each of these three spheres. I devote just one—albeit the longest—chapter of this book to diasporan films. The remaining six chapters treat the much larger corpus of works from the overlapping national and transnational spheres.

It may seem odd to describe a small, Third World country's cinema as transnational, or for that matter, to suggest that Philippine cinema is an exemplary site for observing the imbrication of the national and transnational spheres of cinema. I hope to make a case for these counterintuitive notions in this book and in so doing contribute to a broader discussion of national cinema and transnational film practices.

Films that have been labeled "transnational" by scholars such as Gina Marchetti, Sheldon Lu, and Marvin D'Lugo include those (a) made through "global film finance arrangements" (i.e., international coproductions);[36] (b) produced partly or mainly for audiences outside the nation (i.e., films with transnational appeal and that circulate transnationally);[37] (c) partly or fully set outside the nation (e.g., transnational adventures)[38] or in cosmopolitan spaces within the nation (what Jameson calls "multinational spaces");[39] (d) made by transnational auteurs or international stars who operate across nations and cultures and whose presence signals a foreign element in the work;[40] (e) invested in projecting transnational cultural identities (i.e., diasporan films, films about exiles and migrant laborers);[41] and (f) written in the transnational grammar of narrative film (e.g., a transnational hybrid cinematic form or transnational filmic discourse).[42]

In the case studies within this book, I will be discussing some of the previously mentioned transnational film practices. I also want to contribute to the list two practices of transnational film that I have come to understand by tracking Philippine cinema's American fantasies. First, I posit as transnational those films that make visible the transnational consciousness and structures created by both imperialism and postcolonial cultures. Insofar as movies represent to such nations their common dilemmas and parallel struggles, such works should be considered transnational films. Some of these films militantly take on transnational anti-imperialist causes, functioning as instruments in the tricontinental struggle against neocolonial violence and exploitation.

Second, I call attention to the transnationalism borne out of a practice Dick Hebdige calls "'mundane' cosmopolitanism."[43] Three of my case studies show alternate ways of traversing the real and imagined borders of national cinema, in some instances without even showing the film abroad. One example is an unauthorized remake of an American film in which a Filipina actress "does a Glenn Close" and seizes her Hollywood moment. Although this particular film was rarely shown outside the Philippines, I consider its making a form of transnationalism in cinema. In such kinds of transnational films, the cosmopolitan experience is recreated locally and then explicitly or implicitly offered as an international object or act. This practice is connected with the concept of projection within globality that I mentioned earlier. Lacking the means of mobility, the cultural capital, or the financial resources literally to *go* global, these films put the imagination to work in everyday acts of participation (let us call them cultural citizenship) within transnational culture. One might count this tactic among the "weapons of the weak," to borrow James Scott's popular phrase, within the cultures of globality.

Although some of my conceptions of transnationalism in film may apply only to the specific case of Philippine cinema, I venture that the project of articulating American fantasies could serve as a model for studying other cinemas as well. The value of this study's example lies in its multifaceted approach to conceptualizing the presence of the foreign in national, transnational, and postcolonial cinemas. To account for this foreign presence, I suggest that we look at its many possible guises. As I described earlier, American fantasies pertain, but are not limited to, the following: foreign characters, plots, and settings; the spectral influence of foreign film languages and genre conventions; the film's foreign travails and its international audience; and the transnational and geopolitical relations envisioned and impacted by the film. In the Philippine case, the long history of U.S. colonial rule and neocolonial influence gives a peculiar coloration to American fantasies. While I am sure that those fantasies unique to the Philippines require distinct reading strategies, many American fantasies that cut across national imaginaries could be studied through an array of common reading practices. Indeed, the American fantasies and Philippine films in this book tell a story that is not unfamiliar to other countries. That story tells of how the United States reordered and policed the postwar world, abetted and suppressed nationalist feelings and movements, preserved and endangered democracies and economies, offered an enduring vision of an ideal society, and propagated a language of cinematic fantasy and melodramatic despair that "natives" have repurposed.

To give examples of other cinemas whose American fantasies deserve study, we will turn to a period film from Taiwan and a melodrama from Korea. First, let us consider the intricate picture of postwar geopolitics, postcolonial nationalism, and transnational film form envisioned in Edward Yang's monumental film, *A Brighter Summer Day* (*Guling jie shaonian sha ren shijian*, 1991). The film revolves around awkward teens coming of age in the 1960s. As the children of nationalists who fled to the island when the communists triumphed in China, these youths are oblivious to their parents' nostalgia for the mainland. In their search for identity, the teens look toward the West, specifically by behaving like juvenile delinquents from American movies. They hit their teachers with baseball bats, dress like James Dean, and replicate the sound and feeling of Elvis Presley songs they barely understand.

The strong Western influence is not alone, however, in shaping Taiwanese identity. At various moments in the film, signs of the eight-year Japanese occupation resurface enigmatically alongside American specters. The film's hero, Xiao Si'r, lives in an old Japanese-style house that yields a hidden samurai sword and a tape deck, left there by its former Japanese and American residents. On certain nights, Japanese music wafts in from a nearby fruit vendor. At other times, the radio carries the rants of political commentators, one of whom derides "that young punk" John F. Kennedy for being too green to fight the communists. Even the family's bodily functions are affected by Japanese and American influences. Si'r relieves himself in a latrine covered by a shoji screen. In an earlier scene, we hear his older sister's habit of bathing in the morning described as "American-style." These signs of culture, politics, or war from influential foreign nations figure symbolically in the film's tale of displacement, historical change, and the emergence of a new Taiwanese nationalism. Further interpretive work on this film's American fantasy may lead to a consideration of such issues as the changing significance of the American figure in images of Taiwanese history, this Taiwanese new wave film's curious relationship to Hollywood films such as Nicholas Ray's *Rebel Without a Cause* (1955), and the complex geopolitics of Taiwan's place in the new world order.

In Kim Ki-duk's *Address Unknown* (2001), set in a village outside a U.S. military base, American specters play a negative role in the making of South Korea.[44] Propelled into madness, self-mutilation, and murder, Kim's characters are barefaced symbols of the strain empire places on Korean nationalism. Chang-guk, the film's antihero, is a half-black Amerasian who spends his days stewing in the hatred of himself and everyone around him. His crazed mother, who lives in a bus discarded by the U.S. Air Force, never tires of writing his American father even if her letters keep returning as undelivered mail. One of Chang-guk's neighbors, a young woman with an eye injury, has an American suitor offering to find her a cure. Like Cora in *Of Different Races*, the young Korean woman and the rest of the characters pin their hopes on American benevolence but end up disenchanted. As Kim's convoluted plot unravels, the scenes of disillusionment escalate to moments of horror. Before the end credits roll, we witness all kinds of trauma, all traceable in some way to the U.S. base. These include the butchering of dogs, the exhumation of a communist killed during the Korean War, the piercing of several eyeballs, an episode of incest and bestiality, the wounding of genitals, a gang rape, a murder, and a suicide. The sensationalism of *Address Unknown* seems born out of desperate necessity. Its excesses are founded on the grief of living at the military contact zone.

The affinity of Korean cinema with Taiwan and the Philippines lies in their shared need to speak *of* and *to* empire. Of course, the currency and form of their statements vary widely. Viewed as a constellation nonetheless, their American fantasies lend insight into the exigencies of colonial modernity, development and underdevelopment, domination and resistance, and intimacy and estrangement.

The constellation of approaches that I use in studying American fantasies draws from the innovative projects of other film scholars and cultural critics. Thomas Elsaesser and Tom O'Regan write about the presence of American figures and Hollywood elements in foreign cinemas. Allan Isaac elucidates literary and cultural texts that revolve around American fantasies of its colonies and former colonial subjects. Mette Hjort's work in charting Danish cinema's response to Hollywood provides an imaginative case study of the periphery's response to metropolitan culture. Angelo Restivo and Eric Cadzyn gesture toward new ways of reading the signs of postwar economic development and social upheavals in film and culture. The studies of postcolonial cinema by Roy Armes, Priya Jaikumar, and John Mowitt undertake comparative and transnational critiques of film and empire. Fredric Jameson and Rey Chow give us a range of provocative concepts for thinking about film in relation to geopolitics. In the chapters that follow, I call attention to my intellectual debts to some of these scholars, as well as to many others besides them, whose fine scholarship has enabled my own.[45]

The limitations of this study are also worth acknowledging here. First, this book does not seek to propose a grand theory of postcolonial visuality even if it offers a broadly applicable model for studying postcolonial, national, and transnational cinemas. I cannot imagine a theory both simple and complex enough to account for the imprints left by empire's different stages on the fields of cinema and nation. In undertaking a critique of neglected cinematic formations what is often needed is not so much a theory, new or old, but a variety of approaches that illuminate particular cinematic practices and the stakes of cultural production more generally.

Second, this book does not account for all the manifestations of Philippine cinema's American fantasies. Because they have already been well elucidated in recent scholarship, I opt not to study the many films about Filipinos and Americans fighting side by side in World War II.[46] Also, due to potential overlaps with certain parts of this book, I must forego the chance to discuss some of my favorite comedies about Filipino travelers in the states and parodies of American media figures.[47]

Third, this study deals by and large with commercial films. There are good reasons for this choice. Although belittled by critics, popular movies teem with American fantasies, are generally understudied, and are more likely to acknowledge those wayward desires for America that art cinema or agitprops often deny. Due also to the limited circulation of Filipino avant-garde films both in the Philippines and abroad, I refrain from elucidating the American fantasies in experimental works such as Nick Deocampo's *Oliver* (1983).

The Plan of the Book

I now turn to specific American fantasies and particular workings of decolonization and globalization in a variety of Filipino movies. This study selectively covers American fantasies in films made since the Philippines gained independence from the United States in 1946. To elucidate the cultural work of these fantasies, I perform close readings of the films, zooming in on the textures and strands of the daydreams in light of their historical or social contexts. I will draw upon a wide variety of ideas in cultural theory and cinema studies to frame my interpretations.

This book is divided, according to constellations of American fantasies, into three parts and seven chapters. Part I, "Visions of Empire," studies films that configure Filipino encounters with U.S. imperialism in its past, present, and future guises. In chapter 1, "Terror Is a Man: Exploiting the Horrors of Empire," I explain how the ghosts of imperialism returned to America in the unlikely form of science-fiction horror films made by Filipinos especially for U.S. drive-in theaters. By tapping into the banal political unconscious of an ex-colonized people, these transnational productions exported more than blood, sex, and schlock. They also dispatched images of U.S.-instigated violence in the Third World to a nation often forgetful of its imperial doings. Interestingly enough, these oblique figurations of U.S. imperialism may be counted among the most economically successful Philippine envoys to America and the rest of the world.

A direct representation of the horrors of contemporary U.S. imperialism may be found in the films that compose chapter 2, "My Brother Is Not a Pig: American Benevolence and Philippine Sovereignty." Here

I discuss political films that take up a stridently anti-imperialist stance toward the U.S. military bases. Made between the mid-1970s and the late 1980s, before the dismantling of the controversial installations, these agitprops mourn the fantasy of the benevolent U.S. empire by rendering testimony to its incursions upon the sovereignty of the Philippine nation-state. By proffering sensational images of the maimed, the defiled, and the dead, these films enjoin a contemplation of the biopolitics of U.S. military presence in the former colony. At the same time, the narratives' implicit critique of America's infidelity to its own ideals shows traces of hope in the realization of the intimate ex-colonizer's avowed benevolence.

In chapter 3, "(Not) Searching for My Father: GI Babies and Postcolonial Futures," I turn to specters of future relations between the ex-colonizer and the ex-colonized. Such visions of the future may be glimpsed in three films about Amerasian children seeking to reunite with the white fathers who have abandoned them. Although these films depicting the plight of the "GI baby" are often reductive, I contend that what accounts for this reductive quality is their interest not in social realism but in allegorical representation. I then proceed to show how the films could be read as parables of the nation's fate after empire. Owing to the hybrid identity of the films' Amerasian protagonists, their tales unleash ambivalent feelings toward both empire and nation, thereby offering unusual visions of the postcolonial order of things.

The fantasies in Part II, "Transnational Imaginings," locate Filipinos in America. The two women's films discussed in chapter 4, "The Migrant Woman's Tale: On Loving and Leaving Nations," involve two Filipinas who achieve success in the states but are lured back to the homeland by the appeals of nationalism and romance. One of them turns a critical eye to the emptiness and complacency of her middle-class life. The other sees in that life things more precious than material rewards, namely, emotional strength, personal independence, and social power. Despite their differing views, the decision to repatriate is shown as an agonizing ordeal for both women—an indication that these female melodramas challenge not just the myth of the American dream but also the alibis of Filipino nationalism and patriarchy.

Chapter 5, "Filipino American Dreams: The Cultural Politics of Diasporan Films," attends to the diaspora's broken dreams of assimilation.

The second-generation Filipino American protagonists in this chapter seek their place in U.S. multicultural society by trying to retrieve a usable ethnic identity and cultural inheritance. Instead of stabilizing their identity as American men of color, they discover only repulsive brokenness among an older generation of Filipino men ruined or forsaken by their American dreams. Their fantasy of assimilation turns alternately into a pipe dream of critical Asian American nationalism or a nightmare of ethnic self-allergy.

In Part III, "Global Ambitions," I turn to fantasies of globalization that are elaborated in an ostensibly "American" manner. Chapter 6, "Naked Brown Brothers: Exhibitionism and Festival Cinema," looks at gay-oriented sex melodramas aimed at "American" and First World audiences. In catering to the perceived fantasies of gay foreigners, these films exoticize Filipinos but mitigate the gratuitous display of skin by flashing political agendas on national and global screens. Moreover, the transnational enterprise of appealing to a Western audience benefits the development of both Filipino gay politics and gay cinema. Chapter 7, "Philippine Cinema's Fatal Attractions: Appropriating Hollywood," studies two unauthorized adaptations of American causes célèbres: Lorena Bobbit's mutilation of her husband's penis and Adrian Lyne's 1987 sex drama *Fatal Attraction*. The restaging of these globally popular spectacles permits Filipino actors and spectators to imagine themselves within the mise-en-scène of globalization and to participate in the ecumene of global culture through the entrée provided by an American culture intimate to them.

Across six decades of Philippine films, we find a pervasive recurrence of American fantasies performing diverse cultural work. Culture, after all, is a pivotal site for the processes we call decolonization and globalization. The cinema offers an immense vocabulary of images, scenarios, and allegories for these national and transnational projects. Its commodious language registers the most discrete shifts in culture and lends itself to nearly every kind of social fantasy a people could invent.

I

Visions of Empire

1

Terror Is a Man

Exploiting the Horrors of Empire

The task of rewriting the story of empire is arguably one of the chief projects of cinema during the long era of decolonization.[1] In the case of Philippine cinema, the most widely seen corpus of films about the encounter with U.S. imperialism consists not of historical dramas but of science-fiction horror films. A testimony to fantasy's unpredictable workings, these "B-movies" tell imperialism's history in scenes of blood-curdling terror, mild eroticism, and immensely pleasurable schlock. In what one might call a mundane case of unsolicited postcolonial justice, the films were seen not by the ex-colonized, who knew empire's story well, but by the patrons of American drive-in theaters and grindhouses, many of whom were unfamiliar with their country's doings in the former colony. Moreover, beyond the fact that these films let the ghosts of the imperial past return to haunt a nation that sometimes forgot about its imperial encounters, they sustained a transnational commerce. The monster pictures brought fame and profit to the Filipinos and Americans who made and sold them.

When Quentin Tarantino came to the Philippines in 2007 to receive an award at an international film festival, he told the entertainment press that he wanted to meet two native filmmakers he greatly admired: Eddie Romero and Cirio H. Santiago. He also gushed about the late Gerry de Leon, confessing he was "a huge, huge fan" of the Filipino director.[2]

The American director's affirmation of the three native directors brought to light a chapter in film history that was largely obscure even in the Philippines. Tarantino was giddily paying tribute not to their domestic oeuvres but to the fruits of their two-decades-long adventure shooting low-budget "American" movies in the Philippines. Many

Filipinos had come to know Romero only for his historical epics, De Leon for his prestige films, and Santiago for his commercial movies during the studio era. What Tarantino had in mind were the cheap, somewhat ragged, often sensational genre pictures called "exploitation films" that the Filipino directors supplied to far-flung drive-in theaters, second-run cinemas, and late-night television programming from the late 1950s to the 1970s.[3] Most of these Philippine-produced American fantasies were made especially for the U.S. and foreign markets. Bypassing local theaters entirely, they were exported directly there. This oeuvre of transnational Philippine cinema includes, among others, a string of war films such as *Cavalry Command* (produced by Santiago and directed by Romero, 1963), the science-fiction horror films that will be discussed in this chapter, and successful women-in-prison films such as *Black Mama, White Mama* (Romero, 1973), featuring Blaxploitation star Pam Grier.

Romero, like De Leon and Santiago, never made it big in Hollywood but operated instead within the margins of the American film industry. He entered that industry in 1957, just as the classic B-movies and exploitation films were giving way to the teenpics and sexploitation films that would rule low-budget filmmaking in the following decade and a half.[4] His and the other Filipino directors' American careers flourished during a window of time when the Hollywood majors neglected the expansive youth and rural audiences and failed to meet the staggering demand created by the popularity of double-bill programs, especially at drive-in theaters.[5] The low-budget production outfits that Romero and company worked for, invested in, or helped found catered to these audiences and venues by rapidly churning out new, cheap movies—often violent and racy—or dubbing and repackaging foreign films. For instance, De Leon's vampire film *Kulay dugo ang gabi* (*Blood Is the Color of Night*, 1964) was given English dialogue, tinted, reedited, and renamed *The Blood Drinkers* (1966). As was common in exploitation film production, even their freshly made films were often derivative of older American movies and British literature. Romero himself acknowledged that he sometimes engaged in a "polite steal" of Western cultural productions.[6] Apart from cannibalizing the scenario of H. G. Wells's novel *The Island of Doctor Moreau* several times, he also appropriated the plot of Stanley Kramer's film *The Defiant Ones* (1958) to draw up the scenario of *Black Mama, White Mama* (1973).[7]

Romero recalls participating in the industry as a cofounder of production outfits (Lynn-Romero Productions, Hemisphere) and as a writer-director of films "financed entirely by Americans" and "made-to-order for American distribution prior to production."[8] His work involved "wheeling and dealing" in the states, filming entirely in the Philippines, and maintaining ties to distribution operations in New York or Los Angeles.[9] Sometimes he would supervise productions filmed in the Philippines by American directors or even shoot Filipino-language versions of those films with the same sets, crew, and some of the same actors.[10] While many of the films succeeded at the box office, Romero said he was gypped at times by his U.S. partners. "People were always trying to rip me off," he claimed. "If you think it's bad here [in the Philippines], it's 10 times worse in Hollywood . . . One of our films made a lot of money, and the distributor bought a Mercedes Benz for his wife and included it in his distribution cost."[11]

Though lionized in his native Philippines mainly for such prestige films as *This Is the Way It Was . . . How Is It Today?* (1976), a sprawling meditation on Filipino identity set during the end of Spanish colonialism and the beginning of American empire, Romero had always been rather proud of his success in the less reputable enterprise of making B-movies for the United States. In a 1997 interview for the Asian film journal *Cinemaya*, Romero noted that *Black Mama, White Mama* "made $12 million in the US alone."[12] Two years earlier, he had told film scholar Bliss Cua Lim that his World War II drama, *The Walls of Hell* (1964), "made more money in Scandinavia than any other war film except *The Longest Day*."[13]

For Romero, the success of his low-budget American fantasies was the fulfillment of a dream, nurtured since his childhood in then U.S.-controlled Philippines, to make "some modest films, using some American acting talent, for American distribution . . . to be part of the mainstream of American culture, to be in fact an American."[14] Meeting the standard of American movies, he said, also meant having the opportunity to hone his technical skills. "These B-pictures were in fact very challenging for a Filipino director," he told filmmaker Manny Reyes in an interview. "Their requirements for cinematography, for editing, were much higher than local movies."[15] While Romero admits that some of his exploitation films "were the worst things" he ever did, he stresses that even "a terrible film" like *Brides of Blood* made a "tremendous impression" in the exploitation circuit.[16] By all accounts, he was not exaggerating. Like Santiago and De Leon, Romero's competence in producing American fantasies secured him a place in the pantheon (or capacious ghetto) of American low-budget filmmakers.[17] It brought him deals with some of the most important production and distribution outfits of the exploitation circuit: American International Pictures, Dimension Pictures, and New World Productions.[18] Until his death, Santiago continued to be involved in making low-budget films for foreign markets and, along with Romero and De Leon, his work still commands fanboy admiration from cinephiles such as Tarantino.

The stateside success of these Filipino directors primed the international distribution of their work. These films are the first of several examples I will give in this book of Filipino-made American fantasies that travel widely because of their contrived "Americanness." This oeuvre is also an example of cultural productions made

Eddie Romero confers with Francis Lederer and cinematographer Emmanuel Rojas on the set of Terror Is a Man. Courtesy of Eddie and Joey Romero.

during the period of decolonization that circulate internationally and thus presage the future event of globalization. The traces of the global exportation of these Philippine-made American fantasies survive to this day through the traffic in Mexican, Spanish, Italian, and German posters, lobby cards, and press kits of the films at fan conventions and in the virtual marketplace of the Internet.

The focus of this chapter is a small but prominent group of the low-budget films I discussed previously. My particular interest here is a study of four science-fiction horror movies set in a place called "Isla de Sangre"—later Anglicized as "Blood Island"—an imaginary place somewhere in the Pacific but represented on screen by the Philippines. The four Blood Island films—*Terror Is a Man* (1959), *Brides of Blood* (1968), *Mad Doctor of Blood Island* (1968), and *Beast of Blood* (1971)—are directed alternately or in tandem by Romero and De Leon.[19] These filmmakers engage in what Judith Halberstam calls the "production of monstrosity" by both drawing on and dissimulating the history of empire.[20] Scenarios contrived to bring whites, natives, and monsters together on a nondescript island already set into motion a colonial narrative. In these films, however, what fundamentally shapes the vision of monstrosity is the *ex*-colonial relationship between Filipinos and Americans. To produce ghouls that menace natives and whites, the Filipino auteurs tap into their knowledge of American imperialist ventures abroad as well as into the political unconscious of their ex-colonized people.[21] The filmmakers exploit the versatile technology of monsters—a technology that allows grotesque bodies to signify a plethora of meanings—in order to represent the horrors of colonial and other encounters.[22] As expected of any attempt at repression, the task of muting the specificities of Filipino–American relationships—from the past colonial affair to the present business of coproducing movies—both succeeds and fails.

Chalmers Johnson notes that while "it is typical of an imperial people to have a short memory for its less pleasant imperial acts . . . for those on the receiving end, memory can be long indeed."[23] The ex-colonials' conscious and unconscious recollection of these acts resulted in cultural commodities projecting the history of American empire obliquely to U.S. audiences, while profiting from both Filipinos and Americans.

Several times here I have alluded to the fact that United States culture restricts the visibility of American empire. Its apparitions are sporadic and fleeting. The outward denial or quiet repression of the continuing history of American colonialist enterprise and imperialist conduct is part of the discourse of American exceptionalism. This notion of America's specialness or exemplary nature claims, for instance, that the United States never commits certain kinds of violence (e.g., engaging in colonialism) or, if it does, applies it only for justified reasons (e.g., propping up dictators to preempt communism or to wield nuclear weapons to protect the free world).[24] I wish to suggest that the Blood Island films rectify empire's deficient awareness of itself. They embed narratives critical of empire.

Political scientists and literary critics have shown how the history of U.S. imperialism has been variably occluded through such claims of exceptionalism.[25] Chalmers Johnson has shed light on the "hidden imperial scenarios"[26] of American "global military-economic dominion."[27] Amy Kaplan and Allan Isaac have pointed out the fact that depictions of American empire are all too rare in U.S. culture. Eddie Romero himself suspected that his country, America's only former colony, was somewhat unknown to the U.S. audiences he was catering to. When asked why the Philippines was called "Blood Island" in his films, he speculated that it was done for audiences who "wouldn't know where the Philippines was."[28] Happily, my task here is not the usual one of demonstrating or bemoaning the invisibility of empire. My goal instead is to elucidate the *fantastic* terms of visibility that are the paradoxical result of intent and happenstance. The ex-colonial's fantasy serves to figure (out) empire: to see through its invisibility, to trade in its images, and to bring into relief its unintended consequences.

Appropriately, the figuration of empire in the films discussed here takes the form of a postcolonial commerce in "blood," a mode of visibility proper to the violence of imperialism. In American-produced films that "exploit" Filipino filmmaking labor and the ex-colonial people's political unconscious, empire's past resurfaces. It is interesting—and rather ironic—to note that one of Romero's earlier transnational efforts, *Cavalry Command* (a.k.a. *Day of the Trumpet*, 1963), gave a direct and flattering portrayal of American empire's beginnings. Curiously enough, this war film valorizes U.S. pacification efforts during the Philippine–American War, one of the bloodiest conflicts in modern history. *Cavalry Command* did not enjoy, however, the commercial success of the monster movies that figured the imperial project in a fantastic but unflattering way. It took a lot of blood, some sex, and a little abstraction to make the story of U.S. imperialism viable as an object of attention. Slumming in American B-movies, Filipino auteurs chanced upon a way to market the horrors of empire.

The project of elucidating the figuration of colonialism in the Blood Island films is not without precedent. In her exploratory work on this corpus, Lim characterizes the films as "fantastic representation[s] of colonial history," but she defers a close reading of the films in favor of a historiographic treatment of the oeuvre.[29] Here I will foreground these fantasies' contours while keeping the broader historiographic aim of this exercise within sight.

Before I turn to individual films, I also wish to note that the horror film's potential for tendering figurations of historical trauma is a topic that has been well elucidated by scholars. In her study of Gothic horror fiction and films, Judith Halberstam characterizes the horror film as a "critical genre." For Adam Lowenstein, the horror genre is "very much engaged with, rather than estranged from, traumatic history."[30] Its allegories force audiences to confront historical traumas, serving, he says, as "means of reckoning with the horrible."[31] Robin Wood calls horror "in the 70s the most important of all American genres and perhaps the most progressive."[32] My claim about the figurative possibilities of the science-fiction horror films in question is decidedly more conservative. There is no need to undertake a "redemptive reading" of these films.[33] Nor is there a need to argue that, as Judith Halberstam puts it, they are "somehow larger than [their] low genre classification."[34] As irresistible and often profitable objects of schlock cinema, the Blood Island films already constitute an important contribution, even if they seem merely to have blundered into linking the United States and empire through fleeting images.

The Imperialist's Burden: *Terror Is a Man*

In the annals of B-movie history, *Terror Is a Man* is regarded as an impressively crafted monster movie. A critic for the horror-mystery fan magazine *Scarlet Street* compares it to the work of Val Lewton and argues, in a lengthy review published in the late 1990s, that De Leon's film is "one of the most undervalued chillers of its period."[35] The story is familiar. As one of the standard references for B-movies sums it up, the film is "basically *The Island of Doctor Moreau* with one creature."[36] A closer look shows that *Terror Is a Man* rearticulates the novel's preoccupation with the moral and psychic burdens of an imperialist project. Harry Paul Harber adapted its screenplay from Wells and appropriated some elements from another British novel, Mary Shelley's *Frankenstein*.

The film visits the imperialist project already in progress and then moves forward in time to depict its decline or possible renewal. *Terror* begins two years after a couple—a U.S.-based European doctor and his American wife—moves from New York to a remote island. Though sparsely inhabited by natives, Isla de Sangre feels to Doctor Girard (Francis Lederer) like terra nullius. "I came here to do a very specific piece of work," he cryptically tells the shipwrecked "visitor" to the island, William Fitzgerald (Richard Derr). "I came to this island because it afforded me privacy." The doctor has presumed to conduct a dicey experiment on the island but holds himself accountable neither to the native population nor to the ethical purview of Western science. The experiment involves the transformation of a panther into a man through a series of surgeries and enzyme injections. The ambitions of this project might be described not only as Darwinist but also as imperialist in nature because the doctor aims at nothing less than "to be a father of a new race of man." This desire to fashion a new race coincides with his rather violent appropriation of the island. His experimental creature (played by Flory Carlos) has driven out all the native inhabitants and killed four of them. The transformation of the creature into a human is thus set to coincide with the emergence of a new "native" in the "new" Eden of Isla de Sangre. By design, this native creature will also usher in a new history for the Westerner's island and his future people, thus effacing from memory the brutal process behind the settlement and clearing of the territory. The new human's knack for repressing history is no longer to arise from mere ideological conditioning. In keeping with the Western doctor's megalomaniacal vision, what is to preclude remembrance, rather, is the miracle of neurophysiology and parahuman consciousness. "He alone," Girard says of his ideal creature, "will have a new, fresh mind, capable of thinking his own thoughts with a complete objectivity." The doctor predicts that the new race will not be "dominated by complexes, anxieties, fear, and prejudices of countless generations before them." The implicit irony, however, is that Girard also fully expects his creatures to fear white men who, like him, wield power."[37]

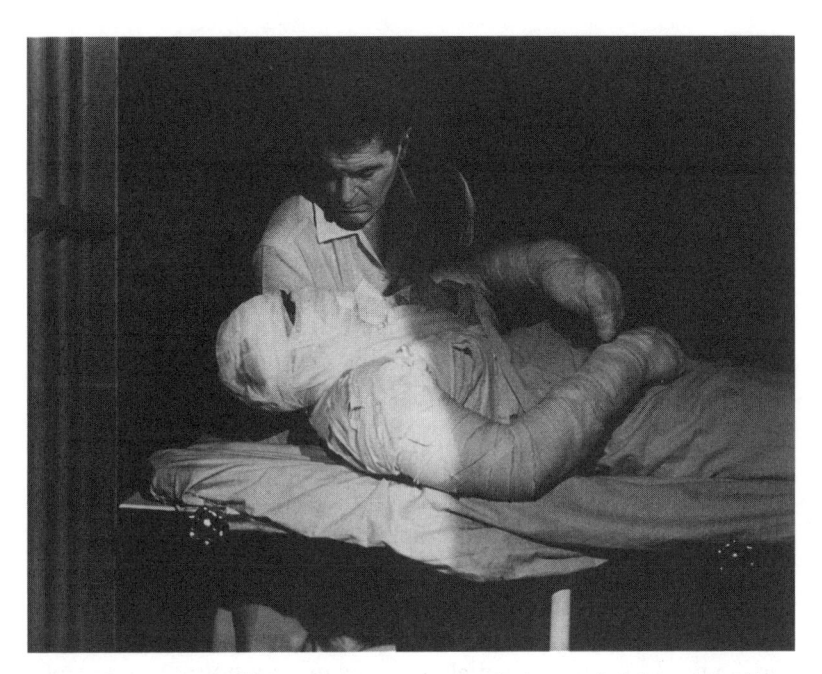

The mad scientist (Francis Lederer) from New York attempts to turn a panther into a new kind of human being with disastrous results. Source: Terror Is a Man.

The doctor's project of creating "a higher, a perfect man" is abetted, if begrudgingly, by a small cabal of aides. They will later find themselves in the midst of an ethical struggle with their own complicity. Apart from his wife, Frances (Greta Thyssen), a nurse who assists his operations, Girard enjoys the support of a Guatemalan factotum named Walter Perrera (Oscar Keesee Jr.). Fitzgerald, the visitor, also finds himself initially drawn to the doctor's work. His curiosity and sympathy may have something to do with his own colonialist background as a gringo who has "lived in South America most of the last ten years." When he hears that the natives had evacuated Isla de Sangre in terror after some of them were mauled by the escaped creature, his reaction is one of strange amusement: "That's fantastic! All while I was asleep!" Later, while enjoying a moment at the deserted beach, he callously tells Frances that he finds the elimination of the natives—particularly the eerie silence of their absence—quite convenient. "I think I'm developing a taste for quietness in my later years," he says. "I like it." Fitzgerald takes pleasure in what Albert Memmi considers the ultimate colonialist fantasy, namely, in seeing the island purged of natives.[38] Only the pliant native servants remain—the siblings Celina (Lilia Dizon) and Tiago (Peyton Keesee), both of whom demonstrate an inexplicable tolerance for Girard's work even though their mother was among those killed by the creature during its first rampage.

Much of the narrative focuses less on the progress of the mad scientist's work than on the crisis of faith that afflicts Frances and, eventually, Girard's other accomplices. This plot line is worth accentuating vis-à-vis my symptomatic reading of imperialism in the film. The moral reawakening among the settlers of Isla de Sangre occurs when, during another escape, the creature kills a native couple. There is a grand exodus of the village folk. Hearing no reprieve from the fugitive creature's pained howling, Frances falls into a hysterical state. "I can't help being afraid!" she screams at Girard. "I'm afraid of this house, this island. I can't stand water. What you're doing is so wrong. I hate it, all of it!" Prior to the creature's latest escape, Frances believed that her distress was solely due to her husband's inattention and her consequent sexual deprivation. She now realizes that the other aspect of her anxiety is her agonized conscience, namely, her growing inability to countenance Girard's terrible work.

It is important to note briefly that Frances's moral anguish makes the film's figuration of empire perhaps more psychologically complex than the one found in *The Island of Doctor Moreau*. In H. G. Wells's novel, it is the castaway who renders judgment on the cruel British scientist. The castaway acts as the scientist's foil but, by replacing him, implicitly conserves the fantasy of imperial succession. In *Terror Is a Man*, as if under the pressure of its moral dilemma, America's imperial subjectivity splits into two figures: one unswervingly faithful to empire's will and another anguished by the recognition of empire's violence. These two figures are at odds within a gendered structure of intimacy. The doctor's closest collaborator, as well as eventual foil, is a woman, no less than his wife.

"I heard it crying," Frances tells Girard. "Sounded like a human. It's known nothing but pain and fear since we came here." In the midst of her hysterical bout, Girard's wife is haunted by the possibility of an intersubjective relationship between the suffering, monstrous hybrid and Western settlers like herself. "Please let the animal go," she begs Girard. "Let it escape. Then we can leave here." Frances realizes that the creature's liberation is ultimately her own as well. Initially, however, she finds herself unable (and perhaps unwilling) to put an end to her husband's work. She threatens to stop assisting him in his surgeries but frequently reports to his clinic anyway. Her hesitation to effect change deepens her anxiety and aggravates her sense of sexual deprivation. Except for her husband and the native child Tiago, the remaining males on the island are affected—as well as aroused—by Frances's hysterical bouts. Writ large in the film, the erotic crises stand in for deeper issues of human subjugation and territorial conquest. Frances assuages her anxieties over her husband's unethical project by seducing Fitzgerald, who she initially believes is a much better man than Girard. She flaunts her vulnerability to the castaway during an afternoon at the beach. "I'm afraid of everything," she tells her strapping companion. "Right now, the darkness and the night . . . I never used to be afraid of the darkness before, but I am now." She also lures him by declaring her intent to jettison her husband. "I'm gonna leave on the next boat," she threatens him, "whether he's finished or not. I have to get away. Sometimes I think like I'm gonna die on this island." On a lonely night, she waltzes into Fitzgerald's room, in her nightie, and makes love to him. The next morning, she regrets what happened, refuses to speak about the tryst, and pushes away her newfound lover. As the plot unfolds, she decides that he is not her white prince after all. Fitzgerald resembles her husband, and he offers her no relief from the ramblings of her conscience and fails to meet her sexual needs.

The Guatemalan Walter is likewise fired up by Frances's histrionics. His sexual attraction to her develops alongside his own existential crisis and resentment toward Girard. After eavesdropping on the cozy moment Frances and Fitzgerald share on the beach, Walter feels suddenly emboldened to pursue her sexually as well as rebel against his domineering master. When he fails to blackmail her into submission, he displaces his urges with a vengeance onto the housemaid Celina. His presumably forced sexual advances leave visible bruises on her body, which others notice. Additionally, in emulation of Frances's unwieldy emotions, Walter's sexual frustration turns into hostility toward the doctor and his work. In an unguarded moment, Walter disparages his superior while speaking to the castaway: "I worked around in hospitals and nut houses since I was twenty-three, back home. And let me tell you that Girard's worse than the rest of them put together!"

Walter is even less sympathetic toward the creature. Unlike Frances, he sees it not as the victim but as the face of Girard's cruel paternalistic imperial ambitions. "Maybe that stinking animal down there is gonna die," he says one time in response to the creature's cries of pain. Later, when the creature is recaptured after its escape, Walter breaks ranks with Girard and calls for the animal to be neutralized. "He's out of his mind, calling that thing a man!" he tells Fitzgerald. "Someone's got to stop him. He'll get us all killed . . . What he's doing is not right!" Walter tries to deal with his sexual frustration and anger at Girard. He holds the doctor at gunpoint, forcing him to give up the creature. Unfortunately for Walter, the creature is likewise stimulated by Frances's distress, freeing itself from the gurney restraints and mauling Walter to death. The creature then abducts Frances—perhaps either to liberate her from the cruel island or, having internalized Girard's instinct for domination, to ravish her. Girard and Fitzgerald pursue the creature. The beast pounces on the doctor and throws him off the cliff, leaving the burden of saving or letting go of the "new native" and Isla de Sangre to fall squarely—or so it seems—on Fitzgerald.

This substitution of Fitzgerald for Girard raises the possibility for the continuity of the latter's imperialist project. As seen earlier in the film, Fitzgerald has taken to Girard's work with curiosity and unusual sympathy. He even comes to Girard's defense after Walter recognizes that his master had already crossed the line. "Do you think Charles is insane?" Walter asks rhetorically. The castaway rushes to defend Girard: "He may be a genius. He's not insane. It's a fine line." Fitzgerald's apologist reply is telling, especially in light of their sexual competition over Frances. Indeed, their ideological similarities appear to overpower their libidinal urges and their sense of masculine pride. Though he admits to not having the wherewithal to fully understand and, much less, to continue the doctor's experiments, he seems to have no qualms about being a settler. We may infer this from the toast he gives at dinner with the Girards. "I'd like to drink to destiny or the fates or whatever it was that put me ashore here on your island," he says. "Thanks for putting me on this island." If, in the film's climactic moment, he is able to wrest from the new native the doctor's wife and dominion over the island, Fitzgerald's victory might effect a return to an older form of imperialism. Whereas Girard envisioned a new Eden based on genetically designed social engineering, Fitzgerald might reluctantly settle for a nostalgic repetition of his golden decade as an entitled gringo

Walter (Oscar Keesee Jr.) makes a pass at Frances (Greta Thyssen) after seeing her flirt with the castaway. Source: Terror Is a Man.

in South America. His earlier statement about the inhabitants of Isla de Sangre hints at his general attitude toward natives and the kind of rapport he might have with them, if they should choose eventually to return to the island under his dominion. Without even having laid eyes on the natives after he arrives, he easily assumes that they "must be a primitive bunch."

Fitzgerald (Richard Derr) develops a keen interest in Dr. Girard's (Francis Lederer) project. Source: Terror Is a Man.

In a final anti-imperialist turn, *Terror Is a Man* presents a rather surprising exit from Girard's technologized imperialism, from Fitzgerald's residual colonial predilections, and even from Frances's empathetic but ineffective maternal protectionism. The creature frees itself again. It whisks an inert Frances away from her husband. The doctor and the castaway hasten in pursuit to rescue her. The creature mauls Girard and throws him off a ravine. Fitzgerald wounds the beast-man with a single gunshot before Frances, now revived, can shriek for him to stop. The creature absconds as Fitzgerald tends to the woman. During the moments leading to the creature's escape, the camera follows the injured creature tottering across the beach and meeting its unexpected rescuer.

In Wells's novel, the castaway Edward Prendick's succession of Moreau leads to his devolution and to that of the creature. Prendick escapes back to London but there he is haunted by "the terror of that [unnamed] island."[39] Of all characters in the film, it is the native child Tiago who finds the resolution to the colonizer's dilemma. Tiago inexplicably rescues the same creature that killed both women in his family. Having silently arbitrated over competing claims of victimhood, he puts the wounded man-animal on the lifeboat, as if the feral creature were the infant Moses. Tiago commends it to an undetermined place of refuge, away from Isla de Sangre where it had been mangled, and away from the fate of death or subjugation that may await it in the hands of the island's new master. "He is gone," Tiago impassively tells Fitzgerald when asked about the creature's whereabouts. The boy then walks away from the couple that he has also saved from their own imperialist predilections. As Fitzgerald scans the horizon, Frances, the merciful Westerner, reminds him that the creature only "wanted to help" her. Such an ending helps us understand that monstrous terror is characteristic of the imperialist as it is of the wretched creature. The film makes it abundantly clear that the creature is simply reproducing the master's evil.

The colonial allegory of *Terror Is a Man* is quite legible. The specificity of this work as a figuration of empire is worth discussing in brief, beyond pointing out the fact that the roles of the natives and the monster are played by Filipinos and that the film is directed by De Leon, an ex-colonial subject. The film's mad scientist, Girard, is European, but he comes from New York. Like the monsters of American horror films, he is both foreign and familiar.[40] He comes to an island that lies somewhere between the Americas and the Pacific, which recalls the vast province of U.S. imperial influence that Allan Isaac calls the "American Tropics."[41] Girard's successors in holding dominion over the territory—his wife Frances and the castaway Fitzgerald—are both marked as Americans (though the former is portrayed by a Danish actress). Finally, Girard's desire to fashion a new native resonates historically with the discourses of U.S. empire in the Philippines. Girard's mad experiment somewhat resembles an infamous transformation project undertaken by Dean Worcester, the University of Michigan zoologist turned Secretary of the Interior in the Philippines. Worcester produced a set of photographs tracing the tribal boy Pit-a-pit's transformation into a gentleman wearing a suit and skimmer hat.[42] The set of images tracking Pit-a-pit's change in clothing and demeanor is one of the ways by which Worcester generated the fantasy of the native's radical metamorphosis under colonial rule.

The story line pertaining to the monster's fortunes bears allegorical force as well. De Leon's "new native" is an insurgent subject reminiscent of the monster in *Frankenstein*. Judith Halberstam describes

Victor Frankenstein's creature as an "allegory about a production that refuses to submit to its author."[43] Like the Philippine "insurgents" who fought the bloody war of conquest waged by the new imperialists, Girard's "new native" not only refuses to submit to him but also wreaks havoc all over his tropic simulacrum of Eden. By fleeing Isla de Sangre, the monster not only manages to survive but, in an unusual fantasy of colonial liberation, also frees himself from the control of Girard's successors, the "new" regime of Western tormentors.

When the movie was released in 1959, the colonial allegory—much less the figuration of a specifically American narrative—escaped critical notice. A famous reviewer for the *New York Times* praised De Leon's film as a "quiet, sensibly restrained and quite terrifying . . . well-photographed little picture."[44] As I have proposed earlier, the fact that the film was able to conjure U.S. empire is already an achievement on its own. Its cultural work should be situated at a time when the public was still largely hesitant to grapple with the notion that Americans, not just their transatlantic cousins, could get caught up in the affair of settling islands and visiting destruction upon their inhabitants.

Although it drew modest praise from the *New York Times*, the film did not do well at the box office. However, due to the enterprising spirit of its American distributors, it was reissued again and again. It continued to haunt U.S. screens like the return of the repressed—first as a feature on late-night television, and later in a double-bill with a Filipino-made World War II film, *The Walls of Hell*.[45] The new title given to the reissue of De Leon's movie could not have been more apt to its discourse on the subject hailed, and at the same time disfigured, by empire. *Terror Is a Man* was renamed *Blood Creature*.

Brides of Blood: The Gift of Love and Death

After Isla de Sangre, another spot surfaced on the map of cinematic gore. *Terror on Blood Island*, the working title of *Brides of Blood*, piggybacked on the cult fame of *Terror Is a Man* and intimated a connection between the old and new settings.[46] That said, *Brides of Blood* actually belongs to another kind of exploitation film. Sexier, tackier, bloodier, and filmed in color but done with less artistry and technical polish, it stages a different scenario for U.S. empire.

The American scientist in *Brides of Blood* behaves more benevolently than his counterpart in *Terror Is a Man*. Paul Henderson (Kent Taylor) stays clear of scalpels and syringes. Instead he investigates the environmental impact of nuclear bomb tests conducted by the United States after World War II. Another visitor on Blood Island is a Peace Corps volunteer engaged in a constructive effort. Jim Farrell (John Ashley) serves as an "instructor of community action" who helps the natives build schoolhouses, health centers, and irrigation systems. Farrell's participation in social engineering resembles the work of an earlier generation of community organizers dispatched by the U.S. Department of State to help stem the communist threat in the barrios of developing countries. The cold war humanitarianism of these two men takes a surprising turn as they learn about the history of Blood Island. Instead of testifying to the goodwill of America, they become witnesses to the tremendous suffering visited in the name of bestowing peace and security upon the free world.

Although Blood Island was, as Henderson points out, merely "on the fringe of the atomic radiation area during the bomb tests in the late '40s," the island seems to be suffering from some kind of plague. Crabs on the island have grown monstrous appendages. Pink flowers spew noxious smoke. The branches and roots of old trees come to life and trap passersby. When an oversized butterfly suddenly attacks and wounds Henderson, he confirms his earlier hunch: "It seems that some living organisms on this island are undergoing drastic mutation." His wife, Carla (Beverly Hills), later adds that the damage is much more pervasive than her husband would care to admit: "I've seen it happen to a banana plant . . . even to the very air we breathe around here!"

Following genre conventions, the real source of the trauma on Blood Island initially eludes the old scientist. Henderson could not explain, for instance, "why the people on this island [have not] been affected by mutation."[47] If the trauma seems elusive to him, it is because the scientific discourse he represents should not have neglected the archive of history. The reference to Bikini Atoll in the film gestures toward such an archive. Esteban Powers (Mario Montenegro) is the half-American, half-Spanish landlord hosting Henderson and his wife. Powers mentions to Henderson that the people "weren't on [Blood Island] when the bombs were exploded on Bikini."

What the film references here is the societal and environmental impact of the tests on one of the territories in the central Pacific. In the 1940s and 1950s, Bikini Atoll was evacuated when the United States conducted nuclear tests there.[48] The tests took place both to ensure that the nuclear devices worked and to show off U.S. power to enemies and allies, but they also affected the territories and lives that were deemed expendable.[49] The inhabitants of Bikini were resettled in locations exposed to radiation and lacking ample food sources. This displacement is implicit in Powers's allusion to Bikini—and so is the imperialist disavowal of its violence. Replying to the information Powers has volunteered, Henderson notes only the superficial benefits of the resettlement to Blood Island. The dramatic irony, portraying Henderson's epistemic blindness, is not too subtle. The old scientist (a researcher of plants and animals) concludes that if the people were not on Blood Island during the Bikini experiment, "then they couldn't possibly have been affected by the bomb tests."

The repressed trauma of Blood Island troubles the social order of its denizens. The village elder Arcadio (Andres Centenera) makes cryptic references to this problem upon welcoming his American visitors. "We are ashamed," the elder tells them. "We wish we had asked you to return where you came from, while the ship was still here. We have gone back to primitive ways. There are things which we do now that we did not do before." When asked to clarify his statement, he clams up. His silence is fitting because the plight of his people frustrates rational speech: they are losing control over their baser instincts and "devolving" into savages. The natives blame their atavism on a green monster (a ridiculously fake-looking, low-budget prosthesis) to which they refer as the "Evil One." Like the tribes of yore, the natives sacrifice women to placate the monster. The elders run a lottery to pick the victims, and on the same night, the Evil One violates and slaughters them. A native woman points out, however, that the monster "does not devour his victims. He merely satisfies himself on them. . . . [Slaughtering a naked woman] is his way of satisfying himself." The denizens' fear of death, as well as their internalization of the monster's perversity, drives them to hold ritual orgies before the sacrifice. They show no mercy toward the ones picked. Arcadio even denounces his own granddaughter Alem (Eva Darren) after she is rescued at the stake by Farrell.

The "Evil One" pounces on one of its victims. Source: Brides of Blood. Courtesy of Hemisphere/The Kobal Collection.

The monster's behavior mirrors the trauma it suffered during the American bomb tests. We learn later in the story that Powers is the human alter ego of the Evil One. Before the film reveals this connection, Powers vividly describes the moment that literally changed him and his wife: "It was our fifteenth anniversary when Beatriz talked me into taking a little vacation. It was a cruise among the islands. We had a thirty-foot boat, no radio. And we learned much later that we had come within range of a radiation area." While Powers claims nonchalantly that a "schoolgirl expression" was all he got from the exposure, he admits that the radiation eventually killed his wife. He recalls further, "She developed a fever. We flew her back to the mainland but the doctors there couldn't do anything for her. And then her complexion suddenly changed . . . discolored. She grew darker by the day, almost by the hour. In spite of the fever, which she couldn't shake off, she seemed quite well otherwise. Then one day, suddenly, she died. She died in terrible pain. The pain came all at once and simply overwhelmed her!"

Henderson apologizes for prying, but Powers quickly asserts his confessional mood, sitting at the table and leaning toward Henderson and Farrell. A medium long shot framing all three men records the ensuing conversation. The tone abruptly turns unemotional and scientific, as the men discuss the damages inflicted by U.S. nuclear testing but previously unknown to American scientists.

Implicit in Powers's recollection to his "fellow Americans" is a cold war narrative about a gift as strange as the mutations on Blood Island. To call this gift "imperial benevolence" only approximates the absurdity of the promise to love and shelter the non-Western world, while harboring the promise to kill. Using the language of cold war tactics, Max Lerner offers us a more precise name for this paradoxical gift. He calls it "the overkill factor," referring to a way of measuring the surplus killing power of nuclear weapons.[50] Thanks to this gift of love, the security of nations becomes contingent upon "how many times America's weapons could kill the entire population of the USSR and, indeed, the world, and how many times the Soviets could do the same."[51]

Because the overkill factor appears to its givers as a gift of protection, its fatal implications are often occluded. Early in *Brides of Blood*, there is a scene shadowed by the prospect of overkill as a gift of death. Late one afternoon, Henderson and his wife come upon the villagers rushing to their homes. The horizon is lit with a spectacle that makes Carla gasp: "Paul, that sunset!" After a pause, she ponders the natives' response: "Why is everything so still?" Carla does not realize that the people are running for their lives. But she, at least, has some intersubjective grasp of native trauma. In contrast, her husband the scientist is oblivious to the early signs of disaster. Henderson dismisses the eerie silence and sunset as a "trick of the atmosphere," a figment of his wife's imagination. Carla, as it turns out, is correct. It is the breathtaking sunset that calls forth the nuclear monster.

It is significant that Powers makes the revelation about his misfortunes to Farrell and Henderson. A figure of what Robin Wood calls the "divided Monster," Powers enjoys an alternate identity that renders his malevolence invisible.[52] As a nuclear mutant and as a "miscegenated" child of two ex-colonial nations, Powers sees that, given their cold war vocations, Farrell and Henderson are just like him. They serve as agents of the fond violence (or violent fondness) of U.S. imperialist conduct. Aware of his monstrosity, Powers keeps his hunters close, calculating the risk that they might discover his predilection for murderous eroticism, but also hoping that they would administer to him the necessary "cure" of death before he gores his next victim. But neither Farrell nor Henderson suspects that the fair-skinned landlord is the green monster. Henderson is killed by the henchman Gorro in the latter's attempt to keep his master's secret. For his part, Farrell learns of the Evil One's identity only after the monster is attacked by the mob of villagers at the end of a long chase. As soon as the monster is killed, the villagers throw themselves into a massive orgy—either to celebrate their liberation or to divert their anxiety over the possibility that the monster's curse would not let up.

The half-American, half-Spanish Esteban Powers (Mario Montenegro) is also a divided monster. Source: Brides of Blood.

The film concludes with this hysterical orgy, no doubt in order to titillate its audiences. At the same time, however, the cultic dread projected onscreen may be interpreted as a gesture in keeping with a tendency in certain modern horror films to let the trauma linger on or to suggest the monster's possible return. Its conclusion banishes and, at the same time, abets the condition of high-anxiety spectatorship during the cold war. It is necessary to recall here the promotional gimmick that the film's distributors launched, encouraging American audiences to identify with the anxiously oversexed inhabitants of Blood Island. Female moviegoers were given a set of plastic wedding rings.[53] *Brides of Blood* simulates for its viewers what the natives of the American Tropics feel, wedded to nuclear destruction, surviving the gift of love and death. The simulation allows these viewers to acknowledge their consent to the vaunted benefits of U.S. nuclear defense, even as they confront the dread of likely ruin.

Mad Doctor of Blood Island: The Fall of *Cacique* Manor

If *Brides of Blood* depicts the effects of imperialism even beyond formal occupation, *Mad Doctor of Blood Island* portrays the state of affairs shortly after empire closes shop. The latter movie follows the fortunes of a pathologist, Bill Foster (John Ashley). Like the famous Victor Heiser, Foster is sent to contain epidemics within the fringes of the American imperium.[54] Dispatched by the "government on the mainland," the doctor visits Blood Island to investigate a disease that causes the inhabitants to vomit green blood before dying. Foster's love interest is a white woman named Sheila Willard (Angelique Pettyjohn), who is also on some sort of salvage operation. Her alcoholic father (Tony Edmunds) has been living a hobo-like existence in the "pest hole" called Blood Island. Holding on to the shards of her family life, Sheila is trying to rescue the broken man whom she has not seen since she was twelve.

A process of decline similarly occurs in the lives of the native protagonists. The family of the late Don Ramon Lopez is unable to recover from his demise. Their filial bonds are fraying just as their colonial way of life on the island is starting to wither. Don Ramon was the great *cacique*, the most politically and economically influential citizen on the island. He lorded over its vast plantation and kept his dysfunctional family intact until a mysterious disease consumed him. As the dead man's secrets begin to unravel, his family anticipates that the worst is yet to come. Like Sheila, the *cacique*'s only son, Carlos Lopez (Ronaldo Valdez), is determined to take his mother away from the "wretched island." Señora Lopez (Tita Muñoz) tends to linger at her late husband's grave while waxing existential. When asked by her son to explain the state of affairs on the island, she says enigmatically, "Nothing... Death, only death... On this island, we struggle desperately and have found our own separate ways to... nothing."

All this stilted talk of ennui, in fact, is merely cover-up for the scandalous events marking her aristocratic family's decline. Señora Lopez has been shacking up with her husband's physician, Dr. Lorca (Ronald Remy), a shady character. Though Señora Lopez never explains her reasons for taking Dr. Lorca as her lover, two reasons seem equally plausible. First, she latches on to him in the hope that he might be able to do something more for her husband. As it turns out, her husband is not dead. Dr. Lorca has been conducting an experiment to discover an elixir for immortality. Life-sustaining chlorophyll infusions have turned the *cacique* into an angry, ravenous monster. Looking nothing like his old self, Don Ramon nonetheless retains a few memories and continues—in a literal and twisted way—his old occupation of preying on poor village folk. Señora Lopez's second motive appears to be revenge for her husband's infidelity. Her husband had once taken for his mistress a thirteen-year-old child. Now an adult, the mistress, Marla (Alicia Alonzo), continues to live in the manor. Adding to this moral quagmire are incestuous episodes between Marla and Carlos that, the mistress later points out, occurred even when Don Ramon was still alive.

Given this scenario, the task of the visiting American pathologist Foster goes beyond the generic routine of exposing the rogue Dr. Lorca and the dangers of this native scientist's misguided work. As Dr. Lorca himself suggests, there is much more at stake in his human experiments than the development of a destructive "native" technology: "They are helping me to save my distinguished and most important patient, Don Ramon. And more—they're contributing to the advent of a new era in geriatrics and internal medicine!" Dr. Lorca's seemingly pathetic and shallow project of discovering a potion for eternal youth is but another aspect of his complicity in resuscitating the old colonial order. As the territory's only remaining lot of *caciques*, the Lopez family represents the native elite who benefited the most from their complicity with the new colonialists and whose grave abuses ironically also hastened empire's decline. By sabotaging Dr. Lorca's experiments, Foster helps to demolish the last vestiges of Spanish colonialism, paving the way for its afterlife in a new regime.

Preparing to liquidate the *cacique*'s legacy, Foster undertakes a prolonged investigation of the Lopez family's affairs. The process teaches him how to help Carlos work through the crisis that has prevented the Lopez heir from severing an attachment to the old regime and from securing his family's future on Blood Island. As the old American scientist suspects, Carlos suffers from a blockage in his psyche. The young man is unconsciously holding back the recognition that the green creature is his father, the *cacique* who already had been a human predator even before he became a monster and whose sins are starting to be visited upon his only son. Foster helps Marla reveal the family's secrets to Carlos. Foster convinces the young Lopez to pry open Don Ramon's tomb, nudging Carlos toward personal deliverance. A confrontation scene between Carlos and Dr. Lorca takes place after the beast mauls Señora Lopez. While Carlos weeps over his mother's corpse, Dr. Lorca asks Carlos if he saw the killer. "A beast," Don Ramon's heir replies. "Walks like a man." Dr. Lorca tells Carlos what the young Lopez already suspects. "There's a man, all right. Or someone that once was a man. Your father." Carlos's acceptance of his father's violence completes the fall of the *cacique*'s house. The goals of both Carlos and Foster are attained, clearing a path through colonial sin toward reform and reconciliation.

Foster's role in the liberation of Blood Island is complemented by Marla's consistent efforts to challenge the Lopezes' hold on the territory. She brazenly uses Carlos for sexual pleasure, imperiously orders the monster around, intimidates Dr. Lorca and Señora Lopez with her arsenal of family secrets, and shadows Foster throughout his mission. Although Marla could have emerged as the island's emancipator, the plot relegates her to a subordinate role. During the movie's finale, the figure of the "new" woman is trapped under the rubble, consumed by fire, and blasted to smithereens. Like Dr. Lorca's modern science, Marla's modern sexual ethos points toward the other unspoken colonial presence, the American presence that must be obliterated along with the *cacique* legacy if Blood Island is to be restored to its idyllic state.

Don Ramon, the cacique-turned-monster, recognizes his son (Ronaldo Valdez) and resists mauling him. Source: Mad Doctor of Blood Island. Courtesy of Hemisphere/The Kobal Collection.

At the end of this fantasy of the *cacique*'s fall, the natives gaze at the horizon as the ship carrying the outsiders—the old wino, his daughter, the pathologist, the liberated son, and the remnants of the monster—fades into the distance. Interestingly, the film's commercial success and the promise of cashing in with a sequel appropriately undermine the fantasized death of imperialism. Both the charred monster and the partially burnt scientist return to Blood Island. And of course, in hot pursuit of villainy, so does the American agent.

Beast of Blood: Tyrants and Assassins

Although *Beast of Blood* purports to be a sequel to *Mad Doctor of Blood Island*, it brackets the history of the Lopez family. It builds its narrative instead on the scaffolding of Joseph Conrad's *Heart of Darkness*. Bill Foster (John Ashley) returns to the island to hunt down a renegade scientist named Dr. Lorca (played in this sequel by Eddie Garcia). Foster suspects that Dr. Lorca is still hiding in the jungle, rather than lying dead and buried as most people believe. Foster, who is no longer working for the unnamed organization he used to serve, does not reveal his true purpose for returning. The other characters suspect—quite accurately—that the liquidation of the monster and the renegade scientist is his secret motive. Through Foster's character, the imperialist traces become legible. Foster embodies the figure of the American secret operative who cunningly penetrates a rogue state's borders, waltzing with a dictator in one moment and then killing him at the first opportunity. This motif of surveillance recurs throughout the plot. The film encrypts in the monster genre an espionage fable—more specifically, a story about America's covert empire during the cold war.[55] In this novel remapping of Blood Island, the terrain's historical and geographic coordinates appear to index the U.S. Central Intelligence Agency's (CIA's) "secret wars" and the love–hate relationships between the U.S. government and the rogue and puppet dictatorships of Latin America and Asia.[56]

Beast of Blood begins with an inquest into Foster's previous stint on Blood Island. Foster is questioned by an American journalist named Myra Russell (ex-Bond girl Celeste Yarnall), who hopped on the boat to Blood Island to get Foster to break his silence. Her professional inquiries about "what happened at Blood Island or what may still be happening there" and Foster's sly reticence about the matter weave into the sci-fi mutant thriller the issues of strategic "intelligence." Foster, mum as a cold war assassin, leads many of the natives to believe at first that he is on a monster chase rather than a manhunt. Myra refuses to accept Foster's explanation. "Doctor, you're a sterling character and a brilliant scientist," she says, lending a convincing American accent to scriptwriter-director Eddie Romero's campy English dialogue. "But this cloak and dagger bitch just isn't your bag!" Through Myra, Romero articulates a suspicion toward U.S. "anti-diplomacy," those covert activities conducted during the cold war to stem the communist threat.[57] Antidiplomacy included not only espionage but also "clandestine operations . . . aimed at overthrowing foreign regimes" or "that shore up repressive regimes," the assassination of foreign leaders, and the waging of "dirty" and "secret" wars in developing countries (like the secret wars in Laos in the 1960s).[58]

When the boat lands on the island, Foster announces his ostensible purpose to the town elder, Ramu (Alfonso Carvajal): "If the beast is still alive, I'll find him. Now I can use your help if you wanna give it, but you won't stop me." The beast he is referring to is the monster formerly known as Don Ramon, a chlorophyll-poisoned mutant that was last seen as a charred zombie on a boat that exploded at sea. Believing that the monster is still alive, Foster asks for help in staking out Don Ramon's old house. The natives are reluctant to join, believing that the Evil One's domain is cursed and truly abandoned. The American, however, persists in helping them outgrow their superstitious ways. He goes to the house with a handful of natives and there finds clues to indicate that the home "hasn't been abandoned . . . [and was simply] rigged up to scare people." He returns to the house at night and, with the help of a gutsy native woman named Laida (Liza Belmonte), discovers that it is occupied by Dr. Lorca's henchman, Razak (Bruno Punzalan). The latter escapes in an ensuing chase led by Foster—who reveals himself to be an unusually trigger-happy scientist, firing at an unarmed man.

Meanwhile, Dr. Lorca's goons abduct the American journalist Myra. The mad doctor informs her that her abduction was meant to parry Foster's aggression. Dr. Lorca implicitly suspects that Foster is out to assassinate him. Foster takes upon himself the mission of saving Myra and arranges for a face-off at Dr. Lorca's new hideout. "I hadn't counted on meeting your friend Dr. Foster again," Dr. Lorca tells Myra. "He is a somewhat reckless sort of person, and I felt that if he was really bent on seeing me, I should give him good reason to approach me with caution." Rogue meets rogue.

The Americans (John Ashley and Celeste Yarnall) confront Dr. Lorca (Eddie Garcia), the mad scientist and warlord who reigns over Blood Island. Source: Beast of Blood. Courtesy of Scepter Industries/The Kobal Collection.

Like Foster, Dr. Lorca no longer seems much of a scientist after his reappearance on Blood Island. With an army of goons and a prison house full of tortured captives, Dr. Lorca resembles the type of Third World despot the CIA would depose (or prop up) during the cold war. In spite of his suave, charming demeanor, Dr. Lorca's freak science makes him a justified target for someone like Foster. The native scientist harvests organs and body parts from chlorophyll-poisoned humans for the "restoration" of Don Ramon, the man he turned into a monster some years back and recently decapitated to guarantee his containment. Besides the harvest of human organs and the *cacique* restoration, Dr. Lorca threatens to engage in a simpler kind of genetic "experiment" with the American journalist. Myra recounts Dr. Lorca's perverted twist on miscegenation: "He suggested that I become his woman for a while and try to give him a child. Nothing personal, mind you, just mutual insurance. It came to him as kind of a passing thought over dessert . . . He said that if I didn't think that that was such a hot idea, it would be okay to have a child by you instead."

The gallant Foster moves to stem the threat of forced miscegenation by offering Myra the gift of his virility. "I've come to help you," he assures her. "Just don't fall apart on me because I'm counting on you." The two make love in the hut. As it turns out, this sexual release is the only kind of liberation that the bungling cold war assassin is able to effect on his own. He and Myra are rescued the following day by the natives, who storm the lair and stage a revolt against the despot. They are led by Laida—as in the film's prequel, a figure of the "new" woman—who makes good on her promise to help Foster even though he rejected her earlier sexual advances.

As the mob closes in on Dr. Lorca's laboratory, he scrambles to escape with a few file folders in tow. At this point, Don Ramon's headless body frees itself from gurney straps, kills Dr. Lorca, and proceeds to destroy the laboratory, sending it up in flames. Moments before everything blows up, Foster reaches the lab and takes Dr. Lorca's folders. He escapes and flees the lair with Myra and the villagers.

As the film ends, the village elder Ramu inquires about the files in Foster's possession: "Doctor, those papers you took, what will you do with them?" The shot resembles the scene featuring Powers's revelation in *Brides of Blood*. It is a medium long shot accommodating, in one frame, the native and the two Americans while they discuss the high stakes of U.S. intervention. Foster replies to the native leader with the usual vagueness: "Nothing at all . . . I hope." The final image of the film zooms in on a wooden trunk borne by a villager at the tail of the exodus. Guided by the conventions of the genre, we would assume that the trunk can only contain treasure, or even Don Ramon's head. The elder, however, assumes that the folders in Foster's possession contain something important, such as intelligence data. The native's implicit recognition of the makings of espionage demonstrates the contaminating effect of Foster's cold war paranoia. Ramu's concern regarding the fate of the secret files appears to suggest that he has taken up Foster's agenda as his own. It ought to be recalled that the American doctor has been pressuring the native to see things from the doctor's point of view and to do as the American says. When Ramu asks Foster about the files, he may simply be expressing concern on the American's behalf.

But the tone of Ramu's query may also be read differently. It may be heard as late-blooming skepticism toward Foster, exposed as having the imperialist knack for causing upheavals in territories he will later flee. After helping unseat the despot and rescue the Americans as Ramu was instructed, the native realizes the importance of prying into the white man's secrets: "Doctor, those papers you took, what will you do with them?" The answer is never given. The native is left to ponder the enigma posed by the humane, charismatic, and quietly menacing cold war agent.

Conclusion

In *American Tropics*, Allan Isaac maintains that colonies "leave a ghostly, and sometimes bloody, trail that haunts the center."[59] The transnational films in this chapter substantiate Isaac's claim with fake blood and with ghosts that look even faker. These films engendered a moment of disjunction in American moviegoing. On balmy evenings, while the cold war stalked the distant tropics, the screens of drive-in theaters in quiet American towns were splayed with the devastation wrought by forgotten imperial projects. The frightening, erotic, and unintentionally farcical images of American scientists and Filipinos hunting or being hunted by fantastic monsters all recalled to America the very real nightmares visited elsewhere by U.S. imperialism. The postcolonial commerce between Filipino moviemakers and American spectators occurred as transactions involving fictive blood, sex, and money—as American fantasies reflecting the economy of violence instituted by empire.

The figurations tendered by these films show that the enterprise of imperialism was abetted *and resisted* by Westerners, alternately ruthless and merciful. In these Philippine-made American fantasies, some natives function as American surrogates and collaborators, while others play victims. Still others, including precocious children and gutsy women, rise as unexpected heroes and heroines. Because these fantasies are tailored for U.S. audiences, the Americans often save the day, if not also the hapless natives. These obligatory liberations notwithstanding, the American presence on these bloody islands is explicitly questioned by natives who resent the intrusion and always seem to know much more than they let on. One of the peculiar ironies in the Blood Island films is that, while the American protagonists confront the object of their pursuit as an enigma, the natives never fail to see into the monster's identity, recognizing either its affinity with imperialists or its origin in imperial ventures.

In his important work on horror films, Robin Wood concedes that while the genre is particularly effective in locating the place of the horrible and exposing "areas of disturbance" within the dominant culture,[60] it often "proposes no solution."[61] The horror film furnishes no "radical alternatives."[62] This lack of unequivocal resolution is not always a bad thing. In spite of the proclaimed closing of the imperial era, as well as the end of the cold war, the greatest superpower continues to use military force in laying claim to leadership of the free world. Long after the American redeemers have left Blood Island, monstrosity survives. Given the vigor of *informal* empire, it seems only fitting that the green creature lives on.

2

My Brother Is Not a Pig

American Benevolence and Philippine Sovereignty

In the previous chapter, I showed how the ghosts of U.S. empire returned in the unlikely form of transnational horror films from the American ex-colony. This chapter studies confrontations with the present forms of empire through two strident political melodramas and one thriller film about the now-shuttered U.S. bases in the Philippines. As in the previous chapter, the films discussed here have a nightmarish quality, depicting imperialism in its ugliest forms. The natives' militant response counters the imperialist's own American fantasy: the dream of empire's benevolence. This fantasy thrives on the belief that the United States' "role in the world is virtuous . . . [and that its] actions are almost invariably for the good of others" as well as of its citizens.[1] The benevolence that these movies refute is simultaneously heard by the ex-colonial nation they represent as a promise whose fulfillment is devoutly wished.

The three films in this chapter belong unmistakably to a cinema of decolonization. Lupita A. Concio's *Once a Moth* (*Minsa'y isang gamugamo*, 1976), Lino Brocka's *PX* (1984), and Augusto Buenaventura's *In the Claws of an Eagle* (*Sa kuko ng agila*, 1989) all share an explicit interest in dismantling the vestigial forms of colonial relations. These films traffic in anticolonial nationalism and exemplify the rarefied militant strain of nationalist cinema. Simultaneously, they participate in the larger tricontinental project of critiquing empire through film. These melodramas portray what cannot be translated with ease or spoken with perfect composure: what different nations know as empire's informality, its impropriety, and its unmapped violence.

There is an understandable objection to the stridency and grimness of the three cases studied here. In a cinema dominated by commercial films, these three movies present an unpopular theme. They bring to the fore questions of sovereignty and openly contradict the state's position over such issues. For Concio and Brocka especially, troubled sovereignty cannot be thought of apart from questions of the heart, metaphorical as well as corporeal—of hearts, rather, lodged in the bodies that live close to the U.S. military bases. I argue, then, that these films' weaknesses are inseparable from their strengths. It should not be surprising that these movies respond to empire's impropriety in a cinematic language replete with its own affective excesses.

Tales of Imperial Benevolence

Until their closure in the early 1990s, the two big American military facilities in the Philippines represented both the superpower's ferocious might and its slowly decaying relationship with the ex-colony. During the periodic renegotiations of the base agreements from the mid-1970s to 1990, the three films I mentioned earlier argued for the closure of these facilities by posing a challenge to the fantasy of U.S. imperial benevolence. This long-lived fantasy was disseminated in the Philippines as early as 1898, through President William McKinley's "Benevolent Assimilation Proclamation." The American government, the edict claimed, assumed control over the Philippines "not as invaders or conquerors, but as friends, *to protect* the natives in their homes, in their employments, and in their personal and religious rights . . . [and to bestow] the reward of its support and protection . . . substituting the mild sway of justice and right for arbitrary rule."[2] Formal colonialism in the Philippines came to an end in 1946. Discourses echoing McKinley, however, justified continued U.S. influence and presence there. The fantasy of benevolence scripted America's pledges of mutual defense, which fueled anticommunist operations in Southeast Asia, as well as of aid, which fostered political and economic dependency.

In clamoring for political change, the movies about the bases traffic in this fantasy of benevolence as much as trouble it. They dramatize American incursions on the territorial and political sovereignty of the Philippines by depicting the fates of the prostitutes, rape victims, and injured trespassers who encounter the violence underwritten by the bases. However, these films do more than serve the necessities of political agitation against continued U.S. military presence or draw out of obscurity empire's violated bodies. What these films do is foreground the oft-ignored biopolitics implicit in questions of Philippine sovereignty. They posit sovereignty not ultimately as a matter of asserting the right to national self-determination but as a politics of life and death.

Beneath all their snarl and denunciation, the former colonial wards still find themselves clinging to the myth of what Richard Nixon once called "the old special relationships" between the two nations.[3] While these films implicitly mourn America's betrayal of its own ideals, they harbor traces of hope in the realization of the benevolence avowed by the ex-colonizer. The obsessive desire to account for the shortcomings of American benevolence is contiguous with the effort to critique empire. It is through this double movement that these films attain their politically exigent figurations of U.S. imperialism in late decolonization. The pragmatic, as well as utopian, cultural work of envisioning a livable relationship between the two parties after decolonization was strictly beyond their purview. It remained for other filmmakers to address at a later time, whose works are the focus of the next chapter. In the following sections of this chapter, I pay close attention to the symbiotic bonds of imperial violence and affection as they emerge in the American military bases' postcolonial frontier.

On All Souls' Day in 2005, a twenty-two-year-old Filipina pseudonymously called Nicole accused a U.S. Marine of raping her inside a van while his three cohorts cheered him on. The alleged sexual abuse happened inside the former U.S. base at Subic Bay in Olongapo City.[4] Filipinos could not help recognizing the incident as a throwback to the days of the American bases. Like U.S. servicemen on a weekend pass, the accused were partying in Subic Bay after conducting military exercises in the southern Philippines. Their access to the port and country was underwritten by the Visiting Forces Agreement (VFA), a thinly veiled continuation of the de facto permanent American military presence once guaranteed by the old base pacts.[5] As before, the custodianship of the offenders was hotly debated. Much to the chagrin of nationalists, the VFA allowed the accused to remain in U.S. custody until the very last appeal was adjudicated.[6] A Manila judge defied the lopsided terms of the agreement and threw the single convicted felon in a Philippine jail. Within less than a month, however, under the cover of night, the Philippine government smuggled the American Marine out of prison and delivered him to U.S. Embassy officials.[7]

The incident caused a furor reminiscent of past controversies over the social and political consequences of the bases. Newspapers, politicians, and citizens expressed nationalist outrage against neocolonialism. They trafficked in talk and images of the native body spectacularly violated as in colonial times. These discourses are present in the three films discussed in this chapter, all of which register the question of sovereignty. Historically, the problem of Philippine sovereignty was the "fundamental . . . [and] front and center"[8] issue that "received the most attention" during several rounds of negotiations for the pact to renew the bases.[9] It is directly linked to the question of imperial benevolence. In the films about the U.S. bases, sovereignty not only concerns the political recognition of an independent Philippine nation-state by the benevolent ex-colonizer but also is understood as the privilege of enjoying individual liberties and, above all, the fundamental right to life. Whenever the sovereignty of self or nation is troubled, whenever it comes to hinge on the decision of the powerful, benevolence is all.

Sovereign Exception and Political Theater: *Once a Moth*

The bases existed in the aberrant space and time of the nation's postcolonial history. Even after Philippine Independence, the bases occupied vast territories upon which America claimed legal ownership as late as 1956. After that year, ownership was ceded to the Philippines, but jurisdiction over these territories remained with the U.S. military.[10] The United States' claims to these spaces were guaranteed by the extension of territorial entitlements enjoyed during the colonial epoch, which should have expired when the United States officially recognized the independence of the Republic of the Philippines (RP) on July 4, 1946. As the American ambassador to the Philippines Stephen Bosworth concedes, America's access to the bases "is a direct legacy of our colonial rule in that country."[11]

It could be said, in the language of political philosophy, that the bases were underwritten by a *sovereign exception*, a temporary suspension of the existing order in one special case.[12] According to cold war ideology and the RP–U.S. mutual defense treaty, the rationale for such a suspension of the territorial integrity and political independence of the Philippine nation-state in one exceptional case (i.e., the base agreement) was the necessity of preserving the state from its own internal enemies and from potential foreign aggressors such as communist China. The influx of U.S. material and financial aid enabled by this exceptional arrangement also crucially guaranteed the security of the Philippines, a client state of America. Seen exclusively from the U.S. military's perspective, the Philippine concessions sustained the "strategic defense perimeter" in the western Pacific, enabling the maintenance of the desirable (i.e., noncommunist) geopolitical sphere of influence called the "free world."[13] The identification of one state with the interests of the other was thus the crucial enabling fiction that justified the taxing demands of the sovereign exception on Filipinos.

The trouble here is that the question of "nation-state sovereignty" is forever and unnecessarily an absolute one, as the philosopher Jacques Derrida tells us.[14] A single transgression—one defiled native woman, one dead scavenger, one Philippine flag raised lower than the Stars and Stripes—could compromise the sovereign right of the nation-state, the facade of Philippine independence. After all, as Carl Schmitt observes, sovereignty is defined in relation to the "borderline case and not with routine."[15] More than the rule, Schmitt adds, "the exception proves everything."[16] Since the extraordinary act of suspending the political order requires supreme authority, the exception undermines the integrity of Philippine sovereign leadership and nationhood. Moreover, if the sovereign is "he who decides on the exception," true sovereign power can be none other than the source of an edict interposing itself between, on the one hand, the accused rapists and killers and, on the other, the juridical system to which the accused must answer.[17] The authority that grants such interposition can be said to exceed even the power of the state—in this case, even if a state may have been "declared" by the colonizer as a state it has freed. The consequence of such interposition is evident. In the geopolitical sphere, true sovereignty on Philippine soil ironically comes to fall not on the independent republic but on the former colonizer. The nation becomes precariously fictive. If rogue U.S. military men can evade the Philippine juridical system, it would seem indeed, as fierce nationalists claim, that the ex-colonizers have never left.

It was not lost on Filipino politicians that the sovereign exception played a significant role in the decolonization process and in sustaining or eroding the integrity of the young nation. From the very inception of the bases agreement in 1946, the question about the sovereign decision already stood out as the most contentious issue.[18] Manila lay in shambles after having been carpet bombed at the close of the war. Even then, when the Philippines was in desperate need of American rehabilitation, Filipino politicians could not help but raise objections over the provisions for extraterritoriality and criminal jurisdiction in the proposed accord. If the relevance of the state, as one political philosopher tells us, rests upon its power to issue a decision, then it was precisely this relevance that the controversial provisions challenged.[19] The terms of extraterritoriality posited U.S. jurisdiction over American servicemen and their families who commit crimes outside the bases as well as over Filipino citizens who commit crimes within the bases. The initial provisions on criminal jurisdiction guaranteed U.S. servicemen and their families certain immunities from Philippine civil law for two kinds of crimes: those committed outside the bases against fellow American military members[20] and those committed in the line of duty against non-Americans within and outside the bases.[21] These extraordinary limitations on Philippine civil law haunted the sentiments of the people and the speeches of politicians. Nation and state were joined by the ghostly hyphen of an intrusive extraterritoriality. As the political scientist Chalmers Johnson acknowledges, extraterritoriality is "one of the historically most offensive aspects of Western (and Japanese) imperialism . . . [It] reflected the belief that Asian law was barbaric and that no 'civilized' person should be subjected to it."[22]

Declared independent by the United States, the Philippines was nonetheless deprived of the sovereign decision by American extraterritoriality. "Filipinos argue," Ambassador Bosworth writes, "that they have never had the opportunity to make a sovereign decision as to whether they want the U.S. military facilities in their country." Bosworth unequivocally acknowledges the paradoxical situation of an ex-colonial state proclaimed sovereign but at the same time constrained by its ex-colonizer in deciding the fate of the bases. "I have some sympathy for the Philippine position," Bosworth adds.[23] His tact and emotional restraint are admirable in the face of what was to become—as the films on the bases show—a source of national anger and mourning.

So divisive were debates over particular sovereign exceptions in 1976 that they stalled preliminary discussions for the renewal of the base agreement. Only after President Ferdinand Marcos set the issue aside did the two sides manage to iron out the points that led to the 1979 agreement. In 1976, Lupita A. Concio (now Lupita Aquino-Kashiwahara) released a film called *Once a Moth* (*Minsa'y isang gamu-gamo*). Concio's film responds with admirable specificity and force to the legal debates surrounding Philippine sovereignty and the U.S. bases. The accords for the bases were renewable every five years. As with *Once a Moth*, the release dates of the other films in this chapter corresponded to the five-year cycles in which base accords were to be renewed and, hence, were being discussed and negotiated.

National failure is at the heart of the motifs in Concio's film. *Once a Moth* depicts the ways in which Filipinos fail to fully express their nationalist sentiments in public spectacles or to perform the mundane aspects of their national identity. The characters in *Once a Moth* are all irremediably guarded in their comportment, incapable of enjoying their jubilation, and largely mute in their grief. They suffer from the failure of articulation. It is a condition symptomatic of the constraints that the sovereign exception places upon the ex-colonized. The sovereign exception, in this particular case, underwrites U.S. presence at and through the bases. When these motifs of constraint are set beside the film's historical moment, Concio's irony is hard to miss.

In 1975, a year before the start of another round of negotiations, Marcos began speaking candidly of his plan to demand greater compensation from the Americans "in keeping with our dignity as a sovereign republic and in keeping with the development of our time."[24] Several factors bolstered the feeling that the Philippines had gained some leverage in the bases negotiations, namely, (a) communist victories over U.S. client governments in South Vietnam and Cambodia, which raised questions about the value of the American security commitment to Asia and the mutual defense treaty with the Philippines; (b) misgivings about the importance of the bases expressed during a U.S. congressional reappraisal of foreign policy; and (c) the Philippine nation-state's need to rethink its relationship to other Asian countries and the Soviet Union. Marcos wished to see U.S. commitment displayed in dramatically rising aid figures. He also told visiting American solons that his government needed to assert more control over the bases so as not to be perceived as a puppet of Uncle Sam.[25]

Filipino nationalists, meanwhile, were drumming up the distinction between possessing actual sovereignty and "the appearance of sovereignty."[26] For them, this difference spelled out unequivocally the need to close the bases, which were an instrument not of the Philippine nation-state so much as of the former colonizer. *Once a Moth* draws upon such nationalist conjuration of apparitional sovereignty. In the film, Philippine sovereignty is so severely compromised that it could not even be represented with a dignity proper to an independent republic. "The appearance of sovereignty" warps the integral image of the nation-state. Concio's film mirrors such distortion with her motif of stunted expression. I now turn to this motif involving scenes of public spectacle.

Once a Moth's protagonist fails to learn the dance called *tinikling*, the country's iconic "bamboo dance." Corazon dela Cruz (played by superstar Nora Aunor) is a Filipina nurse bound for the United States. What is arguably the film's most dramatic scene of hindered expression, the *tinikling* scene, involves a performance of national identity most legible to Filipino viewers as such. Other signs necessary for the performance of this identity are presented early on in the film, leading to the *tinikling* scene. Cora's travel agent (Leo Martinez) advises her to bring her *patadyong* (a native skirt), learn to cook *adobo* (savory pork stew) and *pansit* (rice noodles), and master "one or two *kundimans*" (love songs). The travel agent reasons that she might be called upon to perform her cultural identity in America, since she is embarking on an exchange-visitor program sponsored by the U.S. Department of State. During her farewell party, Cora receives a native dress from her mother, Chedeng (Gloria Sevilla). *Once a Moth*'s director showcases Aunor's talent as a champion singer and has Cora belt out a patriotic ditty with great panache. Cora's friends insist, however, that she also practice the "bamboo dance." Elsewhere, juxtaposed with the scene at the party, her brother Carlito (Eddie Villamayor) is about to perform an act of nationalist self-expression. He is trying to fly a kite over the vast firing range known as Crow Valley. The kite—red, white, and blue, like the colors of both the Philippine and American flags—is a thinly veiled emblem. Cora tries to skip in and out of the gaps of the clashing bamboo poles. But when she miscalculates the rhythm, her leg is caught between the poles at precisely the moment Carlito falls, gunned down by an American sentry for trespassing.

The juxtaposition of the *tinikling* and kite scenes forms a rather pedantic image of cultural conflict. It is a barefaced allusion to the political challenge presented by the bases. The image of clashing bamboo poles points to the difficulty of reaching an agreement according "full respect to Philippine sovereignty" while accommodating the "unhampered United States military operations" desired by the excolonizer.[27] The dance also represents Cora's personal dilemma. As Cora confronts the fact of American violence in the homeland, what awaits her as a nurse-in-training in the states are the benevolent acts of healing and learning from a different culture.

The kite, as I have mentioned, bears colors shared by both the American and Philippine flags. It recalls the moment in history when Emilio Aguinaldo appealed for American recognition of Philippine independence but also asserted his people's prerogative to self-determination. To represent his country's cause, the same freedom that America embodied, Aguinaldo unfurled an emblem steeped in the hues of Old Glory. The kite that Carlito wanted to fly over Crow Valley inherits Aguinaldo's gesture. It also emblematizes the indeterminate sovereignty of the bases. But having entered the firing range against his family's advice, Carlito dies before the colors could be flown there. Likewise, Cora's future performance for "cross-cultural" American spectatorship is marred in advance by her failure to embody the *tinikling*'s rhythm.

Cora's misstep and Carlito's incursion into Crow Valley are depicted as fated moments. Carlito dies during an aberrant lapse of filial affection, when his otherwise doting parents and siblings ignore him as they prepare to celebrate Cora's departure for America. The ironic situation reflects the Philippines' unfounded confidence in its leverage during the negotiations for new base accords. *Once a Moth* marks the impossibility—at least during its historical moment—of parity between the ex-colonizer and the ex-colonized. The outcome favoring the ex-colonial nation-state was not guaranteed because, as Carlito's death shows, the sovereign exception continued to fall within the domains of the U.S. military. Depicting the lapse in national vigilance as an aberrant instance of neglect in Cora's family, Concio's film brings to the fore the conditions that enabled catastrophe, as the ghost of sovereignty waited in the wings of triumphal spectacles.

After Carlito's demise, Grandpa Menciong (Paquito Salcedo) burns the kite. The incendiary act is motivated by the old man's skepticism toward both American benevolence and Philippine sovereignty. Having lived most of his life as a subject of empire, Grandpa recalls the practice in the so-called commonwealth period when the national symbol was banned by the U.S. colonial regime's infamous "flag law."[28] Concio presents Grandpa's character as the figure most adequate to performing an act supplemental to flag burning. It is, after all, this weary man who recognizes the questionable intimacy of Philippine nationalism and American sovereign power. The mutual defense treaty enabling the U.S. military presence in the Philippines marshals the assumption that the security of the free world is at risk. It presumes a worldwide state of siege in order to legitimate the sovereign violence of the military base. This cold war presumption is what Grandpa questions. Early in the film, the old man recalls that American planes sowed bombs over Crow Valley. Young scavengers who happened to be there were instantly killed. As the old man says in vivid Filipino, they died "with skulls blasted." Grandpa protests the brutality of a militarism that has no justification. He asks his daughter Chedeng, "Is there a war in our country? Why are the Marines in Subic shooting people? And why are those pilots dropping bombs over there?" Grandpa's rhetorical questions implicitly refute the legitimacy of the "law-maintaining" violence and benevolent protectionism of the U.S. security apparatus.

Just as Carlito and Cora, however, fail to perform their national identity, Grandpa fails to express his nationalist outrage in the public sphere. During the funeral procession for the young scavengers, Grandpa's memory of World War II is triggered. He relives the infamous death march that began in his hometown of Capas, Tarlac.[29] The death march recalls an instance of solidarity between Americans and Filipinos in the face of another foreigner's atrocity. The involuntary memory is depicted as a cutaway to sepia-toned footage of the event. The footage is shown when Grandpa, thinking aloud, suddenly recalls the historical episode: "I don't understand the American: is he an ally or enemy? I seem to be seeing the death march once more." Throwing off the audience, the abrupt insertion of the historical episode in the funeral scene reproduces Grandpa's puzzlement. Recalled in the context of the scavengers' victimization, the death march is emptied of heroic meaning.

In his lifetime, Grandpa has never really seen Filipinos win over empire. His twilight years have coincided, in fact, with the increasing reach and power of U.S. sovereignty. "Corazon, do they also own the moon now?" Grandpa asks in another scene, as he watches the television broadcast of the lunar landing. The reference to America's successful venture to outer space takes place after the death of the scavengers and before the victimization of his grandson Carlito. The news aggravates his sense of outrage and helplessness over the might of America, this inscrutable foe and friend. Confronted by the victimization of the young scavengers, Grandpa finds little solace in the nostalgia enjoyed by old nationalists who keep themselves, in Fanon's words, "drunk on the remembrance of the epoch which led up to independence."[30] At the same time, however, the affective bonds formed by events like the death march retain enough force to hold in abeyance political grief. Even if Grandpa would like to see Filipinos win over empire, what constrains his nationalist outrage—at least until the death of his grandson—is his belief in American benevolence, a deeply internalized myth sustained by the ties of colonial intimacy. Grandpa does not suffer the same fate as the young scavengers or Carlito, but the old man is perhaps the most tragic figure in the film. Able to bear witness to his nation's emergence from formal empire, but unable to relinquish the myth of American benevolence, Grandpa is denied the freedom to despise America and to mourn his own nation.

Another character in *Once a Moth*, Cora's future mother-in-law, suffers from the constraint that the American fantasy of benevolence imposes upon national selfhood. Yolanda (Perla Bautista) works for the PX (post exchange) commissary at the base. When a Filipina merchandise control guard (Luz Fernandez) becomes jealous of Yolanda's friendship with an American serviceman, the guard subjects Yolanda to false suspicion of smuggling commissary goods. Yolanda is strip-searched during the routine screening of employees as they leave the base. "I just want to be sure," the guard tells her in English, "there are no prohibited items concealed in your bra and your panty." Unable to find anything, the guard confiscates Yolanda's underwear, feigning disgust. Initially, Yolanda keeps to herself the details of the shameful incident. When she finally breaks her pained silence, she reveals that the guard ignored her pleas made in the name of a shared national identity. Yolanda recounts her trauma to her son, Boni (Jay Ilagan), and housekeeper (played by Lily Miraflor), sharing that the guard proceeded to pick the "panty with the tip of her ballpoint pen." The guard then waved the undergarment around and "called the attention of the Americans at the gate . . . They laughed. The Americans even covered their noses and their eyes. As I exited the gate, they were laughing at me. All of them were laughing at me!" As she concludes the account of her shame, we briefly catch a glimpse at the foreground, on a shelf in the living room, of a porcelain figurine of a black child. Like Yolanda, the child mourns the deficiency of white love.

While she gains sympathetic Filipino listeners in her son and the housekeeper, Yolanda fails miserably in expressing her grievance to the Americans. The ill-treated mother files charges of "slander by deed" but is answered with further harassment by the Filipina guard and her two American companions, who confiscate the "smuggled goods" being sold in the family's dry goods store. When Yolanda files a suit against the American base commander for authorizing the illegal raid, the latter obtains an official duty certification that instantly removes him from Philippine jurisdiction. During the inquest, he plainly states, "Since I was acting on official duty, I am answerable to my government, not to a Filipino court." Later in the film, Yolanda's attorney explains another legal concept to her in an attempt to convince her that the case is dead. "We cannot do anything," he insists. "What we are contesting are extraterritorial rights enjoyed by the Americans since 1947. We're swimming against the tide here." The power of American extraterritoriality and criminal jurisdiction, authorized by the base's sovereign exception, shatters not just Yolanda but also Boni, who has long harbored dreams of joining the U.S. Navy and immigrating to America.

The fruitless inquest over the injustice done to Yolanda finds its explosive repetition in the trial of Carlito's killer. Whereas the inquest involves a matter of personal liberty, the trial adjudicates on a matter of life and death. In spite of their disparity, however, the two cases become identical when set against the U.S. military base whose exceptional status Philippine law guarantees. Yolanda's shame and Carlito's death both amount to nothing. The sameness to which these incommensurable forms of suffering are reduced demonstrates, as I will discuss further, the stakes of the sovereign exception.

"A Piece of America": The Base as Sovereign Sphere

The social impact of the sovereign exception went far beyond the context of the Philippine nation-state. The military defense establishment innocuously described the bases as "cut-rate multipurpose Western Pacific pit stops."[31] In fact, collectively, U.S. presence in the Philippines and in other countries "anchored the southern flank of America's strategic position in the western Pacific," sheltering from their enemies not only the Marcos dictatorship but also the rest of the "free world."[32] The bases became staging grounds for U.S. military ventures in China, Siberia, Korea, Indonesia, and Vietnam, visiting life and death upon the Far East region.[33] What allowed these so-called pit stops to operate without hindrance was the principle of the sovereign exception.

In the cold war imaginary, the bases—which may have harbored long-range missiles—were both deterrents to and magnets for communist attacks. For Filipinos, the base represented more than just a "visible symbol of U.S. imperialism." It yielded more than just good fodder for politics and "nationalist posturing."[34] The base became what Giorgio Agamben calls a "sovereign sphere."[35] It became an extraterritorial threshold where the weakest of Filipinos in and around the bases were "abandoned . . . to the most extreme misfortunes" and where GIs could kill without standing trial for homicide.[36] Of the twenty-eight deaths reported in base records from 1947 to 1963, the seven that were attributed to GIs resulted in no convictions.[37] The imposition of a three-year sentence on Larry Cole for shooting Rogelio Balagtas in 1964 was an exception, meted out under the glare of extreme public scrutiny. Most GIs accused of shooting Filipinos at the bases went home scot-free. By contrast, Filipinos who trespassed at the base were, to borrow Agamben's language, "stripped of every right by virtue of the fact that anyone can kill [them] without committing homicide."[38] The host state voluntarily retracted its power in the face of U.S. sovereignty. Due to special privileges granted to the accused GIs and the dispensations routinely given in the face of the most serious transgressions, the Filipino citizen was reduced to bare life—to biological life stripped of all rights.

Of the sovereign sphere Agamben writes, "Men enter into a zone in which they are no longer distinct from beasts."[39] *Once a Moth* demonstrates Agamben's thesis in an uncanny, almost literal way. According to the testimony of the soldier accused of Carlito's death, the shooting was an accident. The native boy, who was about to fly a kite bearing the colors of the American flag, was mistaken for a boar by the American serviceman. When the Philippine citizen strays into the sovereign sphere of the U.S. base, a metamorphosis takes place: he turns into a "non-man," the figure of an "animal in human form."[40] The life of the Filipino trespasser becomes bare life, or the animal life of man. Although bare life had become irrelevant to politics in the long history of human societies, Foucault points out that politics in modernity engendered anew "the bestialization of man achieved through the most sophisticated political techniques."[41] This modern politics capable of suspending the status of human life goes by the more popular name of "biopolitics."[42]

If what the native undergoes upon straying into the sovereign sphere of the U.S. base is a form of bestialization, then the politics of the U.S. military-base complex can be aptly characterized as biopolitics or even as thanatopolitics (a politics of death). All three of the films in this chapter memorialize this sacrificial figure—that of the native scavenger felled by the bullets of an American sentry. *Once a Moth* exploits the power of this figure in drawing a vulgar parallelism between the fate of Carlito and the spit-roasted pig served at Cora's farewell party. The twinning of boy and animal is foreshadowed for the first time when Carlito sits next to Grandpa as they witness the pig's slaughter. The boy gets clingy, and the old man shoos him away. Carlito offers to help with other chores, but everyone in his family asks him to keep out of their way. He decides to join a bunch of kids headed for Crow Valley on the back of a cart pulled by a water buffalo. Later, it is this same vehicle that bears the boy's corpse after Carlito takes a bullet smack in the heart, from an American sentry idly looking for something to shoot. The depiction of the boy as bare life unfolds in a cross-cutting, match-cutting pattern straight out of Soviet filmmaker Sergei Eisenstein's agitprop *Strike* (1925).[43] As Carlito's bloodstained body is loaded onto the cart and covered with banana leaves, the roast pig at Cora's farewell party similarly is brought to the feasting table, and Grandpa Menciong covers it in banana leaves.

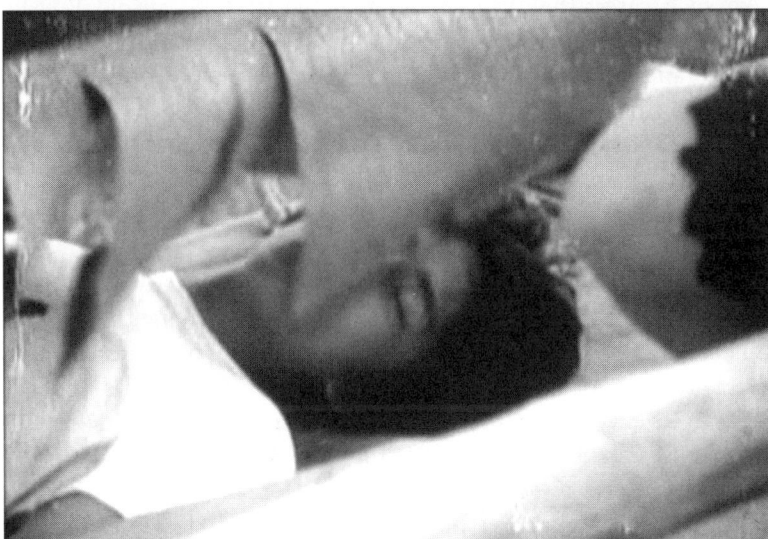

The parallel fates of the pig and Carlito (Eddie Villamayor) are established through intercuts and match cuts. Source: Once a Moth.

If the rendering of Carlito's death seems overly dramatic or heavy-handed, it is because it bears the memory of earlier child killings at Crow Valley. *Once a Moth* asserts that the matters of sovereignty and the bases exceed politics as it is usually known. Crow Valley is a sovereign sphere in which the human life of the ex-colonized is "exposed to an unconditional capacity to be killed."[44] In *Once a Moth*, the political order in the preceding statement by Agamben is specified as an extraterritorial American order. The film points out the resemblance between contemporaneous struggle against the bases and the ones waged against the colonialism that preceded—but also led to the rise of—the "cut-rate multipurpose Western Pacific pit stops." Tracing this history of conflict is an important task. As empire steps up its use of force against citizens, so do global struggles against imperialism intensify in their biopolitical stakes.

Once a Moth assembles a composite of true-to-life fatal incidents connected to the bases. Carlito's plight in Crow Valley draws from two such cases: the 1964 shooting of the sixteen-year-old Rogelio Balagtas by Larry Cole, an off-duty American sentry hunting in Clark Field,[45] and the 1969 killing of another Filipino man by sailor Michael Mooney, who mistook him for a boar.[46] In *Once a Moth*, the GI (not insignificantly named John Smith) escapes trial by being "mistakenly" reassigned to another country. As in the case of Balagtas, the offer of a cheap solatium—a $787 check for a boy's life—only adds insult to injury. The insult doubles quite literally in *Once a Moth*. Cora's family is offered monetary settlement twice. In the first instance, one of two American officers who come to the funeral apologizes for mistaking the child for a boar, handing the grieving sister a check. Fuming in righteous anger, Cora protests, "My brother is not a pig!" Later, when the trial is suspended, the GI's lawyer offers her the humble recompense of loose dollar bills cobbled together by his client. "Did the soldier tell you how much a person's life is worth these days in America?" Cora asks the lawyer. "How much is a kilo of human flesh?" The attorney is about to rehash the boar defense when Cora shows him a wallet-sized portrait of her brother and barks, "Tell Corporal John S. Smith that you saw my brother's picture. Never would he be mistaken for a boar. My brother was a person."

Once a Moth unmasks "the law of the jungle" as the real order of things at the base.[47] In this jungle, there are no distinctions between human and beast. Managed by an ostensibly superior civilization, the base is a jungle in which the native is reduced, as Fanon writes, "to animal level by imperial powers."[48] The willful misrecognition of the native as animal persists within this jungle where, as Derrida reminds us, "the reason of the strongest" carries "the greatest force."[49]

Once a Moth's conjuration of the base as jungle is doubly effective in figuring an oft-ignored aspect of the sovereign sphere. Like many such vast tracts of land within the bases, Crow Valley represents potential agricultural and residential property consigned to unproductive use by the base agreement. The sovereign exception of the bases pact called for the land to be preserved as a jungle where the old and new technologies of killing could be practiced by American soldiers training in order to fight elsewhere.

The magnitude of the country's territorial concessions to the jungle of Crow Valley and the even larger sprawl of the bases was staggering. An American scholar notes that until the closure of the bases in 1992, "the Pentagon was one of the largest holders of agricultural lands in the Philippines."[50] So vast was this territory that "in the mid-1970s, unbeknown to the air force, squatters produced about $5 million worth of sugar cane per year at Clark" and had been dwelling in "an area the size of Ohio State University."[51]

The deprivation of living space and other forms of patrimony—lumber, minerals, and marine life—contributed to the poverty that made scavengers and boars of natives. Here, as in colonial times, the fact of occupation repeated that "original sin of simple robbery," which continues to link imperialism and capitalism together.[52] Marcos, who had the leverage to correct this problem during the negotiations in the 1970s, later recovered about 92 percent of the land area of Clark Air Base and 60 percent of the land area at Subic Bay. The use of this returned territory, however, was restricted by the blanket guarantees exacted by the United States during this round of talks. In exchange for the recuperation of land, the appointment of a figurehead Filipino base commander, and gaining control of base perimeter security, the Philippines guaranteed "unhampered U.S. military operations."[53] The fact that this guarantee involved nothing less than one of virtually unlimited control over the sovereign sphere of the bases was asserted in the succeeding years when Philippine inquiries about the presence of nuclear weapons at the bases were met with a response that was essentially "it's none of your business."[54]

The responsibility for deciding over life and death in the base (and in the western Pacific) thus ultimately remained with the United States. The remarks of a character in *Once a Moth* about Clark Air Base are symptomatic of this fact: "It's a piece of America!" What does it say about the ex-colonizer's benevolence, the film asks, when within this piece of America, death reigns as the fate of the ex-native?

In my introduction to this book and in the previous chapter, I noted the unpredictable nature of fantasy. Even in *Once a Moth*'s grim economy of trauma, one will find an unpredictable turn in the narrative that bears upon the film's fantasy of U.S. imperial benevolence. The film ends with a striking vision of reversal that shows the native for once wielding absolute power over life and death. Having just lost her case, Cora and her people exit the court house. Just then, a uniformed GI on a motorcycle tries to overtake a jeepney and suffers a sudden mishap. Onlookers crowd around him while Cora, escorted by her lawyer, approaches, not looking too happy to help the American. The movie, however, leaves little doubt about her benevolence in wielding the power of biopolitical choice. The scene highlights Cora's medical profession: "Please let us pass," the lawyer announces. "There is a nurse here." One of the closing images in the film frames Cora in a low-angle shot. The heroine looms over the bloodied, motionless American whom her vocation as a nurse requires her to succor.

The fantasy of power and righteousness is a staple in cultural productions of colonized and decolonizing societies. Homi Bhabha writes that "the fantasy of the native is precisely to occupy the master's place while keeping [her] place in the slave's *avenging* anger."[55] What is perhaps not so common in *Once a Moth*'s fantastic reversal is that it is the native woman who fights back on behalf of the weakened men. Cora stages it beyond the politics of lawsuits and in the biopolitical sphere, as a nurse weighing decisions of life and death. She wields a power begotten of the ex-colonizers who established nursing schools in the Philippines and, to this day, continue importing Filipino nurses en masse. Despite Cora's biopolitical leverage in the final scene, as well as her justifiable hostility toward the wounded serviceman, her heroism is underscored. Cora has to be good to the GI, even if he might be incapable of doing so. More accurately, because his kind has not been able to show any benevolence, she shows *him* what benevolence means.

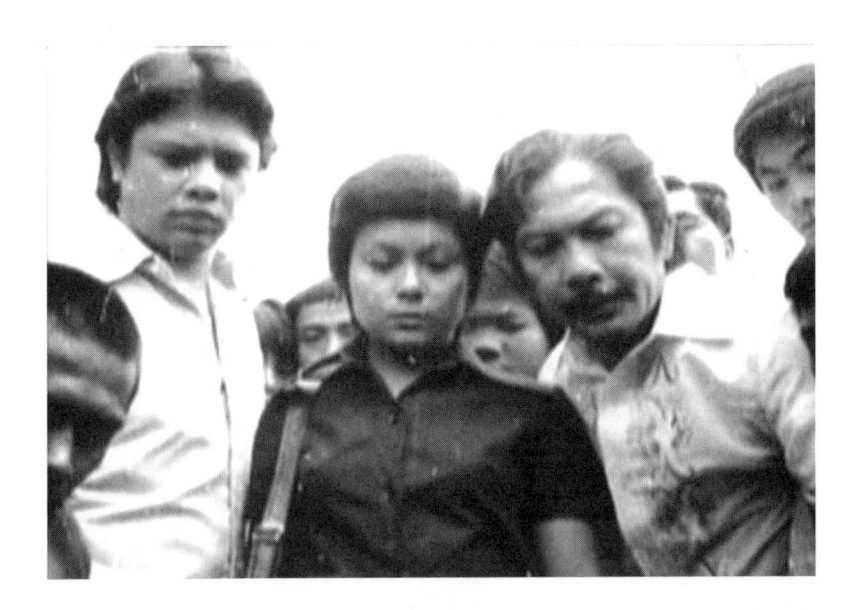

The Filipina nurse (Nora Aunor) stands over the body of an injured U.S. serviceman. Source: Once a Moth.

In a final scene edited out of the video release of the film, Cora follows the wounded American to the hospital. There she learns that he is none other than John Smith, her brother's killer.[56] *Once a Moth* turns the revenge fantasy Bhabha describes into a postcolonial version of the Samaritan parable. Cora's ordeal becomes less a battle waged against the intimate enemy than a struggle to honor *his* sovereignty. Cora redeems the ex-colonizer from *his* lack of benevolence, for the sake of the future and for the sake of others who may yet require the benevolence of empire.

Love and Death in the Periphery: *PX*

The deprivation of space and resources, as we have seen in the previous section, creates a situation in which the native need not be shot in order to be killed. Lino Brocka's *PX* (1984), a thriller designed for crossover appeal beyond the Philippines, departs from the overtly nationalist concerns of *Once a Moth* but succeeds nonetheless in treating the thanatopolitics outside the sovereign sphere of the base.[57]

In *Homo Sacer*, Agamben suggests that "the [concentration] camp, which is now securely lodged within the city's interior"[58] has become "the hidden paradigm of the political space of modernity."[59] If we think of the base as a kind of camp—both are arguably sovereign spheres— we may understand the implicit preoccupation of Brocka's film as querying what the base means for those who live within its periphery.[60] How does the biopolitics of the military base affect those who are inevitably implicated, drawn in, or made complicit by its presence? What does American benevolence mean for people who live on the margins of the bases?

For too long, said a mayor of the city outside Subic Bay naval base, American servicemen had treated the Philippines as little more than "the periphery of the bases."[61] Within the regime underwritten by this mind-set, the "natives" became figures who, in Agamben's scenario, were banned from the base and yet also part of it. Though excluded, they were part of the order; indeed, the ban worked in such a way that they were included precisely in their very exclusion.[62]

The three protagonists of *PX*—two Filipinos and an American serviceman—are literally banished from Clark Air Base in Pampanga. Their fortunes, nonetheless, become bound to the oblique forces emanating from within the territory on which the protagonists cannot set foot. The protagonists become entangled in the order immediately outside it, as with countless natives and foreigners living in the shadow of the base. Unlike the majority, however, the three protagonists find themselves drawn to the very threshold of power. There, in a place that is neither outside nor inside the sovereign sphere, biopolitics and thanatopolitics become interchangeable—the politics of life as one of death.[63]

Brocka's film turns the cinematic thriller genre's stock characters of cop, fallen woman, and outlaw into historically recognizable figures of the base milieu. The historical reality of gangsterism within and outside the base allows for the thriller's genre conventions to be rehearsed even as the film seeks to portray the complex thanatopolitics stalking the periphery of the base.[64]

The first of three liminal figures is a racial hybrid. Lydia (Hilda Koronel) is a half-American prostitute. When she was born, her U.S. serviceman father abandoned her and her mother outside Clark. Before ending up as a prostitute, she hoped to avoid the typical fate of base children and lived with her mother away from Clark until her mother died. However, in keeping with the film's theme of fated repetition, Lydia was drawn back to the same circumstances that shaped her mother's life. In the sense that Lydia is one empire's bastard daughter, she is *returned* to Clark. To borrow Agamben's words, Lydia is "already originarily and immediately subject to a power of life and death with respect to the father."[65]

Lydia's paternity haunts her. She constantly wavers between foregoing and reviving her childhood dream of going to America by hooking up with a GI. *PX*, however, configures the prospect of immigration as contiguous with the fate of prostitution. The double significance of Lydia's patrimony constitutes her ambivalence. Though her entitlement to America remains elusive, Lydia clings to the darker aspect of her father's legacy. As a prostitute, physically alluring yet morally despicable, Lydia is alternately a lover and hater of both American and Filipino men. She embodies the figure of the ex-colonized "as the living haunt of contradictions."[66] Within her thrives the fugitive border between the native self and the foreign ideal.

Lydia's live-in boyfriend, Isidro (Phillip Salvador), also shares the privilege and curse of liminality, though mainly with respect to his indirect sharing of the U.S. military's power over life and death. He is a hired gun who murders both natives and foreigners outside the base. When asked to justify his occupational choice, Isidro tells Lydia that he finds satisfaction in the fact that "in all of Angeles, I know I'm the very best there is." Gomez, the head honcho of the city's most powerful criminal syndicate, shares his opinion. Isidro is his go-to person for the liquidation needs of the drug and prostitution ring Gomez runs with the cooperation of the Americans. As both an instinctive killer and an agent of oblique imperial powers, he is the figure of the native afflicted with a "homicidal melancholia" that Frantz Fanon poetically names in *The Wretched of the Earth*.[67] Isidro constantly receives his kill orders from corrupt Americans and Filipinos, yet he also already possesses a murderous desire that comes from the terror and anger that are, in Fanon's words, the "expression of the natives' unconscious."[68] The source of the negative emotions is the disenfranchisement of one who constantly appreciates what he can never attain. He puts his kid brother, Boy, through school because he believes that "not knowing how to speak English get[s] you nowhere." He expresses great pride in hearing Boy use the conqueror's tongue: "You would think he was some child of an American, speaking their *wers-wers*." In bragging about his brother's achievement, however, he acknowledges that his own lack of an education is one of those things that make him "a throwaway" person. Having himself "hired out" to Americans for his homicidal capacity gives him the compensating (but also corrosive) sense of fulfillment he needs to get through the day.

The third wheel in the relationship, and the discredited authority figure of the genre, is a low-level American serviceman named George Graves (Leonard Urso). Although he serves in the seemingly powerful capacity of an armed sentry, he becomes the weakest of the three protagonists when he inadvertently antagonizes the American–Filipino crime conspiracy. Upon the insistence of Murphy and another of his superiors, Graves shoots at an unseen figure moving in base territory. His unintended victim turns out to be Boy, Isidro's brother, who is yet another one of those pubescent scavengers killed while salvaging shell casings in Crow Valley. The same superiors who prompted the killing secretly turn against Graves, fearing that he would either willfully expose or draw attention to their participation in the same drug trafficking ring under Gomez's protection.[69] They frame Graves for drug possession then later take out a hit on him. With Isidro dead set on vengeance and his superiors anxious to rub him out, Graves is ironically reduced to a status even lower than that of the homicidal native who, though susceptible to being killed, enjoys a measure of control over his life. Suffering a fate unthinkable for a U.S. serviceman, Graves, in this fantasy reversal, comes to resemble the native scavenger boy in *Once a Moth*, a man-animal banned from the base.[70] For his survival, Graves becomes dependent entirely on the kindness of Filipinos outside the base. Lydia, who has resumed entertaining American clients, helps Graves. So does a poor family, offering their home as a safe house despite the fact that the noise of the planes at the base has diminished their duck farm's productivity. Lydia and the poor family harbor the fantasy of a special relationship with America. It is this fantasy—working in tandem with the valorization of an indiscriminately permissive Philippine hospitality—that provisionally sustains Graves's life.

The volatile configuration of opposing forces in the narrative makes the eruption of conflict inevitable, reflecting the similarly intimate and yet explosive coexistence of native and foreign alliances within and outside the base. Hence, in *PX*, the young boy's death is a mere triggering event. Even the love triangle that places the three figures in direct conflict is perfunctory (and thus weak). The film demonstrates that for people who have inherited the resentment created by the colonial situation and sustained in its aftermath by neoimperialism, what holds is the murderous cycle of violence.

The violence that Fanon sees as an inevitable continuation of the oppressive colonial regime seeps out of the base and circulates among the Filipinos on its periphery. Living close to the base, those who are most intimate with—and thus vulnerable to—the agents of empire are the ones who die in the greatest numbers. Before and during Graves's inevitable pursuit by both Isidro and the gangsters serving as proxies for corrupt Americans, three prostitutes are murdered in mysterious circumstances.

At the start of the film, the corpse of a bar girl named Tina is found in an alley. Onlookers at the crime scene, including Lydia, shudder while hearing descriptions of the dead woman's ordeal. "She was probably high," says one woman, when "a lot of men had their fun with her . . . dear God, seventeen of them . . . seventeen." Tina was "brought to a construction site and then guys took turns . . . even a twelve-year-old kid joined the fray." Later at the bar, one of Tina's

Lydia (Hilda Koronel) looks away from the corpse of a mysteriously slain fellow prostitute. Source: PX

colleagues recounts the sad way of life that foreshadowed the manner of her death: "Yes, do you know when she got high, she just spread her legs in the alley, her mouth open, attracting flies?" Later, a woman from the province (Estrella Kuenzler) shows up at the bars with photograph in hand, looking for her runaway daughter named Luisa. Lydia, who is unable to muster the courage to reveal the young woman's fate, turns the mother away after giving her money for the trip home. She then recounts the grim tale to her colleague Josie: "I knew her [daughter]. She did the table dance. A sexy dance. They would inject her with drugs to loosen her up. She had four American boyfriends at any one time because she saw it as a gamble. Maybe one of them would take her to America. She really wanted to go to America. Like me, like all of us . . . But one day she lost that gamble. She was found dead in a motel, her mouth stuffed with a towel. After it happened, I stopped consorting with Americans." Later in the film, just before the opposing forces meet in fatal convergence, Josie herself is killed, found dead on the same bed where Lydia and Graves first had sex.

PX reveals that the murdered prostitutes are not just intimations of Lydia's fate. To use Rey Chow's phrase, the bar girls' mysterious deaths yield "a scene of crime with the woman's body as evidence and witness."[71] To be sure, the bodies in *PX* bear witness to the social costs of imperialist sexual relations: "souvenir babies, sexually transmitted diseases," and "mass transnationalized and institutionalized" prostitution, among others.[72] But there is arguably more to this scenario. The puzzle surrounding the death of the hospitality girls remains unsolved throughout the film. This enigma suggests the elusive quality of the violence that constitutes and maintains order within and outside the base. The orifices of the slaughtered native women "speak" many things unarticulated about the contradictions of neocolonialism and the turbulent decolonizing processes aggravated and at the same time impeded by the bases.[73] These unarticulated messages travel among the fallen women, one living, and several others, dead. Among the characters in the film, these women have been most intimate with the American and Filipino men responsible for neocolonialism and the tumultuous aspects of decolonization. At the scene of the crime, Lydia gazes at the slain prostitute Tina, and a silent dialogue occurs between them. The camera establishes this mute conversation with a chain of looks. A zooming low-angle shot, revealing Lydia's horrified expression, simulates the dead woman's perspective. The successive frame, in turn, represents the impossible response of the dead. It is the perfect inverse of the one that preceded it. Mimicking Lydia's view, a high-angle shot zooms in on the corpse. Through this exchange of gazes, and through the zooming movement of the lens, the women partake of secrecy and knowingness. They share the same fate of substitution in a brutal place and time. The carnage at the base and along its periphery is so rampant that it victimizes even the men there. By the second half of the film, the imperialist–thug alliance from which Isidro and Graves once drew strength turns against them. Killers both, these men become the hunted.

While the violence represented by the grisly killings is sponsored by oblique powers within and outside the base, the nature of that violence is decidedly intimate. It is a result of proximity to a destructive force, or alternately, an intimacy fated to destruction. "Is it nice in the army?" Lydia the half-American bar girl asks Graves, making small talk during her first encounter with the GI. The boyish American replies, "Of course, although the first thing they tell us is not to trust Filipinos." The suspicion and hostility that have become the institutionalized responses to the dubious politesse of hospitality and special relationships: is this not the law of neocolonial relations epitomized by the base? In *PX*, the thanatopolitics of the camp radiates into the polis that lies immediately outside the camp's enclosure. Brocka asks us to reflect on the turbulence of such contamination through a spatial metaphor for the strange relations between decolonization and colonial paternity. *PX* depicts the ways in which the violence begotten in the colonial era persists, and sometimes even intensifies, in the period of late decolonization.

In the final third of the film, prompted by the conventions of the thriller genre, a chase ensues. Isidro trails Lydia to hunt down Graves. When Isidro catches up with them, Lydia risks her life and her relationship to Isidro by begging him to spare Graves's life. Distressed by her infidelity, Isidro asks Lydia, "Did you love the American even then? When Boy was killed, did you love the American even then?" We should recall here that Lydia is half American and half native. The melancholic question concerning Lydia's split longing is clearly evocative of his own divided heart, set loose to empire's affective economy. The title *PX* is short for "post exchange," or the commissary where

American goods could be purchased. The term is metonymic not just of Lydia and Graves but of things American and the mythic Western country. Hence, it is hardly surprising that in spite of Isidro's bitterness toward his American rival, he decides to spare Graves's life. Isidro acts ostensibly out of love for Lydia. But the native's act of mercy is also fraught with his repudiated identification with Graves. Isidro's frustration over Lydia's desire for Graves reflects the Philippines' colonial attachment to the fantasm of imperial benevolence. Loving a half-American native woman who is in love with an American, Isidro is haunted by the nation's disappointed longing for friendship and parity with America.

The chase scene takes place on the base's periphery, but the film implicitly marks the base as the source of violence. While Isidro murderously stalks Graves, they are in turn being hunted down. The corrupt American military men and their Filipino goons maim Graves in a shootout at a bar. Graves heeds Lydia's advice to crawl back into the base. But as he tries to climb the fence, Graves is killed by a fellow American.[74] Here we discover why Isidro has been denied both Lydia's love and Graves's friendship. There appears to be little love in empire except its territorial love for its borders. Despite promises of friendship, there is little parity attained in the exchanges that flow alongside empire's passion for itself. In *PX*, even an American subject is victimized by the informal policy known as "shoot first, ask questions later." Killed by another GI, Graves experiences what Jean-Paul Sartre calls the "moment of the boomerang," the violence that returns to the imperialist.[75] Graves's demise at the threshold of the base echoes and even surpasses the haste and force with which he had killed Isidro's brother. Brocka amplifies the violence of Graves's death by intently training a couple of lengthy handheld shots on the American as he is riddled with bullets and breathes his last. The film's spectator, who remains on the other side of the fence until the scene ends, becomes a witness who not only lacks the agency to help but also seems to derive a perverse satisfaction watching Graves get what he had coming.

Sometime after Graves's death, we find Isidro cruising the neon-lit streets of Olongapo once again. He had earlier sworn to renounce killing, but it seems as if he is back in business. He runs into Lydia, who is also plying her trade outside a night club. She playfully makes her standard proposition: "Overnight, Joe?" It may be surmised that while the

Graves (Leonard Urso) is shot by a sentry while trying to climb back into the base. Source: PX.

two have returned to their old modus vivendi, they have also drawn a lesson out of Graves's demise. Against the dictates of their hearts, too easily loosed by their American fantasy, Isidro and Lydia strengthen their resolve never again to "love the American" from the base.

Reestablishing Sovereignty: *In the Claws of an Eagle*

More than a decade after Concio's *Once a Moth*, skepticism toward the intimacy between the United States and the Philippines became a popular national stance once more. It is quite likely that such skepticism had been fostered by contentious debates about the social, environmental, and political consequences of extending the lease to the U.S. bases beyond its 1991 expiration. When Augusto Buenaventura's *In the Claws of an Eagle* (*Sa kuko ng agila*) appeared in 1989, the myth of "special relations" between Americans and Filipinos already could be questioned without sentimentality. Buenaventura's agitprop film emerges out of the period leading to what would become the final renegotiation of the U.S. bases pact and the failure to reestablish it. To be sure, there are lingering images of colonial intimacy in *In the Claws of an Eagle*. A drunk American serviceman, for example, is defended against Filipino thugs by the righteous jeepney driver Tonio, played by senator and future vice-presidential candidate Joseph Estrada. Absent from the movie, however, are the refrains of "friendship" and romantic love in the two films discussed earlier.

In *In the Claws of an Eagle*, the relations between Americans from the base and Filipinos on the base's periphery are shown to be fundamentally perverse and malevolent. Shirley (Maria Isabel Lopez), Tonio's on-and-off lover, prostitutes herself to sadistic clients, Americans who degrade her or beat her up. A nameless Filipino thug kidnaps Tonio's fifteen-year-old adopted daughter Anna Peralta (Ilonah Jean) at the behest of a middle-aged American. The American rapes Anna and leaves her for dead beside a heap of garbage. The prevalence of these abusive relationships between natives and foreigners reflects the nation-state's complicity with empire.

Central to Buenaventura's film is the intimacy between Americans and their powerful Filipino allies, represented by Morelos (Subas Herrero). Morelos is a local politician who has unseen allies at the base in Subic Bay. It is this corrupt figure who maintains bonds of intimacy with the Americans at the base. Morelos identifies with their interests

Anna (Ilonah Jean) identifies her American rapist. Source: In the Claws of an Eagle.

and mimics their benevolence to sustain his delusions of righteousness and might. He is a figuration of the post-Marcos era's reviled *trapo* (kitchen rag), or "traditional politician," who enjoys "special relations" with imperial power.

In one scene, Tonio asks Morelos, "Do you mean to suggest that I do as you do and lick your master's prostate?" An implicit contrast is made between the righteous native's hypermasculinity and the politico's perverse manhood. Neoimperial alliance is equated with analingus. This scandalous, homophobic equation points to the real political stakes of the bases issue—real in the sense that it involves the bodies of Filipinos: if not as brute force hired by shady Americans, then as native bodies circulating in and around the bases as prostituted bodies of women or as corpses of children mistaken for animals.

Using the familiar motif of equating the bestial and the human, *In the Claws of an Eagle* tries to retain the biopolitical emphasis seen in *Once a Moth* and *PX*. But Buenaventura's lack of sentimentality, whatever its artistic gain, proves to be a weakness beside the experience of Filipinos reduced to bare life. The depth of their pain is what Buenaventura fails to capture. "Why is it that, to this very day, our country is still run by Americans?" Tonio asks an aged nationalist leader (Ruben Rustia). "Theirs are the claws of the eagle that crush our necks!" the leader replies. This substitution of political slogans for dialogue, only one instance among many, undermines the film's claim to particularity and realism. The pageant-like structure of the plot does not help either. As the tale moves from one episode of imperialist oppression to another, character development is sacrificed along with narrative verisimilitude. The film's crudest treatment of biopolitics comes in the form of ascribing bestial status not to the suffering natives but to corrupt Filipino politicos who serve the interests of U.S. extraterritoriality. Such Filipinos are called "lapdogs" (*tuta*). In a rally shown in the second half of the film, the people cry out, "Morelos is a criminal! He's a lapdog of Americans! *Tuta*! *Tuta*! *Tuta*!" The trick of reversing the terms of biopolitics is expedient, even necessary, given its context. The year *In the Claws of an Eagle* hit the screens marked the period when the Philippine Senate faced the task of deciding on the first bases treaty.

Fueled by a revival of the age-old "Philippines for Filipinos" rhetoric in the years leading to the Philippine Senate's vote on the U.S. bases treaty, the anti-imperialist discourse of *In the Claws of an*

Eagle seethes, but it also falls short on insight. Buenaventura naively suggests that empire can be defeated with one of the most clichéd manifestations of political vigilance: the crowd voicing outrage in the streets. The following diatribe on national culture, delivered by a student activist named Caloy (played by Jinggoy Estrada, Joseph Estrada's son), is but one of numerous instances epitomizing this weakness while repeating the motif of the imperial beast-man: "We've lost so many things! Our culture is going to the pigs." *Once a Moth* and *PX* use melodramatic visibility to trace the unspeakable pain and rage, as well as the tenacious emotional reserves, of Filipinos living close to the bases. In contrast to these two films, *In the Claws of an Eagle* turns the inarticulate dimension of bare life into barefaced slogans. Buenaventura ends his movie by showing a political streamer that conveniently summarizes its intent: "Down with the alliance between Morelos and the U.S. bases!"

One of the film's critics attributes *In the Claws of an Eagle*'s wooden rhetoric and cinematic form to star-producer Joseph Estrada's mercenary aims. The anti-imperialist posturing serves Estrada's future bid for the vice-presidential seat. The critic argues that the film stages the antibases crusade as a kind of "spaghetti western," a form reminiscent of Estrada's old films and highly legible to commercial film audiences. "Its oversimplifications are grossly patronizing," the critic writes. "You're being bashed to death with an ideological smugness that's narrow as well as suffocating . . . *Sa Kuko ng Agila* ultimately surrenders to the vulgarities of movie marketing and to the well-oiled personal propaganda machine of one very canny politician."[76] If *In the Claws of an Eagle* was indeed part of Estrada's political strategy, it proved highly successful: Estrada won the vice-presidency in 1992 (and the presidency in 1998).

Despite its hackneyed slogans and incoherent plot, Buenaventura's agitprop deserves credit for reviving and innovating the subgenre of films about the U.S. bases. Most notably, *In the Claws of an Eagle* declines to treat decolonization as a process concerned with "attacking an old form of [imperial] power," which we find in the first two films.[77] Going beyond the usual face-off between American military and Filipino civilians, *In the Claws of an Eagle* broadens the range of means for portraying the conflict around the military base. The film spins a conspiracy plot that involves much more than the business of coddling abusive GIs. The conspiracy plot functions as a rhetorical device for suggesting the different ways that the bases impact Filipino lives, from their corrupting influence on local and national institutions, to their palpable effect on the environment. Equally important, the plot implicates powerful Filipinos, including politicians, businessmen, underworld figures, and law enforcement. In the movie's fantasy of decolonization, the downfall of the American–Filipino conspiracy is precipitated by bad press and people power. Morelos goes to a much-publicized trial for masterminding the killing of a dissident fisherman and, later, for ordering his goons to fire at the mourners at the fisherman's funeral. These scandals prompt unseen "base officials" to withdraw their support for the villainous politician. They fear that should their association with Morelos become known, public sentiment would turn against the bases. Because of his clout among the Filipino elite, Morelos wins the court case. He is roundly defeated, however, in the court of public opinion. At the end of the film, the masses assembled outside the courthouse heckle Morelos and condemn his unknown benefactors inside the base.

The vulnerability of Filipino crooks and their American partners is symptomatic of the political leverage afforded by the inclusion of strict measures concerning the U.S. bases in the 1987 Philippine constitution. The film's narrative, however, directly attributes the weakening of the mighty bad guys to the crumbling of public faith in American benevolence. The film's concluding image, which recalls the iconography of the 1986 People Power Revolution, suggests that the mob of angry and enlightened protesters might just do to the neoimperialist alliance what it did to the Philippine dictator. Interestingly, shortly before the film's release, Estrada claimed in an interview to the *Philippine Daily Inquirer* that an unidentified entity, working through a "third party," offered to pay $2 million to the film's producers (his brother Jesse Ejercito and Raymond Tan) to stop the film from being shown. The same article insinuates that Estrada's ability to sway the masses into taking up his antibases stand caused some concern among "US diplomats."[78] In his defense of the film, Renato Constantino Jr., the son of the eminent historian, also pointed to the significance of the bad publicity generated by the film: "To be sure, the US embassy is probably gleeful over all the flack the movie has received. Yet, it must be a source of discomfiture to them that . . . [the film] is nothing but a box office hit!"[79]

The actual circumstances that led to the ouster of the bases had little to do with the commercial success or the dramatic overthrow fantasized by *In the Claws of an Eagle*. It had much to do, rather, with a composite of factors: the defeat of the bases treaty in the Philippine Senate; the catastrophic eruption of Mt. Pinatubo and its severe damage to the two bases; the express prohibition of nuclear weapons in the 1987 Philippine constitution; and finally, the Philippine demand for higher rent.[80] Not long after the closure of the bases, Philippine politicians and technocrats began converting the old military facilities into a major hub for multinational corporations in the Asia–Pacific region. The decolonized space soon became globalization's *theatrum politicum*, where neoimperialism assumed the seemingly more benign form of neoliberalism.

Conclusion

An American foreign policy consultant believed in 1989 that only the closure of the bases "would provide a wholly satisfactory settlement of all sovereignty problems."[81] The withdrawal of the U.S. military presence from the Philippines was deemed the culmination of an overwrought decolonization process. In 2005, however, the comeback of those problems in the controversy over a young woman's rape belied the prediction. During a related event in the rape fracas, the problem of sovereignty and the question of American benevolence surfaced anew in tandem, in a plucky display of imperialism.

As the media whirled around the conviction of Nicole's alleged rapist, a typhoon hit the southern region of Luzon. About one thousand people perished from the mud slides. This catastrophe ironically gave some purchase for Daniel Smith, the convicted Marine. No less than Kristie Kenney, U.S. ambassador to the Philippines, and Admiral William Fallon, commander of American forces in the Pacific, called for the Philippine government to overturn a local judge's order detaining the convicted rapist in a Philippine jail, instead of handing him over to American custody, pending his appeal.[82] Kenney and Fallon threatened that if the Philippine government failed to do so, then the United States would discontinue giving aid to the typhoon victims. The link between humanitarian aid and the sovereign decision over Nicole's rape echoes Agamben's recent observation concerning the fate of bare life vis-à-vis neoliberalism. Agamben notes that neoliberalism, the "democratico-capitalist project" that operates as a form of neocolonialism, can come to grips with the life of the Third World inhabitant only as bare life.[83] Nicole's dignity is deemed expendable within the same neoliberal calculus that turns Philippine citizens, wracked by a typhoon, into refugees at the tender mercies of the United States for resources and attention. Framed in Agamben's terms, two forms of bare life are weighed incommensurably against each other.

Contrary to all appearances, as the violence and indifference related to the Nicole case and Ambassador Kenney's denial of aid show, the power of the U.S. military complex has not really waned. As Chalmers Johnson reminds us, "The indispensable instrument for maintaining the American empire is its huge military establishment."[84] Even with the "slipping preeminence" of the informal empire, the United States continues to project its power throughout Asia and the rest of the world, keeping about 725 overseas bases.[85] Moreover, David Harvey has pointed out that the complicity between the monopolistic competition of neoliberalism and the "raw militaristic imperialism currently offered up by the neoconservative movement in the United States"—via the invasion of Iraq and "the global war on terror"—is still causing much grief in less-developed nations.[86] It seems that now, more than ever, Filipinos and the dispossessed of the Third World need to place even greater hope in the realization—not just the empty promise—of American benevolence.

At her sibling's funeral in *Once a Moth*, Cora intones a plea for her brother's recognition. It is a prayer in which the reference to the brother can be revised here and in which the act of naming can be heard differently as a way of marking those souls subjected to the blows of the "global military-economic dominion." In this prayer, Cora addresses the American as brother. Hailed by an imagined fraternity, the American is one who, through the intimacy of confrontation and the plea for genuine benevolence, is transformed into kin. "My brother is not a pig," her prayer goes. "My brother is not a pig."

Postscript

In the spring of 2009, the drama of Nicole's case took yet another surprising turn. The Philippine government refused to enforce a Philippine Supreme Court ruling for the immediate return of convicted rapist Daniel Smith to Philippine custody. Thereafter Nicole's lawyer announced her client's departure for the states. As the media fielded unconfirmed reports that the victim had immigrated with an American lover, her mother averred that Nicole had fled "for good," in part because "there is no justice in the Philippines." Smith's lawyer, on the other hand, immediately released an affidavit from Nicole, in which she recanted her previous testimony. The lawyer added that she took about $2,000 from Smith for all her troubles.[87] Within a few weeks, Smith was exonerated by the courts and repatriated by the U.S. embassy.

A Filipina lawmaker raised suspicions that Nicole's flight resulted from a secret, high-level deal between the Philippines and the United States. Another solon commented that regardless of the circumstances of Nicole's departure, she should not be condemned for giving up on the Philippines. "Nicole did not fail us; our justice system did," the male solon said. He added that Nicole's case "represents the tens of thousands of cases languishing in our courts, in the Office of the Ombudsman and our prosecutors' offices nationwide."

The realization and disclosure of Nicole's "secret" American fantasy instantly turned an angry debate about U.S. extraterritoriality into a rebuke of Philippine justice. Nicole's decision to immigrate to the United States bespeaks a former victim's desperate longing to be on the right side of an awesome force. Scripted by fantasy or not, it certainly gives fodder to the affirmation of the superpower's ultimate benevolence.

3

(Not) Searching for My Father

GI Babies and Postcolonial Futures

How does a decolonizing nation fantasize about what is yet to come? In the first two chapters I examined, respectively, films exposing present forms of U.S. imperialism and films exorcizing the colonial past. Here I turn to specters of the future. More specifically, in this chapter, I study some of the ways in which Philippine cinema projects what a decolonizing nation imagines as the future relations between the ex-colonizer and the ex-colonized. This chapter focuses on three movies tracking the figure of the Amerasian: the so-called GI baby who, upon becoming an adult, tries to recuperate part of his or her lost origins and searches for the American father.[1]

The tale of the GI baby is an American fantasy with two conflicting elements. First, it depicts the Amerasian seeking recognition and intimacy from the white father. Second, it shows the offspring airing grievance toward him and ultimately turning away from him.

Frantz Fanon describes the colonial's, or, in this case, ex-native's, desire for closeness with the white man as a kind of "lactification"[2] or "hallucinatory whitening."[3] For the mixed-race children of empire, the quest for the American father rekindles pride in their whiteness and foreign identity. Even if the father's departure resulted in a life of wretchedness for his offspring, the Amerasian child believes the father to be the guarantor of a better future. It was, after all, the American father who bequeathed some of his racial and national identity to his mixed-race child. But while the white father always confers the gift of recognition in the GI baby's tale, he never truly succeeds in rescuing his offspring. Despite this failure—and perhaps also because of it—the child's longing for reunion quietly persists at the story's end. These wayward desires seem to represent the unruly effects of the postcolonial condition.

The second element of the fantasy, the GI baby's acts of confrontation and rejection, calls upon the Amerasian's negative feelings toward the white father and preempts a successful reunion. The GI baby decries his or her abandonment, disparages the parent, seeks vengeance or demands recompense, and then withholds the means of redemption. In spite of the Amerasian's righteousness in the face of the white father's sins, the expression of rancor is held in check by a refusal to deny affection for the parent. But it is at the explosive moment of confronting the white father and mustering the will to repudiate him that the Amerasian truly wrests control of his or her future and leaves the past behind.

The two elements of the GI baby's American fantasy occur in all three films discussed in this chapter. These tropes form the basis of a standardized plot that with some minor variations these films share. The striking conventionality of these narratives, along with their superficial treatment of the Amerasian's plight, makes me suspect that the interest of these films is in allegorical rather than social-realist representation.[4] They use the figure of the mixed-race child—with his or her dual identity and torn allegiance to the white father and the native mother—to reckon with the old colonial relationship and its aftermath. With the tropes of whitening, reunion, and repudiation, this American fantasy concerned with the subject of Filipino–American relations in late decolonization and beyond. It works out scenarios showing how the painful legacy of empire within the postcolonial subject's divided self might be overcome. The films that resort to this fantasy wrestle with the hybrid subject's unruly feelings for the profoundly intimate imperialist. They attempt to tame the contradictions in the mixed-race child's sameness with and difference from the American father and native mother.

The films in this chapter were made in the past three decades. I focus on the variations of the GI baby's American fantasy in Lino Brocka's *Hellow, Soldier*, one of three episodes in the film *Three, Two, One* (*Tatlo, dalawa, isa*, 1975); Chito Roño's *Olongapo . . . The Great American Dream* (*Exit Subic*, 1987); and Jose Javier Reyes's *Phil-American Boy* (*Batang PX*, 1997). *Olongapo . . . The Great American Dream* is something of a transnational production, having been coproduced and coscripted by Americans and Filipinos and released in local and international versions.[5]

Family Romance and Postcolonial Futures

As a fantasy of decolonization, the GI baby's quest for paternal recognition lends itself well to Sigmund Freud's idea of the family romance. The family romance is a fantasy prevalent in the neurotic male child who seeks from his parents a measure of independence but at the same time begrudges what he perceives as their indifference toward him. The child feels slighted at "not receiving the whole of his parents' love, and, most of all . . . regrets at having to share it with brothers and sisters." In retaliation, the boy entertains the notion of "being a step-child or an adopted child" wrested from parents of "a higher social station" by the inferior, neglectful ones who have raised him.[6] For Freud, the seemingly hostile fantasy liberates the child from the authority of parents while strengthening the familial bond. The child, Freud writes, "is turning away from the father whom he knows to-day to the father in whom he believed in the earlier years of his childhood; and his phantasy is no more than the expression of a regret that those happy days have gone."[7] In her celebrated study of family romance narratives in the French Revolution, Lynn Hunt has shown the significance of such "images of the familiar order" in illuminating the operations of the "collective political unconscious."[8] Hunt uncovered tales and images "of family conflict and resolution" through which the polity worked out its political issues of "paternal authority, female participation, and fraternal solidarity."[9]

If the family romance indeed encrypts political and social scripts, then we can read the Amerasian's search for the white father as a fable of parental substitution. In this postcolonial reworking of the Freudian scenario, the mother is often a prostitute living in poverty after having long given up the trade. The child repudiates her identification with the Filipino mother in favor of the American father. The Amerasian's desire for recuperating his or her lost paternal ties is profound and intense. It is founded on the idea of sharing the father's racial substance. Ultimately, however, this neurotic fantasy tends to redeem the disavowed mother and repudiate the American father.

In exploring the political dimensions of the GI baby's tale, it is useful to recall Ann Laura Stoler's illuminating account of the mixed-race offspring in colonial Indonesia. She suggests that the discourse about the métis, the "mixed population of ambiguous positioning and torn affiliation,"[10] concerns not only the visible markers of race but also the contested "invisible bonds"[11] and "internal states" of national belonging.[12] While sincerely altruistic at times, the white man or woman's preoccupation with the fate of mixed-race children is nevertheless implicated in the perpetuation of a racial hierarchy within empire. It involves the policing of the "interior frontier" of national identity, the very "essence of the nation."[13] Following Stoler, I argue that the films' discourses about Amerasians are also concerned with the invisible, the internal, and the national. In films about Amerasians the family romance projects images of the postcolonial order. It contributes to the nation's efforts to reckon with its colonial past and buttresses faith in the future of decolonization. In these films, the grown-up child of the imperialist father renders judgment upon their shared history, wrestles with its desire for the father's inheritance but takes its mother's name, and in the end, proposes a new way of bearing up under the West's conciliatory embrace. The Amerasian child's racial mixture does not prompt a disparaging discourse on miscegenation. Instead, it taps into the Filipino sympathy toward brokenness and proffers the means for postcolonial restitution. While Amerasian identity is a signifier for the "tainted" character that haunts the former subjects of imperial rule, being of mixed race is both sin and redemption.

How does the nation reckon with its colonial past, its purported historical state of sin? Homi Bhabha describes a fantasy similarly operating with the trope of substitution. The ultimate "fantasy of the native," according to Bhabha, works out the contradictory desire "to occupy the master's place while keeping his place in the slave's *avenging* anger."[14] In the films on Amerasians, the reckoning with the colonial past is staged as a face-off that occurs between the angry child and the father. Through a plot device unlikely to occur in social-realist narrative, the GI baby resolves his or her lack of definition vis-à-vis the injunction to belong to one nation or another. Hence, the Amerasian does end up being assigned an identity: the confrontation scene becomes a moment of reckoning between the ex-colonized and the ex-colonizer. Through the Amerasian figure, the ex-colonized fantasizes about settling the score with the ex-colonizer, putting him in *his* place. In the GI baby's version of the revenge fantasy Bhabha describes, the ex-colonizer is summoned as a paternal figure. He atones for his waywardness by redeeming his bastard. The fantasy rehearses the trauma of abandonment but upends the terms of agency. In this fantasy, the perverse source of pleasure comes from the simultaneous righteousness and impropriety of rejecting the father, denying him an opportunity for atonement.

The tale of the Amerasian in search of paternal recognition was not born in World War II. Its origins are further back, in the previous century when the bonds of intimacy with America were forged at the beginning of the colonial relationship. In 1913, within the first fifteen years of U.S. colonial presence, the American Mestizo Protective Association was founded to assist abandoned or destitute part-American children in the Philippines. In the early 1920s, Governor General Leonard Wood observed firsthand the difficulties faced by some of the estimated eighteen thousand Filipino American mestizos in the colony. He tried to improve their lot by marshalling the support of government and of charitable organizations.[15] Sadly, even Wood's modest response was an exception to his government's attitude toward the mixed-race children. In the early 1980s, the U.S. Congress drew up a bill to enfranchise Amerasians, but the amended version signed into law was deeply problematic. The Amerasian Act of 1982 prescribed strict eligibility requirements and offered only special immigrant status (the so-called fourth visa preference) rather than citizenship.[16] More relevant to this discussion, however, is the fact that the law excluded Filipino Amerasians, along with Amerasians from a few other countries. Written in the aftermath of the Vietnam War, the legislation sought to atone for the United States' recent imperialist activities while quietly disclaiming responsibility for older colonial ventures. The puzzling quality of such erasure doubles beside a census reported in 1980 by the Pearl S. Buck Foundation, a private organization concerned with Amerasian children. According to their estimate, the second-greatest number of half-American children (thirty thousand) in Asia was found in the United States' only former colony.[17]

In light of such history, the films on Filipino Amerasians cannot but end in an angry face-off scripted by a long recollection of colonial intimacy and estrangement. The mixed-race characters in the films I discuss insist that the ex-colonizer's forgetfulness is unacceptable and that to speak of the future course for Philippine–American intimacies requires that past intimacies also be mentioned. Yearning for recognition, these characters earnestly attempt to move forward *with and despite* the burden of the colonial past. It is this paradoxical movement that makes the films in this chapter quite fascinating. What might we learn, then, about decolonization from the American fantasies of Filipino GI babies?

A Past and Future without Redemption: *Hellow, Soldier*

The mise-en-scène of Brocka's *Hellow, Soldier* is a virtual representation of the material and spiritual devastation that follows in the wake of colonialism. The rusty wooden shack where our protagonists reside can be found in a shantytown near the crossing of streets that the film, in a bout of vulgar allegory, names North (Hilaga) and Fate (Kapalaran). In contrast to the Third World squalor in which the shack is mired, the interior walls of the dwelling are painted an immaculate white and plastered with colorful cutouts from American magazines. Invariably cheerful pictures of Elvis Presley, Frank Sinatra, Pat Boone, and John F. Kennedy fill the walls. This decor is complemented by a steady flow of American pop music from a small but prized transistor radio. Inside this shack, Gina (Hilda Koronel), a seventeen-year-old Amerasian abandoned by her GI father, Tom (Claude Wilson Jr.), nurtures the American dream with her mother, Lucia (Anita Linda), who professes bitter feelings toward the GI but is visibly excited about his upcoming visit. Mother and child spruce up their house with the finest curtains from their closet. Competitive over who might receive the greater part of Tom's attention, they bicker about the smallest details of the preparation. Strangely enough, the years since Tom's abrupt exit seem to have had the contrary effect on the women he has abandoned. His distance has made him more desirable to them.

The anxious fuss over Tom is suggestive of what Fanon describes as lactification, the desire for a "bit of whiteness" among the colonized or formerly colonized.[18] Gina and Lucia's obsessive longing for the wayward American has been fuelled partly by the misery of their daily existence. Such misery is impressed upon Lucia and Gina each time they lay their eyes on the slum surrounding their shack. Apart from being addicted to American popular culture, Gina often passes by

Lucia (Anita Linda) and Gina (Hilda Koronel) wait anxiously for Tom's return. Source: Hellow, Soldier. Courtesy of Danilo Brocka/CCP Library/Lino Brocka Collection.

travel agencies to daydream, staring at the posters of U.S. cities on their windows. Lucia, for her part, tells Gina every bit of recollection she has managed to shore up of Tom and their short-lived relationship. On the day before Tom's visit, Gina makes her way through the slum, heading for school. She is halted in her tracks by a stream of urine issuing from above her, where a small boy has decided to piss into the narrow passageway cutting into the slope. Later, she steps on feces.

Everything associated with Tom's whiteness and with America has become the idealized foil to the "collective, permanent, immense" wretchedness that for Albert Memmi defines the situation of the colonized.[19] The prospect of being "rescued" by Tom heightens Gina's awareness of the fact that she and her mother are literally mired in excrement, that is, in the conditions of wretchedness that have crossed into the period of decolonization. Although the shantytown has been home to her mother's family, as we learn later in the film, and although she was conceived in the same house she shares with her mother, Gina believes she was never destined to live in the slums. What adds to her alienation is the rudeness of the other slum dwellers who keep taunting her about her "white man father" ("*ang tatay mong kano*"). The racial difference that her neighbors rub into her face, however, only augments Gina's fantasy of lactification. She imagines that Tom's arrival will change her life for good. Her white father from America will swoop down to extricate her from the morass of her present life.

As it turns out later in the film, Gina and her mother are not the only characters invested in the American fantasy. When Tom arrives, the charisma of whiteness is so powerful that Gina's neighbors all suddenly want to share in her redemption. Owing to her paternity, Gina comes to incarnate the slum dwellers' dream of whiteness. When Tom arrives, the natives are so worked up with their lactification fantasy that they start to press against Lucia's shanty. Gina, fearing the house might collapse, implores her neighbors to control themselves.

The desire for parental substitution at the heart of the family romance haunts Gina's American fantasy. Because the shantytown is metonymic of Gina's maternal lineage, her emphatic rejection of the slum easily contaminates her relationship with Lucia. Gina's desire for parental substitution is implicit in the way *Hellow, Soldier* refers to her tireless correspondence with the U.S. embassy, her obsession with tracking down her father, and her efforts to secure her future in America. Gina vows to her mother never to return to the Philippines if she manages to get out of it and never to let anyone in America, once she gets there, know that she "hail[s] from a pig sty." Lucia stoically bears Gina's animosity toward her destitute origins and the implicit hostility toward the postcolonial nation-state. Gina's disaffection is a symptom of the film's historical moment when Filipino nationalists had to confront two unflattering faces of their mother country: Ferdinand Marcos's fascist New Society and the socialist state for which the militant Left was waging a guerilla war. Like Gina's mother, the nation is figured as an utter wreck. The postcolonial subject's resentment toward her mother, her people, and part of herself is so acute that it persists beyond the tale's requisite happy ending. When, midway through the film, Gina tells her mother about her plan to flee to America, Lucia takes to the bottle and behaves hatefully toward Gina. Lucia's propensity for self-sabotage risks abandonment once more, this time by her Amerasian daughter. The film makes it abundantly clear, however, that her brokenness has been caused by her desperate hope for the white man's magnanimity. Lucia is bothered by the possibility of Gina's departure as much as by the certainty that Tom, arriving with his American wife, will not wish to take Lucia along with her daughter. "You're the only one, Gina," she tells her daughter. "Not us both . . . You're the only one they want to see."

The threat of parental substitution drives Lucia to raise the issue of historical debt and to expose Tom's true colors. Lucia quietly hatches a plan to hijack the father–daughter reunion and turn it into a confrontation. Before Tom's arrival, she shares a bottle of gin with her neighbor. Later, with Gina by her side, Lucia takes out her daughter's baby photo and casually mentions how many cans of infant formula she fed her each week. She recalls what Gina wore during a religious procession, a nice twelve-peso lace dress and white shoes she brought all the way from Manila's Quiapo district, which was a good three-hour bus trip from the city of Pampanga. For this and all other sacrifices, Lucia ostensibly expects nothing more from Gina than to send a picture of herself taken in the states.

Having set up Gina to feel guilt over leaving her mother, Lucia prepares to confront Tom about his enormous debts to both Gina and herself. When Tom and his wife, Betty (Barbara Browne), enter shantytown, a paid lookout screams with excitement, "Gina's white father is here!" They wend their way through the innards of the slums while the slum dwellers crane their necks to catch a glimpse of them or look on from atop dilapidated rooftops. Kids trailing behind them scream, "Victory Joe!" The white couple is mobbed by natives.

Brocka's mise-en-scène elevates what should have been a moment of reconciliation between father and daughter to a public spectacle. The children's greetings—"Victory Joe!"—echo the hospitality with which Filipinos welcomed Americans at the end of World War II. At Lucia's shack, however, the Americans are not accorded a hero's welcome. Feeling guilt over her mother's sense of abandonment, Gina decides not to behave solicitously toward Tom and his wife. Lucia, on the other hand, is completely sloshed, hiding in her room at her daughter's request. All hell soon breaks loose, however, when the drunken woman emerges. "Hello, soldier!" she greets him, echoing how the slum children earlier hailed the American. Unlike the children, her greeting is fraught with actual memories of the days during liberation. The reunion is now completely set up to turn into a thinly disguised image of confrontation between the ex-colonizer and the ex-native.

"You have not changed much," Lucia tells Tom. Between drunken fits of laughter, she mocks him. "Oh, but you have a big belly now and your face is lined, too, especially under your eyes. You're not the same brawny soldier I knew. How funny. I didn't know even gods could fade, too." With exaggerated passion, she strokes Tom's face the way a drunken soldier might touch a native prostitute. Lucia bitterly parodies and reverses the old hierarchy of colonial seduction. Gina watches her mother's histrionics demystify the image of the heroic white father. "I was one of the many who poured into the streets to greet you," Lucia tells Tom. "You looked like gods. That's why I had faith in your kind . . . I allowed myself to be fooled by my savior. By my hero! Why, Tom, why?" Lucia bitterly recalls the intimate episode of Philippine–American friendship as having been no more than a ruse. The U.S. soldier's cherished self-image is recast from that of a liberator to that of an opportunist.

Tom's behavior does not redeem him at all. When he recalls his affair with Lucia, his narrative is disjointed and insulting. Back then Tom relied on the services of a laundress in whose living room he happened

Lucia (Anita Linda) confronts Tom (Claude Wilson Jr.) and mocks Gina's (Hilda Koronel) dream of following him to America. Source: Hellow, Soldier. Courtesy of Danilo Brocka/CCP Library/Lino Brocka Collection.

to pass out on one drunken occasion. At that time, the laundry woman's daughter, Lucia, also happened to be there. Tom characterizes his relations with Lucia as mere accident, or what the colonialists from an earlier era would have called "the fruits of a regrettable weakness."[20]

Because of her burning desire to be enfranchised as an American, Gina does not immediately construe Tom's low opinion of her mother as somehow telling of his implicit view of his own daughter. Gina neither defends her mother from Tom nor supports her mother's denunciation of her father. Gina tries to sympathize with Lucia's grief but her commiseration is expressed with a shade of chastisement. Lucia's misfortunes, Gina tells her mother, were her own fault because she allowed herself to be "fooled."

Throughout most of the film Gina has appeared emotionally distant from her mother. Gina's view of Tom, however, begins to change when she overhears a conversation between Tom and his wife, Betty. It dawns on Gina that Tom's sudden interest in finding her may be driven, after all, not by fatherly instinct but by a desire to validate his masculinity. Betty rubs Tom's waning virility in his face as Gina steps out to fetch their drinks. "Oh, Tom, you've won your point," Betty tells him. "Your darling daughter, out of the blue. We never could have a child of our own, but it's not your fault, is it? You have proof positive right in that room!"

Gina's image of her white father is eroded by the composite portrait drawn by Betty and Lucia's characterizations of him. Tom is an irredeemable sort of patriarch. His failure lies not only in his well-concealed ruthlessness but also in his refusal to acknowledge his present insecurities and past misdeeds. Tom's denigration is contiguous with the film's implicit caveat about future relations with the white man. Lucia's grievance does not abate even after the American couple leaves. She denounces Tom for usurping her place in Gina's filial love: "He comes back, wife in tow. And he even wants to take the blood of my blood. Kills me, slowly but surely. Takes everything I have. When will this end? He's a beast. A beast!" Moved by the forceful rhetoric of Lucia's denunciation against Tom, Gina disidentifies with him and gradually relinquishes her dream of whiteness.

In *Hellow, Soldier* Brocka proffers little hope about the future of Philippine–American relations. Its pessimistic view is further underscored by the plight of Gina's alter ego, an Amerasian teen named

Jefferson (Edwin O' Hara). His shantytown fellows, who have internalized the white man's logic of exclusion and denial, mock him for wanting to be an American. Even Gina appears indifferent toward him. Seeking to contact his father, who was Tom's friend during liberation, Jefferson tries to persuade her to help him on the basis that they "share the same skin color," but she only gives him the cold shoulder. When Tom arrives, the white man himself annuls Jefferson's lactification fantasy by refusing to help him locate his father.

Throughout *Hellow, Soldier*, Jefferson's claim to be recognized as an American is repeatedly denied. Through Jefferson, the film warns against putting too much faith in American democratic ideals because of the likelihood that figures like Tom are going to be unable to live up to them. In the penultimate scene, Brocka reiterates this caveat in what is perhaps the movie's most cinematic episode, given its discreetly meaningful mise-en-scène and camera movement. Framing Lucia as she wakes up from her drunken sleep, the scene begins with a collage of John F. Kennedy pictures pasted on the shack's walls. In a sweeping

Tom (Claude Wilson Jr.) declines to help the biracial teen Jefferson (Edwin O'Hara) locate his American father. Source: Hellow, Soldier. *Courtesy of Danilo Brocka/CCP Library/Lino Brocka Collection.*

movement, the camera tilts down toward the floor, alighting on an empty glass tipped over beside Lucia's dangling arm, and then tilts up to reveal her splayed on the bed. This is not the first time the film alludes to Kennedy.[21] The viewer recalls that the early part of the film shows mother and daughter listening to the breaking news about Kennedy's assassination. Kennedy's specter and, through his counterfeit Amerasian alter, that of Thomas Jefferson haunt the dream of freedom implanted among former U.S. subjects.

After exposing the American father's flaws and the native mother's wretchedness, Brocka forces us to wonder what recourse the postcolonial subject has. What is to become of Philippine–American postcolonial relations, as signified by Tom's parental claim over Gina? Conversely, what is to become of Philippine nationalism, as emblematized by Gina's tested loyalty toward Lucia? Owing perhaps to its historical milieu, the first half-decade of martial law, the film ends at an impasse. Gina is close to achieving what she has been yearning for all her life: the promise of reparation from her father and the possibility of building a new life in America. But Betty, given her protestations, stands in the way of full reconciliation between Gina and Tom. Lucia, moreover, the tippling embodiment of mother nation, has already sabotaged the reunion. Beyond Lucia's implicit prohibition against reconciling with Tom, Gina's hesitation comes from knowing that immigrating to the United States can spell ruin for herself as much as for her mother.

The indecisiveness of American hospitality offers no guarantee of a satisfying end to Gina's pursuit of recognition. Moreover, she fears that her quest for belonging would fail because of the lineage and alienation she harbors within her very being. The conditions for Gina's foreknowledge are found earlier in the movie when Gina, complaining about their noisiness, picks a fight with some of her neighbors. One of the women retaliates by pointing out Gina's outsider status in both the shantytown and in America: "Maybe it's better if you just went away with your white man father," the woman says. "No other people will bother with you there [in America]. You'll die alone there."

Gina's postcolonial subjectivity is riven by two sets of prohibitions, turning both America and the Philippines into spaces of exile. The promise, as well as betrayal, of Gina's lactification fantasy bars her from claiming the bright future that possibly awaits her in America. And yet by choosing *not* to leave the Philippines, Gina knowingly condemns herself to a contradictory form of nationalism. Stuck in an ambivalent nationalism, Gina's loyalty to her mother can only be as passionate as her loathing for her motherland.

As if to emphasize this impasse in *Hellow, Soldier*, Brocka abbreviates its denouement. The hysterical Lucia starts to harass Betty, forcing a drink on her and assaulting her. Tom quickly hands Gina his contact information; Gina is to see him at the hotel so that her travel papers to the states can be expedited. The Americans exit the frame, and Lucia passes out. Later she wakes up to find her daughter gone. After searching frantically for Gina in the streets, she spots her walking with her suitor, Rudy.

Rudy is an unlikely match for the GI baby who, earlier in the film, has always expressed dislike for him. But it is Rudy who offers a provisional route to liberation. Gina affirms the traditional recourse, namely, the perpetuation of the family within the nation's borders, enfolding and occluding Gina's American fantasy. In relation to the family romance, however, it is not clear if such substitution is stable enough to quell the lack represented by Tom and Lucia, whom Gina has equally repudiated.

At the end of the movie, Lucia finds Gina but is worried that Gina is still angry with her. Lucia keeps her distance as she watches her GI baby strolling with the native son. The bittersweet ending condenses the atmosphere and tone pervading *Hellow, Soldier*'s decolonization scenario. It inspires sobriety instead of unqualified optimism, alerting its audience to the unruly longings and historical impediments that belong to the decolonizing process. Although Gina has ultimately chosen her mother over her father, and found a native man as her possible mate, the film ends with uncertainty. It is silent about what it truly might mean for a postcolonial nation to love itself, or what might be done to liquidate the fantasy of special relations between ex-colonizer and ex-colonized. We do not hear the voices of the bantering new "couple." The soundtrack's haunting music comes on as night falls over the slums.

Redemption Realized: *Olongapo... The Great American Dream*

In *Olongapo... The Great American Dream*, the child's desire for parental substitution is merciless. Like the character in Rouben Mamoulian's *Applause* (1929), Racquel (Jaclyn Jose) is sent by her mother to the province, shielding the daughter from the sordidness of her mother's occupation in Olongapo, a city close to a U.S. naval base. Martha (Chanda Romero) meets her daughter once more when Racquel comes of age and returns to Olongapo. The daughter feels only disaffection for Martha. Racquel's profound hatred of prostitutes implicitly justifies her coldness toward her mother.

Already in her late forties, Martha still moonlights in the flesh trade. She has spent most of her life entertaining foreign clients. Her carelessness as a sex worker has resulted in pregnancy twice, with two different men. Racquel is half white, while her sister Diana (Kathy Magno) is half black. When she goes through financial straits, Martha relies on dirty money from her friend Mama Charlie (Susan Africa), who traffics drugs, runs a bar called the Great American Dream, and pimps native women to foreigners. Martha's financial instability, loose morality, and bad parenting wreak havoc on her daughters' lives.

Soon after Racquel returns to Olongapo, Diana catches pneumonia. Mama Charlie refuses to lend Martha any money for Diana's hospitalization unless Martha persuades Racquel to work at the bar. The pimp tries to sugarcoat her intent to exploit the daughter's Amerasian charms. She tells Martha that Racquel can opt to work only as a cashier: "She's so pretty the guys will come in just to say hello to her . . . All she has to do is to ring up the tab, smile at the guys, and wear a sexy T-shirt." Anticipating Racquel's likely indignation at Mama Charlie's offer, Martha refuses the bar proprietress's offer. Martha opts instead to turn tricks at cheaper rates to pay for Diana's hospitalization.

Sensing that the family's predicament could lead her down her mother's path, Racquel distances herself further from Martha. She turns to her childhood friend Joel (Joel Torre). Ironically Racquel's attempt to steer clear of her mother and Mama Charlie gets her nowhere. Joel, who plays in the band in Mama Charlie's bar, ends up seeking help from the pimp. He eventually runs drugs for Mama Charlie and even becomes her secret lover. Apart from needing money for Diana's hospitalization, Racquel is trying to make concrete strides to leave the Philippines. To raise the cash needed for a ticket to the United States, Racquel decides to work at Mama Charlie's bar. Racquel strikes a deal with Charlie at the cemetery, where the bar proprietress is visiting the grave of her stillborn child. "No tricks, no customers, not until I say so," Racquel says. "Put me out front in sexy clothes . . . but nothing else. Not until I give up." Racquel has no real interest in working at the bar and starts skimming the cash box each night to quicken the process of raising money for plane fare. Charlie catches Racquel and demands that she repay the stolen amount by turning tricks for her. Racquel returns everything, along with the savings culled honestly at the Great American Dream.

The desire for independence forms the bare bones of Racquel's family romance. This desire is so intense that it works out the fantasy of parental substitution only up to a point. It defines the end point of the family romance neither as the usurpation of the native mother's role nor as the restitution of the white father. Racquel repudiates both parental figures while desiring the authority they embody. Implicit in her coldness toward Martha, Racquel's merciless fantasy includes a secret wish for her mother to be slain. More accurately, it seeks to render Martha's lifeless body as proof of her prior symbolic death. As far as Racquel is concerned, by failing to demonstrate any desire for the independence and stability to which her daughter aspires, Martha has already died.

Racquel's cruel wish is fulfilled. Martha's recent trick turning has resulted in yet another pregnancy. When she breaks the news to Racquel, the daughter upbraids her as a reckless, weak-willed woman. In utter dejection Martha goes to a backstreet abortionist and fulfills Racquel's implicit wish for her mother's death. A rusty wire hanger does the job. Crying hysterically, Emma (Vangie Labalan), a friend of Martha, wakes Racquel from her sleep and informs her of her mother's demise. The daughter shows no sign of remorse or sadness. While maternal melodramas typically end with a positive outcome for only one of the two dueling women, Racquel's treatment of her dead mother is striking for its absolute indifference.[22] Between sobs Emma tries to describe how the abortionist "used a sharp stick" to rid Martha of her pregnancy, but interrupts herself upon realizing that Racquel has scarcely moved from her bed. The sight of the daughter's indifference infuriates Emma: "Jesus, Mary, and Joseph, Racquel! Make the sign of the cross. At least give her that!"

Some nights after the botched abortion, Racquel dreams of her mother. While the decolonizing force of *Olongapo . . . The Great American Dream*'s family romance demands the ultimate affirmation of the native mother, Martha approaches redemption only on a spectral plane. Surrounded by darkness, sitting at a café table, Martha first appears in an immaculate white dress beside a Caucasian man in a white sailor's uniform. Then, as the scene changes, the mother reappears this time in a purple dress beside a black man also dressed in a sailor's white uniform. If the dream represents Racquel's need to mourn her loss properly and come fully to grips with her maternal identification, what do we make of the appearance of two paternal figures and, more important, of the way their difference is marked?

In the form of a haunting, the ex-colonial's American fantasy revives. The spectral fathers in Racquel's dream are both identified as American sailors. The men are similar insofar as they equally represent the Amerasian daughter's dream of mobility. But in the shifting tableau, it is the uncanny fashion sense of Martha's specter that finally racializes the difference between the two men. Martha looks visibly happier in white, sitting beside the white man. But when Martha reappears in purple, which Philippine ritual culture links with Christ's death, she sits beside the black sailor with her eyes lowered, as if in embarrassment. It is a dream without words, speaking eloquently in *color*. While the haunting suggests the doomed relations between American GIs and Filipina whores, it also comments on the yearning

The ghosts of Racquel's parents (Chanda Romero and an unidentified actor) haunt her dreams. Source: Olongapo... The Great American Dream. Courtesy of Frank Vrechek, producer.

for whiteness persisting in the ex-colonial's assertion of independence. Racquel no longer needs to pay any heed to parental figures. But as the haunting suggests, Racquel's desire for mobility threatens to moor her in the narrative of parental substitution once more. The white father, with the implicit approval of the native mother, is calling the headstrong daughter back into his fold.

As it turns out, the film eventually reveals that Racquel's father is not yet dead. The GI baby's father is still alive, after all; he is living in Texas. More tellingly, even before Racquel learns of her father's "resurrection," the records that testify to her American paternity surface. Racquel finds her birth certificate in Martha's filing drawer. Bearing information about her father as well as his signature, the document makes a solid case for acquiring American citizenship.[23] Her Texan father offers to facilitate her immigration process, but Racquel flatly refuses his assistance. The possibility of redemption, as far as Racquel is concerned, comes not from the father but from the mundane work of what Stoler describes as an "archival state that recorded and documented the intimacies of empire."[24] Her father "only did one good thing," Racquel tells Charlie: "He married my mother legally. Left the papers behind and left me a chance."

Having exhumed her father's archive, Racquel moves closer to her dream by digging in her mother's tomb. Racquel returns to the same cemetery where she struck a deal with Charlie. Although she has been forced to return the money she stole from the bar as well as her honest earnings there, Racquel recovers buried loot from Martha's tomb. The loot consists of drug money Joel failed to remit to the bar proprietress. Mama Charlie's boyfriend, Joel's uncle, discovered the secret affair. Joel killed his uncle, and just before Joel went into hiding, he buried the money with Racquel's knowledge. "You take the money," Joel told her. "Go live your dream."

In taking Joel's money but not his love, Racquel avoids the usual route to salvation. Gina at the end of *Hellow, Soldier* submits to the custodianship of a virile, benevolent native patriarchal figure. Racquel's boyfriend, however, suffers from the same weaknesses embodied by her native mother, her American father, and her disavowed homeland. Joel tries several times to offer her a new life. But Racquel turns him away each time, believing that only through the death of her present relationships can any promise of redemption emerge. Racquel sees

Joel as a male version of her mother: morally corrupt and yet invested in casting himself as a victim. Joel, after all, devolves from an honest, struggling band performer to a drug courier, Mama Charlie's secret lover, and finally, the killer of his own uncle. When Racquel claims Joel's buried loot, she ends up relating to him in exactly the same way she did to her parents—that is, through the good wrought by the residues of the deceased relationship.

During one of the rare moments of tenderness in the film, Racquel and Joel are gazing at the dusk beginning to fall on Subic Bay. Joel talks about the possibility of building a future with her. Racquel points to a garish structure in the distance, a floating wooden castle adorned with multicolored party lights. "I dreamt about that castle, even when I was in the province," she tells her boyfriend. Joel thinks that the castle signifies his resilient hope in their relationship. To Racquel, however, the buoyant monument to kitsch is an emblem of her broken dreams. "Maybe I don't have much time left for dreams," she sighs, and finally tries to break up with Joel, telling him that she only loves him as a brother.

Racquel does nurture a dream, however. Borne of her American fantasy, the sudden intrusion of symbolic endogamy dissolves her

In the eyes of an Amerasian child from Olongapo, the floating castle conjures the elusive dream of America. Source: Olongapo . . . The Great American Dream. Courtesy of Frank Vrechek, producer.

erotic attachment to Joel. The fantasy works in excess of her identifications with her mother and with the homeland. It reaches for models of ex-colonial subjectivity beyond the likes of her mother and her boyfriend-turned-"brother." Martha and Joel are too ruined by the past to sire offspring strong enough to replenish a devastated nation. The native patriarch, the native mother, and the homeland offer no future for the ex-colonial subject nourished by the pap of an American fantasy.

One might say that Racquel's rejection of any sort of intimacy with her mother and with Joel is a defense mechanism. Racquel's emotional detachment is a symptom of what Frantz Fanon calls an abandonment neurosis. Full of recrimination toward the past, Racquel distances herself from everyone around her not only out of pride but also out of an acute sense of vulnerability. Echoing Fanon, Racquel seems to say, "I do not want to be loved. Why not? Because once, very long ago, I attempted an object relation and I was *abandoned* . . . [I choose] not to love in order to avoid being abandoned."[25] Racquel projects onto Joel the faults of her mother and also her father's infidelity. Bereft of hope in the ex-colonial nation, her wholesale rejection of the future represented by Joel is a preemptive act. Racquel's exit to decolonization is fraught with a kind of absolutism as untenable as the fantasy represented by the castle floating in the bay.

The film's conclusion takes place in the cemetery on a hill overlooking the city. Using part of a wooden cross snatched from a nearby grave, Racquel retrieves the loot Joel buried beside her mother's tomb. As darkness falls, Racquel lingers over the panoramic view of Olongapo shining below her. Then, in a gesture of jubilation as well as exorcism, she flings the cross toward the city of her mother's birth. This final scene unequivocally suggests that Racquel has found her freedom: this GI baby is going to America.

Predictably, the antinationalist implication of the ending—not to mention its underlying blasphemy—drew a storm of controversy. One of the three screenwriters refused his trophy during an awards ceremony. *Olongapo's* screenplay was a collaborative effort by two Americans, director Frank Vrechek and cowriter Alan Cummings, and a Filipino, the fierce nationalist Ricky Lee. Lee was offended, among other things, by the politics behind the film's resolution. He did not believe in the implicit message that going to America was the proper response to the problems that beset the ex-colonial.

The film's director, Chito Roño, shared and defended Lee's view. Vrechek acknowledges that his serious disagreement with the two over this issue compelled him to dismiss Roño "halfway through the production."[26]

Lee and Roño's objection, it must be noted here, is valid. The repudiation of the mother and homeland is more intensely marked in *Olongapo . . . The Great American Dream* than the ambivalent response to paternal America. Racquel's attitude toward the latter may be described, using Ashis Nandy's words, as a "qualified rejection of the West."[27] Racquel even credits the "American half" of her identity as the part of her that possesses a steely drive and resilience. The rejection of homeland, by contrast, is unqualified. The barest gesture of kindness that Racquel musters toward Martha is to tell her she is "not angry" with her. Her mother's weaknesses incite little or no compassion.

What needs to be emphasized, however, is that Racquel's ultimate repudiation of the ex-colonial family romance cuts both ways. By rejecting Joel and her mother as well as her Texan father, she challenges nationalist visions of hope as much as she questions the promise offered by the revival of imperialist bonds. The film begs us to consider its implicit postnationalist argument. Through Racquel, *Olongapo . . . The Great American Dream* fantasizes about the ex-colonial as a bearer of critical transnationalism. It seems to prefigure a vision of a decolonized subjectivity no longer sustained by national affiliations.

Problematic though its politics may be, as perceived by Lee, *Olongapo . . . The Great American Dream*'s antinationalism cannot be thought of apart from its critique of anti-imperialism. To credit the film as a decolonizing work of fantasy, we must entertain the idea that Racquel disavows not simply her mother's homeland but the idea of national belonging itself. This GI baby seeks to pry herself loose from her American and Filipino identities. What she wants is *another* way to get to America. She dreams of leaving the Philippines without any baggage from its ugly colonial affair. More accurately—more than fantasizing about another path to refuge—Racquel believes that her American dream is one that could be detached from the geography and affect of America proper.

"Joel, do you know what the great American dream really is?" Racquel asks. "It's not Nancy and Dwayne running away to Michigan. It's a dream that you can live anywhere. It's to be whatever you want to be.

And I want that chance." Racquel desires geographic and social mobility and citizenship without sentimental attachments. What she wishes to disentangle are the anxious need for national belonging, the choice implicit in such need, and a pledge of allegiance to one form of belonging over others. As a mixed-race subject who frequently mishears the call of national identity and collective destiny, Racquel pins her hopes on a place other than the Philippine nation, beyond the mythic America, past the itineraries carved by the old colonial relationship.

The Filipino director and coscreenwriter's vehement protest against the film's resolution may well be read as a warning sign. Racquel's chosen exit to decolonization may simply be the result of a fantasy upheld only by Americans like Vrechek and Cummings. But the defections and disaffections in the history of Filipinos at home and in the diaspora show that Racquel's actions and sentiments toward her mother and father are not in fact alien to Filipinos. Reviewing *Olongapo . . . The Great American Dream*, the filmmaker-critic Emmanuel Reyes argues that the film tries to be critical of imperialism and yet ultimately claims that "Filipinos on the whole are incapable of hating Americans." Even if her America is a place of transnational unmooring, Racquel's decision to leave for America proper only confirms "the suspicion that in every Filipino, there is an American struggling to get out."[28]

Beyond this ambivalence about ex-colonial relations, the film's affects prefigure those that would belong to a later historical moment. Contrary to what nationalists like Lee asserted, going abroad was found to be an expedient solution to the problems at home. Less than a year after the film's premiere, Corazon Aquino famously hailed Filipino overseas workers as "the new heroes" of the nation. Remitting funds to their families in the homeland, diasporic Filipinos became responsible for keeping the economy afloat under the incompetent Aquino administration. Succeeding Philippine presidents continued to valorize the daily exodus of its citizens and to posit the expatriate's financial ties to the motherland as the form of nationalist affirmation par excellence.[29] The so-called new heroes became central to the Philippine state policy for building the nation's dollar reserves. The practice of brokering migrant labor became, on the one hand, an expedient means for the Philippines to seek justice under capitalism and, on the other, the state's way of pimping its own citizens.

Olongapo . . . The Great American Dream anticipates the Philippine state's eventual proimmigration discourse. Its contribution lies, above all, in proffering a critical engagement with the mercenary aspect of that discourse. More than the titular American dream, its family romance roots for a form of decolonized comportment in which Filipinos muster enough gumption to seek other loves besides that of their nation and to learn to mourn a motherland alternately as clingy and exploitative as Martha and Mama Charlie. Like Racquel, thousands of Filipinos did end up seeking better futures in other "Americas," other First World countries, without feeling too bad about leaving the homeland.

The New Atavism: *Phil-American Boy*

Olongapo . . . The Great American Dream's repudiation of the mother and of the homeland is absolute. If its decolonization scenario seems too agonized to sustain the fantasy life of Philippine cinema, Jose Javier Reyes's *Phil-American Boy (Batang PX*, 1997) tempers the repudiation found in Roño's film. The decolonization scenario in Reyes's film adopts the critical nationalism of *Olongapo . . . The Great American Dream* but mitigates it with the pathos of nationalist sentiment and the hopeful outlook of popular cinema.

The heroine of *Olongapo . . . The Great American Dream* destroys her mother and abandons the familial and national home. By contrast, the Amerasian protagonist of *Phil-American Boy* reconstitutes the Filipino family after its lactification fantasy is shattered. The family is reinstated, however, without recourse to the traditional nuclear structure. In place of the repudiated white father, the family does not install the native father as the primary figure of authority. An overcompensating figure of nationalist affect and a fantasy of national self-sufficiency paper over the gap left by the father. This hopeful vision of decolonization is founded upon the reformation of the inept mother toward the end of the film. The mother and her precocious male child then form a dyad requiring no distinct paternal figure.

Before her character transformation, the maternal figure in *Phil-American Boy* embodies the worst attributes of the colonized: the fatuous dream of whiteness, the susceptibility to fated repetition, and the knack for self-sabotage. The titular boy in Reyes's film, as well as its narrator, is Christopher (Patrick Garcia), the son of an American serviceman and a Filipina mother, Tessie (Zsa-Zsa Padilla). The family romance in Reyes's film, however, begins not with Christopher but with Tessie herself. At the start of the film, Tessie's mother bickers about her missing husband, blaming his absence for their destitution. The following night, the young Tessie runs away from home. Tessie heads straight for a girlie bar catering to American servicemen. She becomes an "entertainer."

Working for the bar, Tessie replaces her mother with a *mama san* and seeks a supplemental figure for her missing father. She uses sappy ballads and her underage appeal to lure GIs who could take care of her. Since imperial narratives designate the infantilized figure of the native as the ideal for conquest, Tessie's childishness makes her an easy conscript to colonial male fantasy. She is irrational, gullible, and dependent on her man's judgment. She is profligate and thus deserving of both moral uplift and sexual attention. She is poor and thus needful of the white man's largesse. She is powerless to resist authority and thus doomed to fall for the white man's strength.

Tessie, however, is not a victim of necessity. Pursuing her American fantasy, she is a willing player in the hospitality industry. Descended from a line of hostesses, Tessie proves successful at being a trick-turning singer outside the largest U.S. military bases in the Philippines. Eventually Tessie does find a GI to replace her deadbeat father. The American, named Michael Dahoff (Joshua Spafford), gets her pregnant but leaves her upon the birth of their son. Tessie fends for her son by carrying on as an "entertainer" of GIs. When U.S. bases close in the 1990s, however, mother and son are forced to migrate to Manila. There Tessie finds work as a shoe clerk and waitress. As Christopher reveals, she continues to toy with the prospect of returning to her old vocation. Her nostalgia for the old days is as intense as her addiction to the stale romantic fantasies of American soldiers loving Filipina whores. Tessie keeps a cherished photograph of the GI who abandoned her. Every so often, she treats herself to "comforting" remembrances of her liaisons with other American servicemen by singing lonely ditties on her karaoke machine.

The pleasure afforded by Tessie's nostalgia comes ironically from the pain it resuscitates. While it is easy to construe Tessie's willingness to nurture her hurt as an obvious case of masochism, her nostalgic

Tessie (Zsa-Zsa Padilla) waxes nostalgic for the GI who abandoned her. Source: Phil-American Boy. Courtesy of ABS–CBN Film Productions Inc.

attachment to pain is crucial to her psychic survival. Imperial encounters have shaped her subjectivity to such a degree that figural wounds cannot be fully extricated from her idea of selfhood. To feel whole, Tessie must revive the phantom of the "cruel" white man who hurts "helpless" native women like her. As with other heroines of female melodrama, it is the female Oedipus complex that animates her wounded vitality.[30] Her unruly desire for her father and for the white soldier who abandoned her ironically binds her to the dictates of patriarchal authority, even an oppressive one. It sends her off relentlessly to search for paternal substitutes.

When her GI lover abandons her and her son, Tessie ends up with a fair-skinned native, Danny (Edu Manzano). A mestizo salesman of imported luxury cars, Danny convinces Tessie to resign from the shoe store. He moves in with Tessie and Christopher and instantly fills up the rented apartment with spanking new appliances and furniture. "It's my dream come true," Danny tells the two. "I want to have a family." While Danny is able to manipulate Tessie's desire for paternal subjection, the precocious son remains unconvinced. For Christopher, whose nickname is "Amboy" (short for "American Boy"), the sudden realization of Tessie's longing for an ideal family, as well as Danny's display of wealth and magnanimity, is just too good to be true.

Amboy's skepticism proves justified. Soon after the furnishings are delivered, Danny's veneer of wealth and moral rectitude crumbles. The man is fired on charges of theft. He takes to drinking, gives up looking for a job, and eventually takes interest in Amboy's prospective inheritance from his absent father. The situation forces Tessie to find work to support the family. To Amboy's regret, Danny's delusional tendencies echo those of his mother. Danny, as Amboy puts it, wants to make things "look like they're in order even if our life is a mess." When Tessie and Christopher stray from Danny's fantasy of being able to sustain a proper Filipino family, the man beats them up. Because Tessie refuses to acknowledge Danny's incompetence as a native paterfamilias, Amboy's latent fantasy of parental substitution intensifies.

In Amboy's version of the family romance, the son not only takes over the parental duties of his biological mother but also assumes the paternal role itself. Apart from dreaming of being the man who abandons Tessie, Amboy fantasizes about reprimanding his mother for her dissolute ways. As Amboy, through a voice-over monologue earlier in the film, confesses, "I don't really know how I feel about her. Some days I dream of turning quickly into a grown-up and finding a job. I would no longer have to see my mother do shameful things, no longer have to rely on her. And I would leave her because she is so hardheaded."

Amboy's fantasy is validated by their old landlady, Cedes (Nida Blanca). "You are the one with better judgment," she tells the child after one of Danny's turbulent fits, imploring Amboy to convince his mother to leave the abusive man. Cedes presides over the housing compound encompassing Tessie's apartment and the unit Cedes shares with her daughter's young family. Amboy is drawn to this supplemental figure of the mother he wishes he had. By identifying Amboy as "the one with better judgment," Cedes enforces what Stoler describes as the values of middle-class morality and manliness inculcated upon biracial sons during colonial times.[31] While Cedes comes to Amboy's aid out of genuine compassion, the old matriarch also acts as the steward of an old conservative order. Under the gaze of this order, children of mixed race are deemed at "risk of entirely degenerating and being unfit for learning and civilization" because of how they are reared by their subaltern mothers.[32] Through Cedes's real maternal concern, the colonial view of Amerasian children is absorbed into the ex-colonial nation, working to police Amboy and his mother.

Throughout the film, Amboy gravitates toward Cedes's conservative order. The child receives parental attention not only from Cedes but also from her daughter Laura (Gilleth Sandico) and Laura's husband, Jessie (Piolo Pascual). Their daughter Angela (Anna Larrucea) treats Amboy like a brother. Because Cedes's family embodies the security afforded by conforming to the nation's ideals, the instability of the broken family Cedes takes under her wing is implicitly scripted as a problem of national filiation in the racializing terms through which, in Stoler's account, the colonial moral apparatus haunts the ex-colonial nation. It should be no surprise, then, that while Amboy circles around Cedes's "proper" family, he also keeps himself at arm's length from it.

Although Amboy's family romance fantasy is legitimated by Cedes, his ability to assume parental authority is undermined by his age, physical size, and ambiguous nationality. While the abusive Danny keeps Amboy in line at home, village bums poke fun at Amboy's mixed racial provenance and often threaten him with physical harm. Amboy's fantasy of reforming the patriarchy is dashed just when he tries to assert his self-sufficiency. Mechanically savvy, Amboy retrieves a bicycle from a junk pile. After Amboy restores its functionality, the bums steal the bike. Amboy asserts his claim over it, but the bums respond by destroying it in front of him. The kid tries to get even, deflating the tires on the jeep owned by one of the bums. The bums retaliate by chasing Amboy across the neighborhood. Before they can get to the kid, Danny corners Amboy inside their apartment and beats him up as the neighbors, in horror, listen to his cries.

By destroying his bike, the ruffians also trash Amboy's fantasy of patriarchal renewal. The movie, however, presents a compensatory scenario, using their repressive gesture to direct sympathy toward the young man. His fortitude calls attention both to the latent value of his paternal authority and to the nationalist valence of his project. Amboy's restored bicycle speaks to the community's desire to transform the ex-colonial wreckage into a desirable apparatus for collective mobility. The restoration of junk to utility inspires a *knowing* misrecognition of the old and useless as the new and valuable. Danny and the village bums are suggestive of unproductive citizenship, deterring a nation hard at work decolonizing and modernizing itself. Their aggression visibly upsets the neighbors. The neighbors' reaction affirms that Amboy's fantasy is also their own: a fantasy that requires faith in the regenerative work to which decolonization aspires.

At this low but hopeful point, *Phil-American Boy* links the fantasy of parental substitution more unmistakably to the fantasy of decolonization. Cedes and her family all the more take pity on Amboy. Subsumed by the old matriarch's authority, Amboy no longer has to take on the premature burden of founding a new national order. All that is required of him is to inherit proper patriotic values. But as noted earlier, the kid does not fully heed Cedes's call to embrace the conservative aspect of the ex-colonial order. Interestingly, just when the family romance allows Amboy to emerge as a subject, and just when his fantasy is validated as reflective of the communal desire for the ex-colony's magical renewal, the white father unexpectedly turns up.

Michael finds Amboy through a social worker and arranges to meet his son at a hotel in Manila. Amboy turns his father's invitation into an occasion for issuing his mother an ultimatum to depose her lover in order to validate her son's preeminence. "Do you love him more

The neighbors admire Amboy's (Patrick Garcia) restoration of the bicycle. Source: Phil-American Boy. Courtesy of ABS–CBN Film Productions Inc.

than you love me?" he challenges her. "If you do not leave him, I will go away with my white man father." Although Amboy is dead serious about evicting his stepfather, he is ambivalent about his own threat to his mother. He confesses to Jessie and Laura that he "will go with [his American father] only if Tessie can come along." Tessie, however, does not take the threat lightly. "I've made so many sacrifices for your sake," she tells her son. "I should have thrown you out with the garbage. Why don't you follow your white father all the way to hell? You ruined my life!" Even as her lactification fantasy nears fulfillment, Tessie retreats from it in fear. She realizes in advance that her relationship with Michael—as well as with Americans—can no longer be recuperated. Tessie disavows Amboy, the emerging supplement to the American father. She clings to the abusive native patriarch Danny instead of embracing her part-American son's nascent authority.

Amboy's fantasy involves the impossibly sudden transformation of the wrecked Philippine–American relationship into a working familial arrangement. If the nation's fantasy of decolonization and self-sufficiency is echoed by Amboy's ability to transform a piece of junk into an apparatus of mobility, Reyes's film appropriately calls back into the scene the specter of colonial fatherhood. With the arrival of his white American father, Amboy—and his sympathetic community—come to entertain the tempting possibility of returning to the old imperialist relationship.

The dream of mobility in *Phil-American Boy*, the tempting prospect of magical transformation, allegorizes empire's benevolent new guise, neoliberalism.[33] The dream of self-sufficiency and progress is arguably symptomatic of President Fidel Ramos's Philippines 2000 program. Like Amboy's neighbors marveling over the transformation of the wrecked bicycle, the Filipino nation must suspend disbelief when faced with the promises of the miraculous change offered by Ramos. The rhetoric of the West Point–educated president's diplomatic and trade policies trafficked in a millenarian fantasy of development through intensified global exchange. This fantasy required the Philippines to misrecognize knowingly the striking continuities between imperialism and neoliberalism. It called for the revitalization of neocolonial relations with the United States without exposing them as such. Ramos required Filipinos to ignore the colonial junk left to scatter amid the valorized benefits of globalization.

Philippines 2000, for instance, cultivated the notion that Filipinos had much to gain from the prescriptions of U.S. President Bill Clinton's global free trade agenda despite its often-ruinous effects on Third World citizens. Even more aggressively than his predecessors, Ramos coaxed the nation to be optimistic about such novel or previously unsuccessful measures as the privatization of government enterprises, import liberalization, the exposure of local currency to foreign speculation, the prioritization of foreign debt repayment, and the zealous policing of U.S. Intellectual Property Rights. After the closing of the U.S. bases, Ramos's program informally resuscitated colonial bonds by adopting neoliberalist socioeconomic directives from Washington. Filipinos had to *mis*recognize the fact that the advantages conceded to the West by Ramos's policies were not in any way resistant to the old project of empire.

Ramos's neoliberalist vision of statecraft and nation building had a novel facade of state fatherhood. If Reyes's film seems to recall the brutal stewardship of Ferdinand Marcos in the cruelty of Danny, Ramos had to distance himself from the past dictatorial regime and the special relations Marcos enjoyed with the U.S. government. At the same time, however, the progenitor of Philippines 2000 had to secure his brand of state fatherhood from the maternal discourse of his predecessor Corazon Aquino. *Phil-American Boy* registers the cultural effects of Aquino's spineless, chaotic governance by devoting much of what is supposed to be Amboy's narrative to the inept mothering of Tessie. The new facade of Ramos's neoliberal order ceded the Philippines' decolonizing endeavors to the new Philippine–American relations that, fundamentally but invisibly, resembled the old imperial dependencies.

In *Phil-American Boy*, the prospect of Dahoff's return fills the Amerasian son with both anticipation and anxiety. Amboy worries that he might be unable to communicate with his father because of his poor English-speaking skills. "You will understand each other," Tessie reassures Amboy. "You're father and son." If this moment allegorizes neoliberal desires lodged within the movie's fantasy of decolonization, the ties between old and new are naturalized and hence occluded as a paternal bond. The film toys with the return of an extraordinary specter. The colonial father reappears in the flesh, bearing gifts from the land of plenty. When Amboy meets Michael at the hotel, the American father uncannily resembles the cardboard character in Tessie's nostalgic recollections: a man in formal attire, his white face unblemished by time.

Michael (Joshua Spafford) shows Amboy (Patrick Garcia) a picture of his family in the states. Source: Phil-American Boy. Courtesy of ABS–CBN Film Productions Inc.

Echoing the Filipinos' desire for mobility, the Amerasian son asks his American father to take him to the United States. "Not simple, my boy," Michael replies. "I have my own family. They won't understand about your mother. It's not good for you to go with me to America. Not good." Michael withdraws from his son almost as soon as he graces the boy's fantasy with his charming presence. Here the decolonizing skepticism of the film resumes, framing the reappearance of the colonial as the return to abandonment. Michael presents Amboy $100 to settle old debts. As soon as the father exits the scene, his "gift" reduces the otherwise stoic young man to tears.

Avoiding *Olongapo . . . The Great American Dream*'s grim desire for complete parental substitution, Amboy's family romance forbids the child from getting rid of the mother. Amboy knows that Tessie has yet to recover from her colonial hangover. Michael and her missing father still haunt her desires. This time around, however, Tessie turns away from them for good, as well as from their oppressive native substitutes, and locks herself in her son's embrace. The boy becomes the primary object of desire, forestalling the return of the colonial. Unlike Ramos's neoliberal fantasy, *Phil-American Boy*'s family romance adamantly marks as taboo the reinstatement of the ex-colonizer in the seat of paternal authority. This simple gesture makes Reyes's work the most remarkable among the films discussed in this chapter.

In *The Intimate Enemy*, a penetrating analysis of the psychology of colonialism and anticolonial resistance, Ashis Nandy notes that narratives about the demise of empire conclude with the son turning away from the colonial father. The son discovers "the primal authority of the mother."[34] In Reyes's decolonizing family romance, Tessie and Amboy are left to fend for each other. *Phil-American Boy* ends with a sudden recognition of maternal authority. Tessie beats up a drunken Danny and kicks him out of the house. Removing Danny, Tessie deposes the recursion of both colonial and native patriarchy and secures her parental authority. She gloats to Amboy, "So, do you trust your mother now?" As if to compensate for the long history of errant fathers, she develops a stronger Oedipal bond with her son. Amboy voices his approval of this unusual bond: "My mother confessed that she will no longer have boyfriends. She's content with the fact that I am the only man in her life." Amboy and his mother are hailed as the founders of a transformed familial order metonymic of the nation's struggle to continue the work of decolonization in the era of intensified global commerce. Instead of entertaining men, she decides to earn her keep as a cosmetologist, "duping women" by selling them hope in jars.

Amboy's triumphant affirmation at the end of *Phil-American Boy* preempts any doubt concerning the stability of an incestuous dyad. Upon it rests the film's unique, if polemical, call to reject imperialism's perpetuation dressed up, like Michael, in immaculate new clothes. The fantasy of self-sufficiency generated by the mother–son dyad impresses the urgency of exiting the oppressive attachments to patriarchy and empire through relationships that are too easily assumed as inescapable. In the playbook of decolonization, this rhetoric is not altogether unfamiliar. Stoler, drawing from historical records, has shown that the mixed-race offspring's "affective and lasting ties to native women" were seen as potentially subversive by old colonial regimes. The sentiments of loyalty to the native mother were often blamed for creating "enemies of the [colonial] state."[35]

Amboy (Patrick Garcia) and his mother (Zsa-Zsa Padilla) strike back at her abusive lover. Source: Phil-American Boy. Courtesy of ABS–CBN Film Productions Inc.

The primary attachment to the mother at the ending constitutes the film's atavism. Although the resolution of turning away from the American father is present in all three films examined here, only in *Phil-American Boy* do we find the recourse to male Oedipality. Instead of being outgrown, the attachment to the mother is conserved to impede the return of patriarchy and empire. The symbolic form of mother–son "incest" effects a resolute dismissal of all past and future fathers. This recourse to atavism echoes, as recalled by Nandy, Mahatma Gandhi's sly "feminine" responses to colonialism's "ideology of hyper-masculinity and 'normality.'"[36] Through the elimination of both imperialist and native fathers, Reyes's film takes the route of the "feminine" in continuing the work of decolonization. The mother shows her son the fortitude he needs to depose every kind of patriarch he might encounter in the future. The film, however, does not fully echo the reciprocal engagement that animates Gandhi's "feminine" response to colonial authority. The sufficiency of the mother–son dyad in the film suggests that, with the expulsion of the father, the most vital energies of nation making no longer have to be expended on the creation of oppositional tactics toward the West. Mother and son can define the terms of their existence, surviving the pain generated by the wayward father. The film does not spell out those new terms, but it gestures toward the futurity of a nascent "feminine" countervision. While this vision must still be divined, the film's polemical call is clear: the future of decolonization depends crucially on the refusal to continue identifying with the patriarchal powers that threaten to return in foreign as well as familiar guises.

For his part, Amboy's response to the "feminine" works on two levels of identification. As a loyal son *and* as a paternal figure supplementing both old and new American attachments, Amboy undoes the narrative of abandonment and naïve yearning to which Tessie had been addicted. The redeemed mother is granted the authority to generate a vision that is emphatically affirmed even if it is not yet fully articulated. Where patriarchy is inevitably bound to fail, the idealized "feminine"—not the binary opposite of patriarchy but rather all the possible alternatives that patriarchy could never be—holds the only promise of success in the decolonizing fantasy of *Phil-American Boy*.[37] "We have each other's backs," Amboy tells his mother. "Folks like us are hard to beat."

Conclusion

Although the three films discussed here have not lost their relevance, their respective historical situations leave imprints on the scenarios of decolonization they portray. These scenarios are encoded in fantasies of parental substitution, otherwise known as the family romance. To read these fantasies historically is to track the fate of nationalist, postcolonial consciousness in the wake of Philippine and global transformations.

Hellow, Soldier revisits the imperial relationship at a time of national unrest and worldwide anti-imperialist ferment. It emerged at a time when an unqualified rejection of the colonizer was just as difficult to imagine as the wholehearted affirmation of the postcolonial nation-state. Decolonization in Brocka's film positions the ex-colonial subject ambivalently toward both the United States and the Philippines. As allegorized by Gina's story, the American father is repudiated but not entirely deposed as a figure of authority. His promise of succor is rejected only because it threatens to breed in the mother a sense of abandonment. Even if rejected, however, the white father's promise is regarded as a means of holding in check the mother's capacity for self-destruction. Paradoxically the mother's self-worth depends on both repudiation of the father and the affirmation bestowed by his whiteness.

Gina's relation to her mother is equally fraught with contradiction. The mother's attachment to pain mirrors the nation's persistent image of itself in terms of its passage from colonial subjection. The enlightened daughter sees that her mother's sense of victimization is a part of her own identity. Her narcissistic attachment to pain must be acknowledged but not embraced. To move beyond the wretchedness of her mother's slums, and to resolve the conundrum signified by intersecting streets called "North" (Hilaga) and "Fate" (Kapalaran), Gina initially longs to replace her native mother with her white father. Ultimately, however, Gina herself becomes the parental substitute she seeks, and she replaces the white father with a native lad besotted by her. The transition to the postcolonial order of things is staged entirely as a matter of familial substitution. The national family is set up to replace the ruinous colonial affair, even if the contradictions of ex-colonial desires and the vestiges of the old regime impede the decolonizing project. The mother clings heavily to Gina in the same way that the yearning for the American father persistently cleaves the ex-colonial subject.

Olongapo . . . The Great American Dream's scenario of decolonization suggests that the residual affection for the mother must be purged alongside the sentimental attachment to the devastated nation-state. The film posits that there can be no renewal without such purging. It proposes a postnationalist outlook to decolonization. What is striking in this view is its indifference to the surge of nationalist affect during the year-old People Power Revolution.

Racquel, the Amerasian protagonist of *Olongapo . . . The Great American Dream*, rejects her mother and even facilitates her mother's self-destruction. She refuses to be reunited with her American father and also jettisons the idea of regenerating the national family. The ex-colonial subject annuls the fantasy of building a livable future in the homeland. Racquel compares this decolonizing project to a gaudy, floating castle on Subic Bay. She places her bets instead on the dream of global mobility, a fantasy arguably inspired by the colonial encounter.

The film's postnationalist detachment is implicit in Racquel's manner of claiming her future. She adopts her mother's "profession" without assuming its burdens. She uses the benefits of her father's citizenship without affirming a sentimental attachment to her father and to America. Without shedding a tear, she sends her mother to the grave and bids her motherland farewell. Even if Racquel was born there, Olongapo—a metonym for the Philippines—offers no refuge for her dreams: "Auntie says it's the bathroom of the world."

In sharp contrast to the postnationalist scenario of *Olongapo . . . The Great American Dream*, the third film on Filipino GI babies reaffirms the centrality of nationalist affect to decolonization as it enters the era of globalization. In *Phil-American Boy*, the ex-colonial nation is to be renewed through the exclusion of both Filipino and American paternity. The repudiation of paternity is symptomatic of a desire to eliminate inequities transmitted through father figures: the old colonial relationship, its perpetuation in the tyrannical native structures of power, and the afterlife of colonialism in neoliberal economic policies.

Phil-American Boy posits atavism as a way to forestall the return of the father. The protagonists, a Filipina mother and her Amerasian son, realize in the film's striking conclusion that the route to happiness is their retreat to exclusivity. In this decolonizing fantasy, the incestuous mother-son dyad is inaugurated as the new model for the familial discourse of national belonging. Tessie's ascendant matriarchy gestures toward the utopian promise of the feminine: the sum of all possible alternatives to the imperialist, patriarchal regimes of previous imperial and postcolonial states. In risking incest, Tessie and Amboy profess a resounding "no" to the loving embrace of the white father and his patriarchal usurpers.

Owing to the mixed racial identity of the protagonists in all three films, their fantasies of decolonization try to surpass the retrograde forms of anticolonial nationalism.[38] As we have seen in the three works, the offspring's dual identity and torn allegiance inspire complex reckonings of the old colonial relationship and its possible future guises. *Hellow, Soldier* proposes an ambivalent nationalism; *Olongapo . . . The Great American Dream*, a disarming postnationalist vision; and *Phil-American Boy*, a familial sphere shielded from both the foreign and domestic fathers. The importance of these American fantasies rests not in any concrete political program—they offer none—but in their range of postcolonial affects and their various ways of desiring the future of decolonization.

II

Transnational Imaginings

4

The Migrant Woman's Tale

On Loving and Leaving Nations

The previous part of this book studied conjurations of past, present, and future encounters with American empire. My goal in this chapter and the next is to show how such real and imagined encounters shape dreams of belonging to America and the homeland. The particular American fantasy that concerns me here is arguably the most popular and widely assimilated: the American dream, or the myth of an individual's success through sheer hard work in a land of opportunity and social equality.[1]

Filipinos have a complex relation to the fantasy of settling in the former imperial metropole. For some, success in America is both the ultimate validation of one's professional worth and the surest path to a good life. The United States is, to them, not only the land of the ex-colonizer but also the greatest nation in the world. America is so different from their native Philippines and yet also the most culturally familiar foreign country. Coming to America holds the promise of global citizenship, and learning to love America without postcolonial guilt remains one of the most elusive milestones of decolonization. For others, the American dream is a tawdry mirage that lures—and is sure to disappoint—the naïve and desperate. It represents crass materialism, moral degeneration, second-class citizenship, collaboration with imperialism, and national betrayal. Given all these notions, both advocates and critics would agree that the American dream represents the greatest threat to the anticolonial nationalism that scaffolds Filipino identity.

In Gil Portes's *'Merika* (1984) and Olivia Lamasan's *Hopefully, Once More* (*Sana maulit muli*, 1995), the Filipino's American dream—the fantasy of what I call postcolonial immigration—is told as the story of a migrant woman, her romance with a man who may or may not love America as much as she does, and her eventual retreat to the home and homeland. The figure of the migrant woman is especially suitable for the task of representing the ambivalence of Filipinos toward the desire to make it in America in the face of the homeland's endless misfortunes. On one hand, the migrant woman can be nostalgic, forgiving, ever loyal, and self-sacrificing—in short, the perfect embodiment of nationalist affect. On the other hand, her sexual agency, troublesome experiences with patriarchy and nationalism, and stereotypical fickleness permit her to challenge the alibis of the masculinist state by attaining female liberation via First World modernity.[2] The genre of the woman's film, to which 'Merika and Hopefully, Once More belong, also properly serves the representational demands of ambivalence. The genre's focus on articulating "women's deepest unconscious fears and fantasies about their lives in patriarchy" lets unruly desires and feelings into the picture to bring nuance to discussions about the condition of females in a given society.[3]

It would be unwise, however, to read 'Merika and Hopefully, Once More only as allegories of postcolonial immigration. I argue instead that the mise-en-scène of the Filipina's American dream functions as an imaginary resource for pondering not only the ex-colonial's journey to the metropole but also the politics of female independence and the woman's role in the nation. I am not tempted to regard the American dreams of the women migrants in these films as mere scenic backdrops for a domestic romance. While there is a tendency for romances set in foreign countries to work like travelogues, in both of these films, the change in geographic location effects a remarkable shift in the characters' perspectives about their relation to home and to each other.[4]

In her famous essay on women and patriarchal nationalism, Deniz Kandiyoti points to the common view that women are often "relegated to the margins of the polity even though their centrality to the nation is constantly being reaffirmed."[5] But while in the homeland the woman often lacks the influence befitting her role as the privileged bearer of group identity and cultural authenticity, her sexuality could be a source of considerable power when she immigrates to the West.[6] Rey Chow describes this power as a "sexual agency that disrupts the existing boundaries that mark different racial groups apart"[7] and "interrupt[s] community formation with powerful fissures."[8] In this case, because the migrant woman can choose to be or not to be with an American or Filipino man, "her claim ... to being the progenitor of the community to come" poses a symbolic (and, at times, very real) threat to both.[9]

In the two films discussed here, this sexual agency benefits the migrant woman, proving to be a powerful foil to her supposedly primordial loyalty toward the Filipino man. It gives her leverage to demand changes from him, and it also empowers her to be critical of America's promise of hospitality and enfranchisement to outsiders like her. This agency soon reaches its limit, however, when it begins to venture more deeply into the province of nationalist politics. The migrant woman comes to realize that while gender politics is a potentially winnable contest, the game of nationalist politics is rigged to favor men. Since there is still no acceptable alternative to anticolonial nationalism, Filipino patriotic affect must be demonstrated through the migrant woman's repatriation. The fantasy of the Filipina's postcolonial immigration is thus, to a certain extent, conjured only to be dismissed in the end.

But gender politics is not the only avenue of success for the migrant woman in these films. Moreover, her repatriation does not mean that she is totally defeated on the playing field of nationalist politics. The migrant woman succeeds in her representational task within the allegory of postcolonial immigration.[10] In relationships with men and with the nations wooing her, the migrant's affections wax as quickly as they wane. Her passion easily turns into disgust. This volatility mirrors the unruliness of the feelings that postcolonial immigration and female agency beget in nationalist discourse. Having to choose between "suitors" only deepens her attachment to them. The crisis divides her. Thus, even after she has made her choice, the unpredictability of her emotions could still undo the apparent closure of sacrifice, repatriation, and marriage.

In relation to my exploration of Philippine cinema's transnational practices, it is worth mentioning that both films transcend the boundaries of the territorial nation-state through their settings, spectatorial address, and mapping of Filipino experiences. The visionary independent filmmaker Portes's *'Merika* gently calls for transnational solidarity between Filipinos at home and in America during a wave of anti-Marcos protests in the Philippines, while promoting movie superstar Nora Aunor's popularity among overseas Filipinos. Further, the film is meant as a transnational love letter, paying tribute—as the end credits profess—"to those Filipino residents of Manila Drive in Jersey City, New Jersey who just can't seem to lay down roots in their new land and still dream of coming home to the Philippines." *Hopefully, Once More* also does double duty in its transnational address. For domestic audiences, the film showcases San Francisco and depicts the life of Filipino migrants to America. For the overseas audience, the film affirms their sentimental ties to the homeland while also serving as an advertisement for the American presence of Philippine media conglomerate ABS-CBN. Finally, as with *'Merika*, Lamasan's *Hopefully, Once More* celebrates a Filipina's international stardom—in this case, that of Lea Salonga, the singer-actress who went on to star in the Broadway musical *Miss Saigon* and supplied the singing voice of two Disney cartoon heroines.

'Merika: Living the American Dream, or Nursing the Philippine Revolution

'Merika is an independently produced film about a Filipina nurse who, unsatisfied with a migrant's life in New Jersey, ponders a homecoming to tend the wounds of her countrymen and nation. The nurse's tale travels a familiar path in rallying the Filipino middle class to a nationalist cause, playing to anti-American sentiments in order to bolster a middling patriotism. In consonance with the film's quiet nature, this appeal to nationalism is made by subtly denigrating the practice of postcolonial immigration. Through hushed tones and a putatively realistic depiction of the migrant woman's everyday life, *'Merika* systematically argues for the bankruptcy of the American dream. What makes this critique truly interesting, however, is its dialogical purpose. The object of critique is the great American myth, interrogated from the postcolonial woman's perspective. At the same time, the film's deprecation of the migrant woman's American middle-class life aims to evoke the problematic complacency of the Philippine petty bourgeois at home and abroad during a time of national emergency. This latter aim must be tactfully grafted onto the former mainly because of the Marcos regime's lack of tolerance for any form of revolutionary agitation.[11] The contradictions within this dual purpose further complicate the Filipino ambivalence on the issue of postcolonial immigration.

What flaw, then, does the migrant woman find in the American dream? If asked, Mila (Nora Aunor), the protagonist of *'Merika*, would probably cite a number of problems. First, her tale shows us that the individual and civic life that comes with that dream is unbearable. We see just how this is so through the enactment of Mila's daily routine in the film's opening sequence. She takes cold breakfasts in front of the television: usually a bowl of cereal with a side of terrifyingly banal talk-show banter. She takes even colder daily walks along the near-desolate stretch of asphalt and chain-link fences called Manila Drive. Like nearly every resident of New Jersey, she must endure subway journeys with their montage of nondescript faces and staccato play of darkness and light. At work, she faces insufferable multiculturally affirmative niceties: the greetings in Filipino by white doctors and the "hola" she reciprocally owes her Latino colleagues. At night, she comes home to TV dinners and, of course, TV shows—especially the grating perkiness of Dr. Ruth and an obtuse, sleep-inducing discussion of Reaganomics. On weekends, between the banality of opening junk mail and the occasional letter from home, Mila and her roommate, Violet (Marilyn Concepcion), stare absently at the washers and dryers at the laundromat as they wait for the cycles to end.

For Mila Cruz (Nora Aunor), life in America is as empty and alienating as an endless subway ride. Source: 'Merika. Courtesy of Gil M. Portes, producer-director.

Mila attributes her dissatisfaction with the lived American dream's mundane rhythms to something more serious than a textbook case of melancholia. For example, she tells her handsome Filipino suitor Mon (Rafael Roco Jr.) about her fits of agoraphobia that, as she later acknowledges, point to something deeper. While looking out of the viewing deck at the Empire State Building, she tells him, "The skyscrapers loom so high, like they'll come crashing down on you. All the people around you are always rushing." Mon presses her to think of why she has not adjusted to life in the states, despite having lived there for five years. She responds, "Because people here don't care about each other. You feel so cut off from other people, especially at the end of the workday. It's not like the Philippines . . . I find it hard to breathe here." This immigrant woman describes a strange experience of feeling separated from Americans even as their bodies and built environment press so unbearably hard on her entire being.

Mila's experience is a psychosomatic manifestation of an alienated citizenship, the peculiar kind of belonging and nonbelonging felt by immigrants toward the host nations they help build.[12] Her double alienation as an immigrant and worker seems especially anomalous because Mila's job requires her to be in close physical contact with her American patients and to be deeply empathetic toward them. For the Filipinos in Jersey City's Manila Drive, this experience of alienation is met with a response of reciprocal exclusion. Danny (Marshall Factora), Mila's liberal-minded colleague, points this out during a party with only one American in attendance. "Yes, why is it," he wonders, "that in all the parties thrown here in Manila Drive, no Americans are ever invited?" Mon chimes in with the justification: "They never invite us, so why should we invite them?" Throughout the film, Mila wrestles with the question of whether to settle for this kind of economically prosperous but spiritually alienated belonging. She has already satisfied the permanent residency requirement for naturalization, but she hesitates to assume full membership in the land her American fantasy has promised her. Suspecting that U.S. citizenship will not cure her ennui and civic disengagement, she decides to pursue something else: the love of her homeland and compatriots.

Mila's second problem with the American dream is, like the first, somewhat stereotypical. She detests the tawdry material forms of the prosperity, individuation, and social mobility promised by that dream.

Two men in her life—both of whom are, ironically, Filipinos—embody this shallow materialism. Her brother Lando, an absent character in the film, lives the American dream vicariously through her. He treats her as a cash cow, communicating with her only to ask for money and even lying about their father's health just to get to her pocketbook. She admits thinking often that she is working in America primarily to send money back to Lando. Her suitor, Mon, like Lando, sees America solely in terms of its promised affluence. He boasts of getting a spanking new car on nothing but his good credit. He admires his cousin's obsession with buying—strictly for the sake of appearances—an apartment big enough to be admired by his daughter's classmates and located in a building that purposely has "no blacks" and "no Hispanics." During a fancy dinner at the Rainbow Room Grill, Mon gloats about his newfound "American" prerogative to waste food. He advises Mila to discard her leftover steak, telling her, "That's what I like about the states. You can keep on throwing things away without feeling guilty. You can't do that in the Philippines now, can you?" Mila recalls her mother's advice about the wages paid in purgatory by those who waste food needlessly. Although she presses this advice gently, Mon's further pronouncements about things and money contribute significantly to her growing disaffection for him. The migrant woman's alienation from the stereotypical materialism of middle-class life intensifies her desire to work for intangible rewards and spiritual goods that are yet obscure to her. Later, she realizes that social justice—that pearl of great price—is one of them.

The third problem with the Filipino's American dream, in Mila's view, is the complacency it breeds among its followers. The film uses the trope of forgetting as a way of faulting an individualism that shades into apathy. In her apartment building and the nursing home where she works a second job, Mila bears witness to a struggle against senility waged by those whom society has forgotten. Her landlady's mother, Grandma Gorgonia (Dolores Medel), draws pity from the younger Filipinos in their building for completely losing her memory. Without the faintest sense of time and place, the old immigrant woman remembers no faces and wanders Manila Drive, thinking she is still in the old country. Mila acknowledges that her own greatest fear is ending up like Grandma Gorgonia or one of the many abandoned nursing home residents she tends to in her second job. "Do you know what really scares me?" she confides to Mon. "When I see sick people, dying people in the hospital, I get scared that something bad will also happen to me." The fear of that "something bad," the fate of forgetting and being forgotten, makes Mila identify with a nursing home resident she calls Grandpa Caloy (Cesar Aliparo). The old-timer tries valiantly, but occasionally fails, to hold on to his bittersweet memories of being a poor boy in Ilocos province and a jazz musician in Chicago. Mila helps him counter the machine of forgetting by drawing out stories from his past and sharing her own remembrances about her *tatang* (father). She stimulates the old man's reveries by giving him a nostalgia machine, gifting him with a Walkman so that he can, in hearing Louis Armstrong's music, recall his youth and former career. When he forgets *how* to remember, she restores his nostalgia by inventing a game. She challenges him to name "fruits that grow only in our country!" The snappy exchange coaxes long-forgotten words out of memory—*ratiles, rambutan, lanzones, atis, duhat, langka, durian*—and stalls his inevitable descent into oblivion.

One of Mila's (Nora Aunor) greatest fears is ending up like her senile neighbor, Grandma Gorgonia (Dolores Medel). Source: 'Merika. Courtesy of Gil M. Portes, producer-director

The elder migrant's programmed disappearance, a fate that Mila and Caloy battle together, is related to the condition of alienated citizenship that most immigrants share. But this fading from society and estrangement from one's old self affects and speaks volumes about the larger society of nonmigrants. The shadow of the American dream's figure of youthful success falls hardest on the elderly and those who can no longer participate in the valorized activity of production. The systemic forgetting (and self-forgetting) of those who once lived by the creed of work suggests a moral bankruptcy at the heart of the American dream. This situation is glaringly apparent in the eyes of the migrants because they recognize it as a familiar scene of inhospitality and also find it incompatible with their own values, especially their belief in filial piety. Additionally, Filipino migrants like Mila and Caloy know only too well the business of national forgetting, in its double sense as the failure to remember one's people and as the prevalent condition of social and historical amnesia in the Philippines.

Once again, Mon reveals himself as the immigrant who embodies the deplorable kind of forgetting abetted by the pursuit of the American dream. Unlike the senile woman, Mon can remember but refuses to do so. Eager to forget the old country ("What would I do there anyway?"), he is the ugly antithesis of Mila and the other migrants who try to honor their homeland. Mila's other suitor is a portly Filipino American named Henry (Bodgie Abaya), who visits the Philippines annually to grow roots there. Violet, for her part, haunts the ethnic grocery in search of flavors that transport her back to the islands: "dried anchovies . . . green mangoes, rice pudding, cashew nuts from Antipolo." Mon not only refuses to look back toward his homeland but also fabricates memories to keep him away from it. On one occasion, he even makes up a false memory to justify his distaste for the Philippines and what it represents. He relates, "I had a girlfriend back home, but I left her temporarily to immigrate here. Then I came back for her . . . Just before I returned to the states, she came to my house. Said she really couldn't come with me to America but was willing to sleep with me as a parting gift. I slapped her . . . It was good that I met you. Only then did I forget my past with her."

Mon speaks with a forked tongue. This invented memory of his gives the impression that Mon, who is at liberty to travel in and out of the United States, enjoys legal immigrant status. Moreover, it portrays him as a principled man who grants sexual favors only out of love. In truth, Mon is only too willing to forget his national identity and give up his morals just to get his immigration papers in order. He is the type of ugly immigrant (or despicable petty bourgeois) who sells out even before he gets his foot in the door.

In the course of her soul searching, Mila awakens to another form of complacency in her life. Like some members of the U.S. middle class, she has become politically apathetic. She comes to this realization in the course of a transnational subplot about her developing empathy for Luisa (Chiquit Reyes), an emotionally troubled nurse from El Salvador. At first, Mila resents the Latina's truancy (supposedly due to pains and aches of all sorts). When Mila complains to Danny about the hassles of picking up after Luisa, he enlightens her about the crisis in El Salvador. He tells her about the armed conflict in that country: "In El Salvador, many people are dying because of the Americans." In subsequent interactions with Luisa, Mila learns that the Latina has lost touch with her family in El Salvador. Soon enough, the parallels between the turmoil in El Salvador and the impending crisis in the Philippines enable Mila to realize her unconscionable lack of fellow feeling. Her former indifference to a war caused overseas by the United States demonstrates how deeply immigrants like her have internalized the putative complacency of the American middle class. She snaps out of this complacency only when it becomes apparent to her that Luisa's fate (and that of El Salvador) might well befall her own family and nation if nothing is done. Mila's recognition of the parallels between Luisa and herself is aided by conversations and letters from her best friend Cora, a nurse who once entertained her own American dream but opted to stay in the Philippines. It is through her tactful allusions to the social climate in the Philippines that Mila gains perspective on the country's latest political upheavals. Reporting on the spate of public demonstrations in 1984—the year after the assassination of Marcos dissident Ninoy Aquino, who left his placid life in Boston to rejoin the fight against the dictatorship—Cora acknowledges the turmoil without belittling the country. "It's kinda fun," she says on the phone. "There have been rallies . . . You know, things like that."[13]

Through Cora's letters and phone calls to the old country, the film's political stakes are discreetly figured. Cora's life becomes the shining alternative to Mila's American middle-class ennui. Cora's life is an image of what Mila could have had, or rather what she *should* be living, in the Philippines. As Mila herself acknowledges to Mon, Cora's life and hers are practically identical, from their educational background down to their heartaches with men. From Mila's perspective, the simple contrast—but one that makes all the difference in the world—is the place where they lead those lives. Although they are both in the business of helping people as nurses, Mila sees her friend's life as "having a purpose" because it serves their needy compatriots. Cora is "still active in community work." She recognizes that "she is needed more in our country [than in the states]." Additionally, she heroically sacrifices her need for intimate physical relations to the altar of political change. For more than five years, she has waited patiently for the return of her lover, Pete, an anti-Marcos dissident (or communist insurgent) who is out fighting in the mountains. Mila, on the other hand, just plods along in America, doing so-so with her income but quite poorly in love. She describes her condition lucidly early in the film while carrying her groceries along the chilly and desolate stretch of Manila Drive: "Sure, the money is good, but life runs like clockwork. When their workday is over, people here have nothing better to do than watch TV. That's why it scares me that I'm wasting my life here. I feel like a kibitzer: a mere spectator watching things from the sidelines."

Mila's rhetoric in relating this epiphany points to the melodramatic ambition lying beneath the film's veneer of quiet social realism. In a melodramatic manner, the migrant woman draws a polar opposition between the state of national emergency that calls her back to the Philippines and the empty but transfixing television images that lure her to stay put in America. The conflict is pared down to a simple, irresistible choice: will she labor for change in her homeland or just watch its history recapped on the evening news? In 'Merika, the disavowal of the seductive American dream is posited as a kind of overcompensating affirmation of patriotic action. To raise the stakes—as if they were not high enough at this point in the narrative—the film shows Mila's determination to go home (and, implicitly, to resist the Marcos dictatorship) being seriously challenged by her intensifying attraction to Mon. When she sleeps with him on the night Violet leaves town to take her nursing licensure exam, Mila seems poised to scrap her homecoming plans. With romantic love pitted against patriotic duty, the political fuses with the deeply personal, and the melodramatic oppositions become even starker. Does she join the revolution in the Philippines or have sex with Mon in America? Does she choose a nationalist dissident or an unpatriotic seducer?

Mila's (Nora Aunor) romance with Mon (Rafael Roco Jr.) challenges her resolve to return to the Philippines. Source: 'Merika. Courtesy of Gil M. Portes, producer-director.

The moral stakes of her choice between America and the Philippines crystallize when Mon's amorous promises are unmasked as a mere instrument for his American dream of middle-class comfort. Henry, motivated by his rivalry with Mon, verifies Mon's illegal immigrant status and warns Mila that she is being used. When she asks Mon to confess to lying about his immigration record and his true interest in wooing her, he admits to an initial opportunism but insists that he has truly fallen in love. Unsatisfied, Mila lodges a question of nationalism in her challenge to his fidelity: "If I decide to come home to the Philippines, would you come with me?" she inquires. When he responds with an appeal to being "practical" and warns her about the uncertainties of life back home, Mila comes to grips with the end of the affair. "You really don't love me," she tells him point-blank. "It's all about your America. It's America you're really after." Days later, Mila confronts Mon at wintry Lincoln Park to bid him good-bye, but the man makes his final appeal. Instead of arguing with him, she simply rubs the tawdriness of his American dream in his face: "You can't find everything here in America. Some things just aren't here."

In making Mila's choice not just morally legible but also drastically simplified (i.e., patriotism by physical presence in the nation), the film admittedly risks devaluing its own assessment of the American dream. The migrant woman's critique begins to look like a manipulative device for producing nationalist affect.[14] Immigrant life in America is put down simply to portray political action in the Philippines as the paragon of all noble causes. After all, anti-imperialist—or, more to the point, anti-American—affect is perhaps the surest way of firing up a sluggish Filipino nationalism.[15] One of the greatest consequences of this simplification is the occlusion of the woman's role in the patriotic mandate. The active role that the film assigns to the figure of the migrant woman is surrendered in favor of the unseen but valorized male revolutionary, Pete, the lover of Mila's best friend.

Rey Chow, writing in a different context, names this sort of valorization of male agency as a kind of "revolutionary male narcissism."[16] The woman, whose agency is "prohibited, exiled, and deferred," is simply considered "superfluous" to nation making.[17] Something of this narcissism undermines Mila's status as the active protagonist of what, for its time, was a progressive woman's film. For while her psychological point of view dominates the narrative, Mila initially resolves to give up her independence in America to become a subordinate player in the revolution and in the reformed national community to come. She half-seriously mocks Cora for trying to be a Florence Nightingale but ultimately decides to emulate her best friend by flying to the scene of the national emergency to play second fiddle to male revolutionaries. Mila is associated with the revolution only through her friendship with Cora. She does not even have a revolutionary lover like Pete. Adding to Mila's subordination upon returning home, repatriation aims to satisfy not her desires but those of her two beloved patriarch figures: her *tatang* and Grandpa Caloy. After making up her mind to go home, she declares that her *tatang* will be very happy to see her. She pretends to seek Grandpa Caloy's blessing even if her real interest is to simply thrill him with the news that she will be carrying out his aborted dream of return. But the question remains: what does the woman gain for giving up her American dream? What must *she* do at home after she is repatriated? There is a danger here, as Deniz Kandiyoti warns us, of mobilizing women "when they are needed . . . only to return them to domesticity or subordinate roles in the public sphere when the national emergency is over."[18]

At the end of the film, the quandary over the repatriated woman's role in the homeland (and revolution) meshes with the Filipina's highly conflicted feelings about postcolonial immigration. A conspicuous moment of ambivalence at the airport stages these contradictions. The opposing forces, which draw the migrant woman home and also repel her from it, tear at her being. She is split at the very moment she submits to a coercive national mandate that is silent about the action to which she is called. While Mila's repatriation is held up as the ideal response to the national emergency, the film's denouement registers a deep ambivalence about the command to send the woman back home without a specific charge.

In the scene in question, Mila bids silent farewells at the airport to Violet and Henry. She takes only a few steps toward the boarding gate before turning back to look at her friends. The shot freezes for a few seconds on her look of longing before it leads to a montage of scenes showing her friends carrying on in the states without her. Henry enters data into an enormous computer terminal. Danny fiddles with test tubes. Violet fingers her nurse's headpiece. Grandpa Caloy watches television with fellow nursing home residents. Mon wanders about the Big Apple, haunting the places where Mila once lingered. The succession of these images is accompanied by a montage of dialogue from various parts of the film. This moment is significant because it arrests the glorious homecoming demanded by both the migrant's narrative and nationalist sentiment, as if to express a lingering reservation.[19] The technological and thus "masculine" labors performed by her friends in the diaspora conjure the purposeful occupation she once had in America. The absence of a corresponding vocation in the Philippines is signified by the void to which the boarding gate and its collapsible tube lead. Without having even left New Jersey, Mila is already pining for the American dream all over again. The work and life that she is about to reject suddenly look purposeful. After the montage of dignified workers, the frozen image of Mila's nostalgic gaze at America is released. The camera tracks her as she moves farther down the tube. Closing credits roll immediately thereafter, withholding the scene of Mila's triumphant arrival in the Philippines.

The moment of ambivalence signified by the freeze-frame and montage registers the problem of the woman's national vocation, the question of the diaspora's purpose in a state of national emergency, and the Filipino's conflicted desire for postcolonial immigration. In his study of new German cinema, Thomas Elsaesser notes the difficulty of conscripting the woman as a representative figure of any sort. The dilemma, according to him, "is how to give the female character in the fiction film a coherent identity, when the very thing that makes her a woman is the constant struggle and failure to cohere."[20] In the case of 'Merika, that very "incoherence" of woman permits the figuration of ambivalences within the discourse of national emergency—that of the woman's vocation, of living in the diaspora, and of the American dream. One part of Mila responds to the urgency of the nationalist cause by undertaking the obligatory homecoming. Her performance of the supreme nationalistic gesture doubles its emotional force by satisfying melodrama's ethical imperative and playing up the experience of loss at the heart of the woman's film.[21] The gesture of homecoming is shaded with political meaning: Mila's return faintly resembles Ninoy Aquino's self-sacrificing repatriation to offer his country an alternative to the Marcos dictatorship. The other half of Mila's divided self "stays" in America and accepts the migrant's fate. She turns away from the boarding gate because she has learned the diaspora's lesson, which, as John Durham Peters puts eloquently, is about the "perpetual postponement of homecoming and the necessity, in the meanwhile, of living among strange lands and peoples."[22] Like the film, she will not pass judgment on those who, by remaining in exile, are unable to heed the call of the middle-class revolution at home. (Many Filipino dissidents, after all, exiled themselves to middle-class lives in the states when martial law took effect in the Philippines and yet continued to fight the dictatorship.) Moreover, Mila looks back to make sure that Violet and Henry are also gazing at her—a gesture that signifies the Philippine diaspora's role in helping America keep its disciplinary gaze on the crisis-ridden Philippine nation-state. The montage that interrupts Mila's homecoming thus affirms and illustrates the "density of overlapping allegiances" and the "oscillating desires" that keep the nostalgic immigrant always pining for, and yet also retreating from, the homeland.[23]

Violet (Marilyn Concepcion) and Henry (Bodgie Abaya) emerge as doubles of Mila and Mon. They represent the well-adjusted Filipino immigrants. Source: 'Merika. Courtesy of Gil M. Portes, producer-director.

The dramatic splitting of Mila's subjectivity is reinforced by an uncanny doubling at the scene of departure. Unusual doppelgangers of the film's two main figures emerge in the persons of Violet and Henry. Violet is a fortified version of Mila: younger, tougher, and much better at resisting the siren call of Philippine nationalism. While she and Mila do not bear a physical resemblance to each other, the film invariably links their images and personas. Apart from their shared occupation as nurses, their joint rehearsal of gestures and routines (e.g., paying zombie-like attention to the television while similarly dressed and side by side in the same room) render them practically interchangeable. Henry, who once hoped to be Mila's lover, becomes a different sort of double vis-à-vis Mon: point by point, Henry is Mon's converse. He is rotund and unattractive, while Mon is fit and handsome. The former is not quite a Filipino citizen, while the latter is not quite an American. They profess diametrically opposed allegiances to the Philippines. Finally, while Henry is faithful and true, Mon is wayward and dishonest. As embodiments of the successful life Mila and Mon could have lived in America, Henry and Violet implicitly challenge the foregone conclusions of the migrant's repatriation. Moreover, as the two exit the liminal space of the airport, they supplant not just Mila and Mon, but what Mila and Mon's failed affair represents: the polarizing view that sees living in America and being Filipino as mutually incompatible. Through this doubling of the migrant couple, 'Merika rallies overseas Filipinos to heed the call of the national emergency while also leaving room for their secret wish to preserve their American dreams.

Hopefully, Once More, or Immigration and Women's Liberation

Without a national emergency in the offing, Hopefully, Once More (Sana maulit muli, 1995) allows for a more dispassionate look at postcolonial immigration and, more particularly, at how the attainment of the migrant woman's American dream might change her place at home and in the homeland. The woman's film, Maria LaPlace reminds us, is a "'heroine's text,' a story of a woman's personal triumph over adversity."[24] It is a kind of female bildungsroman. Like the novel of a young man's integration into the social order, the female melodrama is a narrative of a heroine's journey of independence and success. The heroine is "forced out of the family and into the world."[25] She "endure[s] a series of hardships completely on her own . . . [and] finds inner resources—will, courage, and intelligence—that permit her to succeed."[26] Hopefully, Once More follows a middle-class girl's development from a fragile, lovesick puppy in Manila to a high-powered career woman in San Francisco. Once she changes for the better, however, a romantic dilemma threatens to pull her back to her old self and former home. By gaining independence through immigration, our heroine becomes incompatible with the man she left back home. When he comes to America and tries to win her back, love and nationalism force her to consider relinquishing her precious gains in America. The ensuing tug-of-war magnifies the disparity between the Filipina woman's pitiful underdevelopment at home and her impressive blossoming in America. As in 'Merika, a moment of ambivalence occurs at the eleventh hour, suddenly bringing a foregone conclusion to a revelatory crisis. Hopefully, Once More's ultimate outcome, however, and its implications for gender and national politics are quite different from 'Merika's.

At the start of Olivia Lamasan's film, the twentysomething Agnes (Lea Salonga) is an emotional wreck. Her father, who cared for her as a single parent, has just died. Her aunt is selling the home in which Agnes grew up, making her choose between relocating to the province with family or staying in Manila and striking out on her own. Her boyfriend of several years, an advertising account executive named Jerry (Aga Mulach), loves her and has promised marriage, but the wedding plans have to be put on hold. Jerry is still financially unstable, and worse, his blabbermouth mother, Lita (Gina Pareño), is expecting him to pay his younger sister's way through school and to finance his brother-in-law's application for migrant work in Japan. With his hands tied, Jerry encourages Agnes to vacation with her mother, Sylvia (Rosemarie Sonora), in San Francisco once her immigrant's petition is approved. Agnes's vacation lasts much longer than expected when both Jerry and Sylvia prevail upon her to extend her stay.

During her first year and a half in America, Agnes learns to get over her resentment toward her mother, who abandoned her at age ten to start a new life in the states. Now that she knows what things are like when relationships fail, Agnes begins to appreciate her mother's rationale for making a new family in America: "I wanted to go on living," Sylvia tells her daughter. Agnes reaches an epiphany after she is nearly raped in an alley while Jerry fails to take her frantic phone calls. She decides to let go of him, toughen up, make friends, and find herself a real career. She quits her old job rinsing old folks' bottoms at a nursing home, and she obtains a position at a realty firm. She retires her crybaby ways in favor of a masculine predilection for spouting real estate lingo and upbraiding her business suppliers. ("No, you shut up and listen!" she barks on the phone to her mortgage broker while whipping up breakfast. "I need to close this loan!") Like her mother, Agnes catches the eye of a white man—her boss, Dave (Bill Recana). Over a very brief period of time, the Filipina lass has thus turned herself into a self-made American woman. (One critic laments that her metamorphosis took too little screen time.)[27] The American dream has fully emancipated her and, unlike Mila, the brooding nurse in 'Merika, Agnes is happy to be where she is.

All is well until Jerry comes to America on a tourist's visa and tries to win her back. To the credit of this film's woman director and team of clear-sighted female screenwriters, Jerry's claim of priority over the

Agnes (Lea Salonga) transforms from a weakling in Manila to a headstrong professional in San Francisco. Source: Hopefully, Once More. *Courtesy of ABS–CBN Film Productions Inc.*

assimilated migrant woman is challenged up to the very end of the story.[28] In contrast to 'Merika, the threat posed by Agnes's sexuality to the prideful Filipino man's standing plays out on different levels. Besides Agnes's success in living the American dream, her closeness with her white boss hastens the process by which Jerry's Filipino masculinity is brought into crisis. Indeed, it is possible to say that Jerry's quest to become worthy of the new Agnes unfolds as a process of spectacular emasculation. In a surprising and welcome reversal of the typical woman's film, it is not the woman but the man who attains virtue through suffering and weeping. Superficially, Jerry's problem is that he is not entitled to the American dream. Without the purchase of female sexuality that makes migrant women like Agnes more easily assimilable, Jerry's American fantasy could only unravel as a narrative of broken dreams. In this respect, he shares the "gender disadvantage" Mon has in *'Merika*.

Agnes's mobility is only the first of many "American" advantages that separate her from Jerry. He literally has a difficult time chasing after Agnes, who is constantly on the move. This differential in mobility is underscored the moment he arrives in the United States to attend an advertising conference and visit Agnes. Jerry, who crashes at the home of his cousin Nick's (William Martinez) American wife, finds that he has no means of getting to Agnes's suburban home by himself. Nick is reluctant to drive Jerry such a long way because he has babysitting duties at home. Later in the film, Jerry resolves to stay behind as an illegal immigrant in the hopes of winning Agnes back. But his status as a TNT (an acronym for *tago nang tago*, an undocumented immigrant who is "always hiding") heavily impairs his movement. Agnes's success forces her to keep changing houses, moving from the East Bay to a townhouse in the city and later to Florida, where she is due to head a new branch of the Century 21 real estate agency. Jerry tells her that he is always willing to move but also has a hard time finding employers who will hire illegal immigrants like him. Apart from the challenge of sticking with Agnes as she changes addresses, Jerry struggles to catch up with her professional mobility on a daily basis. She is always going off on business trips and is constantly being summoned away from Jerry by beeper messages, phone calls, and after-hours appointments. "This is America," she tells him when he complains about their having to eat an anniversary dinner out of a brown bag as she rushes between appointments. "Life is fast here."

Just as unconquerable as the physical distance created by Agnes's mobility is the economic gap that widens between her and Jerry due to the successes of her American dream. Jerry takes up one menial stint after another, chopping wood one day and washing dishes the next. For him, working in America is not just a vertiginous slide down the economic ladder but also a postcolonial subject's regression into the role of vassal within the imperial metropole. Jerry views his job history under a racialized lens. One of the lowest points for him is when he works at a car dealership where an African American manager unreasonably makes him stand in the lot to watch cars in the rain. For a proud, fair-skinned mestizo who imagines himself as superior to blacks, to be ordered about by them is unthinkable. What truly breaks Jerry, however, is when a fellow Filipino—an ugly, little, brown American—confirms Jerry's absolute demotion within the social ranks. Rolly (Raoul Aragon), the proprietor of the restaurant where Jerry works, reprimands him with unbearably harsh words: "You're just a dog I happen to feed!" This remark prompts Jerry to grab a cleaver, threaten his boss, and salvage what little masculinity he retains. Realizing how undignified he has become in his poverty, Jerry resolves to return to the Philippines in spite of Agnes's last-minute offer to marry him and thus give him legal status in her America.

From Agnes's perspective, the upside to Jerry's failure in achieving the American dream is his forced reformation through suffering. He rids himself of many bad macho traits and learns a few things that make him a better man. He recognizes the importance of Agnes's career. He learns to respect her feelings and to make himself more emotionally available. Most of all, he learns to value Agnes's loyalty, something he always took for granted. His transformation is the sort that would make Filipino feminists rejoice.

But now that Jerry has both accepted his failure in chasing the American dream and completed his metamorphosis into a worthy Filipino man, the nationalist patriarchal imperative calls on Agnes to take him back. Moreover, *she* has to return to the Philippines because, after all, his happiness and work are ultimately more important than hers could ever be. There is a slight hesitation on Agnes's part, but it eventually fades. The brokenhearted Jerry returns to the Philippines alone and builds his own advertising agency. With no more female bosses or American slave drivers ordering him around, Jerry feels "manlier" and happier than ever. In the last few minutes of the film, he steps out of his modern office building. A handheld shot frames him as he weaves through the rush-hour crowd. He stops abruptly, as if distracted by a sudden thought. He turns in the opposite direction and dashes off to retrieve some forgotten thing. He finds, standing motionless in the shifting crowd, his beloved Agnes. Her expression is soft and kind. Dressed casually in pale floral fabric, she looks docile and vulnerable, a lot like the young woman who left Manila a couple of years earlier. One critic argued that her sacrifice is so severe it is "unbelievably stupid." Another critic, Noel Vera, concurred and put it this way: "Lea Salonga . . . left a mother, a successful career, and all semblance of common sense for love. Music swells, hearts burst . . . The audience groans out in ecstasy . . . and if there was a mind operating in that multitude, I missed it."[29]

In the preferred reading of the film, Agnes's concession to take Jerry back, along with her seeming regression into her younger self, are foreshadowed much earlier in the story. Significantly, this foreshadowing happens on the same day she moves into her new home in the big city and during a conversation in which he questions her close relationship with Dave. Agnes unwittingly reverts to calling Jerry "babes," their old term of endearment for each other. It is as if Agnes's conscious steps toward independence are being negated by her unconscious wishes. Nostalgia wields its power, deeming the past arrangement the authentic one.[30] Beneath the persona of the materialistic, hardhearted woman, Agnes has always been Jerry's "babes." From this moment on, Jerry, too, starts calling Agnes "babes" again. This infantilizing endearment resumes and appears to signal Agnes's eventual submission to the "patriarchal renewal" prevalent in the woman's film.[31] Following this interpretation, the desire for repetition professed by the film's title—*Hopefully, Once More*—may be read as a secret wish for the return of the father. What Agnes wants all along is to revive, through a changed Jerry, the father she lost to cancer. As it turns out, what she seeks is not so much independence as intimacy: to never be abandoned again and, moreover, to always be with the right man. In this light, Agnes's reconciliation with her mother gives way to disidentification. In the end, Agnes ignores her mother's warning to stay clear of a Filipino man who cannot learn to be at home in America. To recall a point from chapter 3, the heroine's desire for a substitute father is consistent with the "female Oedipal configuration" often found in melodrama.³² Her unruly desire for a patriarchal figure binds her to the dictates of male authority. Jerry, for his part, regains his masculinity and becomes every bit the deserving patriarch. By the film's conclusion, he gains supremacy over the three women who threaten to emasculate him. He does away with his nagging female boss, reduces his overbearing mother to a sobbing mess, and summons the strong-willed Agnes back to his arms.

But things are not that simple in *Hopefully, Once More*. As with *'Merika*'s eleventh-hour gesture, there is arguably much weight in the fact that *Hopefully, Once More* delays portraying Agnes's already belated change of heart. While this film, like *'Merika* and other melodramas, ultimately "recuperate[s] woman to a 'proper place,'" the basis of her repatriation is challenged profoundly.³³ In this light, the repatriation reads as a perfunctory happy ending to an otherwise prolonged argument for two things: (1) the Filipina woman's liberation from her place in a patriarchal society and (2) the nonmaterial or spiritual rewards of postcolonial immigration. The filmmaker's feminist

Agnes (Lea Salonga) unintentionally calls Jerry (Aga Mulach) "babes," their old term of endearment. Source: Hopefully, Once More. *Courtesy of ABS–CBN Film Productions Inc.*

sensibility, the studio's interest in transnational commerce, and the cult of Lea Salonga's transnational stardom all exert pressure on the compulsory redemption of patriarchy and nationalism in this commercial film. The pressure manifests itself temporally, in the plot's hesitation to reach the expected ending, as well as emotionally, in Agnes's resistance to the supplications of love and country. From this standpoint, the film's theme song—not insignificantly sung by a male singer—could be heard not as Agnes's unconscious wish for a substitute father (in the reading I offered earlier) but as Jerry's impossible desire for things as they once were, back in the homeland, before Agnes was freed by her American dream.[34]

Why then, apart from love, does Agnes ultimately forsake her American dream? What is it, finally, that makes her turn away from the astounding benefits of postcolonial immigration? Two reasons come to mind. First, after all is said and done, anticolonial nationalism dies hard. Agnes recognizes her agency as a migrant woman and flaunts it, but only until she begins to see its complicity with American power. Her financial success and legal immigration status give her the upper hand in her relationship with Jerry. But why would she choose to dominate him using privileges bestowed upon her by white male authority? The reason why she must turn away from her best interests as a powerful woman and person of means is because these advantages subtend the inequities of neocolonial privilege. Consequently, within the moral universe of *Hopefully, Once More*, the imperative of righting the wrongs of empire is what justifies repatriation. Through Agnes, the audience is reminded that the refusal of imperial mastery takes precedence over every other kind of dream one's heart could wish for. It is thus the migrant woman's privilege, as much as it is her obligation, to save Jerry from himself and from Dave's sway. Needless to say, in saving Jerry, she also redeems herself from uncritical membership in a society that displays a facade of prosperity, equality, and hospitality but conceals the toll capitalism and chauvinism takes on the powerless. Knowing that they cannot turn away from the lessons they have learned, the Filipino couple decides that the American dream is not theirs to realize.

The second reason for the migrant woman's reversal is both practical and ideological. Agnes decides to come home so that everyone can have it both ways. She rediscovers her true love. Jerry gets the chance to make love happen "once more." Audiences at home can

Agnes (Lea Salonga) comes home to Manila to reunite with Jerry. Source: Hopefully, Once More. Courtesy of ABS–CBN Film Productions Inc.

fantasize these Filipino stars are in America but still lay claim to them as native property. Like the film's two lovers, spectators in the diaspora can dream of being emotionally tethered to the homeland while thriving in the mobility of the West. The latter perfectly serves the film's commercial interest as an advertisement for the San Francisco–based international subsidiary of the media conglomerate ABS–CBN. The company set up shop in the Bay Area to provide communication products that would make Filipinos feel at home while living abroad. In light of the film and its studio's transnational commerce, the conflicts between nationalism and postcolonial immigration are strategically resolved. Nationalism is affirmed but without strongly negating the importance of postcolonial imperatives.

It is worth noting that the trope of repatriation is eschewed in later films about Filipino migration across the globe. In Olivia Lamasan's more accomplished film *Milan* (2004), for example, the Filipino migrants do not return to the homeland. The same is true of the characters in Rory Quintos's *Dubai* (2005), a male melodrama that will be discussed in this book's coda. To some extent, the slackening of the repatriation imperative may be credited to a deeper cultural engagement with globalization and a much more positive view of labor immigration. However, there is a striking exception to this development: for Filipino immigrants to America, the repatriation imperative remains. This is true even of more recent films such as *I Need You* (*Kailangan kita*, Rory Quintos, 2002) and *I Will Always Love You* (Mac Alejandre, 2006). To be sure, this cinematic representation dramatically contradicts reality: the United States continues to be the most preferred destination for Filipino immigrants. Immigration to the United States has long served as an indirect path to globalization for Filipinos, but this fact could not be freely admitted in works of fantasy. In the diegesis of commercial Philippine movies, the fantasy of globalization via the American way can be entertained only after the unfinished business of decolonization is suppressed. As the strange case of *Hopefully, Once More* amply demonstrates, in Filipino movies men could give up their machismo and dignity more willingly than they could ever admit to owning the American dream and losing their love for a country they, in reality, so often dream of escaping.

Conclusion

In the female melodramas '*Merika* and *Hopefully, Once More*, the American dream provides fantasy scenarios of the Filipina's emancipation from the inequities subtended by patriarchy and nationalism. Both films feature heroines who achieve professional success, develop fortitude, and assimilate into U.S. society. Their superior position grants them considerable leverage in negotiating the terms of their romantic coupling. They also get to decide on matters of "national" significance, namely, their national membership (*Hopefully, Once More* and '*Merika*) and their willingness to participate in the patriotic cause ('*Merika*).

In '*Merika*, the migrant woman's realization of her American dream is depicted as materially rewarding but spiritually barren. Like a sham marriage, middle-class life in America supposedly leads to alienation. The inhospitable country seems to give the immigrant none of the fulfillment that patriotic labor bestows. The call of nationalism and the promise of a meaningful existence lure Mila even if her proposed role in the "revolution" remains undefined. She decides to repatriate.

Although she has the power to rejoin or abandon the homeland, it is still the man—a male revolutionary unseen in the film—who will save the nation. In *Hopefully, Once More*, the heroine's American dream fetches both material and spiritual rewards. Her success pressures her Filipino lover to change his macho ways and teaches him to put her first. The fact that she could live with her success makes her eventual sacrifice for the Filipino man all the more difficult and generous. As in the case of *'Merika*, she still could not be happy outside the tight embrace of the Filipino man and nation.

The films, by virtue of generic convention and nationalist ideology, posit the migrant woman's repatriation as the guaranteed outcome. But instead of reading these films for their valorization of homecoming, I have proposed that we account for their prolonged interrogation of patriarchy and nationalism through the figure of the migrant woman. The films press hard on vital issues "working certain contradictions through to the surface," as with all good melodrama, and letting ambivalence challenge the narrative's perfunctory closure.[35] *'Merika* valorizes the migrant woman's repatriation as a laudable nationalist gesture, but the film discreetly represents a moment of hesitation. At that moment, other patriotic acts, such as the diaspora's mundane labors in nation building, are shown to be almost as vital as coming home to a revolution. In *Hopefully, Once More*, the migrant woman relents from policing Filipino masculinity with power derived, in part, from the enduring inequities of capitalism and racism in America. For both postcolonial women—and this is very important—their American dreams create a critical interval that separates them from those men and nations that so insistently court their unruly desires. As figures of Filipino ambivalence toward postcolonial immigration and patriarchal nationalism, these Filipina migrants make loving and leaving both America and the Philippines a tortuous dilemma.

5

Filipino American Dreams

The Cultural Politics of Diasporan Films

In the previous chapter I explored the strains of a feminist challenge to patriarchy and nationalism in two films about Filipina migrant women. I discussed how these ex-colonial immigrants pursued their American dreams and renegotiated their place at home, in America, and in the old country. This chapter is also about Filipinos in America and their ties to both the United States and their homeland, but here I consider a different kind of immigrant fantasy, another story of decolonization, and a small but important corpus of Philippine filmmaking. I am concerned here with second-generation Filipino American immigrants and their fantasies of assimilation into U.S. society. The objects of my study are three films from the diaspora, made in the first half decade of this millennium: *The Debut* (Gene Cajayon, 2000), *The Flip Side* (Rod Pulido, 2001), and *Cavite* (Neill Dela Llana and Ian Gamazon, 2005). The makers and protagonists of these three films are all young men. As in the previous chapter, gender plays a significant role in the stories of identity and national belonging that I discuss here. The tales of Filipino American selfhood that these films unravel are also narratives of coming into manhood.

As works of diasporan Philippine cinema, these movies render national boundaries fluid in different ways. Set in a Southern California neighborhood, *The Flip Side* crosses imaginary borders into the parental homeland, culture, and history. While the narrative of *The Debut* also stays within the territorial borders of America, the film reaches out to the old country by casting actors from the Philippines in supporting roles, partnering with a Philippine television network, and screening in the Philippines three years after its American release. *Cavite*, which also enjoyed Philippine distribution after its success at

American film festivals, is set mostly in the Philippines but begins and ends in California.

The films use fantasies of assimilation to stage the predicaments of seeking and owning a Filipino American identity. *The Debut* and *The Flip Side* variably temper their critiques of the Filipino nation in the diaspora and in the homeland with affirming visions of "proper" Filipino American identities. In contrast, *Cavite* boldly eschews the affirmative cultural nationalism endemic to many diasporan productions. Instead it offers a bleak vision of the Filipino American's struggle to affirm belonging both in America and in the parental homeland.

Decolonization and Assimilation

The assimilation of immigrants from the ex-colony figures prominently in the saga of decolonization. As Albert Memmi usefully points out, the presence of the immigrant is the "residue of a collective mourning"[1] and a punishment for "colonial sin."[2] The former colonizing nation must learn to live with the "bastard of the colonial adventure."[3] Its citizens must deal with the presence of ex-colonials not only to atone for history but also to manage the difference of minority subjects in the service of nation making.[4] For their part, the ex-colonial immigrants and their children must learn to "digest the memory of colonial domination and the exploitation that followed from within the former colonial power and into the present."[5] Apart from bearing the "victim's burden of forgiveness," they also need to find ways of living in a society that often regards them as second-class citizens.[6]

Through its shifting policies of immigration, the United States has alternately enabled and constricted Filipino home founding in the metropole. Most recently, this wish for incorporation has been intoned as the utopia of liberal multiculturalism. By validating the Asian immigrant's cultural distinction, the United States has sought ways of muting "ethnic differences . . . to achieve [such a thing as] a cohesive Asian American identity" within a larger mosaic of ethnicities.[7] In their more progressive forms, U.S. policies on diversity have also sought to promote cultural heterogeneity with the aim of fostering a "radical democracy around differences that are not exclusionary and fixed."[8]

For the subjects of America's pluralist democracy, the path to assimilation involves taking on an identity and seeking recognition in that identity.[9] The hope, Kwame Anthony Appiah tells us, is that subjects will find identities they could "be happy with in the longer run" and that society will also recognize as legitimate.[10] For the children of immigrants, this injunction to fit into a society of many cultures means having to assume and cultivate an identity based upon their parents' national origin. Filomeno Aguilar Jr. puts it succinctly: "Parental nationality becomes the second generation's ethnicity."[11] Since, as Gayatri Spivak points out, "the connections between national origin and 'ethnicity' are, at best, dubious," much cultural work is needed to fashion an ethnic identity out of the parents' national identity and cultural inheritance.[12] To put it in more specific terms, Filipino American ethnic identity is not a given but something that must be constantly produced out of immigrant experiences and the materials of Filipino national history and culture. Driven by multiculturalism's injunction to claim an affirmative ethnic identity, the youthful protagonists of these diasporan films embark on journeys of discovery and invention to seek ways of becoming proper Filipino American men.[13]

As with the films in the previous chapter, the bildungsroman, or novel of development, serves as the general pattern of the films discussed here. But where the immigrants in *Hopefully, Once More* and *'Merika* achieve professional success and some measure of emotional independence in the United States, the American-born Filipinos in *The Debut*, *The Flip Side*, and *Cavite* find themselves still waiting for their dreams or resigned to failure at the end of the films.

This difference is due to a couple of things. First, the three diasporan films compress the protagonists' development into a very short period of time—in the case of *Cavite* and *The Debut*, not even a full day. Since their narrative model is that of an abbreviated bildungsroman rather than the drawn-out versions that we see in *'Merika* and *Hopefully, Once More*, the diasporan films track only small developments or the start of bigger ones to come. Second, the incomplete resolutions in the diasporan films also have something to do with the tendency of some Asian American narratives of formation to take, as Lisa Lowe puts it, an "anti-developmental" turn.[14] Often the immigrant bildungsroman, Lowe goes on to argue, "disrupt[s] the narrative that incorporates the immigrant subject into a national or cultural uniformity."[15] The Asian American protagonist's failure to incorporate himself into the larger society challenges the terms of inclusion proposed by U.S. liberal democracy and by the parental homeland. The portrayal of unsuccessful assimilation in the Asian American bildungsroman thus may be regarded as a gesture of critical citizenship. It indicates the author's critical sensibility and urges readers to cultivate the propensity for "critically receiving and rearticulating [the] cultural traditions" associated with their ethnicity.[16]

For Filipino Americans, the formation of a critical subjectivity is potentially affected by what Rolando Tolentino describes as their postcolonial perspective, their "unique position as diasporic peoples of former colonized subjects in the United States."[17] In this view, the Filipino people's memory of past subjugation and discrimination under empire teaches them to be wary of current promises of inclusion. At the same time, however, the ghosts of the colonial past can heavily burden Filipino American subjectivity. The vestiges of colonial ideology—what Filipinos in the old country call the "colonial mentality"—may move some Filipino Americans to cling fiercely to the promises of the U.S. nation-state even when it fails them. For other immigrants from the ex-colony, the historical trauma of domination negates their ethnicity and cultural inheritance and leads to a "stunting self-contempt."[18] As I will argue in this chapter, the latter tendency seems to haunt the critical subjectivity of the Filipino Americans in these films. This negation of the racialized self and the parental homeland is fueled by the wounds of colonial history and U.S. racism and by the diaspora's corrupt account of Filipino history and culture. Memmi astutely notes that "while all exiles live out a troubled identity, not all of them are children of a father who has been colonized by the country that has become, for better or worse, their own."[19] For second-generation Filipino Americans, coming to grips with their identity means having to deal with the difference of race and nationality and also with the ghosts of a traumatic imperial history that continues to unsettle them in the present.

In tracking each film's depiction of the Filipino American quest for identity, I will pose four questions that might illuminate the cultural politics behind the films' "assimilative" fantasies.[20] First, what do these films posit as the established Filipino American identity and cultural inheritance? Second, how do these films depict the relationship between the Filipino people's past experiences with U.S. empire and the present fate of Filipino American immigrants and their offspring? Third, how do the films suggest the failure or success of assimilation? Finally, what kind of subjectivity and agency do these films construct for their protagonists?

The Debut: There Is No Place Such as Home

Why is Ben Mercado mortified about coming to his sister Rose's debutante ball? His actions ask a different question: is there anything about this display of family and ethnicity that would *not* put him to shame? His father, Roland (Tirso Cruz III), and grandfather, Carlos (Eddie Garcia), will reunite for the first time since the former got Ben's mother pregnant, dropped out of college, and migrated to America. It is unlikely that the paterfamilias from the old country will pass on the opportunity to belittle Roland's failed ambitions and his present job as a letter carrier. Ben himself might also have to take some insults from his grandfather. After all, he was offered a scholarship to take a prelaw course at the University of California at Los Angeles but has quietly decided on going to art school instead. Should the issue come up, Carlos might pronounce both Ben and Roland as major disappointments in front of the Filipino American community in Los Angeles.

Ben Mercado (Dante Basco) poses with his grandfather (Eddie Garcia) and father (Tirso Cruz III). Source: The Debut.

Apart from the potential eruption of family conflict, Ben quietly worries about the likely explosion of Filipiniana kitsch during the debut and the consequent social embarrassment. Anyone who has ever been to an ethnic gathering knows what Ben fears: the deluge of old-timers decked in garish affluence, the tacky display of riches, the throwing of polite insults between revelers, the festival of thick accents and broken English, and the earnest but clumsy program of folk dances.

The debut forces Ben to identify publicly and fully with his family and his ethnicity. The self-consciousness engendered by this identification repels Ben from the event even as his filial obligations very weakly draw him into the affair. Throughout the film, Ben wanders away from both the debut and his family, seeking other gatherings and the company of other ethnicities. Prior to the debut, Ben is shown constantly moving around while his family stays put at home preparing for the event. He cruises with two of his buddies: a white man named Doug (Jayson Schaal) and a second-generation Mexican American named Rick (Brandon Martinez). They travel to Southern Californian places where everyone but Ben seems able to fit in. An incident at a party that Ben attends with his buddies dramatizes, rather clumsily, his outsider status. During a drinking game, Susie (Nicole Hawkyard), a white woman, drunkenly insinuates that Ben is a dog eater. When his friends protest on his behalf, the girl calls him a "fucking chink" and throws up in front of him. Susie's reaction deems repulsive not just Ben's "race" but also his manhood. Interestingly enough, her involuntary cruelty echoes the jab Ben's father makes at the son's manhood, pointing out the fact that Ben does not have a girlfriend. These affronts make Ben anxiously self-aware of the way that he, by virtue of his skin color, inhabits a form of "subordinate masculinity" rather than the "hegemonic masculinity" of white American males.[21]

Ben's relentless shuttling across places and communities that accept and reject, attract and repulse him is symptomatic of the condition David Eng characterizes as "Asian American racial hysteria,"[22] an "illness of assimilation."[23] The "indeterminate locationality" resulting from Ben's compulsive restlessness—"gallivanting," as his father calls it—is an externalization of his "symbolic disenfranchisement from [both] the normative national ideals of white masculinity" and "traditional structures of patriarchal assumption" within and outside his ethnicity.[24] "Suspended between departure and arrival" even in his nation of birth, the second-generation immigrant just shuttles between places without ever finding the solace of home.[25]

Ben's restlessness indicates not just a spatial displacement but also a temporal one. He is out of synch with the vertical time of the Mercado family's patrilineal succession as well as with the horizontal time of the national communities (i.e., Filipino, American, and Filipino American) to which he might claim membership.[26] During the ball, we notice signs that Ben's condition might be shared by other Filipino Americans. The family of the hyper-Westernized Tita Alice (Fe Delos Reyes), whose members all wear ill-fitting identities, testifies to the social rather than individual nature of racial hysteria. As Eng reminds us, this condition is seen not as "individual pathology but [rather] as social dis-ease, a group malaise, even a lifestyle."[27]

The problems that account for Ben's hysterical restlessness are not uncommon among second-generation Filipino Americans. He seeks a Filipino American identity but secretly detests his Filipino heritage. He yearns to be at home in America but resents his status as an ethnic minority. While Ben's problem is apparent to him, the solution is not. The blurred itinerary of Ben's "hysterical" shuttling and implicit quest for identity thus gains coherence not as a journey *toward* a projected destination but a movement *away* from the established (i.e., constricting) stages and scripts of Filipino identity.

As with many Asian American cultural productions, the family in *The Debut* serves as a stand-in for the cultural inheritance and identity scripts that the protagonist initially disavows.[28] The family wears the face of tradition and answers to the ethnic youth's grievances. The typical generational conflict in immigrant family narratives shows the first-generation immigrant parents actively forcing their traditions and values upon their children. At other times, however, this imposition takes a passive or even an invisible form, as when the failures of deadbeat fathers or the shame of long-dead ancestors haunt the fate of troubled Asian American youth. But regardless of the form it takes, this cultural imposition is associated with the parents and their nationality and is often resented by the children of immigrants. This is why in *The Debut* and the other films discussed here the protagonist is most critical of the family.

But what does Ben find so wrong about his family and, by extension, his Filipino American cultural inheritance? First, he seems put off by the gaudy trappings of Philippine culture, particularly as reflected in the mundane rituals and spaces of the diaspora. We see this in the scene where Rick asks to use the restroom at the Mercado house after giving Ben a ride home. Ben gets worked up when his friends notice the seashell-heavy decor, the pungent cooking smells, the Filipino chatter, and that naughty figurine of a tribesman whose gigantic member pops up when one lifts the barrel covering him. Ben panics and drives his friends away from the house just as his mother (Gina Alajar) invites them to stay for a meal. Although Ben's reaction suggests that his Filipino identifications embarrass him, it is also perhaps the case that he wishes simply to shield his ethnic family from the mocking gaze of an otherwise sympathetic multicultural America.

The outmoded tradition of the debut magnifies the aspects of Filipino ethnicity and culture that put Ben to shame. Toward the middle of the film, Ben politely shows interest in "authentic" versions of Philippine culture performed by his family members (i.e., a folk dance from his sister, a *kundiman*, or ballad, from his father), but he never claims them as his own.[29] Ben's unfavorable view of Philippine culture is rather typical, as scholars of Filipino American communities have

Ben's friends (Brandon Martinez and Jayson Schaal) "appreciate" the kitschy decor of the Mercado home. Source: The Debut.

noted. His negative view of Filipino culture loops back to a "sense of inferiority" about his Filipino American identity.[30]

Apart from the shameful old-country culture and its diasporan form, the other aspect of Filipino Americanness that drives Ben away is its seemingly flawed scripts of masculine identity. Grandpa Carlos presents a contemptible image of Filipino manhood that Ben instantly disavows. A tyrannical patriarch with a heavy hand and a sharp tongue, he recalls the stereotypical paterfamilias from the Spanish colonial era. A film critic in the Philippines aptly describes him as "an unrepentant ogre."[31] Ben's grandfather is also the source of everything repulsive about Ben's father, Roland: philistinism, materialism, and the tendency to humiliate their children in public. Roland's blind reverence for Carlos's patriarchal authority emasculates and cripples both him and his son. Roland quivers at the mere notion of meeting his father at the gathering. His apparent spinelessness begs the question regarding the kind of Filipino American masculinity he may end up bequeathing to Ben. To hold emasculation in abeyance and to overcome the difficulty of patriarchal assumption in a predominantly white society, Ben resolves not to be like the men of his family. By extension, he also comes to repudiate the men of his ethnicity.

While scrounging for a livable ethnic and masculine identity, Ben stumbles onto two kinds of cultural alternatives, both of which are generic to Asian American cultural productions. First he visits a scene of uncritical cultural assimilation. Upon the invitation of the other young Filipino Americans at the party, he takes his friends to mingle in the parking lot of the debut's venue. Though described in the continuity script as "the place to be if you're young and Filipino on this Saturday night," the setup of this impromptu gathering comes straight out of a 1950s teen film.[32] At the lot, young men and women chat in groups. Headlights from a row of cars provide the illumination and also circumscribe the space of the gathering. In one corner, young Filipino American men discuss the cost of tricking out cars with their parents' money. One of Ben's cousins—a young man who has taken one too many ethnic studies courses in college—promotes a wacky conspiracy theory about the marginalization of "brown brothers and sisters" from the mainstream of American social life. The parking lot party turns out to be an extremely banal cultural alternative to the debutante ball. The parking lot represents the unelaborated forms of motility that run counter to the stifling euphoria of ethnic affirmation confined to the debut hall. More importantly, it displaces the promise of shifting the subject's circuits of identification.[33]

At a nearby basketball court, Ben's former childhood friend, Augusto (Darion Basco), performs his mimicry of stereotypical urban blackness in front of other Filipino Americans. He addresses them in Ebonics, displays hypermasculine affectations, and flaunts his shiny 9mm pistol. Like Ben, Augusto implicitly rejects his Filipino inheritance. Unlike Ben, Augusto overcompensates for his disenfranchisement from the mainstream by attaching himself to a more established American ethnic identity. Predictably enough, the faux-black Augusto and the faux-white Ben clash with each other. A pathetic simulation of gang violence erupts as Augusto, jealous of Ben's crush on his ex-girlfriend Annabelle (Joy Bisco), challenges him to a basketball game and plays rough. The ensuing brawl is easily contained. Much to Rose's and the other Filipino Americans' disappointment, however, Ben takes off with his friends to a party at a white friend's place, as though to access forms of identifications other than those offered by the debut and the diaspora.

The second cultural alternative presented on the night of the debut is a scenario of a hybrid culture and identity. Here, it appropriates various elements from mainstream American and Filipino culture. Still smarting from his rejection by white America, Ben returns to the debut and attempts to recuperate his Filipino American identity. He begins the process of salvaging his wounded masculinity by giving up on white women and asserting his claim over Annabelle. He offers her a hastily sketched portrait, drawn on a napkin. The gesture prompts another row with Augusto, who accuses him not only of stealing his girlfriend but also of cultural inauthenticity. "Fuck you, white boy!" he screams at Ben. "Who do you roll with that ain't white? Fucking coconut!" The accusation of being white on the inside and brown on the outside hits Ben hard because it is partly true. Unable to deny his tenuous attachment to whiteness, Ben responds by throwing a punch at someone who, also lacking a stable identity, clings to the trappings of black masculinity. The punch sets off a fistfight. Augusto eventually draws his gun, but he and Ben are restrained by the latter's father and uncle. The Mercado fathers wrest the gun from Augusto. As if to complete Augusto's emasculation, his shamed mother smacks him repeatedly and calls him a "rude boy" while he cries in public.

In the midst of this row, Ben suddenly finds himself attaching to the Filipino Americanness and masculine identity he implicitly rejected earlier. By hitting Augusto, he disavows whiteness. By winning the Filipino community's sympathy, he joins them in rejecting blackness as a model of their ethnicity. Since Ben is unable to assume the dominant racial identities of whiteness and blackness, he provisionally latches on to his "brown" ethnic identity and then attempts to reform it. This appropriation of Filipinoness initially seems tendentious and mercenary. In fact, it is necessary for subject formation. It responds to a pluralistic society's coercive demand for its members to have specific ethnic affiliations. Judith Butler observes that even if the identities "given by regulatory regimes as the sites available for attachment" are sometimes agonistic, "a subject will attach to pain rather than not attach at all."[34]

In contrast to Augusto's discredited pseudoblack masculinity, Ben's recuperation of Filipino Americanness and manhood claims an association with cultural authenticity. It is guaranteed, in equal measure, by his righteous Filipino middle-class family and by his budding romance with Annabelle, who speaks Filipino and knows folk dances. This does not mean, however, that Ben will also claim much of the cultural inheritance associated with his recuperated ethnicity and masculinity.

In shopping for a Filipino culture that he can live with, Ben looks to something closer to urban youth culture rather than the old-country culture of folk dances and debutante balls. We see a manifestation of this desire during the dance number that follows the folk presentation. After the young Filipino Americans politely affirm Philippine culture by cheering the ethnic performance, a dance tune by a West Coast–based Filipino American hip-hop group rouses the youth into a dancing frenzy. Groups of young men and women dance sections of the number in unison. Displaying an exuberance unseen in them throughout the film, the Filipino Americans groove approvingly to a familiar cultural beat. The extended treatment given to this inadequately motivated dance number indicates the film's assertive stance toward a local ethnic cultural alternative defined mainly by second-generation Filipino Americans. By indicating their preferred form of cultural expression, Ben and his friends implicitly assert the position that second-generation immigrants should be "active shapers of an [ethnic] American identity" rather than passive "beneficiaries of a prefabricated identity."[35]

Ben's reformation of his family's defective masculinity follows the same route as his nominal recuperation of Filipino cultural inheritance. This process begins when his father performs a haunting Filipino ballad whose opening lyrics declare, "Love, look what you've done to me!" The audience applauds his number and Ben's friend, Rick, gushes, "I don't know what the hell he said, but your dad's the bud! Go, Mr. Mercado!" Ben's uncle Lenny (Ernie Zarate) tells Ben that his father used to sing with a band but gave it up to support his wife and child. The family's immigration to the states permanently ended that career. Ben realizes that his father sacrificed his artistic ambitions for his family's sake. This dream, brought over to the United States during his parents' immigration, is part of what I wish to call "immigrant patrimony." The term refers to the notion among first- and second-generation immigrants of radically paring down their cultural inheritance to its most adaptable elements. Roland's forsaken ambition to become a singer is the immigrant patrimony that Ben seeks to claim. The price of immigration and assimilation, it becomes the tiny part of Roland and the culture of the parental homeland that Ben seeks to salvage for himself. It is fitting, then, that Ben is drawn not so much by the content or language of the song but by the hitherto forbidden act of singing that represents his father's immigrant patrimony.

Roland's secret yearning to become someone other than what his father wanted him to be affirms Ben's resistance to patriarchal imperatives and also gives him a sense of rootedness in the past of his family's aspirations. Ben learns to separate good family members and Filipinos, like his father, from bad ones, like his grandfather. By the end of the debut, Carlos is expelled from the space and affections of the Filipino American family after he turns violent toward his sons. Ben remains cautious, however, about redeeming his father. As the film's ultimate scene indicates, Ben can only identify with his father if Roland shows that he is strong enough to defy Carlos's imperatives for the men of the family and also brave enough to give Ben permission to realize their shared dream of becoming artists.

To highlight Ben's specific mode of perception, illustrations and snapshots recur throughout the film. This iteration alerts us to a set of motifs pertaining to Ben's process of retrieving the Mercado manhood and of finding a substitute for his relinquished Filipino cultural inheritance. At the film's opening, we see snapshots of Ben having fun with his almost exclusively white friends. We also see photographs of the Mercado family, but they remain in the background. Near the film's end, pictures of the coming-out party dominate Ben's room. The contrast between the two sets of photographs is quite obvious: Ben is making an inward turn toward his ethnic identity. But while the family pictures are affirmative of Ben's Filipinoness, the mechanical process of photographic image making still signifies the prescriptive traditions of the parental homeland. The illustrations, on the other hand, represent Ben's creations. They are the product of a liberating artistic process. In this contrasting schema, one medium—photography—merely reproduces what is already given and seen.[36] The picture represents the Mercados performing the rather inflexible role of a Filipino American family, while the aquarelles suggest a more fluid, more imaginative portrayal of self and culture. For Ben, the art of painting holds the elusive promise of individuation.

What further complicates the dialectic of painting and photography is the contrast drawn between the older illustrations in Ben's art school portfolio and the new piece he gives to his father in the film's closing scene. Whereas fantastic comic book figures populate Ben's earlier "paintings," Ben's new work shows the profiles of Carlos, Roland, and himself. Ben's purpose in presenting the illustration to his father is twofold: to demonstrate the range of his draftsmanship beyond cartooning, and to signal his newfound respect for Filipinoness. Moreover, the way the faces occupy the frame, on three planes vertically arranged, implies a sense of temporality. Presenting this gift the morning after the family scorns Carlos at the debut, Ben offers pointed commentary on paternal relationships across generations. In the aquarelle, the recently unseated patriarch Carlos looms over his son and grandson in the picture, but the lines and shades that render him are faint. The portrait memorializes family history as a genealogy of oppression. The artwork registers the anguish that gnaws at the painter as he contemplates three unhappy generations of men. Haunted by the possibility of repeating what Carlos has done to his father, Roland, Ben chafes against the notion of paternal fate. Ben's insistence on disobeying the family's prohibition of art making lends great poignancy to this image of filial oppression. Moreover, the portrait indicates the tremendous promise that lies in the realization of Ben's defiant masculine identity.

Ben (Dante Basco) presents the portrait of the Mercado men to his father. Source: The Debut.

The etherealized background in Ben's aquarelles reveals an implicit desire to rid the cultural landscape of its clutter and to supplant it with a conveniently nebulous filler. The watercolor painting's background is saturated with formless dabs of grey, green, and orange instead of the typical Filipino mise-en-scène of foliage or pastoral terrain. This colorful abstract background signifies the immigrant patrimony that Ben claims for himself. At the same time, its amorphous quality suggests the emergence of a nascent ethnic masculinity that may yet reform the Mercado patriarchal lineage and reunite its estranged members. The notion of reimagining and renegotiating identities—keeping them in motion rather than in place, as Peter Feng puts it—is one of the familiar mantras of Asian American cultural politics.[37] Keeping identities in motion means resisting multiculturalism's predilection for scripting identities too closely.

It bears noting, however, that in the portrait and in the film's other images of cultural shift, rectangular frames circumscribe the areas of potentially dynamic transformation. The geometric form appears in snapshots, illustrations, Ben's portfolio container, the improvised dance floor of the gymnasium, the basketball court where the youth gather, the Mercado ranch, and the discrete boxes within Ben's amateur comic books. The persistence of such frames is a symptom of the film's multiculturalist discourse. It represents the desire to belong to an appealing ethnic category within heterogeneous America, but it also describes the limit point of multiculturalism. The frame defines the rigid boundaries of this category but leaves its center significantly emptied of reference. When Ben accepts his ethnicity at the end of the film, the general idea of being Filipino American is what he embraces. He gravitates toward Roland and Annabelle, two figures associated with Filipino culture. But by painting vacuity into the aquarelle and, by extension, into the frame of ethnic identification, Ben shows little interest in inheriting or engaging what Roland and Annabelle impart as the dynamism of Filipino culture.

In his work on the transnational imagination of Filipino Americans, Filomeno Aguilar Jr. describes an "anti-national transnationalism." This view, which Ben and *The Debut* seem to propose, thrives on an abstract notion of embracing "Filipinoness but not the Philippines." The problem with this mode of belonging is its failure to consider the disadvantage of constructing a Filipino American identity that is just superficially different from other ethnic identities within liberal multiculturalism. Should not those who profess to be Filipino American be able to paint, as Aguilar puts it, a "picture of their social selves" beyond "such simulacra as homeland cuisine (especially *adobo*) and Baguio carvings"?[38] Since Ben hates pungent cooking smells and native handicrafts, what does he like about being Filipino or Filipino American? And if Ben secretly harbors the "anti-national transnationalism" that Aguilar describes, what else can form the basis of his Filipino American identity other than his racial difference, the fact of his parents' national origin, and the trappings of their immigrant patrimony?[39]

The motif of rectangular frames provokes such questions. It signals the anxiety that the basis of Ben's Filipino American identity is not merely amorphous but also destitute. As for the frame itself, we clearly see at the end of the film that the very act of naming and marking Filipino American identity already brings joy to Ben and affirmation to his family and community. The promise of inclusion superficially alleviates his hysterical wandering, but the challenge of filling the frame is bound to keep him occupied for some time.

Despite its lukewarm Filipino cultural nationalism, Cajayon's *The Debut* won support from Filipino American communities. Through an aggressive grassroots publicity campaign and self-distribution by the filmmakers, the first feature-length Filipino American film earned a respectable $1.7 million gross domestically.[40] In the Philippines, this melodramatic opus earned good reviews but obtained no commercial success. The filmmaker attributes the poor box office showing, among other things, to the Philippine audience's "perception that the Filipino American experience in movies is just too 'art house esoteric.'" He goes on to lament that "over there it was treated like a foreign film."[41] The tale of rejection in the old country echoes Ben's lament over his alienation from white society. The filmmaker's melancholy imitation of his own art seems to betray a usurious investment in the bittersweetness of nonbelonging. Unloved by the Filipinos and Filipino Americans upon whom he bestows less love than disapproval, he nonetheless expects all the respect and affection from them.

The Flip Side: Identity Lessons Here and Elsewhere

Like *The Debut*, Rod Pulido's *The Flip Side* (2001) depicts the travails of young Filipino Americans who feel out of place in their native country. The two films could not be more different, however, in both their form and their politics.

The Flip Side eschews the melodramatic mode of Cajayon's film. Instead of depicting the pain of alienation and the solace offered by the community of second-generation immigrants, Pulido stages the quest for identity and belonging as a comedy of manners unfolding in one household. The first Filipino American feature to be accepted at the prestigious Sundance Film Festival, *The Flip Side* emulates the madcap sensibility and low-budget aesthetics of Kevin Smith's breakout independent film, *Clerks* (1994). Like the quirky convenience store employees and habitués of Smith's film who dream of big things while trapped in a small place, *The Flip Side*'s eccentric Filipino Americans pine to change their identities while housebound on summer break. In order to feel fully at home in their native America, each of the three siblings in *The Flip Side* aspires to be some other color in the ethnic spectrum: Marivic (Ronalee Par) desires to be white, Davis (José Sáenz) seeks to be black, and Darius (Verwin Gatpandan) wants an authentic patina of native Filipino brownness.

Anne Anlin Cheng usefully characterizes this nagging self-consciousness about one's ethnic difference as a kind of "Asian

American hypochondria"[42] or a "form of melancholic self-allergy."[43] Because of an ambivalent relationship to America's normative whiteness, the ethnic subject feels self-conscious about his or her own racialized body. Moreover, coming from a family of immigrants, he or she feels anxious about her "absence of origin" and capacity to fully assimilate into American culture.[44] The resulting "confusion between health and pathology"[45] is profound and especially oppressive because it comes from within and without, a "response to the racism not only from others but also from the self."[46]

In the film, daydreams of physical transformation ease the self-allergy felt by the three siblings. Darius frequently wears a tribal loincloth in their house to feel more attached to his Filipino ethnicity. He ridiculously sports this nostalgic costume even when taking out the trash, hoping perhaps to beam his pride across the neighborhood. His younger brother Davis, a hip-hop-addicted, Ebonics-speaking eleventh grader, tries to elongate his body by frequently suspending himself from the topmost step of the stairs. While he hopes this routine will help him dunk basketballs like the diminutive basketball player Spud Webb, he also fears that his racial makeup is seriously impeding his chance of success. "If I had just a ounce a black blood in me, I bet I could dunk on a regulation rim," he tells his Filipino buddy. Blacks, to his mind, are genetically gifted hoopsters: "Y'know, I read dey got an extra bone in dey foot that makes 'em jump higher," he tells his friend.[47] Davis also has a backup plan if his stretching exercises fail to produce results: he could buy a retractable basketball backboard that could be adjusted to lower-than-regulation height. Marivic, the eldest in the family, counts on the tedium of work to keep herself from obsessing over her ethnic physiognomy. Every shift she works at the mall brings her closer to the aquiline nose of her dreams. That nose, she believes, will help her keep her white boyfriend Curt (Dave Brown) from straying. The surgically altered nose, along with the other objects used or coveted during these daily routines (i.e., Darius's g-string, Davis's backboard) serve as prostheses for relieving the questionable injuries and afflictions of these hypochondriac Filipino Americans.

Darius, who seems most self-conscious of his afflictions, believes that the real cure for his own and his siblings' problems is a dose of learning about their Filipino cultural inheritance. In theory, such education would make him and his siblings proud of their ethnicity as Filipino

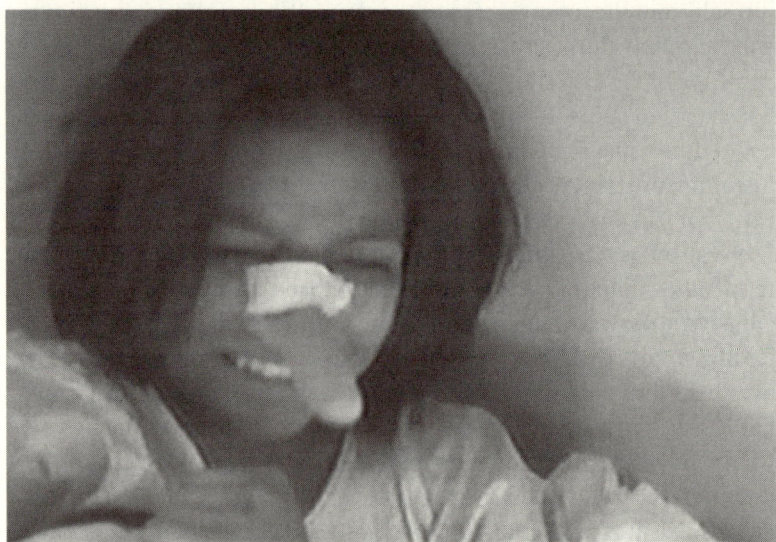

Darius (Verwin Gatpandan) dons a loincloth after coming back from his first year in college. His sister Marivic (Ronalee Par) has a nightmare about a botched nose job. Source: The Flip Side. *Courtesy of Rod Pulido, Puro Pinoy Productions.*

Americans. Darius thus turns their summer vacation into a summer class in Filipinoness. He begins by dressing up his bedroom as a Filipino museum, covering the walls with a map of the archipelago, articles about national heroes and great men, ethnic instruments, and tacky souvenirs. In one scene, Davis finds his older brother staring at the map, trying to pin down the geography of national and family history. "It's weird," Darius tells him, "I can name all these historical sites and geographic locations. Too bad I don't even know where our family's from."

Soon enough, Darius institutes a more formal kind of Filipino education over the dinner table. While passing the rice and viands, he tries teaching his siblings to speak the language that Davis refers to as "Filipinese." The parents, who speak heavily accented but grammatically correct English, are apathetic to his efforts. Although the Filipino lessons grate on the nerves of Davis and Marivic, Darius seems convinced that this sort of education is necessary. He believes it is an important part of helping his psychically unsettled family work out the problem of their disavowed Filipinoness. He believes that lessons in Philippine culture will help them overcome their present recourse to ignorance (Darius himself), denial (especially Davis), complacency (the parents and the grandfather), or even self-hatred (Marivic).

Darius's pedagogical initiative is regarded with indifference by the family's very own icon of Philippine cultural inheritance: the unnamed World War II–era veteran grandfather, or *lolo* (Peping Baclig). Lolo, who is often shown accompanied by a musical cue of ethnic percussive instruments, seems at first totally withdrawn from family life and unresponsive to his grandson's atavist zeal. Darius tries his best to coax the old man into telling the "national story": specifically, Lolo's heroic participation in World War II and the eventual liberation of the Philippines. But the reclusive old man is only interested in betting on the lottery, a habit he finances by stealing money from his daughter. On closer inspection, it appears that the old man's recalcitrance may have something to do with his own unexamined malady. Like a chronic depressive, he is always sleepy and aloof, leaving his room only to buy tickets. His room, in fact, suggests an ethnic ghetto within a suburban home: it is adorned with foreign decor, religious images, military service medals, small national flags, and a wedding portrait. When Darius brings him a dinner tray with his favorite panfried Spam, the grandfather just takes a couple of bites, pulls up his blanket, and turns away.

Darius persists in engaging him, however, since the old man is the guarantor of the cultural authenticity he seeks. His mother, lovable as she is, seems to have retained only the native traditions of domestication, a punitive Catholic morality, and a penchant for gossip. His father, who fancies himself a stern old country patriarch, is a softie at heart whose deepest concerns are getting the family together for meals, getting mushy with his wife at the dinner table, and relishing his favorite condiment of *bagoong* (shrimp paste). When Darius announces that he is petitioning his college to offer Philippine studies classes, his father is the first to object. Perhaps echoing the Philippine middle-class paranoia over student activism during the Marcos era, he asks Darius if his campus Filipino club, Kababayan (conationals), is "some kind of crazy radical group."

Darius's struggle in conscripting Lolo to impart the Filipino lesson and the old man's reluctance to do so seem to indicate a difference in their cultural politics. Lolo's own struggles, as with his fellow soldiers in the Pacific war, have centered on claiming the veteran's benefits due him, including promised American citizenship. His grandson, on the other hand, is concerned with the assertion of his Filipino ethnicity through the auspices of multiculturalist education. To the film's credit, Lolo's quest to be enfranchised is in no way equated with obsequious assimilation. Neither does he evoke that despicable image of the Filipino paterfamilias associated with Carlos in *The Debut*. While Darius initially gains Lolo's sympathy through a bribe (i.e., procuring his lottery tickets), the old man comes to recognize his grandson's sincerity. In a sentimental moment of cultural instruction, Lolo identifies his hometown on Darius's Philippine map and tells his grandson of its riches: "Sta. Maria, Ilocos Sur. My home. Beautiful village. Lots of farmlands as far as the eyes can see." He hints that his obsession with the lottery is linked to his homecoming dreams. Later, he educates Darius about the infamous death march forced upon Filipinos and American prisoners of war by the Japanese toward the end of World War II: "Four days, four nights, we marched. No food, no water, nothing. My comrades who fell were beaten. Many were stabbed with bayonets . . . I wanted to stop, but I can't. Anger kept me on going. Marching, marching." This "national narrative" visibly moves Darius.

"I never learned anything like that in class," he tells him. "I mean, about Filipinos." Lolo's World War II tale affirms Darius's Filipino American identity not only because the narrative speaks of heroism within the family but also because it recalls a historical moment of joint sacrifice and solidarity between Filipinos and Americans.[48] True to the spirit of multiculturalist education, the ex-colonized Lolo's painful history becomes an affirming tale of "national origin validation" for Filipino American youth.[49]

Darius witnesses how Lolo's recollections of the Philippines work like a talking cure, pulling the old man out of his emotional and physical reclusion. The old man starts to eat in the kitchen. He gets even more deeply invested in the lottery after promising to take Darius with him on a dream vacation to his hometown. As for the other grandchildren, their ethnic self-allergy seems to get worse over time. Davis's humiliating attempts at dunking basketballs climaxes in a showdown with a young African American boy at a child-sized basketball court. The black kid flies and dunks with aplomb, making mincemeat out of the much older Filipino ball player. Marivic, for her part, proceeds with her nose job. Despite Darius's attempt to counsel his family about the "mental colonization" and unexamined "shame and insecurity" driving the surgery, the parents hand Marivic a check to do as she pleases. Desperate at the turn of events, and fired up by the nationalist lessons from Lolo, Darius proposes to take the Filipino lesson to the Philippines. Over dinner, he asks his parents to plan a family trip to the Philippines for the sake of the old man and "the rest of us." When his mother reasons that they are "too busy" and that the homecoming is "not important," Darius questions the family's priorities: "And Marivic gettin' a phony nose is important!"

Profoundly disappointed by the family's dismissal of the nationalist activity, Darius seeks other means of furthering his education in Filipino cultural inheritance and the roots of his ethnic identity. Unlike Ben in *The Debut*, Darius refuses to settle for the trappings of immigrant patrimony. Lolo's Filipino lesson, like the decrepit figure himself, strikes Darius as something that could not be confined to the ethnic home. Darius resists entrusting cultural pedagogy to the limited imaginations of the cultural melting pot and the racially diverse university. Moreover, he implicitly refuses the sort of "long-distance nationalism" that insulates the diaspora from the fate of co-Filipinos in the parental homeland.[50]

As it turns out, Darius, while bidding his family good-bye to resume his studies, conceals a plan to ditch college for a while and fly to the Philippines with his grandfather. The trip, he later reveals to the old man, is funded by the financial aid check he recently got in the mail. He is thus not abandoning but holding in abeyance his college education, that much-valued form of learning associated with his parents' American dream. Darius hints at this possibility during the dinner conversation earlier in the film. When his father, citing money problems, votes down the idea of taking a family trip to the Philippines, Darius volunteers to "take some time off school and work." He justifies this recourse by asserting the value of this informal education over the banal lessons of the university: "What's the point [of going to college]? I'm not learnin' anything, anyway." His gesture of deferring one cultural lesson for another also constitutes a reply to Marivic's earlier denigration of ethnic studies in U.S. academia. Upon hearing about the Filipino club's petition for classes, she remarks, "Filipino classes? In college. That's weird . . . I don't know. It just doesn't seem very—collegey." Darius's pursuit of the "uncollegey" defies the complacency instilled in the likes of Marivic by multiculturalist pedagogy's superficial integration of ethnicity and citizenship. Darius's impetus to dislocate himself from the mental and territorial boundaries of racially diverse America is both a product of that pedagogy and at the same time a gesture of opposition to that system. The field trip to the Philippines resists the tendency of liberal multiculturalism to promote what Spivak calls "the museumization of national origin" of second-generation immigrants to the First World.[51] By committing himself to a personal experience and revaluation of his Filipino cultural inheritance, Darius unsettles his outsider perspective on the parental homeland. He also refuses complicity with an insular system of U.S. multiculturalism that engages the cultures of national origin solely through virtual proxies *already* contained within the space of a pluralist democracy. In visiting the Philippines, Darius might even learn the art of forging allegiances to multiple sites of belonging—to construct a transnational identity.[52]

Though somewhat foreshadowed, Darius's sudden "homecoming" is not represented in the conventional cinematic tropes of a romantic return. Hastily announced at the very conclusion of the film, the planned trip is not set up to conjure a promise of anything grand or concrete for Darius. Indeed, it is telling that the film does not make any attempt to represent the journey or indeed to confirm that it was successfully undertaken.

Lolo's sporting of his veteran's uniform indicates his quasi-official assumption of the role of a mentor in this new Philippine lesson. The gesture echoes his grandson's earlier donning of a loincloth to signify his role as the family's "Filipino" educator. Lolo's role is to help Darius find the real-life coordinates of the Philippine map, both the physical one that used to hang in the boy's room and the cognitive map within his diasporan consciousness. This well-established motif of giving an impromptu geography lesson depicts the student's relationship to the parental homeland as a pedagogical one, first and foremost. While the "old country" is at times described in sentimental terms, it is visually represented as a series of coordinates on a graph and not in concrete images of an idyllic place from Lolo's memory. The prize that the itinerant geography lesson holds is thus not cultural authenticity (e.g., acquiring more loincloths), but a keener awareness of one's positionality within what Arjun Appadurai calls the "ethnoscape" of Filipinoness.[53] We know that Darius, like his gambling Lolo, makes a wager on something to be learned elsewhere even as the image and nature of that something are not entirely clear. The lesson could help him discover those inchoate elements of transnational or postnational identity that will fortify his sense of Filipino American selfhood. In relation to his and his siblings' hypochondria, the rewards of the traveling lesson may be something as simple as the affirmative image of the racialized self in a place where one's racial markers tend to fade. If the racialized subject's hypochondria is a nagging hypervigilance about one's "racial difference and national position," as Anne Cheng argues, then the cultural surround of the old country might offer Darius a different object to behold as an affirming ideal.[54] Perhaps an alternative image of normality and centeredness can make him just a bit more comfortable in his own skin. As Darius reminds Lolo, "I got a week before school starts. And it probably won't hurt if I miss a few days—or weeks [of classes]." The lesson, for whatever it is worth, would not take too long. Those last weeks of the American summer hold the promise of an alternative pedagogy that cannot be taken too seriously but that one would be foolish to ignore.

Cavite: Routes of Self-Loathing

As in *The Flip Side*, the protagonist of *Cavite* realizes that he needs to make a trip to the Philippines. But even if the ultimate outcome of both journeys is the consolidation of Filipino American selfhood, the lesson to be learned and the manner of its learning are radically dissimilar. Against the backdrop of the global war on terror, a Filipino American's vacation to the Philippines turns into a nightmare. During his ordeal, the protagonist learns to despise himself and repudiate his parents' homeland to prove himself a worthy American citizen.

The protagonist Adam (Ian Gamazon) is a Philippine-born Muslim who immigrated to the United States as a child. We learn in the beginning of the film that his problems cut across different aspects of his life. At age thirty-two, Adam holds a blue-collar job as a night security guard in San Diego. His white ex-girlfriend (Dominique Gonzalez) hates him and threatens to abort his child, later confessing that she could not stomach the prospect of bearing a Muslim's offspring. Adam's shortcomings as an ethnic man are brought into high relief as he crosses over to the old country on a vacation. The trip instantly devolves into a harrowing rescue mission and a violent educational experience about himself, his family, and his race. During this passage from alienation in America to mad pursuit in the Philippines, Adam's experience of emasculation as a nonwhite American and a not-quite Filipino is the most torturous one among those of protagonists discussed in this chapter. The film posits Adam's psychic unraveling as a harsh but proper corrective to his malformed Asian American manhood. As in Carlos Bulosan's fiction, which repeatedly traces "Filipino men's emasculation in the U.S. empire," Adam's suffering does not annul but rather secures his loyalty to America.[55]

Upon his arrival in the Philippine capital of Metro Manila, Adam discovers that he has been stood up by family members who promised to pick him up at the airport. A call from the cell phone surreptitiously planted in his backpack by an unseen person notifies him that his mother and sister have been kidnapped. A few snapshots planted along with the cell phone lend credibility to the hostage threat. In a plot device straight out of the American thrillers *Cellular* (David Ellis, 2004) and *Phone Booth* (Joel Schumacher, 2002), Adam must constantly take instructions through the gadget in order to fulfill his rescue mission.

The voice from the phone belongs to an enigmatic, all-seeing Muslim bandit associated with the Abu Sayyaf terrorist group. His instructions force Adam to find his way through the roads and alleys of the nearby province of Cavite. Though largely depicted as an enormous slum, the province carries an onus of historical significance. It is the birthplace of Emilio Aguinaldo, the revolutionary general who fought both Spanish and American colonial powers and who designated himself as the president of the Republica Filipina, the First Philippine Republic. Aguinaldo's ancestral home and the surrounding areas lie at the crossroads that lead Adam to the many sites of the young Philippine nation's spectacular failures. The terrorist maps Adam's journey from the very outset. This itinerary takes him to the same places his father visited shortly before his death in a suspicious bus explosion. It ultimately leads his psyche to a place of deep shame and loathing for himself, his family, and his race.

At the site where Emilio Aguinaldo began to plot battles he would lose against two colonial powers in the late nineteenth and early twentieth centuries, *Cavite*'s antihero finds the severed finger of his sister tucked inside a carton of American cigarettes. This bit of flesh is a memento for the decaying aspects of Adam, namely, his castrated identity, his family's miserable lot, and the savagery of the bandit race from which Aguinaldo, Adam's father, and Adam himself are descended. This tradition of patriarchal failure is impressed upon the Filipino American as he begins his journey. Adam vomits upon seeing the finger but regains his composure to retrieve pocket change from the grisly package. By design, the appendage rests on top of the coins he will use as fare on the terrorist's itinerary. In a textbook case of transgenerational haunting—wherein "one generation finds itself performing the unspoken unconscious agendas of the one that went before"—*Cavite* shows how the failure of Philippine national becoming in Emilio Aguinaldo's republic continues to have an adverse impact on the formation of Filipino American masculinity.[56] The sister's severed flesh presages the abjection that Adam must endure throughout his journey.

Within the context of U.S. cultural politics and cultural productions, Karen Shimakawa posits abjection as a condition of minority subject formation. "The conceptual U.S. citizen-subject comes into being," she writes, "through the expulsion of Asianness in the figure of the Asian immigrant."[57] Racial minorities, she contends, "must

Adam (Ian Gamazon) retraces his father's steps at the birthplace of Emilio Aguinaldo. Source: Cavite. Courtesy of Gorilla Films Productions, LLC.

radically jettison parts of themselves in order to be identified as U.S. American" and even to constitute Americanness itself.[58] Examples of those abjected in the United States include Japanese Americans forcibly interned at relocation camps during World War II. Since many of them were U.S. citizens, they represented both the "foreign threat" that was being excluded and, in their submission to the racist edict of containment, the patriotic Americans who made sacrifices to secure the nation from possibly "dangerous" immigrants like themselves.[59]

In *Cavite*, the Filipino American's abjection similarly occurs during a state of national emergency. Adam's journey takes place when the so-called global war on terror that began in Washington after September 11 reaches the American ex-colony. While only 5 percent of the Philippine population is Muslim, the U.S. defense establishment considers the archipelago a significant front in the war against Muslim terrorists. The film indulges in a twisted fantasy of post–September 11 patriotism. Family history and religious–ethnic membership, according to the fantasy, predispose the foreign-born U.S. citizen to terrorism. Hence, oddly enough, the Filipino American subject can profess his loyalty to America by taking on the part of the enemy within the state, the naturalized U.S. citizen with strong ties to Muslim terrorists. To affirm his loyalty to America and to purge himself of the rottenness that lurks within him, Adam rushes down the freeways of self-abnegation outside American borders. He learns to disavow one part of himself after another at every pit stop. This picaresque of self-loathing is seen on screen almost exclusively through wide-angle lenses and handheld shots that emphasize the disorder of the Philippines and the antihero's inner tumult.

The first thing Adam gives up in his ordeal of self-abjection is his affective ties to the old country. Having been born in Mindanao, where most of the Philippines' alienated Muslim population resides, his Filipino nationalism is presumably weak to begin with. That patriotic affect diminishes even more as Adam slips into one of the Philippines' darkest slums. To reach the shantytown, he must hobble across a bridge made out of sticks. The piece of makeshift infrastructure spans a tar-black pond dotted with refuse, scavengers, and bathers. At the other end of the bridge, the slum greets Adam with a placard that reads, "By Order of the Village Chief, It is Illegal to Shit on the Path." The squatter's colony teems with life. Children litter the site. The voice on the phone tells him that half of them are bound inevitably to "sell their dicks and pussies" as underage prostitutes. The scene is calculated to inspire loathing for the modus vivendi of this abject Third World race. "Nothing can be done," the voice solemnly declares. "This is the reality of the Philippines." To go native, to claim Filipino identity, is to end up *here* in the slum. Out of its guts Adam must extricate himself and his family. But just as the hapless native-born subjects bear the taint of having purportedly scatological origins, Adam cannot be cleansed thoroughly of *their* abjection. At the Noveleta wet market, the voice on the phone instructs him to eat *balut* (duck embryo cooked in its shell), a delicacy famously abhorred by Westerners. Although he nearly gags, he swallows all of it nonetheless as the voice on the phone taunts him: "I hate *balut* myself, but you need to experience Filipino culture. That's the taste of your homeland. Shove it down your insides!" With self-allergy far more severe than the kind played out in *The Debut* and *The Flip Side*, Dela Llana and Gamazon shore up their cultural inheritance from the mutilated flesh, slums, garbage, and slimy food of the parental homeland. In *Cavite*, Filipinoness is simply unlivable.

After Adam downs the *balut*, a street urchin runs off with his backpack. Adam chases after him. The appearance of the kid, a Filipino version of the artful dodger, triggers another gustatory motif that extends Adam's punitive consumption. The chase draws us into the interior of the wet market, and along its periphery, where the camera offers glimpses of modern and transnational establishments. Because the plot contrives for Adam to enter a bank, it is through the eyes of the street urchin that we see the obvious traces of advanced capitalism along the fringes of the traditional site for native commerce. Watching the traffic flow haltingly on a congested street, the kid pauses for a meal close to the bank. Inside, Adam is being instructed to withdraw the $75,000 stashed away by his father as bounty for snitching on fellow Muslim guerillas. Apart from bearing witness to the corrosive effect that multinational commerce has on an already-fragile national culture, these spatial contrasts set up a perversely crude dichotomy between Filipinos and Filipino Americans. While Adam is digesting *balut* at the bank, the child outside is relishing what is presumably a reward for assisting the terrorists. McDonald's French fries, the greasy largesse of transnational capitalism, serves as the bounty of an allegedly anti-Western revolution, the Muslim *jihad* or holy war. The terrorist deems fast food an object of pleasure for the half-formed Filipino subject, just as he marks *balut* as an object of universal disgust.

Later in his travails, Adam heads to a cockfighting arena to deliver the ransom. There he is forced to confront his father's lack of principle, treachery, and unheroic death. In the restroom, two heavies show up and call him a "faggot." They retrieve the knife he smuggled from one of his stops and rough him up. As Adam reels from the beating, the voice begins to recount the disgrace of Adam's father. The voice says that Adam's father had returned quietly to the Philippines the previous year to try to recover the money he had stashed away at the bank. His former comrade, the voice on the cell phone, got wind of his return. The comrade forced Adam's father to engage in the suicide bombing of a bus as payback for his betrayal. In exchange for committing the terrorist act and returning the reward, the comrade vowed not to hurt Adam's family.

The comrade's revelation taints Adam's cherished memory of his father. It suggests that Adam's family's life in the United States is built upon a foundation of lies, greed, and dishonor. The revelation also deprives Adam's father of the political and religious martyrdom that guerillas earn through the ultimate sacrifice of self-annihilation. Adam instinctively denies the comrade's allegations, but the narrative painfully hits home. Through his entire ordeal, Adam witnesses how his own life succumbs to the repetition of his old man's failures. Like his father, Adam is unable to protect the women of the family and is thus symbolically and literally deemed unworthy of fatherhood.

An encounter with two anonymous boys, held hostage in a lower-class house, crystallizes the idea of paternal failure. When Adam enters the house, the terrorists' accomplice takes a Polaroid of the boys and hands it to Adam. The photograph is to be taken to the children's father, the bank teller who facilitated the withdrawal of the money belonging to Adam's late father. Adam manages to steal a kitchen knife before exiting the house, but he is unable to use it for rescuing himself or the children. What follows this scene takes place in a cockfighting arena, traditionally a male sphere in Philippine gaming culture. Here Adam is assaulted by goons, but the knife he has pocketed continues to be useless in his impotent hands.

Juxtaposed with the assault in the gaming cockpit, the encounter with the boys may be read as a confrontation with the weak fatherhood operating in Adam's life. In the boys, Adam encounters himself as a son victimized by his father's shady dealings. At the same time, he sees in them a prefigured image of his own child, yet to be born but already compromised by Adam's helplessness as a father. Toward the end of the film, his ex-girlfriend informs him that she had to terminate her pregnancy. When she tells him that she "can't have a baby that's Muslim," Adam remains calm. The ex-girlfriend's revelation merely confirms the abject status that Adam has already come to accept in the old country. The dark epiphany occasioned by the boys and the assault at the cockpit has prepared him to accept the abortion of his child as yet another repetition of his failed paternity.

In the final, and perhaps most excruciating, station in the itinerary of abjection, the impotent protagonist is forced to assume the role of a terrorist. At the gaming cockpit Adam retrieves the backpack stolen earlier by the street urchin. Soon after, he discovers that a time bomb has been placed inside it. The man on the phone orders Adam to plant the backpack inside Quiapo Church, a monument that stands at a historic quarter in Manila where Christians and Muslims peaceably coexist. The prospect of committing this terrorist act gnaws at Adam's conscience. At first he vows to stay inside the church and perish along with his victims. The voice convinces Adam, however, to spare himself for the sake of his family. By assenting yet again to the imperative issued by the anonymous voice, Adam stays within the zone of abjection to which Muslims have been consigned in the wake of the Bush administration's global war on terror. After the attacks on September 11, the American family turns into an entity subsumed by the state, in need of the state's protection against a racially constructed threat of terrorism. In *Cavite*, Adam functions as an obedient subject. The need to shelter his family ironically forces him to be complicit in terrorism. Adam serves to embody the post–September 11 characterizations of the terrorist as the Islamic foreigner within the state, hapless to escape his fate as a killer of multitudes.

As an Asian American youth, Adam's journey of coming into identity is vastly different even from that of *The Debut*'s occasionally self-hating Ben Mercado. For while the latter's hysterics occasionally evince an ambivalent energy that draws him to and repels him from his Filipino heritage, every moment of Adam's ordeal leads him to despise the Philippines and himself. In *Cavite*'s lesson of self-loathing, Adam's harrowing vacation amounts to innumerable credit hours earned in a Third World classroom where the racialized American subject is taught proper comportment during the regime of global terror. The instructional goal of this lesson is revealed to Adam at the end of the film by the voice from the cell phone: "Go to Mecca, Adam. Pray. Better yourself. Face your jihad. This is what I want for you. Have a good life, Adam. A good life." Perversely enough, in this particular situation, being a good Muslim is code for being a good American.

Adam is shown near the end of the film absently rehearsing his bedtime rituals. He brushes his teeth, phones his mother and sister, and recites his evening prayers. His apartment is empty. His white girlfriend has just told him moments ago that she has terminated her pregnancy. His isolation signals the stasis of grief that comes after loneliness feeds on his soul. No longer resisting the story of "thwarted patriarchal assumptions" that defines his national, familial, and personal histories, Adam finds peace as an abject figure in America.[60]

What are we to make of the identity politics that propels *Cavite*'s fantasy scenario, in which a Filipino American gets caught up with

Muslim terrorists? On the surface, Adam's profound brokenness represents the Filipino American subject's feelings of inferiority and alienation. Though exaggerated in the film, such sentiments are not that unusual among Filipino Americans.[61] In *Cavite*, the disdain for the parental homeland is so great that it becomes nothing less than hell on Earth. The film's attitude toward the Philippines confirms the scholarship mentioned above, regarding the "persistent self-hate,"[62] the "lack of self-respect and self-love as Filipinos,"[63] and the "sense of guilt or shame over being Filipino or Filipino American."[64] *Cavite* is all too complicit with imperialist and orientalist discourses that imagine the Third World as an unlivable zone. As I have argued above, it could also be the case that *Cavite* is a strange progeny of post–September 11 U.S. nationalism. In the film, the Filipino American protagonist declares his loyalty to an embattled America by portraying and repudiating the threat posed to national security by Muslims and immigrants of color such as himself. Finally, it is interesting to note that the diasporan subject's fate in *Cavite* is simultaneously able to figure the Philippines' geopolitical relation to America in the war on terror. *Cavite* represents the tricky outsider–insider status in which the Philippines already finds itself post–September 11. Even Philippine president Gloria M. Arroyo, a lapdog of George W. Bush, initially found it difficult to deal with her country's impossible status as both a zealous U.S. ally in the war on terror and a notorious breeding ground for radical Muslim terrorists. For Arroyo to demonstrate her unflagging commitment to the global war on terror, she first had to admit to the significant terrorist presence in her country. In other words, to secure its identification with the American way, Arroyo's Philippines, like Adam, had to consent to its abjection and declare itself as rogue territory. *Cavite* thus inscribes the Philippines within an abject space of loathing while using this very space to form an unlikely afterimage of America besieged by terror.[65]

Despite *Cavite*'s unforgiving depiction of Philippine squalor and turmoil, the film merited a positive review from a Philippine national daily for being "creative and bold."[66] The critic did not take offense at the film's characterization of his country as a land of garbage and terrorism. He neutrally states that "the camera lingers on scenes Filipinos are already all too familiar with . . . [to] serve a foreign audience well." In a gesture of transnational Filipino solidarity, the critic ends by rewarding the Filipino American's bold hate letter to the parental homeland by endorsing the film and recognizing the filmmakers as conationals. "Even though *Cavite* speaks mainly to a Western audience," he goes on to say, "they can probably count on support from their *kababayans* [countrymen]."

Conclusion

The three films discussed here suggest that the injunction to assume a Filipino American identity operates on at least three levels. First, it can speak through a familial call, as in *The Debut*. Second, as in *The Flip Side*, it can tease the subject whimsically into the most banal efforts at self-improvement and the obsession with bodily transformations. Finally, as in *Cavite*, it can pierce through the Filipino American sense of alienation as a telephonic command that, heard in the homeland itself but speaking with accents ill at ease in its vernacular, comes from everywhere and nowhere. This search for ethnic identity in a racially diverse America unfolds on film as an arduous enterprise that, as Lowe observes of the immigrant bildungsroman, "refuses the premature reconciliation of Asian immigrant particularity"[67] and the incorporation of "the immigrant subject into a national or cultural uniformity."[68] At the end of the three films, Filipino American identity eludes its seekers. The young men, however, gain some insight into the means for fashioning their ideals. In the case of *Cavite*, the protagonist realizes he should stop looking altogether.

For the protagonists of *The Debut* and *Cavite*, and two of the three siblings in *The Flip Side*, the problem of assimilating into multicultural America lies with the ostensibly inferior cultural heritage and identity scripts from their parental homeland. The critical subjectivity that some of these fictional Filipino Americans cultivate sees their parents' national origin and culture as the weakness that lies within. To furnish themselves with a usable ethnic identity, even an inferior one, they must eviscerate Filipinoness or identify with it through self-loathing.

Produced and viewed under the heading of "Filipino American," these films suggest that the diasporan imagination awaits another stage in the ongoing project of decolonization. They point to the need for more complex, if not more affirmative, considerations of Filipino and Filipino American identity and history. This diasporan cinema points to open terrain, which not only accommodates but also sees more than the monotonous indictment of the Third World scatter their parents left behind. Beyond the current fascination with the brokenness of Filipinos, what awaits there are the more dynamic notions of Philippine culture and history.

In the stage of decolonization yet to be achieved by Filipino American films, national identifications would no longer be unthinkable without the cartographies of transnational belonging, and even perhaps without the recourse to a more radical possibility: the principled refusal to stand under the banner of a Filipino ethnicity or cultural inheritance.

These diasporan films bring into relief the tensions inscribed in Filipino American identity formation. The limitations made evident by the routes of Filipino American self-loathing force us to consider other dynamic, affirmative modes of constructing ethnicity—or, more radically, to bypass the dream of a stable ethnicity and construct identity at the fluid crossroads of transnationalism. Among these diasporan films, only *The Flip Side* entertains the prospects offered by transnational affiliations. It is also the only film that emphatically refuses to draw an invisible border between the two words in the phrase "Filipino American."

In his study of Asian American film, Jun Xing praises films that help ethnic audiences imagine and construct "layers of multiple and even contradictory identities that defy any dogmatic notion of purity."[69] The protagonists of *Cavite* and *The Debut* face the agony of their contradictory identities and filiations but seek to cultivate only one part of their divided selves, the psychical reserve through which they hope to be reconciled with their stateside identities. In *The Flip Side*, two figures with liminal identities revisit the shared fantasy of being whole and at home at last. They set their sights on traversing that wide but crossable gulf between the old country in the present and a new ethnic America to come.

III

Global Ambitions

6

Naked Brown Brothers

Exhibitionism and Festival Cinema

In part II of this book, I dealt with narratives on the Filipino's place and selfhood in America. My task in the two chapters of part III is to examine how Filipinos use American fantasies to produce films that engage international audiences and global media culture. In these chapters, I will show how these films register the processes of globalization as well as how they provide vehicles for Filipinos to participate in the cultural realm of globality. If the American fantasies of the previous chapter were made of ethnic cuisine, slender noses, and debutante balls in Southern California, here the stuff of daydreams is soap bubbles, skimpy underwear, and the squalor of Manila. In my analysis of Filipino American movies in the previous chapter, I dealt with tales of young Filipino men searching for identity and manhood in America. This chapter also features a cast of Filipino male youths, but these come from the homeland, and what they seek is not a sense of self but an audience in gay America and beyond.

The "American" fantasies that concern us here are three gay Filipino movies exported to the states: Lino Brocka's *Macho Dancer* (1988) and Mel Chionglo's *Midnight Dancers* (*Sibak*, 1994) and *Burlesk King* (1999). These films were also intended for and seen by other international audiences in such countries as Germany and Japan. Nonetheless, I characterize these pictures as "American" fantasies because they employ an American imaginary as a resource to attract local and global spectators. *Midnight Dancers*, the second male stripper–themed film, was, for instance, made upon the prompting of the late American film programmer David Overbey who, half a decade after *Macho Dancer*'s success, "contacted Brocka's friends to come up with a movie of a similar theme" for the Toronto International Film

Festival.[1] That follow-up venture, *Midnight Dancers*, also enjoyed great success, attracting snaking lines of audiences at international and gay film festivals in the United States and throughout the world. The film reached Toronto, New York, London, Japan, Berlin, and Amsterdam before playing to Philippine theaters about ten months after completing postproduction in Manila. The impressive audience for these male stripper films broke a long spell of American indifference toward the cultural productions of its former colony. It established the gay marketplace as a reliable point of entry in the West for Philippine films, inspiring the production of dozens of gay interest films with such lurid titles as *Bathhouse* (Crisaldo Pablo, 2005) and *Service* (*Serbis*, Brilliante Mendoza, 2008), the first feature-length Cannes entry from the Philippines in nearly a quarter century.

Despite their brazen pandering to audiences in the First World, these Orientalist works do not involve a retreat into the old-fashioned manufacture of colonial fantasies but instead represent significant cultural productions of decolonization and globalization. Beyond the self-conscious throwback to playing exotic roles ostensibly desired by white sex tourists, these films try to wrest control of the means of visibility at a time of globalization. Rey Chow uses the terms "visibility" and "visuality" with reference to the mechanics and consequences of being seen in the world.[2] She characterizes visibility as a kind of "menace" because it has become our inexorable fate in globalization to be "exposed, revealed, captured on the screen"—in short, to "be made visible as images"—in ways we can hardly control. Visuality, she adds, has thus "become the law of knowledge and the universal form of epistemological coercion."[3] I argue that in the case of exportable gay films like *Macho Dancer*, Filipino filmmakers have discovered ways to appropriate American Orientalism and thereby reap economic and political benefits from it. In this Orientalist troping of Filipino visibility, brown bodies glimmer with the halo of prostitution, catering to rich foreigners.

This chapter is divided into three sections. First, I discuss how *Macho Dancer* addresses the American/foreign spectator both implicitly and directly, and I then hypothesize on the manner by which that spectator's gaze is partially introjected into the specular and narrative economies of this film. Second, I elucidate the stakes of the film's exhibitionist display in the Philippines post-Marcos and in the international festival circuit. Third, I attend to the transnational gay politics that emerged through *Macho Dancer* and the two follow-ups that it inspired. To sustain a focused discussion, my analysis deals principally with *Macho Dancer* but refers, whenever relevant, to the other male stripper films.

Hail, Queer Foreigners!

An article from the British journal *Films and Filming* quotes Brocka claiming "that *Macho Dancer* is not a festival film" aimed primarily at foreign audiences.[4] "He made it," the article goes on to say, "to compete in the commercial mainstream and believes that his 17-year-old discovery Alan Paule has the kind of face with which Philippine audiences will fall in love." Brocka clearly addresses local spectators with his film, including a gay following that, to his great credit, he never underestimated in his career. But the information that the film was not intended for international festivals was only partly true at the time of the film's production and even less so during its exhibition. The same article even contradicts Brocka's claim by suggesting that he "filmed two versions of some scenes, the more explicit of which are destined for export markets."[5] Moreover, the film was smuggled out of the Philippines without the mandatory censor's "export stamp" in order to be screened intact at the Toronto International Film Festival.[6] Audiences at home were offered a much tamer version and, because of the penalties leveled by the angry censors, only after considerable delay. Brocka's tactical maneuvers thus contradicted his avowed intention of making the film primarily for domestic spectators, effectively designating the North American audience as the first and privileged viewers of his film.[7] In the realm of festival cinema, these claims of priority are routinely made and contested, often with the result that directors have to defend or deny their status as "native informants" speaking in terms determined by a Western audience. In Brocka's later festival films, including *Macho Dancer*, the self-conscious address to the foreign spectator becomes a crucial element of the film's tactic of visibility. The movie's appeal to local audiences remains. But although such appeal is considerable, it is not given as much import as the desire to be seen by the imagined outside. In the next sections, my analysis focuses on the gaze Brocka makes available to American/foreign spectators. Later I demonstrate how this

American/foreigner's gaze interlocks with the mechanics and politics of Filipino spectatorship. My recourse to the ungainly slash linking and separating "American" and "foreigner" is a rhetorical move dictated by necessity. There is no adequate English translation for *"kano*," the truncated form of "Amerikano" in Filipino slang. The word signifies not only "white man" but also "foreigner" in general.

From the very first scene, *Macho Dancer* repeatedly hails its hypothetical American/foreign spectator. When the movie opens, we see a balding, middle-aged white man trailing his lips up the contours of a young Filipino's sweaty torso. He kisses the lad's chest, his neck, and even his lips. The young man's body is familiar territory to the Westerner, and it shows in the intensity of their romance. As they carouse in a seedy motel, the camera moves around to keep up with the action. This time, we see the native perch his lithe body on top of his partner's wide, lumpy frame. Eager to please the white man, the Filipino goes down on him. Moments later, the young man in turn is being fellated by the Westerner. The camera captures the Filipino's expression as he reaches climax. The hustler's groans become finally audible, indicating that but for the native's orgasm, we have been experiencing the event through the interiority of the enraptured foreigner. As the film's historical frame widens, we learn that the white man is an American serviceman named Larry (Mel Davidson) and that the Filipino hustler named Pol (Alan Paule) is his kept boy from the slums outside Clark Air Base.

Using a standard tactic for enhancing the foreign appeal of a film, Brocka establishes a rapport with Western spectators by offering Larry as the first of several onscreen surrogates with whom to identify.[8] Aside from being appropriate to the setting of *Macho Dancer*, having an American—the "quintessential" white man—as the figure of the Westerner enables the film to engage specifically American viewers as well as a broader audience of Westerners and other foreign spectators. A great part of *Macho Dancer*'s American fantasy proposes that the spectacle of exotic dancing, the offstage lives of these Third World characters, and the film itself are in many ways cut to the measure of the gay foreigner's desire. Third World exhibitionism emerges as a floating world ordered by his pleasure.

Now that I have established the American/foreigner's status as the film's privileged audience, it is time to ask what is being looked at and how the looking is done. In a brief article on European art cinema,

Pol (Alan Paule) tricks with a GI (Mel Davidson) from the U.S. military base. Source: Macho Dancer.

Thomas Elsaesser describes one of the interests of the festival film as that of "politico-voyeuristic curiosity."[9] The term captures the way in which the spectacles of sex and Third World underdevelopment are thoroughly enmeshed in delivering erotic pleasure to Western or First World spectators. Though left undefined in the article, Elsaesser's evocative phrase links together the social, the visual, and the erotic: elements that are present in most festival movies but are especially prominent in the sensational sex and poverty of male stripper films. In his analysis of another Brocka film, Rolando Tolentino describes the erotic charge in the First World's witnessing of Third World squalor: the filmmaker, he says, courts Western audiences by "reifying orientalism, exoticizing and aestheticizing poverty."[10] The slums, like bodies, are offered in visual and thus erotic display.[11]

Returning to the two questions posed earlier, what is being looked at in *Macho Dancer* is certainly not just the naked brown bodies on display but the sociopolitical morass in which they thrive. One might speculate that the film's American/foreign spectators, like the American servicemen and international sex tourists in the film, exercise a politico-voyeuristic curiosity that makes a pornography of the Third

World. Through different foreigners' gazes that are reflexively depicted in the film, *Macho Dancer*'s real-life spectators symbolically gain power over, and presumably derive Orientalist pleasure from, Filipino exotics and their turbulent society. The film panders to this politico-voyeuristic curiosity, thereby maintaining the coherency of the film's spectatorial address even after the Western figures exit the story or move to the margins of the frame. After his latest American GI departs, Pol ventures to the capital. With the encouragement of his mother and his former neighbor Greg, a hustler in Manila's red-light district, Pol emigrates to the big city to better support his family's needs. When the narrative shifts to Manila and ventures into a prolonged exposition of the flesh trade, the film both sustains and dissimulates the American/foreigner's gaze by assigning it to other white spectators at the clubs. *Macho Dancer* then reassigns the American/foreigner's gaze to two sets of native informant figures who address not just the film's foreign spectators but also its local audience. Although Pol is the film's protagonist, his relentless objectification by other characters cues the film's spectators to identify instead with these native informants. The first set is a colorful group of gay club owners and pimps who are all addressed with maternal nicknames (Mother, Mama Charlie, Mommy), while the second is composed of more-seasoned macho dancers and hustlers who try to teach the naïve *provinciano* about the perils of city life. Because these native informants substitute for foreign viewers, their inconspicuous presence is deceptive. Their role complicates the relay of looks in the film. These looks shift constantly between the perspectives of Filipino and American characters as well as between the implied gazes of domestic and foreign audiences. In his analysis of a scene from *Macho Dancer*, Angelo Restivo was first to call attention to this unstable point of view, which he describes as "the complex interplay of looks in the film." Specifically, he points to the significance of "the look of the (Western, American) spectator (who is both in and out of the text)."[12]

Simultaneously taking on and catering to the lurid fascination of First World and domestic spectators, the film's native informants introduce the milieu of male hustlers with earnest vulgarity. Mother (Joel Lamangan), the first pimp that Pol meets, instantly orders him to drop his pants in front of other hustlers. Mother then sizes up Pol's qualifications by grabbing his genitals. With the familiar crudity

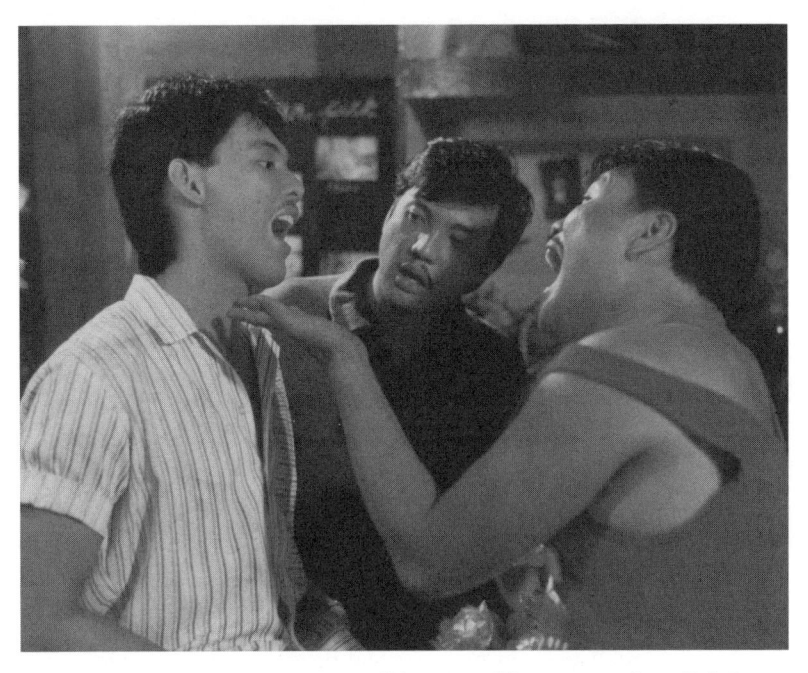

A bar owner (Joel Lamangan) functions as a surrogate of Filipino gays and Western spectators. Source: Macho Dancer.

and scathing humor of the American drag queen and its Filipino counterpart, the catty gay beautician, Mother reports to everyone present the size of Pol's member: "Oh my, it's a biggie!" Mother also makes cruel fun of the lad's supposed "innocence," encouraging the same of spectators who he knows can see through a hustler's act. "Many guys tell me they're virgins," he quips. "The truth is they've been blown by every faggot in Manila!" Reflexively touting his credentials as a native informant, Mother claims to know what else Westerners like besides naked Filipinos: Third World kitsch, in the form of plastic roses with Christmas lights. "They're a hit in Canada," he says. Using the labor of off-duty strippers, he produces the ugly handicrafts in the basement of his strip club for export to North America.

While the orientation provided by the gay *mama san* is useful, wicked fun, the bulk of information and pornographic talk is supplied by the older male and female sex workers. Noel (Daniel Fernando), who serves as Pol's mentor and roommate, emerges as the best informant of them all. He is attractive, affable, and, most importantly, as loose with his lips as he is with his body. While showing off his one-room apartment to Pol, he supplies numerous details about the habitation of sex workers and their petty creature comforts. Over lunch, he freely tells his sordid biography to the newcomer as they dine elbow-to-elbow with other patrons at an outdoor food stand. "I was sleeping at Luneta Park," he volunteers. "A man came up to me, trying to be friendly. I had not yet eaten that day. It was the day I decided to let go of my shame." Still more revelations follow in a scene designed precisely to exploit the appeal of salacious counsel. Congregating at a park in the small hours of the morning, the hustlers talk about their promiscuity ("Noel's best record is servicing eight customers in one night!"), the tricks of the profession ("Try your best not to cum for every customer!"), their hygiene ("Bathe before and after each trick."), and their sexual caprices ("I'm pricey, but when I dig the person, I put out for free.").

The film affirms the legitimacy of these sordid details and the spectator's interest in them by drawing a contrast between "good" and "bad" kinds of sex work. In the film's gay erotic and moral economies, "bad" means nonconsensual and heterosexual prostitution. The "bad" kind of sex trade happens at female brothels—stereotypical dens of white slavery—of the sort protected by a policeman called "The Kid" (Johnny Vicar), who also supplies drugs to the bars. Female sex work, the film suggests, is ethically problematic because women are less able to deal with drugs and violence than male prostitutes. Their participation in the flesh trade is even linked to rape. We see this in the sharp contrast between the female prostitute Bambi's revelation about her turn to sex work and Noel's earlier narration of his own entry into prostitution. Bambi (played by Jaclyn Jose, the star of *Olongapo . . . The Great American Dream*, a film discussed in chapter 3) tells her secret to Pol in a moment of great distress. "I was a whore since the age of twelve," she begins. "My father was my first customer. He would give me a peso to keep me from tattling. He was too poor to hire even the cheapest streetwalker." This incest trauma that Bambi agonizingly channels into her work as a prostitute cannot be more different from Noel's first trick, which he recalls nonchalantly between mouthfuls of rice and viand. Sheltered by a cultural—if not universal—double standard, Noel speaks candidly of his sex work, and the film shows it with little guilt.

The unapologetic depiction of male sex work, which is consistent with the film's privileging of foreign spectators and courting of the local gay audience, follows every step of Pol's initiation into the trade. Fresh off the bus, he lands at D' Pogi Disco (The Handsome Disco) and witnesses an especially racy moment: male performers seated in a row on stage, masturbating for the audience. The first row of tables and chairs is occupied by white men. One of the foreigners is shown leering intently at the strippers while "masturbating" the beer bottle in front of him. Despite Pol's stereotypical *provinciano* "innocence," the sleaze does not cow him one bit. He soon takes a job entertaining patrons at Mama Charlie's Pub but has a difficult time landing as many tricks as the dancers. Later he asks Noel to give him dancing lessons so he can move up at the club. Emboldened by his initiation, Pol joins the group rehearsals onstage and later takes a "chorus role" in the show. One night—just like in American backstage musicals—Pol is forced to substitute for a sick colleague and triumphantly plays one of two featured roles in a routine that involves soaping up Noel and romancing him while they gyrate to lounge music.[13]

Pol (Alan Paule) takes dancing lessons from Noel (Daniel Fernando) and others in order to get ahead in the club. Source: Macho Dancer.

Many critics detected a strong intent to pander to gay spectators, including a foreign gay audience, as the motivation for the film's excruciatingly detailed treatment of Pol's entry into male exotic dancing. The *New York Times* identified the film's "true interest" as that of catering to a gay "lust for soap bubbles."[14] While *Variety*'s reviewer also attributed the film's "frequent and generous dancing routines featuring total nudity and bump n' grind gay foreplay" to "Brocka's lugubrious celebration of gay eros," he nevertheless credits "*Macho Dancer*'s vivid depiction of teenage prostitution" with providing a "daring political perspective."[15] The *Hollywood Reporter*'s critic, Harry Sheehan, made a similar point, insisting that Brocka's "camera never loses sight of the social trap that has ensnared the young man."[16] He went on to argue that the "tension between Brocka's fascination and his criticism"—in other words, the film's seemingly conflicted appeal to a politico-voyeuristic curiosity—"becomes the moving force of the film." Sheehan's characterization of the film as an "eroticized semi-documentary" captures the pairing of eros and epistemophilia, the desire to know. The film serves up both perks to its hypothetical gay American/foreign audience.

The presentation of different practices of stripping (e.g., D' Pogi's vs. Mama Charlie's), the hierarchies of skills and roles (e.g., gigolo, background dancer, lead performer), and the perseverance of the dancers are all important repetitions. Combined with frequent depictions of the hazards of the trade and the hardships faced by the dancers, these recurring images of labor and art implicitly validate a Third World cultural form that might otherwise be seen as tawdry exploitation. The film makes its own appeal for legitimacy along the same lines. *Macho Dancer* rehearses the contextualization of the lurid to insinuate a practice of pornographic social melodrama into the "prestige" market of international festival and art-house circuits. As we shall see in the next section, such rehearsal constitutes "macho dancing" as an unlikely political gesture.

The Politics of (Trans)national Pornography

Pol's evolution into the consummate macho dancer is significantly not the film's resolution, but rather its midpoint. The tale of his initiation into the big city is rounded out by his entanglement, through his mentor Noel, in the local politics of the red-light district. The film's more explicit turn from the erotic to the political occurs as Noel starts dealing drugs to finance his and Pol's costly expeditions into female brothels to locate Noel's missing sister, Pining (Princess Punzalan). Noel's resolve to scour every whorehouse in the metropolis exposes him and Pol to the abyss of the female flesh trade and, by extension, to the ills of the social order that sustains it. The face of this exploitative order is "The Kid," who is involved in running every illegal activity in the district. The social picaresque that leads us to the confrontation between the powerless sex workers and the crooked authority figure is vividly orchestrated by Brocka, who draws here on his expertise as a cinematic poet of Third World oppression.

When the subplot about Noel's forcibly prostituted sister emerges, Brocka quotes liberally from the mise-en-scène and tropes of his widely acclaimed *Manila: In the Claws of Neon* (*Maynila: Sa mga kuko ng liwanag*, 1975). The heroine of that film, Ligaya Paraiso, is also taken prisoner in a brothel. Later, she is bought out by a Chinese businessman who mostly keeps her cooped up in his apartment. Like Noel, the hero of *Manila: In the Claws of Neon* tries to settle the score with the heroine's captor. In both films, the narrative climaxes with the

Pol (Alan Paule) and Noel (Daniel Fernando) search for the latter's sister, Pining. Source: Macho Dancer.

horrifying image of a young man cornered by a hostile mob that swiftly moves in to kill him.

This image of the summary execution of youths by a merciless band is Brocka's oft-used but unfailingly powerful emblem of the civilian's ultimate doom in the clutches of the repressive nation-state. To Filipinos who lived through the dictatorship of Ferdinand Marcos, *Macho Dancer*'s depiction of Noel's killing vividly evokes the deposed strongman's infamous reign of terror.[17] Sadly, the same image of summary execution—what I call the "Marcosian moment"—went on to find new significance in Corazon Aquino's regime, which was marred by the violence of state-tolerated vigilante squads, the massacre of farmers protesting near the presidential palace, and eight coups d'état mounted by the extremists from the political Right.

For those who recognize Brocka's quotation of his martial law–era work in *Macho Dancer*, this gesture of repetition is itself a searing indictment of the Aquino presidency. The recycling of the Marcosian moment is an implicit assertion of Brocka's disenchantment with the much-vaunted People Power Revolution.[18] Brocka declared in interviews to foreign journalists that "the revolution has not changed the system"[19] and that "the system has not changed, because it has been exploiting and victimizing the poor and the underprivileged, and it is still doing it."[20]

That said, the specificity of the film's antiestablishment commentary lies in another area and uses a strategy that is decidedly less generic and better developed. This critique lies in the interpenetration of form, content, and context of spectatorship through which Brocka's film operates. To understand the workings of such a critique, we must invert the logic behind the typical reaction to the film, as exemplified by the *New York Times*' Caryn James. In her brief, scathing review, James faults *Macho Dancer* for pursuing what she believes to be two incompatible goals: wanting "to be a sexy homosexual film and to comment on social conditions in the Philippines at the same time." She concludes by insisting that Brocka's "political reputation can't save *Macho Dancer* from the charge that it is a soft-core sex film masquerading as a political statement."[21] The false dichotomy separating the exploitative nature of pornography from the culturally elevated operation of sociopolitical commentary obscures the fact that the film's pornography *is* its politics. *Macho*

Dancer binds political critique and pornography together in a mutually reinforcing partnership. The possibilities of such an unholy union were already articulated by Thomas Waugh in response to a late Marcos-era festival film titled *Boatman* (Tikoy Aguiluz, 1985). Waugh wrote, "Now there are hints everywhere that sexuality may be connected to the political realm after all . . . sexuality is established as the anguished terrain of politics."[22] As I shall explain later, the fusion of pornography and political critique is contiguous with *Macho Dancer*'s overlapping, dual address, which actively entices an American/foreign audience while also hailing Filipino spectators. The film's pornography is also integral to Brocka's formulation of dissident gay politics during a specific historical moment.

I read this twinning of social exposé and pornography as a gesture of flagrant exhibitionism: a provocative response to the triumphalism and complacency of the Philippines after the 1986 People Power Revolution. Though Brocka routinely disavowed any specific political agenda, his cultural response to the national situation is both appropriate and compelling.[23] My use of the term "exhibitionism" refers to a well-rehearsed concept in studies of national cinema. The concept suggests three important factors: the practice of projecting an image, the intent or significance of the display, and the desired audience toward which the spectacle is directed. Andrew Higson defines an exhibitionist cinema as one that "acknowledges its visibility" and recognizes the "presence of the audience" through the "theatrical presence of the performers" and other "elements of self-display."[24] In his pathbreaking study of the new German cinema, Thomas Elsaesser theorizes the sociopolitical valence of exhibitionism. He finds in the exhibitionist gesture a political recourse to superficiality, a defiant tactic of exposure, and even a practice for "working through" and registering history. Elsaesser writes the following on the possibilities of the "spectacle of self-display": "Film-makers confronted the law of the father on the side of exhibitionism . . . Rather than internalise the latent conflicts which German postwar history and the legacy of a particular culture had programmed into them, feminist and gay film-makers in particular tried to restage traumas in their films, often making the body itself the site of division, transgression and the transformation of sexual identity."[25]

Following Elsaesser, I read the gesture of exhibitionism in *Macho Dancer*, the display of the body and the externalization of the interior self, as political. Brocka responds to the trauma inflicted by the state's continuing exercise of its repressive power by reviving two tactics of dissident cinema from the Marcos era. Both tactics are, of course, studies in grandstanding: the political melodrama, with its spectacular depiction of poverty and despair; and the pornographic film, with its presentation of unwieldy bodies and sexualities. Brocka's unprecedented recourse to explicit pornography in the context of a political melodrama is best seen as an adjustment of stance. His two most provocative films from this period, *Orapronobis* (*Fight for Us*, 1988) and *Macho Dancer*, engage in graphic representations. In its French version, *Orapronobis* initially included a controversial scene of cannibalism. It is performed by a fanatical member of one of many vigilante groups conscripted by the Aquino government to help stem the communist insurgency in the hinterlands.[26] *Macho Dancer*, for its part, showed gangly sex workers beating off to gawking foreigners and locals.

Brocka's pornographic display reworks tropes from a Filipino genre called *bomba*, erotic films that flourished during the dictatorship. Brocka's deployment of this mode is particularly rich because it salvages a historically politicized practice of film pornography. A generic term for moving-image erotica, *bomba* got its name from a Marcos-era tactic of provocative political rhetoric in which speakers unexpectedly "drop a bomb." Uttered in bold defiance of strict censorship and political repression, the bomb consisted of exposés and diatribes against the government or incumbent public officials. The term was thus given to the contemporaneous practice of making hard-core pornographic films, or more accurately, of reinserting ("*singit*") snippets of hard-core sex into soft-core films already sanitized by the censors. *Bomba* films peaked in the early 1970s and again in the mid-1980s, when censorship laws and the monitoring of cinemas were relaxed.[27] Unlike the *bomba* of political tirades, which were swiftly (and often violently) dealt with by authorities, the erotic *bomba* enjoyed a symbiotic relationship with the state. During the latter period, Marcos allowed the screening of uncensored soft-core erotica to sustain the government-controlled Manila Film Center (MFC), built by First Lady Imelda Marcos and partly overseen by their daughter Imee. The art-house enterprise served as the rationale for the exception to censorship, which was later challenged by film exhibitors and moral crusaders.[28] The inconsistent policy with respect to the MFC fueled a game of hide-and-seek between law enforcement and purveyors of erotic films. This game caused the function of pornography to shift constantly between being a state-tolerated safety valve for social unrest and holding up an image of the nation's morally degenerate state of affairs.

The candor of *Macho Dancer*'s exhibitionism is remarkable. Brocka's gratuitous staging of erotic acts supplants not just the *bomba* film but also the reflexive and anxiety-ridden figuration of *toro* (live sex shows)—the virtual emblem of Marcos-era sexual perversity—in such films as *Boatman* and *Private Show* (Chito Roño, 1986). The film's lengthy macho-dancing sequences and group masturbation scene represent a more transgressive kind of sexual perversity than *toro* does, since the homosexual character of the filmed sex acts arguably heightens the scandalous effect of an erotic spectacle. The erotic display of male bodies represents a symbolic turning away from the *toro* and *bomba*'s scenes of heterosexual (reproductive) sex. Moreover, these explicit images of perversity are delivered as part of a dissimulated tale of romance that involves two men, Pol and Noel. Numerous and crucial turns in the plot show that their homosexual relationship is no less than the dissimulated backbone of the film's entire plot.

The narrative of Pol and Noel's friendship is structured like a love story. They click instantly upon meeting. They get personal on their first "date" at the outdoor eatery and then move in together shortly thereafter. Every night they get intimate at the club. Several women enter Pol's life but never "steal" him away from Noel. Pol even rescues a damsel in distress—Noel's sister, Pining—in the film's climactic set piece but sends her packing to the boondocks in the next scene. The film's only heterosexual romantic entanglement, between Pol and Bambi, results in a tearful parting by the breakwater of Manila Bay. The woman, citing her unfulfilled ambitions and desire for independence, resolutely declines the man's invitation to flee the city and start anew in the country. Two significant gestures of homoerotic love lead to the film's conclusion. First, Pol avenges Noel by shooting "The Kid" in the dark of night. The assassination is falsely attributed to a communist liquidation squad. Second, Pol returns to Mama Charlie's newly renamed club in order to dedicate one last dance to Noel's memory. This involves "showering" onstage with Dennis (William Lorenzo), Noel's usual partner. While the final scene shows Pol riding a bus back to Olongapo, the closing title sequence (a sort of flashback) catches him dancing once again with the entire gang of strippers. These final homoerotic moments make it seem unlikely that Pol's return to his hometown would result in a future heterosexual coupling. What awaits him instead are the irritating demands of his family and, most likely, another relationship with an American serviceman.

One may read the macho dancer's turning away from heterosexuality and reproduction as a gesture of defiance and indifference against Corazon Aquino's discourse of nation building and moral rehabilitation. Though initially enthusiastic about her ascent to power, Brocka quickly recognized the stifling conservatism of Aquino's regime and its inability to make good on its promise of change.[29] Much to her consternation, Brocka resigned from his position as one of her appointed constitutional commissioners.[30] He also became a vocal critic of Aquino's old-school chief censor, Manuel Morato.[31]

On film, Brocka's critique of Philippine society under Aquino was especially harsh. His defiant gesture involved circulating images of extreme poverty, military violence, and, in *Macho Dancer*, homosexuality. These scandalous images of social ills and gayness challenged the Aquino regime's projection of itself as a propoor, propeace, and profamily affair installed by the people, the Catholic Church, and the Virgin Mary. *Macho Dancer*'s confrontational stance is reflected in the denunciation of the film by Rev. Nick Cruz, a Jesuit film editor and critic known for his liberalism. Cruz wrote,

> There was nary a single moment in the film that showed Pol or his fellow dancers having any feelings of guilt or revulsion or disgust for the kind of life they were living. For them and for the viewer, the film seems to imply that male prostitution and macho dancing are normal and acceptable ... It is not enough to show at the end of the film that Pol turned his back on macho dancing and went back to his hometown, because those last few minutes of self-realization cannot outweigh the vivid impact and moral damage of one and a half hours of glamorized macho dancing.[32]

Cruz was not speaking for the Aquino administration, of course, but as a liberal cineaste and Catholic priest, yet his reaction about the film's gratuitous homosexual display is a good indicator of the film's transgressive, scandalous quality. So unnerved was he that he came up with a sequel to the review, publishing negative comments about the film from his students at an elite Philippine university.[33] The London Film School–trained Jesuit's reaction is understandable, since *Macho Dancer* is not just sexually explicit but also radically antiestablishment. Instead of condemning sex workers for their "immorality," the film blames the state and society for the crushing poverty that engenders prostitution. It is worth mentioning that morality appears to play no part in Pol's decision to quit the sex industry. He leaves because the flesh trade is being ruined by crooked cops.

As I mentioned earlier, Brocka and his risqué film predictably ran afoul of the censors. The censors initially refused to preview the film because Brocka smuggled it out of the country without their approval.[34] After Brocka and his many supporters made noise, the censors accepted the tamer domestic version of the film. But even in its altered form, *Macho Dancer* was bold enough to challenge the government's political will to uphold the new freedom of expression clause that Brocka himself put into the 1987 constitution.[35]

Equally significant as the film's turn to gay pornography, as I mentioned earlier, was Brocka's decision to direct this exhibitionism to audiences in the West, installing them as its first and privileged spectators. *Macho Dancer*'s particular mode of exhibitionism takes a different stance than what Rey Chow observes in contemporary Chinese cinema. Expanding on the political valences of what she calls, after Thomas Elsaesser, an "affect of exhibitionism," Chow sees the self-display of Chinese cinema as a response directed to the "voyeuristic aggression" of both the Chinese state and the West.[36] In relation to the latter, the "very excessive modes" of this cinema contain "a critique of the voyeurism of [Western] orientalism itself."[37] Brocka's gesture is more arguably collusive with the West than a tacitly anti-imperialist stance would permit. By seducing Western spectators, Brocka's film effectively turns the international art-house circuit into a chain of temporary exhibitionist sites. On those global screens, *Macho Dancer* shows the world his nation's shame: the state's failed project of social change in the aftermath of the People Power Revolution. In Brocka's tactic of visuality, pandering to the West becomes the means of conscripting international witnesses, the exploitation of Filipino bodies is marshaled into exhibitionism, and a morally questionable cultural form (pornography) is put to the service of a sociopolitical critique. Indeed, it matters little if the *New York Times* reviewer perceived the film's political critique as being less successful or prominent than Brocka's other goal of titillating gay audiences in the West. As Elsaesser reminds us, a film's meanings are inevitably reassigned in export by "audiences who could ignore the peculiar historical inscription or economic determinants that might have marked the films."[38] Festival films like *Macho Dancer* could lose their critical edge in their cross-cultural reception, but they may also acquire a different "political meaning [albeit] in ways not always controlled by their directors."[39] As it turns out, the film's American reviews acknowledged the legibility of Brocka's social critique. That they also unanimously commented upon the film's pornography—whether or not they saw it as something more than just a queer confection—means that its exhibitionist gesture succeeded in the fundamental and simple task of getting the attention of foreigners and exposing to them the perverse state of Aquino's postrevolutionary nation.

Exportable and Reimportable Gayness

The homoerotic defiance of *Macho Dancer* serves yet another political function besides implicitly critiquing the general social conditions in postdictatorship Philippines. Gender politics is an equally important category of analysis, not only for *Macho Dancer* but also for other festival films from the Philippines. I have already described how the homoerotic depictions sharpened the scandalous effect of *Macho Dancer*'s pornography. What remains to be discussed here is how Brocka's exhibitionism prompted the formulation of a gay politics that could be legible and appealing both at home and abroad. The challenge of this cross-cultural exchange calls for this sexual politics—a kind of transnational gay politics—to be considerably elastic. I shall stick to the term "gay" instead of "queer" even if the latter conveys a wider range of sexualities. Indeed, "queer" is more appropriate to the variety of "nonstraight" sexualities (including bisexuals, transsexuals, lesbians, and straight-identifying men and women) engaged by this politics and these films, but the term has little purchase in the Philippines and, because of that, will not serve the interest of this transnational critique.[40]

My first point on this issue is that the film seems to respond to the challenge of a transnational gay politics by reforming the masculine ideal of Filipino gay erotics under the hypothetical scrutiny (or sympathetic witnessing) of an imagined foreign gaze. For this politics the site of negotiation is the body of the Third World male prostitute, on whose contours various forms of perversity can be realized. The transactional nature of the gay sex purveyed in the film is balanced by the homosexual rapport that develops between Pol and Noel. The relationship is initiated when Pol offers a handkerchief to Noel after seeing him get beaten up by two drug pushers inside a gay bar restroom. When the two become colleagues at Mama Charlie's Pub, their physical closeness forges bonds of emotional intimacy. As one of the strippers describes it, a special kind of understanding develops between coworkers who "grab each other's balls nightly." The relationship deepens significantly when Noel, desperately needing emotional succor, seeks intimacy from Pol in the only way familiar to him. Noel starts to kiss him while crying on his shoulders. The startled Pol deflects the advance and subsequently tries to prove his manhood by taking Bambi as his lover. He even brings Bambi to their apartment, prompting an understated display of jealousy on Noel's part. This gesture of boundary setting with Pol ends quickly, however, when the two find themselves in a most intimate situation: having sex with one another in a Japanese-produced porn video. Moreover, Pol puts his life on the line to help save Noel's sister, affirming his ultimate commitment to his friend. His later decision to hunt down "The Kid" in vengeance for Noel's killing may thus be read as a lover's act. By shooting the bad closet queen who harasses his "lover" (Pol and Noel talk early in the film about "The Kid" being gay), Pol's murder of "The Kid" becomes as homoerotic as the final dance that pays tribute to Noel.

It is worth noting that the homosexualization of the two central figures is accomplished even while maintaining a facade of masculinity normative to Filipino gay erotics. Consistent with Filipino preferences for manly but sexually cooperative hustlers, none of the dancers is effeminate or marked as homosexual and yet neither Pol nor Noel lives up to the machismo suggested by the film's title.[41] This calculated ambiguity allows them to perform gay erotic acts for foreign spectators without losing the masculine image prized by domestic audiences. Moreover, the film manages to impute to its two male leads homosexual desires that seem to develop from necessity to a fully consummated erotic and emotional bond. Indeed, their coupling is the most complete in the film. It is characterized by a life-and-death commitment that easily surpasses the intensity of Bambi and Pol's tender but casual romance. The bond between Pol and Noel quietly fuels the tragic love story at the center of the film.

Filipina critic Chit Domingo, writing in the vernacular, observed that "the macho dancers seem to enjoy what they are doing."[42] She adds that "Noel's prostitution is not the problem. It's his sister's prostitution that's the problem." Across the Pacific, Lawrence Chua's stateside academic critique of the film also read this sexual ambiguity, albeit in a decidedly positive way: "The characters in *Macho Dancer* elude easily defined categories of sexual identity." The film's representation of sexual identity is one that, the Asian American critic argued, could "enable us to imagine ourselves as new kinds of revolutionary subjects."[43]

For lack of a better term—and to riff on an old one—we may refer to the macho dancers' homosexuality as "latent" because it is initially "buried" in the plot and the film's visual field. This synthetic sexual formation (this "latent homosexuality") accommodates expectations of masculinity and homosexuality within and beyond the national imaginary. Significantly enough, especially for our understanding of the relay between domestic and international gay politics, this "latent homosexuality" achieves its full realization under the cinematic gaze of foreign spectators. Returning to the scene of the porn video shoot mentioned earlier, we find the two dancers strapped for cash, kicked out of "The Kid's" drug trade, and now hired for a sexual tryst in front of the camera. They mutually consent to the encounter and, we infer, consummate it without making a fuss. The foreign gaze intervenes here not only to legitimize the activity as a business enterprise but also, more importantly, to give the two permission to realize their desires within a contained extranational and temporary space: namely, the audiovisual temporality of the foreign sex video. The condition of this video-recorded encounter is homologous to the catalytic effect of the film's self-conscious display of Filipino gay sexuality to foreign spectators. The speculative anticipation of the Westerner's gay politics and the notion that one's sexuality is being subjected to surveillance engender the imaginary reformation of Filipino sexualities and the production of more progressive sexual politics for display abroad and reimportation back home.

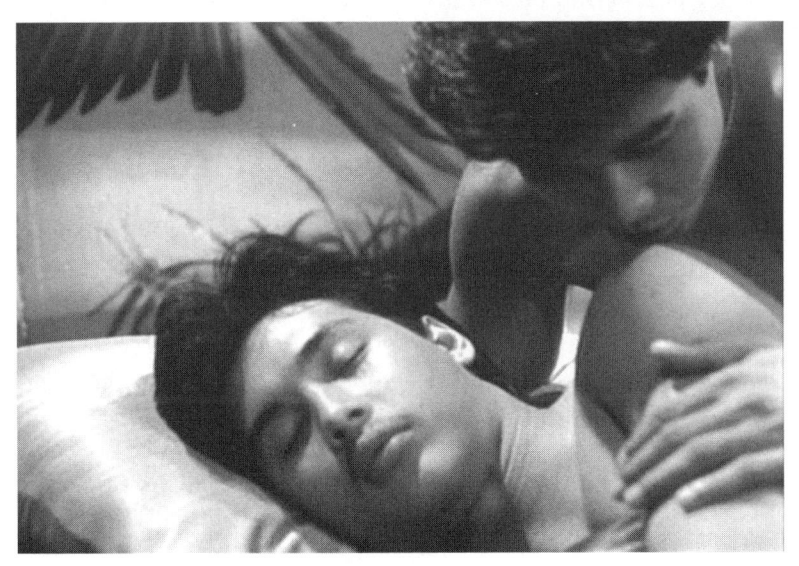

Pol (Alan Paule) and Noel (Daniel Fernando) consummate their homoerotic relationship at a shoot for a Japanese-produced porn video. Source: Macho Dancer.

Joel David argues that *Macho Dancer* flounders in advancing a truly progressive gay politics by refusing to make explicit the homosexuality of its male protagonists. David writes, "The issue of credibility at this point centers on how Pol could have retained his heterosexuality all this time . . . Nowhere is this reluctance to pursue obvious logic displayed [more fully] than in the excuses summoned for sexual encounters between Pol and Noel."[44]

It seems to me that Brocka's subtle approach to this issue favors a desirable versatility: Pol and Noel's "latent homosexuality" plays to a wide range of gay desires, suitable to heterogeneous gay and straight audiences at home and abroad.

The success of *Macho Dancer*'s gay politics in crossing national borders and pushing the envelope at home is affirmed by the film's warm reception in America and the reimportation of that success at home. Its strong showing at festivals happened just before the new queer cinema's watershed years in the early 1990s, anticipating the progressive gay politics and bold sexual content that marked American gay independent films in the succeeding decade.[45] Brocka's gay film even contributed materially to the development of First World gay cinema. The distribution of *Macho Dancer* was the founding activity of Strand Releasing, which was to become one of the most important distributors and producers of gay independent cinema in the states.[46] Arguably, *Macho Dancer*'s foreign success also contributed directly to the slow but significant development of a gay cinema at home. Brocka's film opened new prospects. Playing to the gay market became an expedient way of penetrating the foreign film festival circuit and even landing modest distribution deals. Many independent filmmakers followed Brocka's suit, tackling domestic gay subject matter with "foreign" standards of sexual content and liberal gender politics.

Midnight Dancers, the follow-up to Brocka's film, projects the fantasy of an even more progressive state of affairs for Filipino gays while also upping the ante on its transnational erotic appeal.[47] Chionglo's movie boasts three male stripper characters as its lead protagonists, brothers who each represent a different physical type. In following the brothers' exploits in and outside the gay bars, the film eschews even *Macho Dancer*'s passing concern about the progressive moral degradation of its female subjects. It is only at the very end of *Midnight Dancers* that the moral cost of the sibling callboys' sexual excesses is articulated. As the brothers walk a dark street, one of them suddenly exclaims, quite out of context, "Something is lost [to us when we entertain so many sexual clients]. I don't know exactly what it is, but I know that it is something." Prior to this, the opposite moral premise, established early in the film, prevailed: when one of the characters asks the boys' mother if she had any reservations about their involvement in the sex trade, she replies, nonchalantly, that she had none. "They really have nothing to lose," she says. "After all, they're men." The heightened sexual plenitude is matched by a liberal attitude toward gayness. The film shows the youngest of the three brothers openly having a relationship with the club's drag queen while one of his older siblings romances both a wife and a gay lover. So "liberal" indeed is this opening up of Filipino gay sexuality that a reviewer for *Variety* found it "almost too-good-to-be-true."[48]

The rousing success of *Midnight Dancers* inspired a further attempt by the same director and writer (Ricky Lee cowrote *Macho Dancer* and penned three other male stripper films) to cash in on *Macho Dancer*'s formula. *Burlesk King*, financed by a production company that made its fortune on "straight" soft-core pornography, does not try to surpass

Midnight Dancers *replicates the gay attractions of Brocka's film.* Source: Midnight Dancers.

Midnight Dancers' depictions of gay sex. In fact, it introduces a heterosexual romance into its plot in an attempt to cater to the mainstream (heterosexual) audience at home. But the film tries to compensate for this heterosexual infusion by pushing its liberal politics even further than *Midnight Dancers*' and taking a page from American gay independent films. *Burlesk King* incorporates the U.S. gay indies' bleeding heart liberalism and such melodramatic staples as the sympathetic portrayal of gay couples, an appeal on behalf of people living with AIDS, and a scene of reconciliation with family. The film dutifully features one pair each of loving gay and lesbian couples, an American expatriate dying of AIDS, and a scene of instant absolution for an American patriarch who once pimped and beat his wife as well as their child.

The pursuit of revenge sets *Burlesk King* into motion. Hustler and male stripper Harry (Rodel Velayo) vows to hunt down his American father who, when Harry was a boy, sold him off to a pedophile. Leaving Olongapo for Manila, Harry works as an exotic dancer and continues the search. He finds his old man in a scavengers' colony, aims a gun at him, but hesitates to pull the trigger. He cannot bring himself to kill the man now afflicted with AIDS. As Harry prepares to leave, his father tells him that his mother—once thought dead—still lives. She works as a prostitute outside Clark Air Base. When Harry tracks her down, she mistakes him for a client. She tries to lure him with the advertising pitch that her "female parts are still tight." Raising the specter of incest, the film quickly puts the viewer at ease: Harry clears up his identity as he follows his mother to a dark alley. In a later scene, she implores Harry to take her to his father so they can nurse him. Harry agrees, and they all reconcile at the garbage dump. The final image is an extreme long shot that shows the reunited family leaving the mountainous filth of the scavengers' colony. The implausible resolution echoes the film's artless hodgepodge of mimic "American" gay politics, exotica, and Third World squalor.

A film critic who writes for the Internet recognized the film's liberal politics and commended its "pansexual positivity, with a sympathetic lesbian couple and no real gay villains."[49] Other critics ignored the politics and panned the film wholesale. *Variety* critic Emmanuel Levy, who earlier gave *Midnight Dancers* a sympathetic review, declared *Burlesk King* "inept on every level." He did not appreciate the reunion between the Amerasian son and his AIDS-ridden American father, characterizing the ending as an "unlikely note of forgiveness."[50]

The protagonist (Rodel Velayo) points a gun at his AIDS-afflicted American father but, moved by pity, forgives him instead. Source: Burlesk King.

According to scant exhibitor data, the film's theatrical opening-week gross reached 65 percent of *Midnight Dancers*' impressive take (selling about two thousand tickets vs. *Midnight Dancers*' three thousand) but slid considerably in subsequent weeks. At some point during its run in the United States, the film earned only $251 on a week's engagement.[51] Suggesting perhaps that the "stripper films" had worn out their welcome, *Burlesk King* did not merit a follow-up effort for more than half a decade, until the same director-writer team made *Twilight Dancers*, their fourth and last male stripper picture. Chionglo, who directed the last three of the male stripper films, said in an interview that the exotic dancing and personal relationships in *Twilight Dancers* (2006) were "symbolic and metaphorical" of social issues.[52] "I am interested in the idea that you are dancing for life, for survival," he said. Ricky Lee, screenwriter of all four films, added, "The country dances to the music dictated by others." Lee's rationale also succinctly captures the twinning of politics and commerce that sustains the very enterprise of Third World festival filmmaking in which their increasingly less political and more sensational gay films participate.

In the aftermath of the male stripper film's decline, Filipino festival entries have alternately resumed the older practice of offering social problem and avant-garde films, continued the mix of flesh peddling and neorealism, or kept on selling liberal gay politics and poverty minus the sex, as in the case of *The Blossoming of Maximo Oliveros* (*Ang pagdadalaga ni Maximo Oliveros*, Auraes Solito, 2005), the first Filipino-language film to compete at the Sundance Film Festival. Despite the modest success of these contemporary festival films, few if any of them are given the American theatrical runs that the first three male stripper films enjoyed. The prohibitive cost of American theatrical distribution means that outside of festivals, Filipino film exports to the United States mainly compete for distribution in the straight-to-video market. This is not necessarily a bad thing. While leaving festival theaters, these films are also moving into far more intimate spaces in the world's various gay communities.

Conclusion

In order to be visible on global screens or gain agency over one's image in the vast theaters of globalization, ex-colonials from Third World Philippines must allow themselves to be seen in ways that are both familiar and novel to the West and also to domestic audiences. The "menace" of this visibility under globalization, as Rey Chow tells us, is that its terms and meanings could be very difficult to control and alter.

For Philippine cinema since the late 1980s, playing the international festival circuit has meant trafficking a pornography of young male bodies, societal woes, and Third World squalor. Like the protagonists of the male stripper films, Philippine filmmakers understand what playing to foreign audiences entails: espousing the sexual politics of their imagined gay American and First World spectators and stimulating not just the foreigners' libidos but also their sense of pity, fear, and outrage about the Third World.

In conjuring gay fantasies for the First World, Filipino filmmakers and their male stripper characters often imagine playing to the intimate American spectator: the audience that has been viewing their bodies and society through the inured seeing practices of voyeurism and surveillance. As in the case of the horror films discussed in chapter 1, globalization in this instance has a contrived American accent and passes through an imaginary American route.

As I have shown in my reading of the three films, this Filipino negotiation of global visibility through cinema has brought its share of both nonmaterial and palpable gains. In *Macho Dancer*, for instance, Brocka mobilized gayness as a form of dissident politics. By using tropes of pornography associated with the Marcos regime and ambivalently showing the perversities inflicted on young Filipino men, Brocka represents Philippine society's stagnation after the vaunted 1986 People Power Revolution. If earlier in his career, Brocka taught Filipinos the political value of shaming one's society in front of the world by picturing slums, prostitution, and tortured bodies, in *Macho Dancer* he designed a critique of the status quo that proceeds by flaunting gay perversions at home and in the world.

The breakthrough success of the American and international runs of the male stripper films continues to inspire many Filipino filmmakers to develop the field of gay cinema. The filmmakers' investment in the fantasy of playing on global screens means that they and their critics often judge the achievement of these films by the scope and commerce of their transnational exhibition. I have proposed in this chapter that we also pay heed to their other vital achievements. In the realm of gender politics, for instance, these films negotiate local and global agendas. Through the international circulation of these movies, Filipinos become actional subjects, helping to construct a transnational imaginary of gay politics and desires. These progressive visions of sexuality detour through the outside, winning validation abroad in order to gain wider acceptance at home.

7

Philippine Cinema's Fatal Attractions

Appropriating Hollywood

In the previous chapter, I showed how Filipino filmmakers engage in the global commerce of festival cinema. Specifically, they aim their movies at imagined American or foreign spectators and purvey fantasies that appeal to gay men. These purposely crafted fantasies capitalize on the historical and contemporary specular relations, the practices of looking and being looked at, between Filipinos as ex-colonials and Americans as ex-colonizers. In this chapter, I consider movies that use a different tactic for participating in global film culture.

In 1990, one of the top studios in the Philippines released its unabashed rip-off of the Hollywood sex drama *Fatal Attraction* (Adrian Lyne, 1987). The film's title, *Is It a Sin to Worship You? (Kasalanan ba'ng sambahin ka?,* Chito Roño, 1990), fittingly suggests an apologia to Hollywood because the picture's obsessive fidelity to the American original could have been easily construed as shameful opportunism. To cite just one example, the elevator sex scene that stands as one of the American film's memorable set pieces is restaged in the Philippine version using humbler technology but in a manner that remains strikingly true to the spirit of the original. Rather than copulating vigorously as the lift slowly ascends a grungy building, the Filipino stars feverishly thrust their way up the concrete stairs of a middle-class apartment, stopping momentarily—as did Glenn Close and Michael Douglas in *Fatal Attraction*—to reach orgasm.

Instead of excoriating *Is It a Sin to Worship You?* on the familiar grounds of unoriginality, the Manunuri ng Pelikulang Pilipino, a circle of old-guard Manila film critics, rewarded the film with nominations in six major categories, including best screenplay, best direction, best actress, and best supporting actress. A group of younger critics gave

199

The famous elevator sex scene in Fatal Attraction *is rehearsed, Third World style, on the stairs.* Source: Is It a Sin to Worship You?

the film one of the four "silver prizes" they handed out that year, citing "its throbbing atmospheric bravura that conjures startling images of eerie alienation, quirky psychosis and impending doom."[1]

It is unlikely that both groups of critics missed the film's numerous "allusions" to *Fatal Attraction* because the American sex drama was a box office hit in the Philippines and circulated widely on pirate video. The old guard's decision to nominate the film in so many categories— and, moreover, to hand it the plum for best production design—perhaps suggests their wise recognition of Third World cinema's entitlement to such tastefully executed cultural pillage. Because what, one might ask, is so wrong about such unauthorized appropriations? When global corporate capitalism bombards Third World denizens relentlessly with American entertainment, it becomes impossible to clear the impressions the latter makes from the visual field of local culture. Should *Is It a Sin to Worship You?* be regarded as cultural theft or as the act of profound and faithful devotion that its title seemingly professes?

In this chapter, I look at Philippine cinema's engagement with the most ubiquitous kind of American fantasies: U.S. motion pictures. In attempting to answer the question of what Filipinos do with these American fantasies, I will discuss two popular Philippine films adapted from American movies: Roño's *Is It a Sin to Worship You?* and Mel Chionglo's *Loretta* (1994), a pseudobiopic based on the genital mutilation scandal involving Lorena and John Wayne Bobbitt. While no Hollywood feature films were ever made of the penis-chopping scandal, a semifictionalized porn video starring John Wayne Bobbitt himself was released in 1994. Additionally, news coverage of the incident and the ensuing trials constituted some of the most widely seen television events in America and the world during the 1990s.[2] My treatment of the Philippine appropriations of these American fantasies draws from the scholarship on national cinema criticism and the larger body of discourse about globalization and culture.

I turn to *Is It a Sin to Worship You?* and *Loretta* because they represent a kind of transaction between Philippine movies and world cinema that is more common and yet less studied than local films with new wave or avant-garde trappings. As with the previous chapter, my broadest aim here is to show how American fantasies serve as imaginary resources for Filipino participation in the cultures of globality. More specifically, I demonstrate how Filipino appropriations of globally popular American movies constitute acts of what Dick Hebdige calls "'mundane' cosmopolitanism."[3] By conscripting American fantasies in the scheme of projecting Filipino movies onto global screens, by insinuating Filipino cosmopolitan reveries in the dream time of globalized culture, these two films generate creative interactions between the periphery and the center. My analysis of *Is It a Sin to Worship You?* and *Loretta* expounds on the methods and accomplishments of these case studies of Philippine cinema's globalization, particularly (a) the simple and complex modes by which American pictures are appropriated in these Filipino movies, (b) the ways in which these appropriations figure the transformations wrought by globalization, and (c) the distinctive contributions of these Filipino movies to domestic audiences and to global cinema and culture.

As regards decolonization and globalization, two terms I am tracking in this book, I posit that the response of these two films to the "cultural imperialism" or dominance of Hollywood follows a tricky approach to cultural decolonization that opens up into the realm of cultural globality. I characterize this approach as tricky because it involves negotiating both a real fidelity and a trenchant corrective to American cultural material.

"Peripheral" Cinemas and Global Hollywood

As with most nations and national cinemas, one finds many traces of Hollywood embedded in Philippine cinema and in the Philippine national imaginary. Hollywood's long-standing dominance of the global film market and the concomitant popularity of such characters as Rambo, Dirty Harry, and Mickey Mouse among the world's moviegoers make it difficult for us to think of American films as the exclusive cultural property of the United States. If we accept Néstor García Canclini's estimate that Hollywood takes up "between 80 and 90 percent of the screen time in nearly the entire world," we must recognize not just the great monetary investment worldwide audiences make in American films but also their legitimate claims of symbolic ownership over the Hollywood repertoire.[4] This repertoire includes not just the films but also the conspicuous details of costuming, comportment, and dialogue, as well as the more invisible "American conception of the world" available within these cultural productions.[5] That "American" worldview includes such elements as the practice of consumerism (which Fredric Jameson equates with the "American way of life"), a cheerful optimism in resolving social conflicts, and an unshakable faith in the righteousness of the American hero.[6]

Notwithstanding the exclusive proprietary claims of its various, mostly American, corporate parents, Hollywood cinema is perhaps one of the most active zones of engagement in what one theorist of globalization describes as the "global ecumene of persistent cultural interaction and exchange."[7] Each national cinema has its own unique corpus of Hollywood movies, a configuration determined by the whims of local media gatekeepers, the meanings available to people in that society, the friction caused by the interaction between American and local films, and the relative significance of "America" within that national imaginary. At the same time, Hollywood is also "within" each local film because the classical Hollywood style of filmmaking is the code of cinematic legibility, because local films cite and evoke figures and moments from American films, because people in various nations often dream of America in the image of Hollywood, and because "so much of any nation's film culture is implicitly 'Hollywood.'"[8] Thomas Elsaesser writes that "national cinemas and Hollywood are not only communicating vessels, but (to change the metaphor) exist in a space set up like a hall of mirrors, in which recognition, imaginary identification and miscognition enjoy equal status."[9] This image of a hall of mirrors evokes the distortions of meaning and form that result from the interactions between American and foreign films.[10] Equally important—and fundamental to this study—the image suggests a realm beyond cinematic style and subject. It evokes a mise en abyme of identifications and misrecognitions created by the ceaseless, bewildering fugue of images of the self and other, and of local and global cultures, in the interplay between national cinema and the Hollywood film. Questions that seek to delineate the borders between national cinema and Hollywood must thus give way to more provocative queries. What do the deepening similarities between Hollywood and domestic films say about a particular nation's experience of the global and the local? How do non-Americans fantasize themselves through Hollywood images?

Despite its overwhelming typicality, the intimacy with Hollywood among ex-colonials, Third World citizens, and other non-Americans is rarely explored.[11] Studies of pan Chinese (especially Hong Kong) cinema's two-way transactions with Hollywood comprise the most significant exceptions to a slowly growing body of scholarship within cinema studies on these asymmetrical relations of exchange. This paucity leads us to the work of globalization theorists and their useful vocabulary of concepts and abstractions for describing "global cultural interactions."[12] The "destruction of other people's national culture industries" and the "McDonaldization" of the world are typical scenarios in studies of the "cultural imperialism" supposedly abetted by globalization.[13] The more hopeful notions of indigenization and hybridization, which ascribe agency to local cultural forms and local cultural entrepreneurs, paint a happier picture of cultural transactions.[14] These concepts are inadequate, however, in describing cases like *Is It a Sin to Worship You?* and *Loretta*. I will cite two reasons here.

First, the asymmetrical exchange suggested by the cultural imperialism thesis applies to the case of *Is It a Sin to Worship You?* and *Loretta*, but the dynamics and results of the transnational exchange are quite different. Because of the country's former status as a U.S. colony, Philippine cinema draws heavily from American cinema and culture. But the transactions are largely unilateral; the Philippines is rarely able to export its own films to the U.S. marketplace. This one-way street is not always such a bad thing. In a symbolic reversal of colonial exploitation, Philippine cinema is able to plunder the resources of Hollywood with impunity. For Filipinos who have been taught to desire things American, the staggering riches of Western culture serve as both the motivation and source of material for practicing what Canclini calls "economic and symbolic reconversion strategies."[15] As in the case of the Filipino *Fatal Attraction*, American cinema's cultural signs are altered in the process of symbolic appropriation and transmuted into economic resources—into Third World films or television programs from which Hollywood could not derive any material benefits. On an economic level, cultural imperialism thus becomes an insecure project, vulnerable to hijacking by cultural pirates. Defense or reprisal on the part of Hollywood is preempted by the relative invisibility of these extremely marginal practices and their meager profits. One might think of appropriation as a sly, pragmatic cultural response to what George Yúdice describes as the hypocrisy of American trade policy: "free-trade rhetoric combined with increased trade barriers."[16] To be sure, the end result of appropriating dominant culture may be less than desirable especially when, as Fredric Jameson puts it, the good of the "cultural realm" enters "into conflict with the economic."[17] As the cultural imperialism or McDonaldization thesis reminds us, the material gains of reconversion must be weighed against the possibility that they might reinstate some of the most pernicious First World consumerist fantasies into Philippine culture. Symbolic reconversions of American films could also reaffirm the superiority and preeminence of the emulated Hollywood product, thus keeping secure the hegemony of American filmmaking.

There is another reason why I think the hybridization thesis is inadequate. The conspicuous similarity and referentiality of copycat films to their American counterparts disallow the fiction of indigenization. In his famous essay on global culture, Arjun Appadurai describes how "at least as rapidly as forces from various metropolises are brought into new societies they tend to become indigenized in one way or the other."[18] The terms and consequences of indigenization are, however, unclear, for as he reasons in the mid-1990s, they "have just begun to be explored systematically."[19] The dictionary definition of "indigenization"—an "act or process of rendering indigenous or making predominantly native"— suggests the long-term process of cultural forgetting necessary to occlude the foreign origin of a cultural artifact.[20] The other keyword, "hybridization," is relatively less problematic but equally imprecise.[21] Hybridization suggests either an all-encompassing mélange effect on cultures (i.e., "we are *all* 'Moroccan girls doing Thai boxing in Amsterdam,'" as one scholar of globalization puts it)[22] or an undefined, highly variable "process of intersection and transaction" to which "one can gain access and which one can abandon."[23]

Ulf Hannerz's essay "Scenarios for Peripheral Cultures" applies the various concepts of cultural appropriation mentioned earlier to the more particular realm of one-way exchanges between the cultural transmitters in the metropole and the cultural receivers at the periphery. I will present some of Hannerz's concepts here in relation to *Is It a Sin to Worship You?* and *Loretta*'s repurposing of American fantasies.[24] In the first scenario, the resulting copycat product becomes an indicator of the *global homogenization of culture*, wherein cultural production in such Third World countries as the Philippines "will by and large be a version of contemporary Western culture."[25] Down the road, a *saturation tendency* can be predicted, as "relentless cultural bombardment"[26] effaces cultural specificity, rendering Third World cultures "gradually indistinguishable from the center."[27] In these triumphalist visions of globalization, a Filipino "remake" of *Fatal Attraction* may be deemed an ultimately desirable product. It reproduces the kind of text and spectatorship forged by the all-powerful cultural imperialist. Apart from bearing the imprimatur of Hollywood, *Is It a Sin to Worship You?* becomes the sort of copy that gets locals hooked on the real thing. The more dynamic but equally totalizing scenario of *peripheral corruption* evokes the corrosive effect of cultural appropriation on the Hollywood original and the cultures of globality. In this view, *Fatal Attraction* and other Western cultural goods are turned into defaced local versions. As Hannerz puts it, "The periphery first adopts [Western originals] and then soon corrupts them." With such fundamentally "bizarre" objects as a Filipino *Fatal Attraction* stealing Hollywood revenue and vandalizing Western culture, this view predicts that "the center, in the end, cannot win; not at the periphery."[28] Alternatively, or perhaps in the long run, a "maturation tendency" might be observed as the Third World periphery "takes its time reshaping metropolitan culture to its own specifications." The prospect of cultural corruption fades in this scenario because "local cultural entrepreneurs have gradually mastered the alien cultural forms . . . taking them apart, tampering and tinkering with them." The end result is some kind of harmonious assimilation, as Hannerz writes, wherein "metropolitan forms are somehow no longer so easily recognizable—they become hybridized."[29] It is also possible, as Hannerz notes, to imagine the incomplete realization of these different scenarios and tendencies in a continuum, an "ongoing, historically cumulative cultural interrelatedness between center and periphery."[30] In this *creolization scenario*, already impure cultures interact with one another in "a gradation of living syntheses," resulting in various unpredictable outcomes.[31] They are in the process of realization and therefore are, as yet, incomplete.

What remains undecided, then, is whether the Filipino remake of *Fatal Attraction* should be deemed "corrupt," "mature," or "creolized," or whether it should be lodged firmly within any of these descriptors. My quibble with these distinctions and with the scenarios discussed in the previous two paragraphs is their tendency to invoke extreme outcomes in cross-cultural interactions. Diverse cultural elements are either pitted against each other so relentlessly as to repress instances of complicity or negotiation or, in the case of the hybridization outcome, seem to be forced into impossibly dramatic synthesis. I am less interested in taking the typical route of emphasizing cultural domination or resistance than in exploring those relationships to Hollywood that are not so much confrontational as they are complicit. I wish to explain more moderate (and arguably more typical) outcomes of cultural transactions. I also wish to uncover elements that link rather than sunder foreign and domestic texts, as well as global and local subjects. In the following sections, I elaborate the ways in which Filipinos use American fantasies as an imaginary resource to accumulate cultural possessions, to engage in mundane cosmopolitan acts, and to project themselves as participants in global culture.

Fidelity, Commensurability, and "Taking It on the Face": *Is It a Sin to Worship You?*

Indigenization does not adequately name the cultural work implicit in the unauthorized Filipino remake of *Fatal Attraction*. From its opening credits, *Is It a Sin to Worship You?* declares its fidelity to the American film by presenting close substitutions for numerous details of the Hollywood original. The camera tracks the gorgeous stockbroker Catherine Posadas (Vivian Velez) as she commutes to her office in the financial district of Makati. Though she does not share the profession of Glenn Close's character, Alex Forrest, who works as an associate editor at a New York publishing house, Catherine holds the quintessential yuppie job in the Philippine equivalent to Manhattan. Similarly, the counterpart of the lawyer Dan Gallagher (Michael Douglas), though reimagined as a real estate developer, is the perfect Philippine yuppie figure of the "Makati executive." In a playful allusion to the American film, this role, played by Julio Diaz, is assigned the name Alex Katigbak, after the first name of Close's character. The Filipino substitute for Anne Archer, who plays Gallagher's spouse, is Dawn Zulueta (Grace). Instead of playing a housewife like Archer, Zulueta inhabits the role of another yuppie figure: a gym owner and aerobics instructor. These substitutions of the lead characters' occupations are closer to the spirit of the original than we think. What is *Fatal Attraction* after all but a parable of urbanite decadence and the career folk whose privileges, neuroses, and decline came to be associated with the epithet "yuppie" in 1980s argot? As Janet Maslin writes in the *New York Times*, "Years hence, it will be possible to pinpoint the exact moment that produced 'Fatal Attraction,' Adrian Lyne's new romantic thriller, and the precise circumstances that made it a hit. It arrived at the tail end of the having-it-all age, just before the impact of AIDS on movie morality was really felt."[32]

The small details announcing the petty bourgeois excesses of the "having-it-all age" in *Fatal Attraction* are easily grafted by *Is It a Sin to Worship You?* onto the affluent Third World metropolis of Makati. Local color and the topography of uneven development spell the variance between the two films. Their disparities notwithstanding, we find the same markers of yuppie material culture in both. In both *Fatal Attraction* and *Is It a Sin to Worship You?*, the husbands sport eyeglasses with trendy oversized rims, while the mistresses swoop into the frame in striking all-white ensembles. In both films they dine in white tablecloth restaurants where they flirt while soaking up the classy ambience. These yuppie folk also insist on their distinction by using white telephones—those worldwide icons of bourgeois melodrama—to trade intimacies, insults, and grave threats.[33] Even these yuppies' sense of casual refinement is strikingly commensurable across such seemingly distinct cultures, as evinced by how the Filipino characters emulate their American counterparts' preparation of fancy spaghetti. Glenn Close's character makes her pasta while listening to Puccini's *Madama Butterfly* and then consumes the dish as Michael Douglas's character talks about his and his father's bittersweet childhood outing at the Metropolitan Opera. For her part, Vivian Velez's character heightens the Italian accent on her spaghetti by preparing it in a slightly uncommon, upper-middle-class way: *alla carbonara*, instead of the sweetened Bolognese style preferred by most Filipinos. The trappings of a "dominant imaginary of global capitalism" account in part for these correspondences between bourgeois cosmopolitan lifestyles in the First and Third Worlds.[34]

If we think of the Filipino rendition of *Fatal Attraction* as an exercise in cultural appropriation, the phrase "expedient translation" seems particularly apt in characterizing this case. John Tomlinson, who finds the term in a study of transnational advertising, uses it to describe how formulaic global ad campaigns are effectively localized by plainly substituting local symbols for foreign ones.[35] I wish to retain this idea of a simple but highly effective substitution, but what I want to emphasize at this point are the underlying conditions that allow for such commensurability. In *Is It a Sin to Worship You?*, the expediency of translation seems to have as much to do with the similarity in the cosmopolitan trappings of the New York–Makati petty bourgeois lifestyles as with the translatability of a mode of experience that is fundamentally characterized by its globality. The modularity of the "specific significance inherent in the original," which Walter Benjamin identifies as the precondition of translatability, is in this case traceable to some of the leveling effects of transnational capitalism on the formation of such subjects as the New York yuppies and "Makati executives."[36] These subjects from two geographic divides are in reality placed by multinational corporations in top-floor offices with abstracted views of the city. The view from those offices mimics the perspective of global bosses who imagine the Earth's terrain as an interchange for the transnational flow of commerce. Whether existing in the form of a Filipino stockbroker or an American intellectual property lawyer, yuppies are compelled to make projections of the global consequences of their local actions (or vice versa), and in some ways they all share the common fate of worrying about the health of the U.S. dollar. These impositions of advanced capitalism's global spread define not just the way yuppies do their work but also how they live.

The similarity between the American and Filipino species of yuppie is partly inflected by the historical moment that produced *Is It a Sin to Worship You?*: the increasing adoption of neoliberal economic policies in the Philippines and the concomitantly growing ease with which the nation accommodated both the flexibility of global capitalism and its cultural impact.[37] "Makati executives" had long been recognized for their cosmopolitan tastes that, to cite an example, sustained "exotic" German, Korean, Japanese, and Thai restaurants in a culinary environment once dominated by burger and fried-chicken joints. But the intensification of the state's "import liberalization" program starting in the 1980s made it easier for even the petty bourgeois to enjoy the trappings of a cosmopolitan lifestyle.[38] For many years during the Marcos regime, protectionist trade barriers had made Hershey bars and Washington apples precious even to the middle class. During the waning years of the dictator and following Corazon Aquino's takeover, the adoption of neoliberal economic policies intensified. With "import liberalization," everything from big cans of Planters' brand cheese curls to Nintendo video games and Swatch watches began to flood supermarkets and newly constructed malls at dramatically more affordable prices.

It is from within this "scene" of Filipinos ingesting, wearing, and being surrounded by such forms of American and "international" cultures in an intensified manner that certain details emerge and become culturally legible in films such as *Is It a Sin to Worship You?* Indeed, this "scene" is what gives rise to a moment of self-consciousness about globalization that can only be expressed through a cultural product whose surface and sensibility are visibly wrested from cosmopolitan cultures. It would not be too much of a stretch to say that the similarities in the operations of transnational capital between New York and Makati engender a noticeable sameness in the symbols that represent them. The mise-en-scène of movies is certainly one of the forms such symbols or figurations might take.[39]

There are many deep as well as superficial similarities between *Is It a Sin to Worship You?* and *Fatal Attraction*. That said, one cannot wholly reduce them to the sameness that globalization breeds. One must also account for the methods of transculturation or cultural translation involved in turning *Fatal Attraction* into a Filipino movie.[40] I mentioned earlier that *Is It a Sin to Worship You?*'s substitutions and minor alterations to the plot of the Hollywood film seem to follow the principle of an expedient translation. I will discuss this process more fully in the next paragraphs. In *Fatal Attraction*, the smart, intense, and emotionally unstable female executive falls hard for a married man; in *Is It a Sin to Worship You?*, she falls for the man just when he is two weeks away from getting hitched. That the Filipina yuppie has just missed the train intensifies her desperation to get married and also deepens her obsession with Alex (because he could have easily been hers). When he pulls away from Catherine, the Filipina mistress, like her American counterpart, works the phone relentlessly, hounding his secretary by day, and rousing the couple from sleep in the small hours by making crank calls and throwing stones at their windows.

A cosmetic substitution is made for the scene in *Fatal Attraction* where Alex exacts revenge on Dan by introducing herself to his wife and, later, harassing her. Glenn Close's character presents herself as a prospective buyer of the couple's apartment. Later, she terrorizes the entire family by kidnapping their child for an afternoon at the carnival (they take a hair-raising roller-coaster ride) and boiling the family's pet rabbit in their kitchen. In *Is It a Sin to Worship You?*, Catherine uses the office messenger to send the wife a series of progressively hostile gifts: a bouquet of white flowers, a bouquet of rotten flowers, and finally—in lieu of the rabbit—a cake box containing dead frogs. *Is It a Sin to Worship You?*'s transculturation of a Hollywood film calls for numerous but easy substitutions and changes to the story and visuals. Inasmuch as it involves performing simple acts of recoding cultural signs and reconciling minor cultural differences, "expedient translation" seems to me a fitting description of Roño's work.

It is important to note that *Is It a Sin to Worship You?*, like other transculturated objects of Philippine globalization, flaunts rather than hides the traces of its cultural borrowing. Apart from its mercenary aims, I interpret this flaunting as a gesture of mundane cosmopolitanism. It shows off the "cultural competence" of the filmmakers and performers in interpreting a work of global import.[41] Let me offer a specific example. One of the highlights of the revenge plot in *Fatal Attraction* finds the mistress spilling a corrosive substance over the husband's Volvo station wagon. This ruins the hood and roof, rendering the car useless. In what might, on the surface, seem like a radical substitution, the mistress in *Is It a Sin to Worship You?* redirects the dangerous fluid to the wife's face instead of her early model Mitsubishi Galant. What do we make of the fact that the Filipina actress (and her character) takes it on the face? While it might be tempting to read this act as unintended metacommentary on the self-destructive tendencies of overzealous copycat filmmaking, the self-punishing displacement of the acid onto the Filipina's face ought to be recognized as a convention of Philippine melodrama. Among the scorned women of Philippine cinema, it is the quintessential form of revenge. Like playing a mental patient or a brain cancer survivor, getting doused with acid is a reliable way of earning critical praise. Taking it on the face is an actress's ultimate challenge. It gives her ample room for histrionics without grating on the viewers' nerves. By taking it on the face, Dawn Zulueta gets to take on the sort of go-for-broke acting challenges that Anne Archer tackles in two scenes from *Fatal Attraction*. Apart from the rabbit-boiling scene, which requires Archer to telegraph an emotional breakdown in an instant of absolute terror, the American actress must also register extreme dread in a flash when she realizes that her daughter has been kidnapped by her husband's deranged mistress. Sans rabbit and kidnap scenes, Zulueta gets to try her hand at projecting horror, convulsing in excruciating pain, and letting out an eardrum-piercing scream. What is more, she outdoes Archer by getting to play "blind" (actually, her eyes are just covered with patches) and having to grope and limp her way all over the hospital as the mistress tries to kill her and her husband.

Vivian Velez, who plays Glenn Close's character, also gets to do her own equivalent of "taking it on the face." One of Glenn Close's acting moments involves a scene that shows her compulsively switching the lamp on and off as she sulks in a corner of the room. Her expression, posture, and behavior signal with striking efficiency and great dramatic impact her total descent into madness. In *Is It a Sin to Worship You?*, the moment is showier and enhanced with dialogue. After hiding Grace's drugged body in an empty room, Catherine slips into a darkened conference hall where, by switching the light in the rostrum

A corrosive substance is thrown at the face of the wife (Dawn Zulueta) rather than on the husband's car, allowing the Filipina actress to play her Anne Archer role to the hilt. Source: Is It a Sin to Worship You? *and* Fatal Attraction.

on and off, she alternately emerges from and vanishes into the dark, all the while cursing Alex for his deceptive ways. The intermittent flashes of illumination from the rostrum light makes Velez's expression seem more murderous than Close's blank look. Moreover, the escalating anger in the former's delivery of curses—which goes from restrained teeth gnashing to full-blown histrionics—takes a flashier route than Close's absentminded lamp-switch fiddling. To "take it on the face" is, therefore, to play it to the hilt, to overzealously emulate, or even to have the temerity to outdo the Hollywood original. The self-consciousness of the reproduction, revealed by the overcompensating local substitution of the original gesture, allows these Filipina actresses to "do a Glenn Close" or "do an Anne Archer" in ways that both evoke and try to outclass (rather than efface) the original performance.

As I have noted earlier, the appropriation of these American roles into opportunities for projecting the self as world-class talent may be regarded as a form of "mundane cosmopolitanism" for the filmmakers and, especially, the Filipina actresses.[42] Interestingly enough, magazine articles about the two actresses play up their real-life pursuit of the cosmopolitan lifestyle. Velez, they say, drives "down Sunset Boulevard in a top down Cadillac,"[43] opened the Sepulveda Clinic in Los Angeles, and travels abroad to recharge her batteries and gain "new insights on things and people."[44] Reports also mention that she is looking forward to "be doing an ala-Kim Basinger role" in *Computer Man*, a television series that looks and sounds like the 1980s' *Automan*, starring Desi Arnaz Jr.[45] Zulueta, for her part, has Palestinian blood, is the "articulate, 21-year-old daughter of the Makati upper middle class,"[46] and would like to "pattern her life after those of her idols—Jacqueline Onassis, Elizabeth Taylor and Grace Kelly."[47]

The Filipina actresses' substitute performances for Close's and Archer's are not only recognizable as such through their overcompensating zeal in "taking it on the face." The minor plot alterations and scrupulous reproduction of the Hollywood film's surface produce a screen upon which the Filipina actresses' portrayals are projected as "global" or "international" instantiations of *Fatal Attraction*. The play of fidelity and minor difference thus allows the film and the performances to be seen as sophisticated cosmopolitan acts rather than as irredeemably corrupt Third World imitations—or, to borrow another writer's phrase, "the defaced, spurious image of . . . valuable metropolitan originals."[48]

When the Third World "does" Hollywood—for example, taking *Fatal Attraction* "on the face"—it engages in a mundane and oft-ignored kind of global cultural citizenship that is arguably no less important (and no less "global") than the Metropolitan Opera doing a really great *Madama Butterfly*. Cultural citizenship, according to the anthropologist Lisa Rofel, is a way of expressing affinity to a group through cultural, rather than political, acts.[49] In an era of globalization, myriad desires for belonging and forms of inclusion take shape through a wide array of "transcultural ideas and practices."[50] The practice of appropriation that *Is It a Sin to Worship You?* represents is an expression of bourgeois desires for cosmopolitan belonging and even the fantasy of economic and cultural commensurability between the metropole (New York, Glenn Close) and the periphery (Makati, Vivian Velez).

But there is another nuance to "taking it on the face" that begs discussion, one that points to another possible meaning of expedient translation. "Taking it on the face" also points to a tendency not to internalize the more alienating or unacceptable elements of the American fantasy being reproduced and thus to mark one's ownership and control over a certain cultural import or vision of globality. For instance, in terms of the plot, the violent act of Volvo-trashing depicted by the American film is not fundamentally transformed or repurposed in the Filipino version but merely stretched out for spectacular purposes, recoded to enhance its familiarity, and staged with a minimum of damage to property. (Yes, some of the "acid" purposely lands on the car to produce smoke, but no car hoods were trashed, as was probably the case in *Fatal Attraction*.) My notion of the externality that is represented by the gesture of "taking it on the face" is partly inspired, as in the previous chapter, by a deliberate repurposing of the following quote from Elsaesser: "Rather than internalise the latent conflicts which German postwar history and the legacy of a particular culture had programmed into them, feminist and gay film-makers in particular tried to restage traumas in their films, often making the body itself the site of division, transgression and the transformation of sexual identity."[51]

Elsaesser's description of the logic behind the exhibitionism and narcissism of the new German cinema is an especially rich section of his monograph. Here I would like to focus very narrowly on his notion of the filmmakers' recourse to superficiality and specularization as

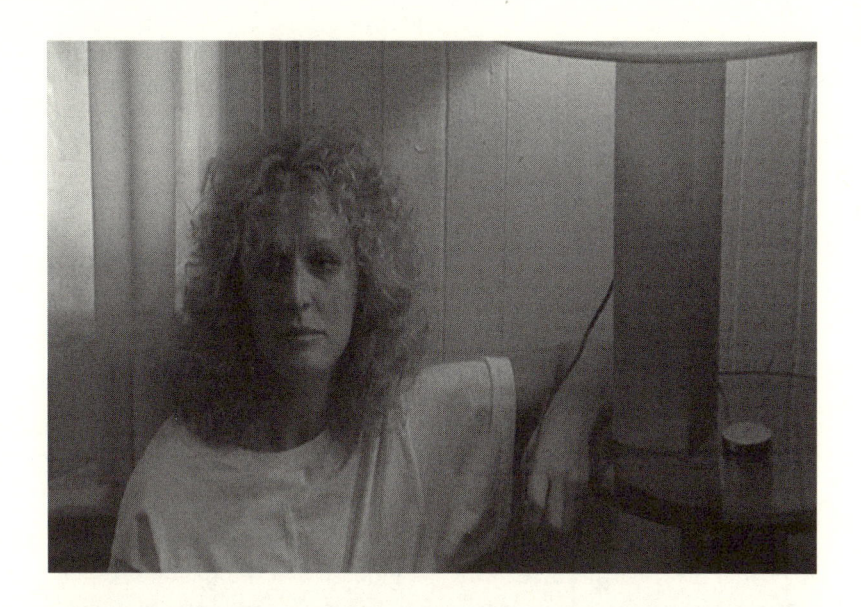

Vivian Velez "does a Glenn Close." Source: Fatal Attraction *and* Is It a Sin to Worship You?

a way of refusing to internalize certain cultural, historical, or ideological elements. Elsaesser's description of the politics behind this refusal of internalization points to a much more serious, even agonistic, valence to the gesture than I would recognize in the Filipina actresses' taking it on the face. I think of this move in *Is It a Sin to Worship You?* to keep things at face value as a specific practice of expedient translation. Taking it on the face is a way in which Philippine cinema engages in the "rapid" and "incomplete" retransmission of Hollywood's globalizing culture.[52]

Hannerz identifies a way of engaging selectively with global culture that results from a "sense of mastery" and control: "The cosmopolitan may embrace the alien culture, but he does not become committed to it. All the time he knows where the exit is."[53] I suggest that "taking it on the face," as a recourse to superficiality, is an assertion of such mastery and control, even if it comes from a very marginal place within the cultures of globality. "Taking it on the face" can also mean not taking it to heart. This tactic attempts to effect a truncated and selective globalization.

Our understanding of this significance of "taking it on the face" is important in apprehending the more dramatic alterations to the film's plot and moral discourse. In *Is It a Sin to Worship You?* we see a refusal to delve deeply into the moral quagmire sitting just below the surface of the adultery plot. First, Catherine does not internalize the complex psychological and moral afflictions of her New York counterpart. The American mistress goes mad because of an implied overattachment to her father whose death she supposedly witnessed as a young child. In the film's account of the female yuppie's madness, Alex Forrest may have been taken to the edge by the tremendous pressures of her career. She seems to be hitting the glass ceiling at work and even in her personal life, where the marital status of the men she likes sets a socially imposed limit. Like many yuppies, she fully believed that she could make great things happen with her youthful charm and Ivy League pedigree. But, as it often turns out, her ascent up the corporate stratosphere is stalled by an unsupportive male boss. Moreover, in her love life Alex suffers the indignity of getting dumped by her very own yuppie ilk, in this case a suit who shares her father issues and love of culture. The married couple, played by Douglas and Archer, are not much better off. Like Alex, their neuroses stem from the yuppie's delusions of entitlement. The husband wants a disposable mistress while the wife wants to move their ostensibly joyful existence piecemeal into a nice suburban house.

Is It a Sin to Worship You? ignores the yuppie neuroses in the Hollywood film. Catherine goes mad simply because mental illness runs in the family. Her mother, Emma (Angie Ferro), is as crazy as they come, and Catherine is candid about the great likelihood of her eventual descent into madness. "I am the daughter of a madwoman," she screams at the funeral of her aunt, whose death she blames on her mother, the last caretaker of the deceased. "Death is my only escape from such a curse!" A visual reminder of this fate is conveniently planted within the mise-en-scène, in the form of clown and jester dolls strewn all over Catherine's house. By reducing Catherine's illness to a hereditary affliction, *Is It a Sin to Worship You?* misses the opportunity to transmit *Fatal Attraction*'s commentary on the misogyny of yuppie culture. The Filipino picture finds a different moral statement to make, however, as I will discuss shortly.

Apart from not having Catherine internalize the American woman's hysteria, *Is It a Sin to Worship You?* also excises the thorny issue of the mistress's pregnancy. Unlike the American mistress, the Filipina mistress does not get pregnant from the affair. In *Fatal Attraction*, the mistress's death at the hands of the married couple has the (un)intended effect of killing her unborn lovechild. The tub drowning scene, vaguely inspired by Henri-Georges Clouzot's *Les Diaboliques* (1955), shows the husband almost drowning his mistress before the wife intervenes and shoots her. With the bullet that Beth fires at the mistress's forehead, the wife bails out her husband and also causes the abortion that Alex refused to have. By killing Alex and her unborn child, Beth reinstates herself and her daughter Ellen into their secure place in Dan's life. By leaving out these complicated and disturbing plot turns, *Is It a Sin to Worship You?* comes up with a version that is more acceptable to Philippine censors and also unburdened of the stigma of a double homicide.

In the second vital alteration to the plot, the film moves the final confrontation from the suburban home in *Fatal Attraction* to a large hospital in *Is It a Sin to Worship You?*, where the wife, Grace, is confined after the mistress's attack. Catherine, dressed as a nurse, attempts to finish off the wife, who is still under sedation and has bandaged eyes. Alex locates the two women just as his wife is about to be killed. A struggle ensues, which ends with the mistress—not the wife, as in *Fatal Attraction*—pulling the trigger of the gun being pointed at her by the husband. The shot blasts through Catherine's head, spilling her brains and blood everywhere (some of it landing on the Filipina wife's face and also on her husband's). The more gruesome execution in *Is It a Sin to Worship You?* is matched by a simple but important detail in the film's last shot that radically departs from the intent of the American original. *Fatal Attraction* ends by reinstating the patriarch and restoring his suburban family. After the mistress's body is taken away and the cops leave, the husband and wife embrace each other and stay in each other's arms as they exit the frame. The camera pans to focus on a framed photograph of the happy family. Clearly the disturbance has been safely pushed back to the distant past.

Is It a Sin to Worship You? tellingly omits the Hollywood ending. The Filipino movie concludes with the wife rejecting her husband's succor. Grace makes this gesture when Alex tries to push her wheelchair and take her back to her hospital room. Though visibly enfeebled by trauma, Grace stalls the wheels of the chair, stands up and walks to the elevator, leaving her husband speechless. Instead of conniving with the errant husband in disposing of the mistress, as did the wife in *Fatal Attraction*, the Filipina wife hangs on to the words of the fallen mistress. Moments before Catherine pulls the trigger that will end her own life, she chides Alex for being an expert at "picking things to destroy," for pitilessly "crushing my heart to pieces," and for having "no balls." Her words make Grace see her husband for who he really is: a man unworthy of the fatal attraction that drove Catherine to her grave. Far from being an abrupt development, Grace's sensitivity to the other woman's predicament is depicted earlier in the film. When Catherine begins her destructive streak, Grace asks Alex to recount how he had mistreated the hysterical lady. When he refuses, telling her that she simply would not understand, Grace voices her suspicion that he had a big hand in the sordid mess: "Well, maybe it's better that I don't try to understand because it seems that what happened between the two of you would just make me throw up." Later, when the reprisal from Catherine escalates, Grace blames her husband once more: "I'm a woman, too. I can somehow imagine what that crazy woman is going through. You let her fall in love with you even if you knew you were already spoken for. You kept her hopes high and then you abandoned her. That would drive anyone nuts! Damn it!"

Is It a Sin to Worship You?'s ending, along with the film's other sharp feminist touches, may be attributed to the female cowriter (Raquel Villavicencio) and the smart U.S.-educated male director (Roño) and cowriter (Reyes), all of whom possess a good track record of producing gender-sensitive representations. A review by film scholar Joel David praised the film for having female lead characters that "are not your traditional faithful-loving-long suffering types, but as bad as contemporary local female bad can be."[54]

In the spirit of an expedient translation, *Is It a Sin to Worship You?* takes as much as it can from *Fatal Attraction*. It leaves out what is messy and expensive and only tries to improve upon a few vital things. In sum, what the Filipino rendition gives back to American cinema is nothing shabby: a tribute, a corrective, and a picture of the sameness that Hollywood and global capitalism have wrought upon the mise-en-scène of Third World lives and movies.

Complex Transmutations and Global Acts: *Loretta* and the Bobbitts

If "taking it on the face" describes *Is It a Sin to Worship You?*'s route to the cultures of globality, the Filipino reworking of Lorena Bobbitt's saga adopts a different strategy. Recoding the American tale of spousal abuse and genital mutilation into an instrument of Third World feminist pedagogy, the Filipino picture avoids the faithful reproduction of superficial details in favor of taking its pressing subject to heart.

On June 23, 1993, Lorena Bobbitt mutilated her husband John's penis. The lurid details of the incident, as well as the timing of its news coverage, made it an easy target for appropriation by Philippine cinema. The Bobbitts' story appeared in the newsstands and on television at a time when true crime stories were all the rage in Philippine cinema. The local multiplexes hit pay dirt with films based upon sensational tabloid-based fodder, like *The Vizconde Massacre Story: God Help Us!* (Carlo J. Caparas, 1993), a docudrama about a triple murder in an upper-middle-class subdivision.[55] As the Bobbitt cases went to court, a biopic about Lorena Bobbitt was publicized in Philippine media. Ruffa Gutierrez, a Filipina American actress and runner-up in the Miss World beauty pageant, reported to the media that the project was in development and that she was attached to star in it. Months later, when it came time to publicize the completed film, Gutierrez contradicted her previous statements. She emphatically stressed to entertainment journalists that the project had nothing to do with the American incident. It appears that the producers did not bother or did not think they could afford to secure the rights to the Bobbitts' story.

Probably to fend off legal action, the film dispenses with many of the details of the Bobbitts' marriage and trials. A disclaimer at the beginning of the film echoes the star's claim that the story line is fictitious, but the simple change in the last syllable of the protagonist's name, the retention of her initials ("Lorena Bobbitt" becomes "Loretta Bautista"), and the press's constant mention of the Bobbitt case in relation to film made the intertextual relation between the two fairly obvious. The packaging for the VCD (video compact disc) release of the film even contradicts the disclaimer in the opening credits by indicating that the film "was based upon real events."

In his book *Globalization and Culture*, John Tomlinson writes of the "complex transmutations of cultural practices and forms" occurring in globalization.[56] What Tomlinson describes is the process of hybridization, a term preferred by many scholars of global culture but that I find inadequate to describe the example at hand. Because the makers of *Loretta* bear the burden (and possess the freedom) of reimagining the entire story line of the film, they are called to perform one of those truly "innovative acts of cultural brokerage" that is of a substantially different nature than the expedient translation of *Fatal Attraction* into *Is It a Sin to Worship You?*[57] Once again, I wish to adapt a term in order to name a process that has not been adequately described in current literature. The second word in the term "complex transmutation" is more accurate than "translation," which I used previously to describe the Filipino rendition of *Is It a Sin to Worship You?* In the case of *Loretta*, there is not an "original" film for which it serves as a commensurable rendition in another language. "Transmutation," on the other hand, suggests a "conversion into something different" and thus additionally captures the nuance of the Bobbitt incident's appropriations into a porn video and a Third World movie.[58] What is interesting, as I will explain in the following sections, is how the drastic transformations in *Loretta* seem to result not so much in the cannibalization of the Bobbitt "text" but in a deep engagement with it. The Third World film serves as a critical interlocutor both of the "text" of the mutilation incident and of the American video.

In the same year that *Loretta* played the big screen, a well-publicized American film about the incident hit adult theaters and home video. In contrast to the Filipino adaptation's focus on the battered wife, *John Wayne Bobbitt Uncut* (Ron Jeremy, 1994) revolves around the husband and his surgically reattached penis. In spite of John Wayne Bobbitt's proprietary claim over his life story, this video—which is equal parts docudrama, biopic, and porn movie—also leaves out most of the details of his marriage with Lorena. Even the scene of genital mutilation is staged in a campy manner appropriate to porn. Additionally, the video box comes with the following fine-print disclaimer: "The fantasies of John Wayne Bobbitt . . . are not under any circumstances to be construed as real or factual portrayals of persons and incidents." Strange as it may sound, *Loretta* and *John Wayne Bobbitt Uncut* are united not only by their "factual" basis but also by their forced recourse to fictionalization. They divulge what it might mean to fantasize under duress. However, there is a great divergence of interests in their "filmization" of the Bobbitt story. *John Wayne Bobbitt Uncut* projects a compensatory fantasy. The protagonist's working-class masculinity is synecdochically repaired through the reattachment of the penis and through its concomitant rebirth as a prized entity among social dilettantes, adult film vixens, and medical professionals. For its part, *Loretta* tries to offer something more substantial than the delectations of true crime material. Among the various things the film attempts is to draw elements from the American incident, recode them in the local idiom, and use them to expose the operations of patriarchy across a class-divided Philippine society.

What kind of transcultural dialogue takes place between *Loretta* and Lorena? What does *Loretta* do for Lorena? The U.S. media coverage of the Bobbitt incident raised questions of culpability: Did she do it in self-defense or as a vendetta? Should he be acquitted for abusing her just because she cut him? *Loretta* makes it unmistakably clear that the woman is the victim. The film is fueled by polemical and pedagogical intent, its plot unraveling as an exposé. Its itinerary is organized by an attempt to exhaust the permutations of how women are exploited within the film's Third World milieu. To lend coherence and emotion to the composite narrative of the Filipino Bobbitt story, the tale of

Loretta is narrated in voice-over by the victim, who recalls her harrowing experiences as a battered wife in contemporary Philippine society.

Given that Loretta and Lorena (a native Venezuelan) are both Third World women, it is fitting that the movie begins at one of the most familiar dwelling places of subaltern women. *Loretta* opens at a garment factory where our heroine works behind one of countless sewing machines, making pretty dresses for export to the West. The scenario faintly resembles Lorena Bobbitt's lowly occupation at a nail salon where the immigrant performed her share of alienated labor for the pleasure of American clients. But whereas Lorena Bobbitt supposedly enjoyed the occasional privilege of skimming the nail salon's earnings, her Filipina counterpart suffers the alienation of the quintessential sweatshop employee. Loretta and her coworkers are pressed into nonstop service. As she describes it, the awful working conditions make them feel "like prison inmates" whose only wish is to escape from their "cages." So oppressive is her lot that the film's story can only offer her a fantastic escape: the possible fulfillment of her childhood dream to win a beauty pageant. "Ever since I was a child, I had had the ambition to become Miss Universe," she says in the narration while still ensconced within the "cage" of the factory. Initially, she thinks that attending beauty school will be the route to this dream. She quits her factory job and gives her ambitions a shot.

The luckless woman soon discovers that like sweatshops, the glamour business of pageants can also be oppressive to females. The film demonstrates this through a lesson in female objectification. Not having finished beauty school, Loretta sees the opportunity to live out her beauty contest dreams, albeit on a drastically smaller stage than the Miss Universe pageant. While window shopping at a mall, she is spotted by a talent scout named Chiki (Manny Castañeda), who encourages her to compete in a small-time beauty contest called Pearl of Metro Manila. Loretta and her aunt spend considerable money on her makeover, clothes, and publicity shots, but all of it is for naught. Loretta loses the pageant all because, Chiki alleges, of her "cheapo competitors'" maneuverings.

Despite her loss, Loretta succeeds nonetheless in effecting her own commodification. She catches the eye of the handsome and wealthy Richard Eloriaga (Gabby Concepcion), a friend of one of the pageant judges. The next day, Richard drives up her street in a Mercedes, and behind it is a van full of expensive clothes, shoes, and gifts. Loretta, her talent scout, and Aunt Remy are instantly convinced that the young woman has found her Prince Charming. The film reminds us however that, as with the widely imported American fantasy of beauty pageants, the business of trading on your looks encourages people to treat you like an object. The uncouth aunt calculates the price of the Charles Jourdan shoes given to Loretta while the couple stands in front of her. Loretta herself acknowledges a week later that she has been bought. When her suitor takes her to the rooftop of the building owned by his late father, he proposes to her and tells her jocundly that he will jump to his death if she does not accept his offer. Too weak to resist his charm and money, Loretta asks him, "Hey, who do you think I am; something you bought at the takeout counter?" Indeed, like a carryout item, he immediately brings her to the family home, where she is introduced to his mother. Mrs. Eloriaga (Rosemarie Gil) instinctively begins to treat her like his trophy wife. Instead of asking Loretta questions about her work or family background, the future mother-in-law tests her worth by posing in front of the mirror with her. "I want to know what we'll look like when people see us together in public," she tells her.

Richard (Gabby Concepcion) buys out Loretta (Ruffa Gutierrez) with a trophy and expensive gifts. Source: Loretta.

Upon getting married, Loretta Bautista begins to resemble Lorena Bobbitt more closely. Though the latter was married to a working-class husband and was perhaps much less of a trophy wife than her fictitious Filipina counterpart, both find themselves in lonely marriages to abusive and emotionally distant men. In the case of the real-life example, the lesser of these abuses included John Wayne Bobbitt allegedly harping on Lorena about the size of her breasts (he protested that what he really said was that "her butt was too big"), his lack of consideration for her sexual needs, and his habitual drunkenness.[59]

In a characteristic all-out effort to drive home a moral lesson, the film deliberately overplays most of the scenes that represent Loretta's alienation within her marriage. As the protagonist narrates, her mother-in-law does not even allow her to speak when visitors are present. To make the point absolutely clear, Loretta says it out loud: "Richard and his family are strict with me. Outside the house, he treats me like a piece of decor, something pretty he can show off to people. Inside the house, I feel that they still look down on me, especially Mrs. Eloriaga." Perhaps the most literal-minded portrayal of the young wife's isolation comes in a montage showing Loretta wandering around the farm while her husband and his macho buddies conduct illegal cockfights on the estate. In one shot, a glamorously overdressed and sullen-faced Loretta is seen crossing a shed packed with chicken coops. The comparison between Loretta and the caged hens that exist solely to lay eggs foreshadows her pregnancy. As the mother-in-law's pronouncements make clear later in the film, it is she, the family's grand matriarch, who assigns that pregnancy its existential meaning. To the elder Mrs. Eloriaga, Loretta's child is supposed to be a male heir who could realize Richard's failed ambition to perpetuate the family's political dynasty. When Loretta gives birth to a baby girl instead, the mother-in-law declares that the infant should grow up to become a nun so that she may redeem the "countless transgressions committed in the name of this family."

The film's serious political investment in the issue of spousal abuse is evinced by how it represents Lorena Bobbitt's claims of marital rape through a vocabulary of torture drawn from Philippine cinema's lurid true-crime movies. In the film, the frequent battery of the young wife is not only witnessed by household servants but also echoed a few doors away by Richard's equally heartless cousin, Odie (Toby Alejar). Odie routinely pounces on his diminutive wife, Adela (Jacklyn Jose). This abuse occurs in the singular space of a family-owned compound where fenceless houses are arranged close to each other in a semirectangular configuration. Within this closed little feudal society, powerful kinsmen impose their own law upon the weaker sex.[60] The beating of wives in *Loretta* is thus presented as a form of institutionalized violence. Loretta points this out to Adela, telling her that they have become part of a society of women who "always need to wear long sleeves" in order to conceal their bruises.

A different way of hyperbolizing domestic violence is employed in a scene where a combination of physical abuse, mental torture, and moral degradation calls into question a husband's sense of entitlement to his wife's body. In one of the lower points of the Bautistas' marriage, an inebriated Richard insists on having sex with his pregnant wife on top of his office desk. When Loretta reasons that it might harm their unborn child, the drunkard callously persists in entering her, while assuring her that "the baby would know how to dodge" its father's penis.

The film also makes the point that Loretta, like many women, suffers less severe but nonetheless traumatic forms of abuse on a daily basis.

Loretta (Ruffa Gutierrez) suffers the blows of an abusive patriarchy. Source: Loretta.

Early in her marriage, Loretta asks her aunt why "it hurts" when she has sexual intercourse with her husband. Aunt Remy pooh-poohs her grievance as the result of "not relaxing properly" and assures her by saying that "some women have a hard time during their first intercourse . . . [but] you'll start feeling pleasure as time passes." The young wife firmly insists, however, that the pain never goes away. Loretta's complaint echoes the extreme feminist position that every act of intercourse is inherently violent. As Barbara Ehrenreich puts it in her updating of the argument, "all too many women go home to Bobbitt-like fellows who regard the penis as a portable battering ram."[61]

John Wayne Bobbitt Uncut implicitly disputes Lorena's narrative of physical and sexual abuse. The porn video suggests that it is the female's unfulfilled desire for sexual pleasure that leads to violence against men. Moments before she lops off her husband's penis with a fillet knife, the porn video shows Lorena (Veronica Brazil) complaining about her husband's lack of interest in helping her reach orgasm. She grabs a knife from the kitchen, approaches her sleeping husband, and hisses, "If I can't have you, no one will!" The implicit justification for this scenario is something the traumatized wife supposedly said to the police during her questioning: "He always [has an] orgasm . . . He doesn't wait for me. He's selfish. I don't think it's fair."[62] Cynthia Fuchs notes the problem with the video's "hysterical revision" of the Bobbitt story: "Needless to say, perhaps, John is the hero here, an innocent jarhead menaced by the demonized Lorena."[63]

Upon closer inspection, it becomes clear that both motion pictures deal with the same issue of sexual pleasure and its relation to spousal abuse. *Loretta* makes the case that Richard derives pleasure from women's pain. The American porn video's Lorena, on the other hand, only seeks some mutuality. For the sexually deprived wife in the porn video, John Wayne's penis is not an injurious battering ram but a source of pleasure that is cruelly denied her. While I do not think the video is necessarily remiss in raising the question of the woman's sexual pleasure, the Filipino film version, not surprisingly, offers a more politically responsible depiction of the incident.[64]

In keeping with its didactic goals, *Loretta* takes pains to avoid endorsing violence as a response to spousal abuse. At the same time, it seeks to steer us away from faulting the protagonist for her husband's injury. The film depicts a series of events that mitigate her crime, namely, Richard's unrelenting cruelty leading up to the mutilation of his penis. Richard intensifies his habitual beating of Loretta. He pushes her down the stairs, and as a consequence, Loretta tries to end her life by slitting her wrists. Her mother-in-law arrives just in the nick of time and takes her to the hospital. Shortly after her physical recovery, however, Loretta witnesses her ordeal mirrored in the plight of Adela, her cousin-in-law and neighbor. Adela phones Loretta for help after suffering one too many beatings from her own husband. Loretta rushes to her only to find Adela's lifeless body splayed on the floor near a can of insecticide. The suicide shakes up Loretta, and she flees with her child after Adela's funeral. Richard and his posse catch up with her but, fortunately, not until she is able to entrust her baby to an old woman. The woman agrees to deliver it to Loretta's friend.

Loretta depicts an escalation of the heroine's trauma after the botched escape attempt. Tightening his grip on Loretta, Richard takes her to a provincial estate. There Loretta meets another victim of male violence. Like Adela, this new victim becomes Loretta's proxy. The new victim is referred to as "Ineng" (Jennifer Mendoza), a vernacular term for "young woman." Ineng is a "class-A certified virgin" who is offered

Adela (Jaclyn Jose) seeks Loretta's help moments before her death. Source: Loretta.

by the governor as prey in a cruel hunting game with his buddies, including Richard. She is instructed to run as fast as she can and hide herself in the bushes as the men pursue her for the chance to deflower a virgin. After the rape, as Loretta tends to Ineng, Richard comes out of the blue and drags Loretta away. The next scene shows the two women separately fleeing the estate before dawn. The film withholds Richard's "castration" and the immediate circumstances. It invites our momentary speculation that Loretta maimed her husband to avenge Ineng's abuse at the hands of Richard and his friends.

Details of the unspeakable event that led to the mutilation are disclosed only through court testimony, thus lending assurance that the law is bearing witness to the battered wife's plight. The first of the court testimonies is given by a slightly more effete Richard, whose penis is not reattached like his American counterpart's member. He admits to beating his wife "but only infrequently and within limits." The rest of the tale comes straight out of Loretta's mouth. She says the unplanned mutilation was the result of a series of abuses by Richard. First, he made her sexually available to the governor in exchange for helping him realize his own political ambitions. Richard thus converted his wife into economic and social capital in order to fill the most elusive gap in his masculine identity: his failure to sustain the family's political dynasty. Second, after subjecting Loretta to this traumatic experience, Richard violently reasserted his ownership of her body and her status as chattel by subjecting her to humiliating and cruel punishment. He anally raped her, then spat on her, and finally urinated all over her battered body. It was thus in an act of poetic justice that Loretta took away his prized masculinity with the help of a straight razor.

Interestingly, the female judge's decision, which she delivers directly to the camera, does more than validate Loretta's irresistible impulse to maim her husband as self-defense. She makes the enlightened point that Loretta resorted to violence not only to save her life but also "to defend her womanhood and her dignity." The law's sentence affirms the victim's reasoning, which Loretta earlier articulates in a voice-over: "I can suffer the physical wounds; those can be treated. But the wounds that lie within me, buried within my very self, will remain forever. If I don't finish this [fight], my child will have to inherit it. I don't want her to grow up ashamed of being female—always being molested, always being used by men. I am not mad at all men; just those who did this to me."

In the film's ultimate scene, Loretta is shown triumphantly exiting the courthouse when, from out of nowhere, a real-life lady politician (Senator Dominique Coseteng) occupies the foreground of the frame to trumpet her own achievements in women's rights advocacy.[65] While the lady politician's appearance wrests the spotlight away from Loretta, it also reaffirms the law's sympathy toward the abused woman's plight. Unfortunately, this rosy vision of feminist solidarity triumphing in court over patriarchy is an unlikely outcome. Certain Philippine laws—such as those on concubinage and adultery—are still much harder on women than on men. But insofar as this "fantasy" of Loretta's unequivocal success is meant to empower Third World women to step forward and fight spousal abuse, the exaggeration might be justified.

The triumph of the female victim in *Loretta* contrasts sharply with *John Wayne Bobbitt Uncut*'s ending. In the porn video, the abusive husband restates his claim to victimhood and reports soberly on his ongoing recovery. After ejaculating on porn star Tiffany Lords, John directly addresses the camera with this parting message: "Suddenly the old days seemed like another life, another person, a bad dream, a nightmare . . . This is my new life now. I like people and parties. Will it last? I dunno. I may even settle down soon, but until that day . . . let's party!" That calculated last note of bravado comes only after he speaks of his trauma, in the same way that his anecdote about living the high life is qualified by his working-class self-identification.

Despite its questionable gender politics, there is something to be learned from the porn video's ending. The video's upbeat portrayal of John Wayne's good fortune reflects the advantages he enjoyed over Lorena during and after the trial. John "grossed about $250,000 from his various scandal spin-offs" and was reported by tabloids to have purchased "a $45,000 Toyota Supra twin turbo" during a break from one of the trials. Lorena, on the other hand, was subjected to a month of psychiatric observation under strict confinement and, heavily burdened by hundreds of thousands of dollars in legal fees, received only "about $50,000 for television appearances that aired in her native South America."[66] *Loretta* jettisons this sad reality and militantly deprives the abusive husband of any claim to success. Leaving him with a permanently severed penis, the film poses a corrective to real life and also to the American porn video. "This," the Third World film says, "is how it ought to be."

The idea that the Third World film "talks back" to the metropole is something that cannot be discounted. To see the feminist lesson constituted by *Loretta* as a purely local act is to disavow the global significance of a peripheral culture's actions. Recovering from her suicide attempt, Loretta seeks help from her friend Nelia (Jenette Fernando), a former coworker at the factory who now works at the local women's crisis center and takes courses in women's studies at the university. Nelia counsels Loretta at the crisis center. Behind them posters about spousal abuse crowd the wall, many of them internationally produced, featuring English and Spanish captions: "Sisters, we've been silent long enough;" "You are nobody's property; you are yourself;" "The hidden weapons of abuse;" "He wouldn't hurt a flea but he would put his wife in a coma;" and finally, "Have we really gone a long way baby?" Nelia encourages Loretta to leave her husband and offers to help her resettle elsewhere. But Loretta still hesitates to end her marriage. "Are there really many others like me?" she asks Nelia. The friend reassures Loretta that she belongs to a global sisterhood of abused women who are now seeking strength in each other: "Yes, be they rich or poor, Filipino or not, they are not spared this kind of violence."

Loretta's friend Nelia (Jenette Fernando) assists her at a battered woman's shelter funded by international feminists.
Source: Loretta.

Loretta holds on to the validation and empowerment she finds in the rhetoric of this global female solidarity. Later in the film, her court testimony repeats almost verbatim some of the talk she hears at the women's center about the importance of preserving her dignity and fighting on behalf of her daughter. It is significant that Loretta receives this feminist lesson in a space of transnational sisterhood. This moment self-consciously thematizes the dialogue between local and global agents of feminism in which this film participates. The movie is an implicit cross-cultural reply to the question Loretta asks Nelia at the women's center: "Are there really many others like me?" In light of this transnational feminist dialogue, *Loretta* should be regarded not only as a cultural piracy of Lorena Bobbitt's life story but also as a Filipino expression of solidarity with her. In returning a more sympathetic retelling of her story, *Loretta* speaks to Philippine women while also performing an act of global sisterhood and thus engages in an unusual form of transnational activism.[67] As in the case of *Is It a Sin to Worship You?*, the Third World film gives something back to the First World and does so with a great sense of urgency and purpose.

Conclusion: Fatal Attractions and the Afterlife of American Fantasies

The scholarship on globalization and culture is correct in pointing out that a wide range of complex responses emerges in the encounter between local cultures and globally exported cultural forms. Where this academic corpus generally falters is in its paucity of specific case studies, often a result of scholars' unwillingness to closely study peripheral cultures and elucidate the complexity they acknowledge in theory.

In my analysis of the Filipino adaptations of *Fatal Attraction* and the Bobbitt incident, I have shown the advantages and limitations of concepts such as the *peripheral corruption scenario*, which envisions marginal cultures adopting and then defacing metropolitan culture. Both *Is It a Sin to Worship You?* and *Loretta* seem at times to succeed in improving upon vital aspects of the American texts rather than simply imitating or despoiling them. These improvements, however, do not point to the realization of the maturation tendency, wherein "the metropolitan forms are somehow no longer so easily recognizable."[68] In both of the films discussed in this chapter, very substantial elements of the American texts and the fact of their U.S. provenance are never fully occluded but are instead constantly invoked. I have suggested the value of two concepts—expedient translation and complex transmutation—in thinking about the different modes of cross-cultural appropriation that *Is It a Sin to Worship You?* and *Loretta* represent.

I have argued that the films reference their intertextual relations to the American originals because the local versions often gain legibility and value from being compared to their metropolitan sources. Opportunism is at work here, but it is an opportunism that is already a tactical response to those cultural impositions that have given prominence to the foreign originals. But it seems to me that there are other reasons besides mercenary ones that could explain why the foreignness of American fantasies is somehow preserved in their local renditions. One that I have explored in my reading of both films is the promise of cosmopolitan enfranchisement that comes with preserving some of the foreignness of appropriation. Acts of appropriation materialize fantasies of commensurability with metropolitan cultures and create opportunities for participating in the global realm of culture. I have shown how such desires for enfranchisement animate *Is It a Sin to Worship You?* The film envisions cross-cultural and transnational commensurabilities between Manhattan and Makati, revels in the filmmakers' self-conscious enterprise of remaking an American film, and suggests the actors' entitlement to the Hollywood repertoire. In their cultural translation of *Fatal Attraction*, the makers of *Is It a Sin to Worship You?* claim the prerogative to set the terms of cultural importation and retransmission (i.e., the prerogative of "taking it on the face") of global cultural objects.

In *Loretta*, we also see the desire for enfranchisement and the demand for comparison in the systematic transformation of a sensational American cause célèbre into a film that is both an instrument of Third World feminist pedagogy and a response of transnational feminist solidarity sent from the Third World to the First. The unintentional but still important corrective that the film poses to a politically irresponsible American porn movie is an assertion of global agency from those who are consigned to the margins of world cinema.

I have also proposed a shift away from a reading practice that views cultural appropriation as theft to one that tracks how and what these appropriated cultural productions give back. In this closing note, I submit that we can push this argument a bit further and say that we could also read, in the achievement of *Is It a Sin to Worship You?* and *Loretta*, not the maturation of the periphery but the decay of American originals as revealed by the emergence of their (un)faithful reproductions.[69] In a famous essay, Walter Benjamin describes the translation of a text as "a transformation and a renewal of something living."[70] The text, he says, enters its "afterlife" through the act of translation. The text survives beyond "the age of its origin"[71] and enjoys another life in a different language and culture. The homage and critique proffered by *Is It a Sin to Worship You?* and *Loretta* disclose problems with the American texts that Hollywood, for all its power, could not resolve. As such, these Third World renditions testify not simply to their secondariness as translations but to the decay of the originals—the reverse, in other words, of the peripheral corruption scenario. Thanks to the two Filipino movies, Lyne's film and Bobbitt's tale are revitalized by having been rerendered as instruments of Third World entertainment and pedagogy. These insights are easy to miss if we ignore the afterlife of Hollywood texts just because those cultural productions seem to have minor and local impact. These two films from the Third World show us that the global fate of American fantasies rests, in part, upon the imagination of local cultural entrepreneurs.[72] In their role as brokers of transnational cultures, Third World filmmakers create an afterlife for Hollywood movies, but not mainly through the acts of theft imagined by the Motion Picture Association of America. Sometimes the impoverished Third World also gives back, and what it returns to metropolitan culture is not just the flattery of imitation but the precious gift of a transformative renewal.

CODA

A Tale of Two Brothers

In the male melodrama *Dubai* (Rory Quintos, 2005), two Filipino brothers reunite in the desert country after spending five years apart. There, Raffy (Aga Mulach) and his younger brother Andrew (John Lloyd Cruz) find time to reassess their cosmopolitan ambitions. When they were growing up in Manila, the brothers had shared an American fantasy that was quite different from what I have been discussing in this book. Their fantasy brings into view a split image of the northern dreamland, another "kind" of America. When they were boys, Raffy and Andrew dreamed of migrating to Canada, the country where their late mother used to work. A snapshot of their mother reminds the Alvarez brothers of that dream. Significantly, it was taken at Niagara Falls, the fugitive border between the two North American countries.

For Raffy, however, the fantasy of going to "America" has already lost its allure. After nine years in Dubai, he has found community among his Filipino clients at the freight business where he works. He has even found love in Faye (Claudine Barretto), one of the two Filipinas he has been dating simultaneously.

Andrew feels betrayed by his brother's abandonment of their old plans. He also quickly falls in love with Faye, and until he musters the courage to confide in his brother, he becomes his brother's secret rival for her affections. But the brothers' conflict over romance and dreams of national belonging finds a surprisingly painless resolution in the course of the narrative. Besides affirming Raffy's claim over Faye, the film portrays Raffy's inclination to remain in the Middle East as a sound one. Life in Dubai is good, the film tells us. We see Filipino migrant workers barbecuing and frolicking at the beach, strolling casually in Western clothing, and talking giddily about their sexual relations with both Filipinos and Arabs. Raffy's fellow migrants speak constantly of the nearly zero crime rate in Dubai and of the world-famous seven-star hotel.

On a sandy beach in Dubai, two Filipino brothers ponder their future as immigrants. The older brother (Aga Mulach) plans to remain in the Arab state. The younger (John Lloyd Cruz) is bound for North America—not the United States but the more hospitable Canada. Source: Dubai. Courtesy of ABS–CBN Film Productions Inc.

Andrew tries his best to convince his brother to stick to their "American" fantasy. It is easy, he says, to gain citizenship in Canada. Taxes are high there, he admits, but the social services are exceptionally good. And, yes, Canada is great for sentimental reasons: their beloved, self-sacrificing mother once built a life there and had always dreamed of bringing her family together in that country. But Andrew ultimately fails to persuade Raffy. At the end of the film, the older brother reclaims his woman and declares that he will remain in Dubai. Andrew concedes and, without bitterness, leaves the Middle Eastern desert to follow his dream on the North American continent.

Dubai was made by the same company that, fifteen years prior, released *Hopefully, Once More*. The striking differences in their rhetoric about migration and the West suggest just how far, in the interim between the films, Filipinos have traveled along the divergent and convergent paths of decolonization and globalization. Whereas *Hopefully, Once More* settles for nothing less than repatriation for its protagonists, neither of the two brothers is summoned back home at the end of *Dubai*. Moreover, the film optimistically suggests that the brothers' dreams of seeking happiness and justice under capitalism are capable of being realized abroad. Whereas *Hopefully, Once More* foregrounds the American dream and portrays the agony of leaving San Francisco, the older brother in *Dubai* gives up "America" without a flicker of hesitation. The possibility of a final parting, which raises the stakes in *Hopefully, Once More*, is never entertained in *Dubai*. With the mobility afforded by their First World incomes, reuniting anywhere on the globe can no longer be seen as a problem for the Filipino brothers. Finally, in *Dubai*, the First World East is named alongside the West as a coveted haven for immigrants. The film challenges the myth of America's preeminence as the land of dreams. (In real life, a sharp economic downturn and high unemployment rate would prove hostile to foreign workers in Dubai—including many Filipinos—just a few years after the film's release.)

I end my study with this tale of the two brothers not to imply that, like Raffy Alvarez, Filipinos are jettisoning their American fantasies as they cross over from "the past" of decolonization to "the present" of globalization. Instead, I make the modest claim that Raffy's choice is suggestive of how the "American" question has become less central and tortuous in the face of what globalization presents as a diversity of cultural and geographical alternatives. If the challenge of reassigning the ex-colonizer's place in the national psyche is central to culture's work in decolonization, *Dubai* shows that remarkable progress has been made and that some colonial phantoms have already been banished from the map.

Of course, in exceptional cases, the colonial bonds may suddenly appear to be as strong as ever. For instance, in times of trouble for America or the Philippines, the ex-colony suddenly reattaches itself to the former colonizer. This scenario is not unfamiliar—such as when the Philippines deploys peacekeeping forces to help fight American wars, or when the ex-colony seeks American aid in rescuing the state and its people from coups d'etat and natural catastrophes. But when contentious issues relating to imperialism arise—as shown by the debates over the presence of U.S. forces, the rape of a Filipina by GIs, and the denial of Filipino World War II veterans' benefits by the U.S. Congress—Filipino sentiment instantly turns against their figural America with a vengeance.

This volatile relationship to American fantasies may be observed in other areas of Philippine media culture besides the cinema. Two cases illustrate this point. Michael Jackson's *Thriller* music video, to cite a recent example, has reemerged as a prison yard performance in Cebu province. Viewed through the video-sharing site YouTube, the choreography involved more than a thousand inmates. By spring 2008, the routine enjoyed fourteen million views on the Web site. The video shows how American popular culture has become so deeply entrenched that the mimicry of its scripts and rhythms can be used to regulate errant bodies. Even more striking, disciplinary power in a Philippine provincial jail has turned into pleasure and worldwide spectacle. American fantasy comes to be shown as a crucial means for drawing global interest to Third World cultural productions.

Several months after Jackson's death in June 2009, one of his former choreographers traveled to the same prison for a publicity stunt. The choreographer taught the inmates a new number based on *Michael Jackson's This Is It* (Kenny Ortega, 2009) to create a buzz for its home video release. The new routine enacted one of the film's highlights, a futuristic scene involving hundreds of dancing soldiers. Although simpler costumes and steps were used in the Philippine version, it surpassed the original in one respect. The dancing army in Ortega's film was the result of digital replication. Among the ex-colonized, however, one of Jackson's most extravagant visions attained its belated fulfillment. The Philippine version marshaled nearly 1,500 real persons, all of whom were paying a heartfelt tribute to the American star. And the tribute was nothing less than the wondrous image of rehabilitation in the ex-colony. Once again, the playbook for the globalization of Philippine culture draws heavily from an American fantasy.

The second case, a contrast to videos going viral, pertains to serialized television. Taking part in the international commerce of *telenovelas*, Filipinos act as receivers and transmitters of global culture without having to rely on American scripts. They dub Taiwanese soap operas, produce Filipino remakes of Korean and Mexican filmed entertainment, and export original serial dramas to countries such as Indonesia and Malaysia.

While I have shown why it is useful to try to mark the differences between American fantasies of decolonization and globalization, I wish to close by reiterating the diversity of the fantasies that could be found *within* these two categories. In this book's tour of the many American fantasies that have been conjured across the decades in

Philippine movies, I have shown the different valences and uses of the ex-colony's daydreams about the United States. As imaginary resources in the material form of national and transnational cinema, American fantasies have produced countercritiques of empire. They have aided the ex-colonized in weaving new fables of identity as they seek homes and fortunes outside their nation. They have coaxed a feudal, macho society into dreaming of alternatives to patriarchy and masculinist nationalism. They have provided the intangible capital for making cultural objects that speak to "universal" desires and sensibilities. They have opened up ways of mapping the self onto the playing fields and crossroads of globalization. No account of postcolonial and transnational cinema would be complete without recognizing the wide array of concerns taken up by the dream factories of the postcolony.

By contemplating the recurrence of certain kinds of American fantasies, I have also shown how the history of decolonization and globalization impinges upon these representations. Often, the relationship between the concerns of the day and the substance of the fantasies is not too obscure, such as when a nation's triumph in revolution engenders spectacular images of victory against neoimperialism. But there are instances, too, when the sociohistorical meanings of these fantasies seem largely inaccessible. For instance, it has proven difficult to interpret the significance of Amerasian tales of disaffection toward deadbeat white fathers and wayward Filipina mothers. But even such moments of fantasy's illegibility could be valuable in figuring the complexities of history and generating visions of novel cultural alternatives. Indeed, the capaciousness of fantasy inheres in its candid, imaginative language.

In my account, I cannot emphasize enough that the affects generated by these American fantasies—the feelings stirred by the depictions of decolonization and globalization—are *not* reducible to the flat, unequivocated anger of anticolonialism. Indeed, if there is something that characterizes American fantasies generally, it may be the complex and often sharply conflicted affects they bear. With its richly mimetic apparatus, able to accommodate a range of attitudes toward its objects of fantasy and to include even those modes in conflict with each other, cinema has proven to be a crucial site for the expression of these myriad, erratic affects. Toward the various American figures conjured by these cinematic fantasies, the Filipino characters have shown suspicion, fear, and pity (as in the monster movies); hopefulness (as in the dramas about the bases); spite (as in the Amerasian sagas); admiration and gratitude (as in the migrant woman's tales); melancholy and embarrassment (as in the diasporan narratives); tenderness and eroticism (as in the male stripper erotica); and empathy, ambivalence, and oneness (as in the appropriations of American movies and figures). The diversity and complexity of these affects suggests that, for Filipinos, a productive sense of the undecided (or the undecidable) characterizes their real and imagined relations to America and the First World. In the Filipino, ex-colonial, and Third World daydreams of the United States that I have drawn from the films discussed here, the figure of the American is never quite the same, and it rarely stays in place.

Cinema is one of the most popular forms of Third World culture. Its potential efficacy consists of the way in which the filmic medium places its viewers and practitioners in a mode of simultaneous vigilance and reverie. My hope is that this study of Philippine cinema's American fantasies will encourage readers and scholars to pay attention to the American fantasies of other nations and to Third World visions of the West. It is in sustaining dialogue within and across cultures that the Philippine films of decolonization and globalization, and those visions I have been calling American fantasies, find their most vital and urgent tasks. It is in the province of such fantasies about or directed at the other that we—as audiences and critics, as national and global citizens—are invited to dwell on the fugitive border of nations and selves, of local and global cinemas, and of dreams militantly pursued by one people or secretly longed for by many in the world. It is in such cinematic fantasies about the other that national histories are drawn in parallel; that the collective fate of global subjects is pondered; and that dreams of transforming subjects, nations, and world powers are bravely conjured. In the fantasies of Philippine cinema, the American specter begs the need for watchfulness from those whom it haunts and more so from those who summon it. Such watchfulness is invaluable if, as I have argued here, American fantasies are to succeed in their mundane work of registering national and geopolitical fractures and transformations.

Notes

Introduction

1. Nick Cullather, *Illusions of Influence: The Political Economy of United States–Philippines Relations, 1942–1960* (Palo Alto: Stanford University Press, 1994), 34.
2. Teodoro Agoncillo, *A History of the Filipino People* (Manila: Garotech, 1990), 432–34.
3. My use of the term "transcultural" follows Mary Louise Pratt. For her, "transculturation" denotes "what people on the receiving end of empire do with metropolitan modes of representation." See her *Imperial Eyes: Travel Writing and Transculturation*, 2nd ed. (New York: Routledge, 2008), 7–8.
4. Albert Memmi, *Decolonization and the Decolonized*, trans. Robert Bononno (Minneapolis: University of Minnesota Press, 2006), 97.
5. Jacqueline Rose, *States of Fantasy* (Oxford: Oxford University Press, 1996), 5.
6. Colin McCabe's introduction to *The Geopolitical Aesthetic: Cinema and Space in the World System* by Fredric Jameson (Bloomington: Indiana University Press, 1995), xi.
7. It is in the political unconscious that one finds the "repressed and buried reality" of history. It is also the province of "our collective fantasies about history and reality." See Fredric Jameson, *The Political Unconscious: Narrative as a Socially Symbolic Act* (Ithaca, N.Y.: Cornell University Press, 1981), 20, 34.
8. The ability of postcolonial films to draw new maps of imperial power may well be a feature of the elusive aesthetic of cognitive mapping that Fredric Jameson describes in his book *Postmodernism, or, the Cultural Logic of Late Capitalism* (Durham, N.C.: Duke University Press, 1991), 51.
9. Neferti Xina M. Tadiar, *Fantasy-Production: Sexual Economies and Other Philippine Consequences for the New World Order* (Quezon City: Ateneo de Manila University Press, 2004), 7.
10. Ibid.
11. Ibid., 23.
12. Ibid.
13. Ibid., 18.

14. Ibid., 22.
15. Rose, *States of Fantasy*, 15.
16. Ibid., 14.
17. Ibid., 15.
18. Jan Nederveen Pieterse and Bhikhu Parekh's introduction to *The Decolonization of Imagination: Culture, Knowledge, and Power* (London: Zed Books, 1995), 4, 6.
19. Ibid., 2–3.
20. Memmi, *Decolonization and the Decolonized*, 95.
21. Albert Memmi, *The Colonizer and the Colonized*, trans. Howard Greenfeld, expanded ed. (Boston: Beacon, 1991), 151.
22. John Mowitt, *Re-takes: Postcoloniality and Foreign Film Languages* (Minneapolis: University of Minnesota Press, 2005), 172.
23. Roy Armes, *Postcolonial Images: Studies in North African Film* (Bloomington: Indiana University Press, 2005), 25. Very similar to this notion of a double approach is Ella Shohat's concept of a "cinematic counter-telling" that engages in "reclaiming and re-accentuating colonialism and its ramifications in the present in a vast project of remapping and renaming." See her "Post-Third-Worldist Culture: Gender, Nation, and the Cinema," in *Rethinking Third Cinema*, ed. Anthony R. Guneratne and Wimal Dissanayake (New York: Routledge, 2003), 51.
24. "Empire" is the formulation of the new, decentered apparatus of rule that is "dynamic and flexible," "spread out over world space," and invested in the "production of [its] legitimacy." See Michael Hardt and Antonio Negri, *Empire* (Cambridge, Mass.: Harvard University Press, 2000), 13–15. In David Harvey's *The New Imperialism* (Oxford: Oxford University Press, 2003), the eponymous term pertains to the "imperialist organization of capital accumulation" (172) that operates worldwide through "wholly new mechanisms of accumulation by dispossession" (147).
25. Frantz Fanon, *The Wretched of the Earth*, trans. Constance Farrington (New York: Grove Press, 1963), 315–16.
26. Jameson, *The Political Unconscious*, 79.
27. Spivak writes, "Is decolonization possible? In the broadest possible sense, once and for all, no . . . postcoloniality is a failure of decolonization . . . [decolonization is] presumably a condition before *post*coloniality or *post*-colonialism." See her "Teaching for the Times," in *The Decolonization of Imagination: Culture, Knowledge, and Power*, eds. Jan Nederveen Pieterse and Bhikhu Parekh (London: Zed Books, 1995), 178.
28. Marion O'Callaghan, "Continuities in Imagination," in *The Decolonization of Imagination: Culture, Knowledge, and Power* (London: Zed Books, 1995), 22. The second quote is from Charles Oman, *Globalisation and Regionalisation: The Challenge for Developing Countries* (Paris: Organization for Economic Cooperation and Development, 1994), 56. A useful summary of different perspectives on globalization is given in Jan Nederveen Pieterse, *Globalization and Culture: Global Mélange* (Lanham, Md.: Rowman & Littlefield, 2004), 14–21.

29. John Tomlinson, *Cultural Imperialism* (Baltimore, Md.: The Johns Hopkins University Press, 1991), 175.

30. Roland Robertson, "Mapping the Global Condition: Globalization as the Central Concept," in *Global Culture: Nationalism, Globalization and Modernity*, ed. Mike Featherstone (London: Sage, 1990), 19.

31. Jean-Paul Sartre's introduction to Albert Memmi's *The Colonizer and the Colonized*, trans. Howard Greenfeld, expanded ed. (Boston: Beacon, 1991), xxviii.

32. Rey Chow, *Primitive Passions: Visuality, Sexuality, Ethnography, and Contemporary Chinese Cinema* (New York: Columbia University Press, 1995), 56.

33. Jameson, *The Geopolitical Aesthetic*, 31, 26.

34. For a succinct discussion of Jameson's famous gloss on "cognitive mapping," see ibid., 2–3. Briefly, "the desire for cognitive mapping" is the "operation of some banal political unconscious" that maps "our fellows in class terms day by day and fantasize[s] our current events in terms of larger mythic narratives." What this desire aspires to is a consciousness of class, space, and self in a "system so vast that it cannot be encompassed by the natural and historically developed categories of perception with which human beings normally orient themselves."

35. Chow, *Primitive Passions*, 10; Rey Chow, *Sentimental Fabulations: Contemporary Chinese Films* (New York: Columbia University Press, 2007), 43, 2.

36. Marvin D'Lugo, "Authorship, Globalization and the New Identity of Latin American Cinema: From the Mexican 'Ranchera' to Argentinian 'Exile,'" in *Rethinking Third Cinema*, ed. Anthony R. Guneratne and Wimal Dissanayake (New York: Routledge, 2003), 103.

37. Ibid., 106.

38. Sheldon Hsiao-peng Lu, *Transnational Chinese Cinemas: Identity, Nationhood, Gender* (Honolulu: University of Hawai'i Press, 1997), 24.

39. Jameson, *The Geopolitical Aesthetic*, 154.

40. Lu, *Transnational Chinese Cinemas*, 14.

41. Gina Marchetti, *From Tian'anmen to Times Square: Transnational China and the Chinese Diaspora on Global Screens, 1989–1997* (Philadelphia: Temple University Press, 2006), xii.

42. D'Lugo, "Authorship, Globalization and the New Identity of Latin American Cinema," 105; Lu, *Transnational Chinese Cinemas*, 7.

43. Dick Hebdige, "Fax to the Future," *Marxism Today* (January 1990): 20.

44. For a postcolonialist critique of this film, see Chuck Kleinhans, "Dog Eat Dog: Neo-imperialism in Kim Ki-duk's *Address Unknown*," *Visual Anthropology* 22, no. 2–3 (2009): 182–99.

45. Eric Cadzyn, *The Flash of Capital: Film and Geopolitics in Japan* (Durham, N.C.: Duke University Press, 2002); Thomas Elsaesser, *New German Cinema: A History* (New Brunswick, N.J.: Rutgers University Press, 1989); Mette Hjort, *Small Nation, Global Cinema* (Minneapolis: University of Minnesota Press, 2005); Priya Jaikumar, *Cinema at the End of Empire: A Politics of Transition in Britain and India*

(Durham, N.C.: Duke University Press, 2006); Tom O'Regan, *Australian National Cinema* (London: Routledge, 1996); and Angelo Restivo, *The Cinema of Economic Miracles: Visuality and Modernization in the Italian Art Film* (Durham, N.C.: Duke University Press, 2002).

46. See Jean Vengua Gier, "The Filipino Presence in Hollywood's Bataan Films," in *Geopolitics of the Visible: Essays on Philippine Film Cultures*, ed. Rolando B. Tolentino (Quezon City: Ateneo de Manila University Press, 2000), 35–60.

47. I provide a brief discussion of one of Philippine cinema's Hollywood parodies in my essay, "Philippines: Cinema and Its Hybridity (Or 'You're nothing but a second-rate trying hard copycat!')," in *Contemporary Asian Cinemas: Popular Culture in a Global Frame*, ed. Anne T. Ciecko (Oxford: Berg, 2005), 32–44. The substantial corpus of films about Filipino tourists in America remains to be elucidated. Noteworthy films of the genre include *Lollipops and Roses* (Artemio Marquez, 1971), featuring Don Johnson, and *John and Marsha '86: Illegal Aliens in America (John & Marsha '86: T.N.T. sa Amerika*, Apollo Arellano, 1986), in which President Ronald Reagan offers U.S. citizenship to the protagonist, the wacky slum dweller John Puruntong.

1. Terror Is a Man

1. In her introduction to an anthology of Francophile postcolonial cinema criticism, Dina Sherzer cites the "imaginings and refigurings of colonial culture and life and of colonial wars" as part of the agenda of postcolonial films. See her *Cinema, Colonialism, Postcolonialism: Perspectives from the French and Francophone World* (Austin: University of Texas Press, 1997), 8. Similarly, Roy Armes notes the depiction of "the heritage of colonialism" and the documentation "of the abuses of the colonial past" in the postcolonial films he examines. See his *Postcolonial Images: Studies in North African Film* (Bloomington: Indiana University Press, 2005), 25.

2. Constantino Tejero, "Tarantino Raves over Pinoy B-Movies," *Philippine Daily Inquirer*, August 12, 2007, http://showbizandstyle.inquirer.net/breakingnews/breakingnews/view/20070812-82114/Tarantino_raves_over_Pinoy_B-movies (accessed June 19, 2010).

3. According to Thomas Doherty, "Exploitation refers . . . to the advertising and promotion that entice an audience into a theater . . . [to a movie] that caters to its target audience by serving up appetizing or erotic subject matter . . . [and to] a particular *kind* of movie." See his *Teenagers and Teenpics: The Juvenilization of American Movies in the 1950s*, rev. and expanded ed. (Philadelphia: Temple University Press, 2002), 2.

4. For a fuller treatment of the classical exploitation film and its transition to the new wave of low-budget filmmaking, see Eric Schaefer, *Bold! Daring! Shocking! True! A History of Exploitation Films, 1919–1959* (Durham, N.C.: Duke University Press, 1999), 325–42.

5. Paul Monaco, *The Sixties: 1960–1969, History of the American Cinema*, vol. 8 (Berkeley: University of California Press, 2001), 46. For a brief treatment of the history of "postclassical" exploitation films, see Yannis Tzioumakis, *American Independent Cinema: An Introduction* (New Brunswick, N.J.: Rutgers University Press, 2006), 135–66. Romero estimates that he was catering to "about 2,000" drive-in theaters in his heyday. See Manny Reyes, "I Want to Define My Nation for Its People," *Cinemaya* 36 (1997): 51.

6. Reyes, "I Want to Define My Nation for Its People," 52.

7. Ibid. *The Island of Doctor Moreau* rip-offs include *Terror Is a Man* (1959), *Mad Doctor of Blood Island* (1968), *Beast of Blood* (1971), and *The Twilight People* (1972).

8. Bliss Cua Lim, "American Pictures Made by Filipinos: Eddie Romero's Jungle-Horror Exploitation Films," *Spectator* 22, no. 1 (Spring 2002): 24.

9. Reyes, "I Want to Define My Nation for Its People," 51.

10. Lee Server, "Eddie Romero: Our Man in Manila," *Film Comment*, March–April 1999, 49.

11. Reyes, "I Want to Define My Nation for Its People," 36.

12. Ibid., 52.

13. Lim, "American Pictures Made by Filipinos," 29.

14. Ibid., 26.

15. Reyes, "I Want to Define My Nation for Its People," 51.

16. Server, "Eddie Romero," 49; Clodualdo Del Mundo, "Dossier: Eddie Romero," *Cinemaya* 36 (1997): 48; Lim, "American Pictures Made by Filipinos," 39.

17. Todd McCarthy and Charles Flynn, *Kings of the B's: Working within the Hollywood System* (New York: E. P. Dutton, 1975), 518.

18. Fred Olen Ray, *The New Poverty Row: Independent Filmmakers as Distributors* (Jefferson, N.C.: McFarland, 1991), 63–88.

19. Romero recalled their collaboration this way: "We would divide up scenes. I might take care of the dialogue with the American actors . . . He had a wonderful eye for visuals, a very good sense of editing. He was very good with action things." See Server, "Eddie Romero," 49.

20. Judith Halberstam, *Skin Shows: Gothic Horror and the Technology of Monsters* (Durham, N.C.: Duke University Press, 1995), 88.

21. The political unconscious is a site of repression for the intolerable contradictions of history and society. Since repression is never fully successful, the symptoms of these buried realities appear discreetly in various features of literary and cultural texts. See Fredric Jameson, *The Political Unconscious: Narrative as a Socially Symbolic Act* (Ithaca, N.Y.: Cornell University Press, 1981), 20.

22. The phrase "technology of monsters" comes from Halberstam, *Skin Shows*, 21.

23. Chalmers Johnson, *Blowback: The Costs and Consequences of American Empire* (New York: Henry Holt, 2004), 12.

24. For an extensive treatment of American exceptionalism, see Seymour Martin Lipset, *American Exceptionalism: A Double-Edged Sword* (New York: W. W. Norton, 1996).

25. See Johnson, *Blowback*, 66; Amy Kaplan, "'Left Alone with America': The Absence of Empire in the Study of American Culture," in *Cultures of United States Imperialism*, ed. Amy Kaplan and Donald Pease (Durham, N.C.: Duke University Press, 1993), 3–21; and Allan Isaac, *American Tropics: Articulating Filipino America* (Minneapolis: University of Minnesota Press, 2006), 1–19.

26. Johnson, *Blowback*, xi.

27. Ibid., 8.

28. Lim, "American Pictures Made by Filipinos," 35.

29. Ibid.

30. Adam Lowenstein, *Shocking Representation: Historical Trauma, National Cinema, and the Modern Horror Film* (New York: Columbia University Press, 2005), 10

31. Ibid., 36.

32. Robin Wood, *Hollywood from Vietnam to Reagan . . . And Beyond*, rev. ed. (New York: Columbia University Press, 2003), 76.

33. Charlotte Brunsdon, "Text and Audience," in *Remote Control: Television, Audiences, and Cultural Power*, ed. Ellen Seiter, Hans Borchers, Gabriele Kreutzner, and Eva-Maria Warth (New York: Routledge, 1989), 121.

34. Halberstam, *Skin Shows*, 148.

35. John Brunas, "Shock Drive-In Presents *Terror Is a Man*," *Scarlet Street* 23 (1996): 97.

36. Michael Weldon, *The Psychotronic Encyclopedia of Film* (New York: St. Martin's Press, 1983), 700.

37. In Wells's novel, the effacement of the creatures' memories implies something less dramatic than the psychological aporia described by Girard in the film. Moreau describes it simply thus: "He began with a clean sheet, mentally; he had no memories left in his mind of what he had been." See H. G. Wells, *The Island of Doctor Moreau*, ed. Steven Palmé (New York: Dover Books, 1996), 57.

38. Albert Memmi, *The Colonizer and the Colonized*, expanded ed., trans. Howard Greenfeld (Boston: Beacon, 1991), 66.

39. Wells, *The Island of Doctor Moreau*, 102.

40. Wood, *Hollywood from Vietnam to Reagan*, 77.

41. Isaac, *American Tropics*, xxv.

42. Dean C. Worcester, *The Philippines Past and Present*, vol. 2 (New York: Macmillan, 1914), frontispiece facing page.

43. Halberstam, *Skin Shows*, 12.

44. Howard Thompson, review of *Terror Is a Man*, *New York Times*, July 14, 1960, reprinted in *New York Times Film Reviews*, vol. 5 (New York: The New York Times and Arno Press, 1970), 3201.

45. Ray, *The New Poverty Row*, 66.

46. Ibid., 82.

47. Susan Sontag observes that science-fiction monster movies typically begin with only one character foreseeing, witnessing, or believing in the catastrophic attack. See her "The Imagination of Disaster," in *Against Interpretation and Other Essays* (New York: Picador, 2001), 210.

48. For a recent account of the first wave of tests at Bikini, see Jonathan Weisgall, *Operation Crossroads: The Atomic Tests at Bikini Atoll* (Annapolis, Md.: Naval Institute Press, 1994).

49. Ronnie Lipschutz, *Cold War Fantasies: Film, Fiction, and Foreign Policy* (Lanham, Md.: Rowman & Littlefield, 2001), 85.

50. Max Lerner, *The Age of Overkill: A Preface to World Politics* (New York: Simon and Schuster, 1962), 23.

51. Lipschutz, *Cold War Fantasies*, 85.

52. Wood, *Hollywood from Vietnam to Reagan*, 73.

53. See the poster of the double-bill that includes this film in Ray, *The New Poverty Row*, 67. The copy reads, "Free. Free. Beautiful ring sent to every woman attending the showing of these two attractions." Promotional gimmicks like this were a common part of the showmanship strategies of exploitation film distributors and exhibitors. See Schaefer, *Bold!*, 96–135; and Doherty, *Teenagers and Teenpics*, 137–44.

54. For more on Victor Heiser, see his famous memoir *An American Doctor's Odyssey* (New York: W. W. Norton, 1937).

55. Johnson, *Blowback*, 68.

56. For an account of U.S. interventions in Latin America, see Walter LaFeber, *Inevitable Revolutions: The United States in Central America*, 2nd ed. (New York: W. W. Norton, 1993). For a thinly fictionalized account of 1950s U.S. policy in Southeast Asia, see William Lederer and Eugene Burdick, *The Ugly American* (New York: W. W. Norton, 1999).

57. Lipschutz, *Cold War Fantasies*, 8.

58. Johnson, xi, 11; Lipschutz, *Cold War Fantasies*, 140.

59. Isaac, *American Tropics*, xxv.

60. Wood, *Hollywood from Vietnam to Reagan*, 92.

61. Ibid., 94.

62. Ibid., 80.

2. My Brother Is Not a Pig

1. Chalmers Johnson, *Blowback: The Costs and Consequences of American Empire* (New York: Henry Holt, 2004), 216.

2. James H. Blount, *The American Occupation of the Philippines, 1898–1912* (New York: G. P. Putnam's Sons, 1913), 148–49.

3. William E. Berry Jr., *U.S. Bases in the Philippines: The Evolution of the Special Relationship* (Boulder, Colo.: Westview, 1989), 141.

4. Seth Mydans, "U.S. on Trial in a Philippine Rape Case," *International Herald Tribune*, September 10, 2006, http://www.iht.com/articles/2006/09/10/news/trial.php (accessed June 19, 2010).

5. Thom Shanker, "U.S.-Philippines Tensions Flare over Custody in Rape Case," *International Herald Tribune*, December 22, 2006, http://www.iht.com/articles/2006/12/22/news/military.php (accessed June 19, 2010).

6. Carlos Conde, "U.S. Soldier in Manila Receives Life Term," *International Herald Tribune*, December 4, 2006, http://www.iht.com/articles/2006/12/04/news/phils.php?page=1 (accessed June 19, 2010).

7. Veronica Uy, "Smith Returned to Custody of US Embassy," *Philippine Daily Inquirer*, December 30, 2006, http://newsinfo.inquirer.net/breakingnews/nation/view/20061230-40832/Smith_returned_to_custody_of_US_embassy (accessed June 19, 2010).

8. Fred Brown, "The Future of U.S.-Philippine Relations," in *U.S. Bases Overseas: Negotiations with Spain, Greece, and the Philippines*, ed. John W. McDonald Jr. and Diane B. Bendahmane (Boulder, Colo.: Westview, 1990), 123.

9. Julian Madison, "American Military Bases in the Philippines, 1945–1965: Neo-Colonialism and Its Demise," in *Trans-Pacific Relations: America, Europe, and Asia in the Twentieth Century*, ed. Richard Jensen, John Davidann, and Yoneyuki Sugita (Westport, Conn.: Praeger, 2003), 129.

10. Ibid., 130.

11. Stephen Bosworth, "Thinking the Unthinkable: The Bases Review and the Future of U.S.-Philippine Relations," in *Military Basing and the U.S./Soviet Military Balance in Southeast Asia*, ed. George K. Tanham and Alvin H. Bernstein (New York: Crane Russak, 1989), 177. Bosworth was U.S. ambassador to the Philippines at the end of the Marcos era.

12. Carl Schmitt, *Political Theology: Four Chapters on the Concept of Sovereignty*, trans. George Schwab (Chicago: University of Chicago Press, 2005), 12.

13. Madison, "American Military Bases in the Philippines, 1945–1965," 128.

14. Jacques Derrida, *Rogues: Two Essays on Reason*, trans. Pascale-Anne Brault and Michael Naas (Stanford, Calif.: Stanford University Press, 2005), 141–42. Schmitt likewise notes the absolute nature of a sovereign decision, which is ultimately "created out of nothingness" (Schmitt, *Political Theology*, 66).

15. Schmitt, *Political Theology*, 5.

16. Ibid., 15.

17. Ibid., 5.

18. Berry, *U.S. Bases in the Philippines*, 20.

19. This idea of Joseph de Maistre is noted in Schmitt, *Political Theology*, 55.

20. Berry, *U.S. Bases in the Philippines*, 26.

21. Ibid., 113. The legalese pertaining to these crimes encrypts the naming of sovereign state boundaries: the first set of crimes being inter se or "among us," and the second being those often deceptively classified as acts committed "in the line of duty."

22. Johnson, *Blowback*, 43.
23. Bosworth, "Thinking the Unthinkable," 177.
24. The quote is from a speech given by Marcos during his first trip to China in June 1975. See Berry, *U.S. Bases in the Philippines*, 160.
25. Ibid., 161.
26. Jacob Ulvila, "Turning Points: An Analysis," in *U.S. Bases Overseas: Negotiations with Spain, Greece, and the Philippines*, ed. John W. McDonald Jr. and Diane B. Bendahmane (Boulder, Colo.: Westview, 1990), 97.
27. Berry, *U.S. Bases in the Philippines*, 233.
28. The "flag law" of 1907 forbade the display of the Philippine flag. See Teodoro Agoncillo, *A History of the Filipino People*, 8th ed. (Manila: Garotech, 1990), 378.
29. After the Filipino and American troops surrendered Bataan in World War II, the Japanese forced them to walk to a prison camp about eighty miles away. Many Filipinos and Americans died of exhaustion, bayoneting, gunshot wounds, or beheading. See ibid., 394.
30. Frantz Fanon, *The Wretched of the Earth*, trans. Constance Farrington (New York: Grove, 1963), 169.
31. Hans Indorf, "The 1988 Philippine Base Review in the Context of U.S. History," in *Military Basing and the U.S./Soviet Military Balance in Southeast Asia*, ed. George K. Tanham and Alvin H. Bernstein (New York: Crane Russak, 1989), 98.
32. Robert J. Hanks, "The Strategic Importance of U.S. Bases in the Philippines," in *Military Basing and the U.S./Soviet Military Balance in Southeast Asia*, ed. George K. Tanham and Alvin H. Bernstein (New York: Crane Russak, 1989), 120.
33. Madison, "American Military Bases in the Philippines, 1945–1965," 128.
34. A. R. Magno, "Cornucupia or Curse: The Internal Debate on U.S. Bases in the Philippines," in *Military Basing and the U.S./Soviet Military Balance in Southeast Asia*, ed. George K. Tanham and Alvin H. Bernstein (New York: Crane Russak, 1989), 151.
35. Giorgio Agamben, *Homo Sacer: Sovereign Power and Bare Life*, trans. Daniel Heller-Roazen (Stanford, Calif.: Stanford University Press, 1998), 83.
36. Ibid., 159.
37. Berry, *U.S. Bases in the Philippines*, 104–5.
38. Agamben, *Homo Sacer*, 183.
39. Ibid., 107.
40. Giorgio Agamben, *The Open: Man and Animal*, trans. Kevin Attell (Stanford, Calif.: Stanford University Press, 2004), 37.
41. The quote from Foucault appears in Agamben, *Homo Sacer*, 3. Foucault writes, "Modern man [is] an animal whose politics places his existence as a living being in question," in *The History of Sexuality, Volume I: An Introduction*, trans. Robert Hurley (New York: Vintage Books, 1990), 143. He begins to develop this concept in *Security, Territory, Population: Lectures at the Collège de France*, ed. Michel Senellart, trans. Graham Burchell (Houndmills, UK: Palgrave Macmillan, 2007).

42. Agamben, *Homo Sacer*, 4. My juxtaposition of Foucault and Agamben in these last two sentences may give the impression that their notions of biopolitics are similar. They are not. As Rey Chow and other scholars point out, Agamben emphasizes the negative aspects of biopolitics (such as the sovereign's prerogative to kill or let live), whereas Foucault exposes the ways in which power articulates and manages every aspect of human life. See Rey Chow, "Sacrifice, Mimesis, and the Theorizing of Victimhood (A Speculative Essay)," *Representations* 94, no. 1 (Spring 2006), 132–33.

43. In *Strike* (*Stackha*, 1925), the violent suppression of picketing workers is intercut with nondiegetic inserts of a steer being slaughtered.

44. Agamben, *Homo Sacer*, 85.

45. Madison, "American Military Bases in the Philippines, 1945–1965," 138.

46. Berry, *U.S. Bases in the Philippines*, 111.

47. Derrida, *Rogues*, xiii.

48. Fanon, *The Wretched of the Earth*, 100.

49. Derrida, *Rogues*, 6.

50. Madison, "American Military Bases in the Philippines, 1945–1965," 132.

51. Ibid., 133.

52. Hannah Arendt, *The Origins of Totalitarianism* (New York: Harcourt, 1973), 148.

53. Berry, *U.S. Bases in the Philippines*, 233.

54. Madison, "American Military Bases in the Philippines, 1945–1965," 129.

55. Homi Bhabha, *The Location of Culture* (New York: Routledge, 1994), 44.

56. I thank Jojo DeVera for this description of the film's ending, which, along with the opening titles and end credits, cannot be found in the home video version.

57. As I mentioned earlier, the film was produced by Cirio H. Santiago, a Filipino filmmaker and producer who enjoyed some international prominence by directing low-budget films shown in U.S. drive-ins and distributed in other countries.

58. Agamben, *Homo Sacer*, 176.

59. Ibid., 123.

60. The military use of the concentration camp, according to Agamben, is traceable to Spanish colonial warfare in Cuba in the 1890s. (See ibid., 166.) During the Philippine–American War Filipinos were subjected to *reconcentrado* policies similar to those for which the United States criticized Spain. While the bases and the reconcentration camps are not the same, both are biopolitical spaces created in the Philippines by U.S. empire.

61. Richard Gordon, "Philippine Military Bases: Economic and Social Implications," in *Military Basing and the U.S./Soviet Military Balance in Southeast Asia*, ed. George K. Tanham and Alvin H. Bernstein (New York: Crane Russak, 1989), 137.

62. Agamben, *Homo Sacer*, 170.

63. Agamben notes that the distinction between biopolitics and its converse, thanatopolitics, dissolves in the camp. See *Homo Sacer*, 150, 153. The relation

between the two terms is explicated further in Roberto Esposito, *Bios: Biopolitics and Philosophy*, trans. Timothy Campbell (Minneapolis: University of Minnesota Press, 2008), 10, 110–45, 184–85.

64. Berry, *U.S. Bases in the Philippines*, 142.

65. Agamben, *Homo Sacer*, 89. Agamben uses these words in reference to the subjects' absolute subordination to the power of the sovereign, who holds their lives in his hands. One of the models of such unconditional authority is the father's power over his son's life in ancient Rome. The son becomes subject to this awesome power simply by virtue of his birth.

66. Fanon, *The Wretched of the Earth*, 218.

67. Ibid., 299. As Fanon puts it, "The melancholic Algerian does not commit suicide. He kills."

68. Ibid., 18.

69. This incident in the film's narrative recalls various cases of drug use and trafficking by U.S. servicemen. See Berry, *U.S. Bases in the Philippines*, 150–51.

70. Agamben, *Homo Sacer*, 102.

71. Rey Chow, *Primitive Passions: Visuality, Sexuality, Ethnography, and Contemporary Chinese Films* (New York: Columbia University Press, 1995), 26. Chow uses the phrase in her reading of Yonggang Wu's silent film *Goddess* (*Shen nu*, 1934). The film's image of the modern woman (who is a prostitute, mother, commodity, and figure of the divine all at once) registers "the repressions and brutalities" of modern life with unprecedented clarity and depth, offering not a "mirror" of reality but "a new type of ethnographic picture" that encodes details through the disposition of the woman's body.

72. Magno, "Cornucupia or Curse," 162.

73. In passing, we should note that what is left "unsaid" by these orifices may also be the tale of indirect relays between the violence of U.S. military presence and the state terrorism of Marcos. Marcos was one of several Third World autocrats supported by the United States in pursuit of its anticommunist campaign. See Johnson, *Blowback*, 79. In his reading of Kidlat Tahimik's *Perfumed Nightmare* (1977), Fredric Jameson cites an instance in which the United States functions as a surrogate for Marcos. See his *The Geopolitical Aesthetic: Cinema and Space in the World System* (Bloomington: Indiana University Press, 1995), 191.

74. It is difficult to tell from the video copy I studied if the sentry is Filipino or American, but the synopsis on the film's promotional flyer indicates the latter.

75. Jean-Paul Sartre, "Preface" to Fanon's *The Wretched of the Earth*, trans. Constance Farrington (New York: Grove, 1963), 20. Aimé Césaire famously uses the term "boomerang effect" to describe the same phenomenon in his *Discourse on Colonialism* (New York: Monthly Review Press, 2000), 36.

76. Melissa G. Contreras, "Erap and Nikki in a Pancit Western," review of *Sa kuko ng agila*, *Manila Chronicle*, July 8, 1989, 13. A more sympathetic critic, writing in Filipino, not only praises the film's timely intervention in political matters but also echoes Contreras's observations about the film's poor execution, its

blatant pandering to the requirements of commercial cinema, and Estrada's messianic posturing. See Mara P. L. Lanot, "Sa kaninong kuko?" (In whose claws?), *National Midweek*, August 2, 1989, 48.

77. Michael Hardt and Antonio Negri, *Empire* (Cambridge, Mass.: Harvard University Press, 2000), 146.

78. Ceres Doyo, "*Sa Kuko ng Agila*, $2-M Bribe Bared to Abort Project," *Philippine Daily Inquirer*, June 12, 1989.

79. Renato Constantino Jr., "'Kuko' in Perspective," *National Midweek*, August 16, 1989, 27.

80. The perspective of one of the lead negotiators for the Philippines is given in Alfredo R. A. Bengzon and Raul Rodrigo, *A Matter of Honor: The Story of the 1990–91 RP–US Bases Talks* (Pasig: Anvil, 1997).

81. Indorf, "The 1988 Philippine Base Review," 112.

82. Shanker, "U.S.–Philippines Tensions Flare."

83. Agamben, *Homo Sacer*, 180.

84. Johnson, *Blowback*, 222.

85. Ibid., 255; Chalmers Johnson, *The Sorrows of Empire: Militarism, Secrecy, and the End of the Republic* (New York: Henry Holt, 2004), 24.

86. David Harvey, *The New Imperialism* (New York: Oxford University Press, 2003), 211.

87. The information and quotes in this section are from Julie M. Aurelio and Norman Bordadora, "'Nicole' Recants, Clears Smith," *Philippine Daily Inquirer*, March 18, 2009, http://newsinfo.inquirer.net/inquirerheadlines/nation/view/20090318-194696/Nicole-recants-clears-Smith (accessed June 19, 2010).

3. (Not) Searching for My Father

1. While I have reservations about the term "Amerasian," I use it interchangeably with "mixed race" in this chapter because of its historical significance and specificity.

2. Frantz Fanon, *White Skin, Black Masks*, trans. Charles Lam Markmann (New York: Grove, 1967), 47.

3. Ibid., 100.

4. My point about these facile and unchanging representations will become clearer as I discuss the very similar plots of the films. For now, let me cite a similar opinion about one of the films. Gino Dormiendo, in his review of *Phil-American Boy*, faults the "unrealistic handling of the social milieu" and "regrettable commercialism in tackling a subject that has deep implications for Philippine-American relations and is rooted in our history." Gino Dormiendo, "Ina, kapatid, anak" (Mother, sister, son), review of *Phil-American Boy*, *Filipino Magasin*, June 2, 1997, 32. Other than citing the need for specificity and texture, I would be hard-pressed to describe a better way of representing the Filipino Amerasian's plight. I must admit that my rather unfair expectation of a richer treatment of their interiority

is fueled by my appreciation of "On Being Mixed," chapter 12 of Linda Martín Alcoff's *Visible Identities: Race, Gender and the Self* (New York: Oxford University Press, 2006), 264–84.

5. The film was made by a short-lived outfit ambitiously called The Asian American Film Institute (TAAFI), which planned—but failed—to make other films about transnational experiences and encounters, including adaptations of Carlos Bulosan's *America Is in the Heart*, a historical drama about the Balanginga massacre during the Philippine–American War, and a film about an American journalist who falls in love with a Filipina labor activist in Hong Kong. See Joe Quirino, "*Olongapo: The Great American Dream*, Metaphor for Bar Girls and US Bases," *Sunday Times Magazine*, December 27, 1987, 10–11. The film's producer, cowriter, and uncredited codirector, Frank Vrechek, indicated in e-mail correspondence that the international version "went into distribution in 23 countries . . . and was an entry at the Cannes Film Festival." Frank Vrechek, e-mail interview by author, March 11, 2009.

6. This quote, as well as subsequent citations of Freud on family romance, is extracted from Sigmund Freud, *Collected Papers*, 5th ed., ed. James Strachey (New York: Basic Books, 1959), 75–76.

7. Ibid., 78.

8. Lynn Hunt, *The Family Romance of the French Revolution* (Berkeley: University of California Press, 1992), xiii.

9. Ibid., xv.

10. Ann Laura Stoler, *Carnal Knowledge and Imperial Power: Race and the Intimate in Colonial Rule* (Berkeley: University of California Press, 2002), 90.

11. Ibid., 95.

12. Ibid., 114.

13. Ibid., 80.

14. Homi Bhabha, *The Location of Culture*, repr. ed. (London: Routledge, 2005), 63–64.

15. Lewis Gleeck Jr., *The Manila Americans: 1901–1964* (Manila: Carmelo & Bauermann, 1977), 96–100. See also Ronald Fettes Champan, *Leonard Wood and Leprosy in the Philippines* (Lanham, Md.: University Press of America, 1982), 101, 132; and John Shade, *America's Forgotten Children, The Amerasians* (Perkasie, Pa.: Pearl S. Buck Foundation, 1981), 22–23.

16. Sue-Jue Lee Gage, "The Amerasian Problem: Blood, Duty, and Race," *International Relations* 21, no. 1 (2007): 86–102. See also U.S. Congress. House. "A Bill to amend the Immigration and Nationality Act to provide preferential treatment in the admission of certain children of United States Armed Forces Personnel." 97th Cong., 1st sess., 1981, H.R. 808.

17. Shade, *America's Forgotten Children*, 135.

18. Fanon, *White Skin*, 42.

19. Albert Memmi, *The Colonizer and the Colonized*, trans. Howard Greenfeld (Boston: Beacon, 1991), 117.

20. Stoler, *Carnal Knowledge and Imperial Power*, 94.

21. This is not the only reference to Kennedy in the films studied in this book. *Once a Moth*, a film I discussed in the previous chapter, also alludes to the tragic event even if the movie is set half a decade after the assassination.

22. More often than not, it is the mother who loses out, thus the prevalence of the "maternal sacrifice theme" in mother and child melodramas. See E. Ann Kaplan, "Mothering, Feminism and Representation: The Maternal in Melodrama and the Woman's Film, 1910–1942," in *Home Is Where the Heart Is: Studies in Melodrama and the Woman's Film*, ed. Christine Gledhill (London: British Film Institute, 1987), 122–35.

23. Shade, *America's Forgotten Children*, 48.

24. Stoler, *Carnal Knowledge and Imperial Power*, 8.

25. Fanon, *White Skin*, 75–76.

26. Frank Vrechek, e-mail interview by author, March 11, 2009.

27. Ashis Nandy, *The Intimate Enemy: Loss and Recovery of Self under Colonialism* (New Delhi: Oxford University Press, 1983), 75.

28. Emmanuel Reyes, "*Olongapo*, the Film, Has Nothing New to Say," in *Notes on Philippine Cinema* (Manila: De La Salle University Press, 1989), 147. Interestingly, in another part of his book, Reyes seemingly contradicts himself by describing the film as "the picture with the thickest aspirations yet to come out in the post-Marcos era" (104).

29. Jo-Ann Maglipon, "DH in HK," in *Primed: Selected Stories, 1972–1992* (Pasig: Anvil, 1993), 45–53.

30. Mary Ann Doane, "The 'Woman's Film,' Possession and Address," in *Home Is Where the Heart Is: Studies in Melodrama and the Woman's Film*, ed. Christine Gledhill (London: British Film Institute, 1987), 294. For a brief account of the female Oedipus complex, see *The Cambridge Companion to Freud*, ed. Jerome Neu (Cambridge: Cambridge University Press, 1991), 168–70, 230.

31. Stoler, *Carnal Knowledge and Imperial Power*, 62.

32. Ibid., 117.

33. David Harvey writes that neoliberalism, which has "long dominated the U.S. stance towards the rest of the world," proceeds from the "assumption that individual freedoms are guaranteed by freedom of the market and trade." Such freedoms "reflect the interests of private property owners, businesses, multinational corporations, and financial capital" and "facilitate conditions for profitable capital accumulation on the part of both foreign and domestic capital." For a thorough discussion of neoliberalism, see his *A Brief History of Neoliberalism* (New York: Oxford University Press, 2005), 7; his analysis of U.S. neoliberalism may be found in *The New Imperialism* (New York: Oxford University Press, 2003).

34. Nandy, *The Intimate Enemy*, 91.

35. Stoler, *Carnal Knowledge and Imperial Power*, 70.

36. Nandy, *The Intimate Enemy*, 29.

37. In a different context, Ranjana Khanna also characterizes the abstract "feminine" as something incalculable, "the excess, a profound enunciation or crisis or cut in representation." See her *Algeria Cuts: Women and Representation, 1830 to the Present* (Durham, N.C.: Duke University Press, 2008), 106.

38. Sharon Delmendo observes that "Filipino nationalism is, to some extent, necessarily anti-American." See her monograph, *The Star-Entangled Banner: One Hundred Years of America in the Philippines* (New Brunswick, N.J.: Rutgers University Press, 2004), 7, 141–67.

4. The Migrant Woman's Tale

1. In his study *The American Dream: A Short History of an Idea That Shaped a Nation* (New York: Oxford University Press, 2003), Jim Cullen examines several varieties of the American dream, including upward mobility, equality for African Americans, home ownership, and personal fulfillment. In *The Epic of America* (New York: Triangle Books, 1941), 405, James Truslow Adams famously explains the purchase of the American dream among immigrants: "The American dream that has lured tens of millions of all nations to our shores in the past century has not been a dream of merely material plenty, though that has doubtless counted heavily . . . It has been a dream of being able to grow to fullest development as man and woman, unhampered by the barriers which had slowly been erected in older civilizations, unrepressed by social orders which had developed for the benefit of classes rather than for the simple human being of any and every class."

2. The phrase "masculinist state" comes from Ranjana Khanna, *Algeria Cuts: Women and Representation, 1830 to the Present* (Durham, N.C.: Duke University Press, 2008), 4.

3. E. Ann Kaplan, "Mothering, Feminism and Representation: The Maternal in Melodrama and the Woman's Film 1910–40," in *Home Is Where the Heart Is: Studies in Melodrama and the Woman's Film*, ed. Christine Gledhill (London: British Film Institute, 1987), 117.

4. Writing in a different context, Viet Thanh Nguyen notes that such imagined excursions from "the political and cultural space" of the nation permit the expression of the "most critical" views on an issue. See his *Race and Resistance: Literature and Politics in Asian America* (New York: Oxford University Press, 2002), 63.

5. Deniz Kandiyoti, "Identity and Its Discontents: Women and the Nation," in *Colonial Discourse and Post-Colonial Theory: A Reader*, ed. Patrick Williams and Laura Chrisman (New York: Columbia University Press, 1994), 377.

6. Ibid., 388.

7. Rey Chow, "The Politics of Admittance: Female Sexual Agency, Miscegenation and the Formation of Community in Frantz Fanon," in *Ethics after Idealism: Theory, Culture, Ethnicity, Reading* (Bloomington: Indiana University Press, 1998), 69.

8. Ibid., 63.

9. Ibid., 71.

10. The figure of woman "challenges notions of representational politics and restitution" and "confounds already existing forms of representation," writes Khanna in *Algeria Cuts*, xvi, 237.

11. So deeply couched, it may have been that the film's critics, writing before and after the fall of the dictatorship, failed to read the political meaning of the film. Emmanuel Reyes, for instance, regarded the film as a sentimental paean to immigration. See his "Tender Effort: One from the Heart," review of *'Merika*, in *Notes on Philippine Cinema* (Manila: De La Salle University Press, 1989), 116–18. Joel David counts the film among several melodramas that have "an atypical framework of social disillusionment." He does not, however, offer an elaboration of the film's politics. See his *Fields of Vision: Critical Applications in Recent Philippine Cinema* (Quezon City: Ateneo de Manila University Press, 1995), 25.

12. See a relevant gloss on alienated citizenship in Allan Isaac, *American Tropics: Articulating Filipino America* (Minneapolis: University of Minnesota Press, 2006), 6–7.

13. Screenwriter Clodualdo del Mundo Jr. notes in the introduction to the film's published continuity script that he and cowriter Gil Quito wrote the screenplay in three months, either beginning or ending in January 1984. Ninoy Aquino's assassination on August 21, 1983, was thus still very much in the mind of many Filipinos such as the two screenwriters when the script was written and filmed. See Clodualdo del Mundo Jr., Herky del Mundo, Gil Jose Quito, *Maynila . . . 'Merika, Alyas Raha Matanda: tatlong dulang pampelikula* (*Manila . . . 'Merika, Alias "Old Rajah": three screenplays*) (Manila: De La Salle University Press, 1992), xi.

14. Peter Brooks suggests that melodrama can clarify moral issues without reducing their complexity. See his *The Melodramatic Imagination: Balzac, Henry James, Melodrama, and the Mode of Excess* (New Haven, Conn.: Yale University Press, 1995), 145.

15. Sharon Delmendo notes that Philippine nationalism is frequently conflated with anti-American sentiments. See her *The Star-Entangled Banner: One Hundred Years of America in the Philippines* (New Brunswick, N.J.: Rutgers University Press, 2004), 19.

16. Chow, "The Politics of Admittance," 73.

17. Ibid.; see also Rey Chow, *Primitive Passions: Visuality, Sexuality, Ethnography, and Contemporary Chinese Cinema* (New York: Columbia University Press, 1995), 140.

18. Kandiyoti, "Identity and Its Discontents," 376.

19. I borrow the phrase "glorious homecoming" from Hamid Naficy, *An Accented Cinema: Exilic and Diasporic Filmmaking* (Princeton, N.J.: Princeton University Press, 2001), 229.

20. Thomas Elsaesser, *New German Cinema: A History* (New Brunswick, N.J.: Rutgers University Press, 1989), 61.

21. Tania Modleski notes that "the heart of melodrama" is loss—that is, "those moments when the heroine relinquishes all that has mattered in her life." See her

"Time and Desire in the Woman's Film," in *Home Is Where the Heart Is: Studies in Melodrama and the Woman's Film*, ed. Christine Gledhill (London: British Film Institute, 1987), 335–36.

22. John Durham Peters, "Exile, Nomadism, and Diaspora: The Stakes of Mobility in the Western Canon," in *Home, Exile, Homeland: Film, Media and the Politics of Place*, ed. Hamid Naficy (New York: Routledge, 1999), 39.

23. Bruce Robbins, *Secular Vocations: Intellectuals, Professionalism, Culture* (London: Verso, 1993), 183; Ann Colley, *Nostalgia and Recollection in Victorian Culture* (New York: St. Martin's Press, 1998), 58.

24. Maria LaPlace, "Producing and Consuming the Woman's Film: Discursive Struggle in *Now, Voyager*," in *Home Is Where the Heart Is: Studies in Melodrama and the Woman's Film*, ed. Christine Gledhill (London: British Film Institute, 1987), 151.

25. Ibid., 156.

26. Ibid., 151.

27. The "incompetent script," the critic writes, "glosses over a very important development—the transformation of Lea's character . . . [indicating] that the writers indeed have a very thin grasp of their material." See Eric Cabahug, "Sana huwag nang ulitin" (Hopefully, never again), review of *Sana maulit muli*, *Manila Times*, August 16, 1995, 21.

28. The screenplay is credited to the director, Olivia Lamasan, and cowriters, Mel Mendoza-Del Rosario and Shaira Mella-Salvador. Jose Javier Reyes shares story credit with the three women.

29. See Cabahug, "Sana huwag nang ulitin," 21; and Noel Vera, "I Left My Brain in San Francisco," *Manila Chronicle*, August 12, 1995, 19.

30. Janice Doane and Devon Hodges, *Nostalgia and Sexual Difference: The Resistance to Contemporary Feminism* (New York: Methuen, 1987), 9.

31. Christine Gledhill, "The Melodramatic Field: An Investigation," in *Home Is Where the Heart Is: Studies in Melodrama and the Woman's Film*, ed. Christine Gledhill (London: British Film Institute, 1987), 12.

32. Mary Ann Doane, "The 'Woman's Film,' Possession and Address," in *Home Is Where the Heart Is: Studies in Melodrama and the Woman's Film*, ed. Christine Gledhill (London: British Film Institute, 1987), 294.

33. Annette Kuhn, *Women's Pictures: Feminism and Cinema*, 2nd ed. (New York: Verso, 1994), 35.

34. The eponymous theme song, "Sana maulit muli," was licensed for use in the film. Originally sung by Gary Valenciano, it was a hit in the late 1980s. Some of the subsequent versions were recorded by female artists, including Lea Salonga and Regine Velasquez.

35. Laura Mulvey, "Notes on Sirk and Melodrama," in *Home Is Where the Heart Is: Studies in Melodrama and the Woman's Film*, ed. Christine Gledhill (London: British Film Institute, 1987), 79.

5. Filipino American Dreams

1. Albert Memmi, *Decolonization and the Decolonized*, trans. Robert Bononno (Minneapolis: University of Minnesota Press, 2006), 78.

2. Ibid., 82.

3. Ibid., 78.

4. These two projects of mourning imperialist history and promoting integration through multiculturalism are related. As Victor Bascara points out, in the case of Asian American cultural production, the "recovery of U.S. imperialism emerged in the era of multiculturalism at the very moment when Asian American literature became mobilized to reproduce narratives of liberal inclusion." See his *Model-Minority Imperialism* (Minneapolis: University of Minnesota Press, 2006), xxv.

5. Memmi, *Decolonization and the Decolonized*, 115.

6. The phrase comes from Viet Thanh Nguyen, *Race and Resistance: Literature and Politics in Asian America* (New York: Oxford University Press, 2002), 108.

7. Ibid., 16.

8. Henry Giroux, "Insurgent Multiculturalism and the Promise of Pedagogy," in *Multiculturalism: A Critical Reader*, ed. David Theo Goldberg (Cambridge: Basil Blackwell, 1994), 326.

9. Charles Taylor characterizes the politics of multiculturalism as one of "equal recognition" for individuals and different cultures. See his famous essay "The Politics of Recognition," in *Multiculturalism: A Critical Reader*, ed. David Theo Goldberg (Cambridge: Basil Blackwell, 1994), 81. For Sayla Benhabib, the state's recognition of identities should be influenced by the individual's agency of "self-identification" and "self-ascription" (i.e., controlling his or her membership in a group). See her book *The Claims of Culture: Equality and Diversity in the Global Era* (Princeton, N.J.: Princeton University Press, 2002), 131.

10. Kwame Anthony Appiah, *The Ethics of Identity* (Princeton, N.J.: Princeton University Press, 2005), 110.

11. Filomeno V. Aguilar Jr., "Is There a Transnation? Migrancy and the National Homeland Among Overseas Filipinos," in *State/Nation/Transnation: Perspectives on Transnationalism in the Asia-Pacific*, ed. Brenda S. A. Yeoh and Katie Willis (London: Routledge, 2004), 109.

12. Gayatri Spivak, "Teaching for the Times," in *The Decolonization of Imagination: Culture, Knowledge and Power*, ed. Jan Nederveen Pieterse and Bhikhu Parekh (London: Zed Books, 1995), 192.

13. The struggle to find a "usable" Filipino American masculinity is treated in a discussion of Carlos Bulosan's *America Is in the Heart* in Nguyen, *Race and Resistance*, 63–85.

14. Lisa Lowe, *Immigrant Acts: On Asian American Cultural Politics* (Durham, N.C.: Duke University Press, 1996), 50.

15. Ibid., 51.

16. Ibid., 65.

17. Rolando B. Tolentino, "Identity and Difference in 'Filipino/a American' Media Arts," in *Screening Asian Americans*, ed. Peter X. Feng (New Brunswick, N.J.: Rutgers University Press, 2002), 123.

18. Frank Chin, Jeffery Paul Chan, Lawson Fusao Inada, and Shawn Wong, *Aiiieeeee! An Anthology of Asian-American Writing* (Garden City, N.Y.: Anchor, 1975), x.

19. Memmi, *Decolonization and the Decolonized*, 115.

20. The term "'assimilative' fantasies" comes from Anne Anlin Cheng, *The Melancholy of Race: Psychoanalysis, Assimilation, and Hidden Grief* (New York: Oxford University Press, 2001), 128.

21. Nguyen, *Race and Resistance*, 67.

22. David Eng, *Racial Castration: Managing Masculinity in Asian America* (Durham, N.C.: Duke University Press, 2001), 181.

23. Ibid., 202.

24. Ibid., 181–82.

25. Ibid., 204.

26. My gloss on the times of vertical and horizontal relationships comes from Jun Xing, *Asian America through the Lens: History, Representations, and Identity* (Walnut Creek, Calif.: AltaMira, 1998), 133. Benedict Anderson famously refers to the "horizontal-secular-transverse-time" of nations in *Imagined Community: Thoughts on the Rise and Spread of Nationalism*, 2nd ed. (London: Verso, 1991), 37.

27. Eng, *Racial Castration*, 195.

28. Lisa Lowe writes that "the question of the loss or transmission of the 'original' culture" is "represented in a family narrative, figured as generational conflict" between first- and second-generation immigrants. See Lowe, *Immigrant Acts*, 62.

29. In an interview coinciding with the release of the DVD of the film, Cajayon admits that he did not grow up with Filipino American culture: "There are a lot of Filipino Americans who moved to white neighborhoods, getting as far away from the Filipino American community as they could . . . That was me. I grew up in Orange County; there were very few others around." He notes, however, that his cowriter lived in Filipino American neighborhoods "right on a suburban–urban cusp." See Eddy Crouse, "Interview: Gene Cajayon: The Director on His *Debut* and Filipino Americana," *Barnes & Noble.com*, September 16, 2003, http://video.barnesandnoble.com/search/interview.asp?z=y&CTR=901985 (accessed April 4, 2008).

30. Leny Mendoza Strobel, "Coming Full Circle: Narratives of Decolonization Among Post-1965 Filipino Americans," in *Filipino Americans: Transformation and Identity*, ed. Maria P. P. Root (Thousand Oaks, Calif.: Sage, 1997), 70. See also a similar claim in Linda A. Revilla, "Filipino American Identity: Transcending the Crisis," in the same anthology, 95–111.

31. Joey Hisamoto, "Home Sweet Home in LA: *The Debut*," *Philippine Graphic*, August 25, 2003.

32. Gene Cajayon, John Manal Castro, and Dawn Bohulano Mabalon, *The Debut: The Making of a Filipino American Film* (Chicago: Tulitos, 2001), 71.

33. I owe this insight to John Labella, who commented on an early draft of this chapter.

34. Judith Butler, *The Psychic Life of Power: Theories in Subjection* (Stanford, Calif.: Stanford University Press, 1997), 61.

35. Peter X. Feng, *Identities in Motion: Asian American Film and Video* (Durham, N.C.: Duke University Press, 2002),105.

36. My treatment of the disparity between these two media is inspired by Rey Chow's discussion of painting and identity in the film adaptation of David Henry Hwang's *M. Butterfly*. See her *Ethics After Idealism: Theory, Culture, Ethnicity, Reading* (Bloomington: Indiana University Press, 1997), 95.

37. Feng, *Identities in Motion*, 3, 20.

38. Aguilar, "Is There a Transnation?" 109.

39. Ibid., 106.

40. Hisamoto, "Home Sweet Home in LA," 59. See also Justin Lowe, "Debut Performance," *Filmmaker* 10, no. 4 (Summer 2002): 32–34.

41. Crouse, "Interview," no pagination.

42. Cheng, *The Melancholy of Race*, 72.

43. Ibid., 65.

44. Ibid., 89.

45. Ibid., 69.

46. Ibid., 72.

47. Here I quote the dialogue from the published script of the film. See Rod Pulido, *The Flip Side: A Filipino American Comedy* (Chicago: Tulitos, 2002), 108–9.

48. *Once a Moth*, a film discussed in chapter 2, offers a strikingly different view of this historical episode and its implications for contemporary Philippine–American relations.

49. Spivak, "Teaching for the Times," 186.

50. The term is from Benedict Anderson, *The Spectre of Comparisons: Nationalism, Southeast Asia, and the World* (New York: Verso, 1998), 58–74.

51. Spivak, "Teaching for the Times," 183.

52. Feng stresses the importance of resisting the unchallenged opposition between immigrant and transnational identities. The notion of keeping multiple allegiances might pose a better alternative. See Feng, *Identities in Motion*, 180.

53. Ethnoscape refers to "the landscape of persons who constitute the shifting world in which we live: tourists, immigrants, refugees, exiles, guestworkers, and other moving groups and persons." See Arjun Appadurai, "Disjuncture and Difference in the Global Cultural Economy," in *Global Culture: Nationalism, Globalization and Modernity*, ed. Mike Featherstone (London: Sage, 1990), 297.

54. Cheng, *The Melancholy of Race*, 35.

55. Nguyen, *Race and Resistance*, 83.

56. This gloss on transgenerational haunting comes from Jacqueline Rose, *States of Fantasy* (Oxford: Oxford University Press, 1996), 31. Rose adapts Nicolas Abraham and Maria Torok's concept, which is succinctly expressed in the following lines: "This unknown phantom returns from the unconscious to haunt its host and may lead to phobias, madness, and obsessions. Its effect can persist through several generations and determine the fate of an entire family line." See Abraham and Torok's *The Shell and the Kernel*, ed. and trans. Nicholas T. Rand (Chicago: University of Chicago Press, 1994), 140n1.

57. Karen Shimakawa, *National Abjection: The Asian American Body Onstage* (Durham, N.C.: Duke University Press, 2002), 5.

58. Ibid., 86.

59. Ibid., 11.

60. Eng, *Racial Castration*, 194.

61. Antonio J. A. Pido, *The Pilipinos in America: Macro/Micro Dimensions of Immigration and Integration* (New York: Center for Migration Studies, 1986), 100–102.

62. Nilda Rimonte, "Colonialism's Legacy: The Inferiorizing of the Filipino," in *Filipino Americans: Transformation and Identity*, ed. Maria P. P. Root (Thousand Oaks, Calif.: Sage, 1997), 41.

63. Revilla, "Filipino American Identity," in *Filipino Americans: Transformation and Identity*, 101.

64. Strobel, "Coming Full Circle," in *Filipino Americans: Transformation and Identity*, 68.

65. This interpretive move borrows from Allan Isaac's work. On the ex-colony as an afterimage of empire, see his *American Tropics: Articulating Filipino America* (Minneapolis: University of Minnesota Press, 2006), 11.

66. This and all subsequent quotes from this one-page review are from Jet Damaso, "Creatively Profound Indie," *Business World*, August 4, 2006, S3.

67. Lowe, *Immigrant Acts*, 48.

68. Ibid., 51.

69. Xing, *Asian America through the Lens*, 144.

6. Naked Brown Brothers

1. See Melissa Contreras, "*Sibak*, a Film with an International Calibre," *Manila Bulletin*, July 14, 1995, AT 1–2.

2. Rey Chow, *Primitive Passions: Visuality, Sexuality, Ethnography, and Contemporary Chinese Cinema* (New York: Columbia University Press, 1995), 9.

3. Ibid., 10.

4. Alan Stanbrook, "Crackdown in the Philippines," *Films and Filming*, June 1988, 20–22. One of Brocka's screenwriters, Jose F. Lacaba, speculates that the director made the film after getting into a relationship with a real-life macho dancer, who appears in a supporting role in the film. Jose F. Lacaba, e-mail to

Plaridel Papers mailing list, May 19, 2007, available at http://groups.yahoo.com/group/plaridel_papers.

5. The alternate scenes may have also been illicitly spliced into the film after it began circulating beyond the closely monitored screens of the nation's capital, as was customary in the distribution of Philippine adult movies.

6. Ian Victoriano, "Much Ado Over *Macho Dancer*," *National Midweek*, January 18, 1989, 20.

7. This was also the case with the *Macho Dancer* follow-up, *Midnight Dancers*, which had a running time of two hours and fifteen minutes in its international version as opposed to the one-hour-and-fifty-six-minute length of its censored Philippine version. See Susana de Guzman, "*New York Times* Praises *Sibak*," *Philippine Daily Inquirer*, August 2, 1995, C1.

8. Tom O'Regan notes the inclusion of foreign characters in Australian cinema as a way of appealing to international audiences. See his *Australian National Cinema* (London: Routledge, 1996), 52–53.

9. Elsaesser, "Putting on a Show: The European Art Movie," *Sight and Sound*, April 1994, 26.

10. Rolando B. Tolentino, "Transnationalization as Affected from Within: Contestation of the Nation-Space in Lino Brocka's *Jaguar*," *Asian Cinema* 9, no. 1 (Fall 1997): 42.

11. If, as Fredric Jameson suggests, "the visual is essentially pornographic . . . [asking] us to stare at the world as though it were a naked body," then the claustrophobic, slum-dotted Third World may well be pornographic to Western eyes. See Jameson's *Signatures of the Visible* (New York: Routledge, 1992), 1.

12. Angelo Restivo, *The Cinema of Economic Miracles: Visuality and Modernization in the Italian Art Film* (Durham, N.C.: Duke University Press, 2002), 155. Restivo makes his point about the film's economy of looks in the service of a broader, more sophisticated argument about postmodern visuality than what I am discussing here.

13. In the American "backstage musical," the song and dance numbers occur only in situations where the characters are supposed to be performing or rehearsing. The highlight usually involves the chorus girl's eleventh-hour conscription to assume the lead role in a stage show and her resulting triumph over adversity. The depiction of the arduous apprenticeship and rehearsal period teaches audiences to better appreciate the climactic performance. For more on the backstage musical, see Jane Feuer, *The Hollywood Musical*, 2nd ed. (Bloomington: Indiana University Press, 1988), 17–22.

14. Caryn James, "Mingling Sex and Politics in a Gay Bar in Manila," review of *Macho Dancer*, *New York Times*, March 16, 1990, CC 12.

15. Richard Gold, review of *Macho Dancer*, *Variety*, September 14, 1988, 31.

16. Harry Sheehan, review of *Macho Dancer*, *Hollywood Reporter*, April 19, 1997, 7.

17. Tolentino notes that different kinds of "entrapment" (including claustrophobia and "preventive class mobility") signify the horrors of the Marcos regime ("Transnationalization as Affected from Within," 35).

18. Emmanuel Reyes makes a similar argument about Brocka's return to the images of military violence associated with the Marcos regime: "What makes *Orapronobis* remarkable is that it was imagined in a time when most people had ceased to think about such macabre Marcos related issues as human rights abuses." See "Lino Brocka's *Orapronobis*: The Film of the Decade," in *Lino Brocka: The Artist and His Times*, ed. Mario Hernando (Manila: Cultural Center of the Philippines, 1993), 196.

19. Anon., "Film and Revolution," *Cinema Papers* 59 (September 1986): 16.

20. Hamid Naficy, "The Americanization and Indigenization of Lino Brocka through Cinema," *Framework* 38/39 (1992): 152.

21. James, "Mingling Sex and Politics in a Gay Bar in Manila," CC 12.

22. Thomas Waugh, "Sex Beyond Neon: Third World Gay Films?" in *The Fruit Machine: Twenty Years of Writing on Queer Cinema* (Durham, N.C.: Duke University Press, 2000), 152–53.

23. In an interview with Hamid Naficy, Brocka reiterated his familiar disavowal of the suggestion that his work is consciously political: "I am not a political filmmaker, this is just a label they have given me and I am not being modest." See Naficy, "The Americanization and Indigenization of Lino Brocka through Cinema," 153.

24. Andrew Higson, *Waving the Flag: Constructing a National Cinema in Britain* (Oxford: Oxford University Press, 1995), 154.

25. Thomas Elsaesser, *New German Cinema: A History* (New Brunswick, N.J.: Rutgers University Press, 1989), 280.

26. Melissa Contreras, "Pro and Contra *Orapronobis*," *Manila Chronicle*, November 11, 1989, 17.

27. A progovernment account of censorship policy in the Marcos era may be found in Guillermo de Vega, *Film and Freedom: Movie Censorship in the Philippines* (Manila: Guillermo de Vega, 1975).

28. Lena Pareja and Justino Dormiendo, "Censorship," in *CCP Encyclopedia of Philippine Art*, ed. Nicanor Tiongson (Manila: Cultural Center of the Philippines, 1994), 102–4.

29. Brocka was present at the airport to welcome Corazon's husband, Benigno Jr., on the day of the latter's assassination. He put his career on hold for two years to engage in protest work against Marcos. He campaigned for Corazon's presidential bid in the 1986 "snap elections." When she assumed power, Brocka was disappointed with her regime's policy on both cinema (including censorship) and social justice (i.e., her support for the interests of the upper crust and multinational corporations). See an incisive account of the director's politics in Jo-Ann Maglipon, "The Brocka Battles," in *Lino Brocka: The Artist and His Times*, ed. Mario Hernando (Manila: Cultural Center of the Philippines, 1993), 118–54.

30. On his initial enthusiasm about Aquino and cooperation with her administration, see Monique Neubourg, "Lino Brocka: de Marcos à Aquino," *Cinématographe* 120 (June 1986): 13; and also Stanbrook, "Crackdown in the Philippines," 20–22.

31. For a general picture of the censorship situation in the early years of the Aquino presidency see Anonymous, "People Power Loses Some of Its Bloom," *Cinema Papers*, November 1986, 4.

32. Nick Cruz, "*Macho Dancer*: A Postscript," in *Lino Brocka: The Artist and His Times*, ed. Mario Hernando (Manila: Cultural Center of the Philippines, 1993), 193.

33. Nick Cruz, "More on *Macho Dancer*," *Philippine Starweek*, March 5, 1989, 19.

34. Behn Cervantes, "*Macho Dancer*: A Sensitive Film Subject is Treated Sensibly," in *The Urian Anthology, 1980–1989*, ed. Nicanor G. Tiongson (Manila: Antonio P. Tuviera, 2001), 242.

35. In an interview with film scholar John Lent, Brocka describes how he worked for the expansion of the constitution's free speech provision by adding the term "expression," which could be interpreted to encompass cinema. See Lent, "Lino Brocka as Filmmaker, Dissident, and Constitutional Commissioner," *Asian Cinema* 8, no. 1 (Spring 1996): 78.

36. Rey Chow, *Primitive Passions: Visuality, Sexuality, Ethnography, and Contemporary Chinese Cinema* (New York: Columbia University, 1995), 169.

37. Ibid., 171.

38. Elsaesser notes the "reassignment of meaning" that occurs when foreign films travel. See his essay "Putting on a Show: The European Art Movie," *Sight and Sound*, April 1994, 25. The direct quote in the paragraph above is taken from Thomas Elsaesser, *New German Cinema: A History* (New Brunswick, N.J.: Rutgers University Press, 1989), 300.

39. Elsaesser, *New German Cinema*, 303.

40. As Alexander Doty puts it, "queerness can also be about the intersecting or combining of more than one specific form of nonstraight sexuality . . . [and also] evokes complex, often uncategorizable, erotic responses [to films and figures] from spectators who claim all sorts of real-life sexual identities." See his *Making Things Perfectly Queer* (Minneapolis: University of Minnesota Press, 1993), xvi–ix.

41. Martin Manalansan IV discusses the significance of this masculine ideal in *Global Divas: Filipino Gay Men in the Diaspora* (Durham, N.C.: Duke University Press, 2003), 25–26.

42. Chit Domingo, "*Macho Dancer*: Baklang anyo ng buhay" (*Macho Dancer*: A perverse life), *Philippine Currents*, February 1, 1989, 29.

43. Lawrence Chua, "Queer 'n' Asian," *CineVue: A Publication of Asian Cine-Vision*, December 1992, 8–9.

44. Joel David, "Macho Dancer: Text vs. Texture," *Kultura* 2, no. 2 (1989): 29.

45. B. Ruby Rich, "New Queer Cinema," *Sight and Sound*, September 1992, 30–34.

46. Leslie Camhi, "Strand and Deliver: Celebrating a Decade of Risky Business," *The Village Voice*, June 22, 1999, 156.

47. The four male stripper films were made by different film companies, and the only person involved in all of them was screenwriter Ricky Lee. Mel Chionglo directed the last three films. The publicity for the films, however, stressed the connections among them not only in terms of their subject matter but also in terms of the foreign demand that encouraged producers to make them. See, for example, Frank Mallo, "*Midnight Dancers*: A Worthy Sequel to Brocka's *Macho Dancer*," *Manila Chronicle*, July 11, 1995, 16.

48. Emmanuel Levy, review of *Midnight Dancers*, *Variety*, October 24, 1994, 71.

49. Richard von Busack, "Brought to Bare," *Metroactive*, November 16, 2000, http://www.metroactive.com/papers/metro/11.16.00/burleskking-0046.html (accessed June 19, 2010).

50. Emmanuel Levy, review of *Burlesk King*, *Variety*, February 7–13, 2000, 60.

51. Incomplete U.S. box office reports give the following grosses: *Macho Dancer*, $9,419 on a one-week run, selling about 2,372 tickets; *Midnight Dancers*, $22,480 on a one-week run, selling about 3,247 tickets; *Burlesk King*, $40,468 on several engagements, selling about 7,508 tickets. I accessed these figures on July 20, 2006, during a free trial of a now-discontinued feature of *Variety.com*. The database does not indicate whether or not these figures include earnings from film festival screenings. A free database, *The Numbers* (http://www.the-numbers.com), reports a slightly different gross ($39,036) for *Burlesk King*. Strand Releasing, which distributed *Macho Dancer* and *Burlesk King*, did not respond to several requests to verify the figures for the two films.

52. Roel Hoang Manipon, "Dancing in the Half-Light of Life," *The Daily Tribune*, August 10, 2006, http://www.tribune.net.ph/20060810/life/20060810lif1.html (accessed September 10, 2006; site now discontinued).

7. Philippine Cinema's Fatal Attractions

1. Young Critics Circle Film Desk, *Sampúng taóng sine: Philippine Cinema 1990–1999* (Ten years of movies) (Manila: National Commission for Culture and the Arts, 2002), 7.

2. According to a *Newsweek* poll, "60 percent of the country was following the trial." See David A. Kaplan, "Bobbitt Fever," *Newsweek*, January 24, 1994, 52–55.

3. Dick Hebdige writes that "everybody—willing or otherwise, whether consciously or not—is more or less cosmopolitan" because of their (differential) access to "late-20th century consumer culture." See his "Fax to the Future," *Marxism Today* (January 1990): 18–23.

4. Néstor García Canclini, *Hybrid Cultures: Strategies for Entering and Leaving Modernity*, trans. Christopher Chiappari and Silvia López (Minneapolis: University of Minnesota Press, 1995), xl.

5. Stuart Hall, "The Local and the Global: Globalization and Ethnicity," in *Culture, Globalization and the World-System: Contemporary Conditions for*

the Representation of Identity, ed. Anthony King (Minneapolis: University of Minnesota Press, 1997), 28.

6. Fredric Jameson, "Notes on Globalization as Philosophical Issue," in *The Cultures of Globalization*, ed. Fredric Jameson and Masao Miyoshi (Durham, N.C.: Duke University Press, 1998), 64.

7. Ulf Hannerz, "Scenarios for Peripheral Cultures," in *Culture, Globalization and the World-System: Contemporary Conditions for the Representation of Identity*, ed. Anthony King (Minneapolis: University of Minnesota Press, 1997), 107.

8. Thomas Elsaesser, "Chronicle of a Death Retold: Hyper, Retro or Counter Cinema," *Monthly Film Bulletin* 54 (1987): 166.

9. Thomas Elsaesser, "Putting on a Show: The European Art Movie," *Sight and Sound*, April 1994, 22–27.

10. Elsaesser uses the term "map of misreadings" to describe the often very different meanings and values assigned by audiences to foreign films. Ibid., 25.

11. One notable exception to this lack is Jeffrey Himpele, "Film Distribution as Media: Mapping Difference in the Bolivian Cinemascape," *Visual Anthropology Review* 12, no. 1 (Spring 1996): 47–66.

12. Arjun Appadurai, *Modernity at Large: Cultural Dimensions of Globalization* (Minneapolis: University of Minnesota Press, 1996), 46.

13. Jameson, "Notes on Globalization as Philosophical Issue," 61; George Ritzer, *The McDonaldization of Society* (London: Sage, 1993).

14. In an earlier piece I explored the usefulness of "hybridity" to Philippine film historiography. I still believe that the concept is valuable. It has explanatory force, especially when scholars define their particular use of the term. See José B. Capino, "Philippines: Cinema and Its Hybridity (Or 'You're nothing but a second-rate trying hard copycat!')," in *Contemporary Asian Cinemas: Popular Culture in a Global Frame*, ed. Anne T. Ciecko (Oxford: Berg, 2005), 32–44.

15. Canclini, *Hybrid Cultures*, xxvii.

16. George Yúdice, *The Expediency of Culture: Uses of Culture in the Global Era*, trans. Gabriela Ventureira (Durham, N.C.: Duke University Press, 2003), 359.

17. Jameson, "Notes on Globalization as Philosophical Issue," 70.

18. Appadurai, *Modernity at Large*, 32.

19. Ibid., 32.

20. *Oxford English Dictionary*, 1989 ed., s.v. "indigenization."

21. While the concept of hybridity acknowledges the agency of "cultural receivers," it has been criticized for occluding "the material dynamics of nationalism in neocolonial globalization"; see Pheng Cheah, "Given Culture: Rethinking Cosmopolitical Freedom in Transnationalism," in *Cosmopolitics: Thinking and Feeling Beyond the Nation*, ed. Pheng Cheah and Bruce Robbins (Minneapolis: University of Minnesota Press, 1998), 292.

22. Jan Nederveen Pieterse, *Globalization & Culture: Global Mélange* (New York: Rowman & Littlefield, 2004), 109.

23. Canclini, *Hybrid Cultures*, xxx–xxxi.

24. For the sake of brevity, my discussion will ignore the other fine distinctions Hannerz makes among these various concepts.
25. Hannerz, "Scenarios for Peripheral Cultures," 108.
26. Ibid., 123.
27. Ibid., 122.
28. Ibid., 108.
29. Ibid., 124.
30. Ibid., 126.
31. Ibid., 127.
32. Janet Maslin, "Film: 'Fatal Attraction' With Douglas and Close," *New York Times*, September 18, 1987, C10.
33. Angelo Restivo makes interesting observations about white telephones and Italian bourgeois dramas in his *The Cinema of Economic Miracles: Visuality and Modernization in the Italian Art Film* (Durham, N.C.: Duke University Press, 2002), 27.
34. Lisa Rofel, *Desiring China: Experiments in Neoliberalism, Sexuality and Public Culture* (Durham, N.C.: Duke University Press, 2007), 129.
35. John Tomlinson, *Cultural Imperialism* (Baltimore, Md.: The Johns Hopkins University Press, 1991), 114. The study he cites is John Sinclair, *Images Incorporated: Advertising as Industry and Ideology* (London: Croom Helm, 1987).
36. Walter Benjamin, "The Task of the Translator," in *Illuminations*, trans. Harry Zohn, ed. Hannah Arendt (New York: Shocken, 1969), 71.
37. Apart from expanding on Marcos's experiments with import liberalization, Corazon Aquino began the extensive privatization of government-owned companies. Her economic policies acquiesced with the neoliberalist programs of the International Monetary Fund (IMF) and World Bank.
38. For a detailed account of how the IMF influenced the Marcos administration's phased relaxation of import controls (including restrictions on nonessential consumer goods) during the early to mid-1980s, see Robin Broad, *Unequal Alliance: The World Bank, the International Monetary Fund, and the Philippines* (Berkeley: University of California Press, 1988), 78–79.
39. Fredric Jameson, in his readings of Edward Yang's *The Terrorizer* (1986) and Kidlat Tahimik's *The Perfumed Nightmare* (1977), skillfully demonstrates how the (uneven) impact of advanced capitalism's global spread registers in the spaces and architecture captured in the two films. See Jameson's *The Geopolitical Aesthetic: Cinema and Space in the World System* (Bloomington: Indiana University Press, 1995), 114–57, 186–213, for the two films, respectively.
40. Mary Louise Pratt uses the term "transculturation" to describe how "people on the receiving end of empire" appropriate "metropolitan modes of representation" so that they may, among other things, "talk back" to "dominant culture." See her *Imperial Eyes: Travel Writing and Transculturation*, 2nd ed. (New York: Routledge, 2008), 7.

41. Anthony King, introduction to *Culture, Globalization and the World-System: Contemporary Conditions for the Representation of Identity*, ed. Anthony King (Minneapolis: University of Minnesota Press, 1997), 17.

42. Tomlinson, *Globalization and Culture*, 133.

43. Ricardo Lo, "An Imeldific Role for Vivian V.," *Philippine Star*, January 21, 1990, 13.

44. M. L. Celestial, "Vivian Velez: Bewitching," *Woman's Home Companion*, November 8, 1989, 56.

45. Ibid., 57.

46. Eric Caruncho, "Women of Independent Means," *Sunday Times Magazine*, March 18, 1990, 5.

47. Benjamin Pimentel Jr., "The Dawning of Dawn Zulueta," *National Midweek*, April 19, 1989, 42.

48. Frederick Buell, *National Culture and the New Global System* (Baltimore, Md.: The Johns Hopkins University Press, 1994), 27.

49. In cultural citizenship, "belonging is not merely a political attribute but also a process in which culture becomes a relevant category of affinity." See Rofel, *Desiring China*, 94.

50. Ibid., 106.

51. Thomas Elsaesser, *New German Cinema: A History* (New Brunswick, N.J.: Rutgers University Press, 1989), 280.

52. Hannerz, "Scenarios for Peripheral Cultures," 135.

53. Ulf Hannerz, "Cosmopolitans and Locals in World Culture," in *Global Culture: Nationalism, Globalization and Modernity*, ed. Mike Featherstone (London: Sage, 1990), 240. Hall also invokes the notion of "selective response"; see Hall, "The Local and the Global," 89.

54. Joel David, "Woman-Worthy," review of *Kasalanan ba'ng sambahin ka?*, *National Midweek*, October 17, 1990, 28–29.

55. Bliss Cua Lim discusses one of these true crime hits in "True Fictions: Women's Narratives and Historical Trauma," *Velvet Light Trap* 45 (Spring 2000): 62–75.

56. Tomlinson, *Globalization and Culture*, 147.

57. Hannerz, "Scenarios for Peripheral Cultures," 125.

58. *Oxford English Dictionary*, 1989 ed., s.v. "transmutation."

59. Kaplan, "Bobbitt Fever," 54.

60. Newspaper critic Manuel Pichel interprets this family tradition of wife beating as a preposterous suggestion that "the fault is in the genes." I disagree with his interpretation even though I concur with other points in his review. See Manuel Pichel, "Cashing In on the Sensational," review of *Loretta*, *Manila Times*, June 27, 1994, B6.

61. Barbara Ehrenreich, "Feminism Confronts Bobbittry," *Time*, January 24, 1994, 74.

62. Kaplan, "Bobbitt Fever," 55.

63. Cynthia Fuchs, "'Looks Like a Dick!'" review of *John Wayne Bobbitt Uncut*, *Philadelphia Citypaper*, n.d., http://www.mith2.umd.edu/WomensStudies/FilmReviews/bobbitt-uncut-fuchs (accessed June 19, 2010).

64. The problem of the woman's pleasure would inevitably be raised in *John Wayne Bobbitt Uncut* because it is a central issue in heterosexual pornography. See Linda Williams, *Hardcore: Power, Pleasure, and the "Frenzy of the Visible"* (Berkeley: University of California Press, 1999).

65. One of the films in chapter 2, *In the Claws of an Eagle*, features Coseteng in a lead role. She even shares an on-screen kiss with the protagonist. My brief treatment of that film, however, omits her only because that chapter's argument does not require a discussion of her character.

66. David Grogan and Joyce Wagner, "Cashing In," *People*, August 8, 1994, 28; Kaplan, "Bobbitt Fever," 54.

67. The term "transnational activism" is used in Richard Falk, "The Making of Global Citizenship," in *Global Visions: Beyond the New World Order*, ed. Jeremy Brecher, John Brown Childs, and Jill Cutler (Boston: South End Press, 1993), 47. The work of Amnesty International—which, for instance, campaigned globally in 1995 for a stay of execution on behalf of the Filipina maid Flor Contemplacion, who was accused of murder and executed in Singapore—is one example of transnational activism.

68. Hannerz, "Scenarios for Peripheral Cultures," 124.

69. My use of the term "decay" is inspired by Tomlinson who evokes "the spread of a sort of cultural decay from the West to the rest of the world" in *Cultural Imperialism*, 164.

70. Benjamin, "The Task of the Translator," 71.

71. Ibid., 79.

72. Sandra Bermann's gloss on Benjamin is illuminating in this regard. "According to Benjamin," Bermann writes, "translation is essential to the 'living on' of texts. Indeed, without translation, and its close kin, interpretation, the original will die. As translation reinterprets the original for different audiences, it provides for its continual flourishing and, in the process, for the future of national and transnational cultures." See her introduction to *Nation, Language, and the Ethics of Translation*, coedited with Michael Wood (Princeton, N.J.: Princeton University Press, 2005), 6.

Filmography

Beast of Blood (Eddie Romero, 1971, English), IE.
Brides of Blood (Gerardo de Leon and Eddie Romero, 1968, English), IE.
Burlesk King (Mel Chionglo, 1999, Filipino, subtitles), STR.
Cavite (Neill Dela Llana and Ian Gamazon, 2005, English and Filipino, subtitles), MP.
The Debut (Gene Cajayon, 2000, English), SN.
Dubai (Rory B. Quintos, 2005, Filipino, subtitles), SR.
The Flip Side (Rod Pulido, 2001, English), NLA.
Hellow, Soldier, in *Three, Two, One* (*Tatlo, dalawa, isa*, Lino Brocka, 1975, Filipino, subtitles), CF.
Hopefully, Once More (*Sana maulit muli*, Olivia Lamasan, 1995, Filipino, subtitles), SR.
In the Claws of an Eagle (*Sa kuko ng agila*, Augusto Buenaventura, 1989, Filipino, no subtitles), AV, KC.
Is It a Sin to Worship You? (*Kasalanan ba'ng sambahin ka?*, Chito Roño, 1990, Filipino, no subtitles), NLA.
Loretta (Mel Chionglo, 1994, Filipino, no subtitles), IV, KC.
Macho Dancer (Lino Brocka, 1988, Filipino, subtitles), STR, VE.
Mad Doctor of Blood Island (Gerardo de Leon and Eddie Romero, 1968, English), IE.
'Merika (Gil Portes, 1984, Filipino, no subtitles), SM, KC.
Midnight Dancers (*Sibak*, Mel Chionglo, 1994, Filipino, subtitles), FR.
Of Different Races (*Magkaibang lahi*, Ramon Estella, 1947, Filipino, no subtitles), KC.
Olongapo . . . The Great American Dream (*Exit Subic*, Chito Roño, 1987, English and Filipino, no subtitles), NLA.
Once a Moth (*Minsa'y isang gamu-gamo*, Lupita Aquino-Concio, 1976, Filipino, no subtitles), VE, KC.
Phil-American Boy (*Batang PX*, Jose Javier Reyes, 1997, Filipino, subtitles), SR.
PX (Lino Brocka, 1984, Filipino, no subtitles), NLA.
Terror Is a Man (Gerardo de Leon, 1959, English), WS.

Key to Filmography Abbreviations

AV	Aquarius Video, Philippines, available at Kabayan Central (KC)
CF	CineFilipino, http://www.cinefilipino.com
FR	First Run Features, http://firstrunfeatures.com
IE	Image Entertainment, http://www.image-entertainment.com
IV	Ivory Music and Video, Philippines, available at KC
KC	Kabayan Central, http://kabayancentral.com
MP	Magnolia Pictures, http://www.magpictures.com
NLA	No longer available
SM	Solar Multimedia Corporation, Philippines, available at KC
SN	Sony Pictures Home Video, http://www.sonypictures.com/homevideo
SR	Star Recording, a division of ABS–CBN, http://www.starrystarry.com
STR	Strand Releasing, http://www.strandreleasing.com
VE	Viva Entertainment, Philippines, available at KC
WS	Wellspring (now defunct), remainders at http://www.amazon.com

Index

Note: All titles refer to films unless otherwise specified. All locations pertain to the Philippines unless otherwise indicated.

abandonment, 70, 73, 76, 77, 88, 99, 102
Abraham, Nicolas, 261n56
ABS-CBN Film Productions Inc., 110, 131
Adams, James Truslow, 255n1
Address Unknown, xxix–xxx
adultery, laws regarding, 229
Agamben, Giorgio, 45, 46, 48, 52, 53, 65–66, 250n42, 250n60, 250n63, 251n65
agitprop films, xxxi, 46, 60, 63
Agoncillo, Teodoro, xvi
Aguilar, Filomeno, Jr., 137, 149
Aguiluz, Tikoy (*Boatman*), 183, 185
Aguinaldo, Emilio, 41, 159
AIDS, 194, 207
Alejandre, Mac (*I Will Always Love You*), 132
alienation, 222, 224; from American dream, 113, 115–16, 132; Filipino American feelings of, 112, 150, 158, 161, 165, 166
allegories: colonial, 17–18, 97; in horror films, 9; of mixed-race children, 70; neoliberal, 98; postcolonial, xv–xvi, xx
ambivalence, feelings of, 53, 90, 108, 110–23, 133, 151
Amerasians, xxix, 69–104; American citizenship restrictions, 73, 86, 90; American dream of, 74–90; American fantasies of, 92, 104, 239, 240; colonial view of, 94–95; search for fathers, 69, 71–74, 76
American dream: of Amerasians, 74–90; dissatisfaction with, xix, 107–8, 110–23, 130, 132, 237; of Filipino Americans, 135–62; Hollywood image of, 203; immigrants', xiv–xv, 156, 255n1; women's success through, 123, 124, 126, 127, 130, 132–33. *See also* daydreams; *Olongapo . . . The Great American Dream*
American Mestizo Protective Association, 73
Americans. *See* anti-Americanism; cinema: American; fathers,

273

American; Philippine–American relations; United States
Amnesty International, 269n67
Anderson, Benedict, 259n26
Ang pagdadalaga ni Maximo Oliveros. See *Blossoming of Maximo Oliveros, The*
anti-Americanism, 110, 119, 255n38, 256n15
anticolonialism. *See* nationalism/nationalists, anticolonial
antidiplomacy. *See* cold war, U.S. tactics of
anti-imperialism, xxiii, xxvii, 49, 62–63, 89, 119, 187
antinationalism, 88–89. *See also* nationalism/nationalists, Philippine
apathy, 113, 116
Appadurai, Arjun, 157, 204
Appiah, Kwame Anthony, 137
Aquino, Benigno, Jr., assassination of, 263n29
Aquino, Corazon, 90, 98; administration of, 186, 188, 263n29; economic policies of, 209, 267n37; repression by, 182, 184
Aquino, Ninoy, assassination of, 116, 121, 256n13
Aquino-Concio, Lupita (*Once a Moth*), 33, 34, 39–52, 55, 62, 63, 66, 254n21, 260n48
Archer, Anne, role in *Fatal Attraction*, 207, 211, 213, 216
Armes, Roy, xxiii, xxx, 244n1
Arroyo, Gloria M., 165
art houses, Philippine films made for, 171–97
Asia, U.S. presence in, 28, 34, 45, 66
Asian American Film Institute, The (TAAFI), 253n5

Asian Americans, 136, 148, 167, 253n5. *See also* Filipino Americans
assimilation: cultural, 143, 151, 206; fantasies of, 135–36, 138; immigrant, 136–39, 140, 146, 154, 166
atavism, new, 91–102, 104, 153
audiences, domestic, 110, 173–74, 176, 189, 192, 194, 196–97, 201. *See also* censorship, Philippine
Aunor, Nora, 109
avant-garde films, xxxi, 196, 201

Balagtas, Rogelio, murder of, 45, 48
balut (Philippine food), 161, 162
Bascara, Victor, 258n4
bases, U.S. military, 33–67; closing of, 60, 65, 98; films about, xxiii, 240; life on periphery of, xxix, 52–60, 61, 62, 63; negotiations to renew agreement, 36, 38–39, 41, 49, 60, 62, 237; nuclear weapons on, 45, 49, 65; protests against, 34–36, 38, 40, 48, 63–64; as sovereign sphere, 37, 38, 41–42, 44, 45–46, 48–52, 53
Bataan death march, 42–43, 154–55, 249n29, 260n48
Batang PX. See *Phil-American Boy*
Bathhouse, 172
Beast of Blood, 7, 27–31
belonging, 268n49; Filipino American, 107, 149, 150; national, 72, 89–90, 104, 135, 235; transnational, 156, 167, 214. *See also* homeland
benevolence: American, xiii, xxix, 33, 34, 41, 42, 43, 65–66, 67; of empire, 22, 33–36, 50, 52, 59, 97
Benevolent Assimilation Proclamation of 1898, 34

Benhabib, Sayla, 258n9
Benjamin, Walter, 208, 233, 269n72
Bermann, Sandra, 269n72
bestialization. *See* natives, Filipino: seen as animals
Bhabha, Homi, 50, 52, 72–73
Bikini Atoll, 19–20
bildungsroman, immigrant, 123, 137, 166
biopolitics, 35, 46, 48, 50, 53, 62, 250n42; of concentration camps, 52, 250n60, 250n63
Black Mama, White Mama, 4, 5
blackness, 145, 151
Blood Creature. See *Terror is a Man*
Blood Drinkers, The. See *Blood Is the Color of Night*
Blood Island (Isla de Sangre) films, 7–32
Blood Is the Color of Night (*Kulay dugo ang gabi*), 4
Blossoming of Maximo Oliveros, The (*Ang pagdadalaga ni Maximo Oliveros*), 196
B-movies, 3, 4, 5–6, 9. *See also* science fiction horror films
Boatman, 183, 185
Bobbitt, John Wayne and Lorena, films based on story of, 201, 219–31
bodies: empire's violation of, 35–36; male, 184, 185, 189, 196; native, 62, 172, 175, 187; tortured, 7, 197
bomba films, 184–85
boomerang effect, 251n75
borders, cinematic, 109–10, 135, 235, 240
Bosworth, Stephen, 36, 38–39
Brides of Blood, 6, 7, 18–24, 30, 247n53
Brighter Summer Day, A (*Guling jie shaonian sha ren shijian*), xxviii–xix

Brocka, Lino, 186, 263n23, 263n29, 264n35; *Hellow, Soldier*, 70, 74–82, 86, 102–3, 104; *Macho Dancer*, 171, 172–92, 193, 197, 265n51; *Manila: In the Claws of Neon*, 181–82; *Orapronobis*, 184, 263n18; *PX*, 33, 34, 52–60, 62, 63
Brooks, Peter, 256n14
Buenaventura, Augusto, *In the Claws of an Eagle*, 33, 60–65, 251n76, 269n65
Bulosan, Carlos, 158, 258n13
Burlesk King, 171, 193–95, 265n51
Butler, Judith, 146

Cadzyn, Eric, xxx
Cajayon, Gene, 259n29; *The Debut*, 135, 136, 137, 139–50, 154, 155, 161, 164, 166, 167
callboys, 192–93. *See also* prostitution: male; sex workers
Canada, Filipino migration to, 235–36
Canclini, Néstor García, 202, 204
Cannes film festival, Philippine films shown at, 172, 253n5
Caparas, Carlo J., *Vizconde Massacre Story: God Help Us!, The*, 219
capital accumulation, 242n24, 254n33
capitalism: American, 133; global, xxiii, 200, 208, 209, 219, 267n39; imperialism's relationship to, 49, 130; justice under, 86, 90, 237; transnational, xxi, xxv, 162, 209
Cavalry Command, 4, 8
Cavite, 135, 136, 137, 158–66, 167
Cellular (film, U.S.), 158
censorship, Philippine, 173, 184–85, 187, 217, 262n5, 262n7, 263n29

Césaire, Aimé, 251n75
Cheng, Anne Anlin, 150–51, 157
children: forced into prostitution, 161, 180; mixed-race, 69–70, 72, 73, 94–95, 100, 104; precocious, 32; resulting from prostitution, 83, 84, 92. *See also* Amerasians; Filipino Americans
China, 37; cinema in, 187, 203
Chionglo, Mel, 265n47; *Burlesk King*, 171, 193–95, 265n51; *Loretta*, 201, 203, 205, 219–31, 232, 233; *Midnight Dancers*, 171, 172, 192–94, 262n7, 265n51; *Twilight Dancers*, 195
Chow, Rey, xiii, xxiv–xxv, xxx, 57, 108, 119, 172, 187, 196, 250n42, 251n71
Chua, Lawrence, 190
cinema: American, 3–32, 192, 194; Asian American, 167, 253n5; Australian, 262n8; Chinese, 187, 203; counter-telling concept of, 242n23; Filipino American, 150; German, 121, 183, 214; peripheral, 202–6; Third World, 200, 240; transnational, xxi, xxvi–xxviii. *See also* Hollywood films; *and specific film genres and titles*
cinema, Philippine: American influences in, xviii–xxxi, 150, 204, 216, 240; gay, 171–97; nationalist, 33, 239–40; studio-era, xiii; transnational, 3–32, 33, 70–71, 109, 135–67, 171–97, 199, 201, 250n57. *See also* audiences, domestic; decolonization: cinema of; *and specific film genres and titles*
citizenship, 95–96, 112, 115–16, 138, 214; Amerasian's status of, 73, 86, 90; American, 154, 158, 159–60, 161; cultural, xxvii, 156, 268n49; global, 107, 214

Clark Air Base, 49, 50
Clerks, 150
Clinton, Bill, 97–98
Close, Glenn, role in *Fatal Attraction*, 199, 207, 208, 210, 211, 213, 214, 215
Clouzot, Henri-Georges, *Les Diaboliques*, 217
cognitive mapping, 241n8, 243n34
cold war: end of, 32; films during, 19, 23, 24, 45; U.S. tactics of, xxviii, 22, 28, 30–31, 37, 42
Cole, Larry, murder of Filipino by, 45, 48
colonialism: aftermath of, xxii, 31, 55, 70, 72, 74; devastation from, 74–82, 103–4, 244n1; end of, xvii–xviii, 34; fantasies of, 92, 172; films of, xxii–xxiii, 7, 242n23; history of, xxviii, 7–9; mentality of, 138, 155; struggles against, 18, 48; vestiges of, 25–26, 36, 91, 94–95, 99–100. *See also* ex-colonized, the; ex-colonizers; neocolonialism
comedy films, xviii
commerce: postcolonial, 8, 31; transnational, xx, 100, 130–31, 162
communism, U.S. containment of, 19, 28, 34, 45, 184
complacency, 110, 113, 116, 156, 183
complex transmutations, 219–31, 232
Computer Man (television series), 213
concentration camps, 52, 250n60, 250n63
Concio, Lupita. *See* Aquino-Concio, Lupita
concubinage, laws regarding, 229
Constantino, Renato, Jr., 64
consumerism, 202, 204, 265n3
Contemplacion, Flor, 269n67
Contreras, Melissa G., 251n76

Coseteng, Dominique, 229, 269n65
cosmopolitanism, 216, 232;
  bourgeois, 207, 208, 209;
  mundane, xxvii, 201, 206,
  210–11, 213
creolization scenario, 206
criminal jurisdiction, American
  exceptions to, 35–36, 38, 45–46,
  48, 67, 248n21
Cruz, Nick, 186–87
Cullather, Nick, xvi
Cullen, Jim, 255n1
cultural appropriation, xix, 205, 231–33
cultural inheritance, 146–47, 156,
  161, 167
cultural transactions, 203, 206
cultural translation, xix, 210, 220,
  232, 259n28, 269n72
culture(s): American, 7–8, 136, 149,
  151, 237–38; Asian American,
  258n4; assimilation of, 143, 151,
  206; colonial, 244n1; conflicts
  between, 41; consumer, 202, 204,
  265n3; decay of, 269n69; global,
  171, 199, 201–3, 206, 209, 216,
  219, 220; homogenization of,
  137–38, 205–6; hybrid, 136, 141,
  144–45, 266n21; local–global
  encounters in, 200, 231–33;
  peripheral, 205, 230, 231;
  Philippine, 63, 138, 142–43, 149,
  161, 167, 238; politics of, 138,
  148, 154, 159; Third World, 180,
  205–6, 238, 240; transnational,
  xxvii, 233, 269n72
Cummings, Alan, 88

David, Joel, 192, 219, 256n11
daydreams: consumerist, xviii–xix;
  in Filipino films, xx, xxxi, 151,
  171; national, xviii, xxi–xxii;
  Third World, 240. *See also*
American dream; fantasies,
  American
Day of the Trumpet. See *Cavalry Command*
Debut, The, 135, 136, 137, 139–50,
  154, 155, 161, 164, 166, 167
decolonization: assimilation and,
  135, 136–39; cinema of, xx,
  xxii–xxv, xxxi–xxxiii, 3, 7,
  33, 63, 69, 84, 88–89, 91, 132,
  166–67; cultural productions
  of, 172; fantasies of, xvii–xviii,
  64, 96, 97, 98, 102, 104, 238–41;
  future of, 72, 91, 102, 104;
  globalization's relationship to,
  xxii–xxvi, 65, 201–2; history
  of, xx, 239; nationalism and,
  91, 104; postcolonialism and,
  82, 242n27; postnationalism
  and, 103–4; progress in, xxi,
  107, 236, 237; skepticism of,
  99; U.S. imperialism in, 35,
  38, 57; women's role in, 101–2;
  wretchedness of, 75, 76. *See also*
ex-colonized, the; ex-colonizers
Defiant Ones, The, Philippine movie
  based on, 4
Dela Llana, Neill (*Cavite*), 135, 136,
  137, 158–66, 167
De Leon, Gerardo, 3, 245n19; *Blood
  is the Color of Night*, 4, 7; *Brides
  of Blood*, 6, 7, 18–24, 30, 247n53;
  Mad Doctor of Blood Island, 7,
  24–27; *Terror is a Man*, 7, 9–18,
  19, 246n37
Delmendo, Sharon, 255n38, 256n15
del Mundo, Clodualdo, Jr., 256n13
democracy, American pluralist,
  136–37, 138, 156
Derrida, Jacques, 37, 49
diaspora, Filipino, xxiii, 90, 120, 121,
  131, 133; films of, 135–67, 240

Flip Side, The, 135, 136, 137, 150–57, 158, 161, 166, 167
foreign markets, Philippine films made for, 4, 6, 171–97, 199, 264n38, 265n47, 266n10
forgetting: cultural, 205; trope of, 113–16
Foucault, Michel, 46, 249n41, 250n42
Frankenstein (novel, Shelley), 10, 17–18
free world, the, xxi, 19, 37, 45
Freud, Sigmund, 71
Fuchs, Cynthia, 226

Gamazon, Ian (*Cavite*), 135, 136, 137, 158–66, 167
Gandhi, Mahatma, 101
gay films, 171–97, 214
gender, 12, 135; politics of, 109, 123, 188, 192, 197, 229, 256n10. *See also* feminine, the; manhood; masculinity; women
generations, conflicts between, 139–50, 259n28
genital mutilation, 201, 219, 221, 228
geopolitics, xx–xxi, xxv, xxviii–xxix, 37, 165
Germany. *See* cinema: German
GI babies. *See* Amerasians
globalization, 132, 210, 219–31, 266n21; American fantasies of, xx, 238–41; cinema of, xxv, 7, 171, 199, 202–6, 210–11; culture of, xxiv, 172, 216, 219, 220, 231, 238; decolonization's relationship to, xxii–xxvii, 65, 201–2; progress in, 104, 236, 237; U.S. as figure of, xix, 196–97
Goddess (*Shen nu*), 251n71

guerilla warfare, Philippine, 18, 76, 162–63
Gutierrez, Ruffa, 219–20

Halberstam, Judith, 7, 9, 17–18
hallucinatory whitening. *See* lactification fantasy
Hannerz, Ulf, 205–6, 216
Harber, Harry Paul, 10
Harvey, David, 66, 254n33
Heart of Darkness (novel, Conrad), Philippine movie based on, 27
Hebdige, Dick, xxvii, 201, 265n3
Hellow, Soldier, 70, 74–82, 86, 102–3, 104
heterosexuality. *See* eroticism: heterosexual
Higson, Andrew, 183
history, xxii–xxiii, 10, 241n7; of American imperialism, 3, 7–8, 9, 31–32, 245n21; Philippine, 138, 167
Hjort, Mette, xxx
Hollywood films: global nature of, xxix, 201–6, 216; Philippine remakes of, xviii, xxvi, xxvii, 240. *See also Fatal Attraction*, Philippine remake of
homeland: belonging to, 107, 108, 110, 112, 115–16; outsider status in, 81, 156; parental, 135–36, 138, 147, 155, 157, 158; repudiation of, 76, 82, 86, 88–89, 91, 103–4, 161, 164–66; returning to, 117, 120–21, 123, 130–31, 133; violence in, 41
homosexuality, 171–97, 214, 264n40
Hong Kong, cinema in, 203
Hopefully, Once More (*Sana maulit muli*), 107, 108, 110, 123–33, 137, 236, 237, 257n27, 257n28

horror films. *See* science fiction horror films
hospitality: lack of in America, xv, 80, 115; Philippine, xv, 55, 58, 77
Hunt, Lynn, 71
hustlers. *See* prostitution: male
hybridization, 203, 204, 205, 206, 220, 266n14, 266n21

identity, 103, 258n9; fables of, xxiii, 135; Filipino American, 135–67, 239; hybrid, 144–46; immigrant, 260n52; national, 5, 39, 40, 42, 72, 90, 167; politics of, 164–65; sexual, 190, 214, 264n40; transnational, 156, 157, 260n52. *See also* Amerasians; Asian Americans; feminine, the; Filipino Americans; masculinity; race/racism, issues of
imaginaries: American, 171, 197, 201; cold war, 45; Filipino American, 149; national, xxi, 202; postcolonial, xix, 244n1
immigrants/immigration: alienation of, 112, 115–16, 119; by Amerasians, 73, 86, 91; American dream of, xiv–xv, 156, 255n1; assimilation of, 136–39, 140, 146, 154, 166; identities of, 260n52; illegal, 118, 126; intergenerational conflicts among, 139–50, 259n28; patrimony of, 146, 155; postcolonial, 107–10, 120, 121, 129, 130–31, 133, 135; prostitution as path to, 53, 57; second generation of, 135–67; U.S. policies on, 73, 136. *See*
also migrant women; migrant workers; repatriation
imperialism, 9–18, 27–31, 38, 92; cultural, 201–4; end to, 32, 100; films about, xxiii, xxvii; globalization's relationship to, xxiv, 104; struggles against, 48, 62–63; subjectivities of, 12, 93. *See also* anti-imperialism; empire
imperialism, American, 24, 35, 45, 65–66, 258n4; films about, 3, 9–18; issues related to, 12, 23, 31–32, 237. *See also* empire: American; social engineering
incest, xxix, 25, 178, 194
indigenization, 203, 204–5, 207
Indonesia, mixed-race children in, 72
I Need You (*Kailangan kita*), 132
International Monetary Fund (IMF), 267n37, 267n38
In the Claws of an Eagle (*Sa kuko ng agila*), 33, 60–65, 251n76, 269n65
intimacy, 12, 88, 189; colonial, xv, 43, 60–61, 73–74, 86
Iraq, U.S. invasion of, 66
Isaac, Allan, xxx, 8, 17, 31
Is It a Sin to Worship You? (*Kasalanan ba'ng sambahin ka?*), 199–201, 203, 205, 220, 231, 232, 233; *Fatal Attraction* compared to, 207–19
Isla de Sangre. *See* Blood Island (Isla de Sangre) films
Island of Doctor Moreau, The (novel, Wells), 16, 246n37; Philippine films based on, 4, 10, 12
Israel, nation making in, xxi
I Will Always Love You, 132

Jaikumar, Priya, xxx
James, Caryn, 182
Jameson, Fredric, xii, xix, xxv, xxvi, xxx, 202, 204, 241n8, 243n34, 251n73, 262n11, 267n39
Japanese Americans, internment of, 160
Jeremy, Ron, *John Wayne Bobbitt Uncut*, 221, 226, 229, 269n64
Johnson, Chalmers, 7, 8, 38, 66
John Wayne Bobbitt Uncut, 221, 226, 229, 269n64
justice, 90, 113, 263n29

Kailangan kita. See *I Need You*
Kandiyoti, Deniz, 108, 119
Kaplan, Amy, 8
Kasalanan ba'ng sambahin ka?. See *Is it a Sin to Worship You?*
Kennedy, John F., xxix, 80–81, 254n21
Kenney, Kristie, 65, 66
Khanna, Ranjana, 255n37
Ki-duk, Kim (*Address Unknown*), xxix–xxx
Kleinhans, Chuck, 243n44
Kramer, Stanley (*The Defiant Ones*), 4
Kulay dugo ang gabi. See *Blood Is the Color of Night*

lactification fantasy, 69–70, 74, 76, 80, 81, 91, 97. See also whiteness: desire for
Lamasan, Olivia: *Hopefully, Once More*, 107, 108, 110, 123–33, 151, 236, 237, 257n27, 257n28; *Milan*, 131
LaPlace, Maria, 123
law of the jungle, 48–49
Lee, Ricky, 88–89, 193, 195, 265n47
Lerner, Max, 22

Les Diaboliques, 217
Levy, Emmanuel, 194
liberalism, 194, 196. See also neoliberalism
life, loss of rights to, 36, 45, 46, 48, 50, 53, 66, 251n65. See also biopolitics; thanatopolitics
Lim, Bliss Cua, 9
Loretta, 201, 203, 205, 219–31, 232, 233
love, interracial, xiv–xv. See also miscegenation
low-budget films, American, made in Philippines, 3–4, 5–6, 7
Lowe, Lisa, 137, 166, 259n28
Lowenstein, Adam, 9
Lu, Sheldon, xxvi
Luzon region, typhoon in, 65, 66
Lyne, Adrian (*Fatal Attraction*), 199–201, 204, 205–6, 207–19, 220, 231

machismo, 132, 189
Macho Dancer, 171, 172–92, 193, 197, 265n51
Mad Doctor of Blood Island, 7, 24–27
Magkaibang lahi. See *Of Different Races*
Makati financial district, New York City compared to, 207, 208, 209, 232
male stripper films, 171–97, 240, 265n47
Manalansan, Martin, IV, 264n41
manhood, 62, 135, 143, 158. See also masculinity; patriarchy
Manila: flesh trade in, 176; World War II devastation in, xvi, 38
Manila: In the Claws of Neon (*Maynila: Sa mga kuko ng liwanag*), 181–82

Manila Film Center (MFC), 184–85
Manunuri ng Pelikulang Pilipino (Manila film critics), 199
map of misreadings, 266n10
Marchetti, Gina, xxvi
Marcos, Ferdinand: base agreement negotiations and, 39–40, 49; dissident cinema under, 184; fall of, 256n11; New Society of, 76; protests against, 64, 109, 110, 117, 121, 263n18, 263n29; reign of terror, 182, 251n71, 251n73, 263n17; relations with U.S. government, 98; sexual perversity under, 185, 197; trade policies of, 209, 267n37, 267n38
marriage, interracial, xiv–xv. *See also* miscegenation
martial law, 81, 121, 182
masculinity, 228; American, 140; colonial view of, 92, 94, 101; Filipino, 62, 140, 143; Filipino American, 137, 144–46, 159, 258n13; homosexual, 189, 190, 192; renewal of, 127–28, 129, 133, 146–48; validating, 79, 119. *See also* emasculation; manhood; patriarchy
Maslin, Janet, 207
materialism, 107, 112–13, 143
Maynila: Sa mga kuko ng liwanag. See *Manila: In the Claws of Neon*
McCabe, Colin, xix
McDonaldization thesis, 203, 204
McKinley, William, 34
Mella-Salvador, Shaira, 257n28
melodramas, xviii, 194, 211, 256n11, 256n14, 256n21; bourgeois, 208; female, 93, 121, 123, 129, 132, 133, 254n22; male, 131, 235–36, 237; political, 33, 184; pornographic, 180

Memmi, Albert, xix, xxii, 11–12, 75, 136, 138
Mendoza, Brilliante (*Service*), 172
Mendoza-Del Rosario, Mel, 257n28
'*Merika*, 107, 108, 109–23, 124, 126, 129, 132, 133, 137, 256n11
metropole, the: cultural transmission from, 205, 241n3; Filipino American settlement in, 136; periphery and, 214, 229–30, 231, 232–33
Michael Jackson's This Is It, 238
middle class: American, 110, 113, 116, 118, 123, 132, 208, 209; Filipino, 94, 110, 121, 132, 145, 154, 219
Midnight Dancers (*Sibak*), 171, 172, 192–94, 262n7, 265n51
migrant women, 107–33; films about, 240; liberation of, 123–33; repatriation of, 109, 110–23, 127, 128–32, 133; sexual agency of, 108–9
migrant workers, 90, 132, 235–36, 237, 260n53
Milan, 131
minorities, 136, 141, 159–60, 161, 210
Minsa'y isang gamu-gamo. See *Once a Moth*
miscegenation, xv, 23, 30, 72
mobility: dream of, 85, 86, 90, 95, 97, 99, 103; Western, 126–27, 131, 237
modernity, xxx, 46, 52, 108, 249n41
Modleski, Tania, 256n21
monster films, 3–32, 239, 247n47
Mooney, Michael, murder of Filipino by, 48
morality, 12, 94, 95, 186, 187

mothers, Filipino, 70, 254n22; recognition of, 95, 100, 101, 103, 104; redemption of, 71, 82, 91; repudiation of, 76–77, 83, 89, 94, 96–97, 103, 239; weakness of, 86, 88

movies. *See* cinema; cinema, Philippine; Hollywood films; *and specific genres and titles of films*

Mowitt, John, xxx

Mt. Pinatubo, eruption of, 65

multiculturalism, 258n4, 258n9; American, 136, 137, 142, 148–49, 166, 208, 209; education in, 154–55, 156

murders, of Filipinos by American military, 45, 48

musicals, American, 179, 262n13

Muslims, 158, 160–61; terrorist activities of, 159, 162, 163–64, 165

Nandy, Ashis, 89, 100, 101

narcissism, 119, 214

narratives: of abandonment, 102; of empire, 7, 92, 100; of formation, 137–38; of immigrant families, 141

nationalism/nationalists, Philippine, 39, 80, 256n15; ambiguous, 82, 95; anticolonial, xxiii, 33, 104, 107, 109, 130, 239; attraction of, 119, 120, 121–23, 132; cultural, 63, 136; decolonization and, 91, 104; failures of, 39, 159; immigration and, 131, 155; middle-class, 110; neocolonial, 36, 266n21; patriarchal, 108, 127, 133, 159, 239; politics of, 109, 123; post–September 11, 165; protests against U.S. bases, xxviii–xxx, 36, 38, 40, 42, 43, 48; women's roles in, 108, 119–20, 121. *See also* anti-Americanism; antinationalism; postnationalism

nationality, 137, 138. *See also* Amerasians; children: mixed-race; Filipino Americans

national origin validation, 155, 156

nation building, xxi, 98, 101, 119, 133, 136, 186

nation-state, Philippine, 109–10; postcolonial, 61–64, 76, 102, 103; sovereignty of, 36, 37, 40, 45, 255n4

natives, Filipino, 36, 61, 92; fantasies of revenge, 50, 52; homicidal melancholia in, 54, 58–59; loss of rights, xxii, 7, 46, 48, 50, 52–53; new, 17–18, 29, 30; in Philippine films, xxiii, xxviii, 11, 15, 24–25, 28–32, 176–78; seen as animals, 46, 48–49, 55, 62–63. *See also* ex-colonized, the

neocolonialism, xxiii, xxvii, xxviii, 66, 130; nationalism and, 36, 266n21; U.S. bases as symbol of, 57–58, 64. *See also* colonialism

neoimperialism, xxiii, 55, 62–63, 64, 65, 239. *See also* imperialism

neoliberalism, 65, 66, 97, 98, 104; economic policies of, 98, 100, 209, 254n33, 267n37. *See also* liberalism

New York City (NY), Makati compared to, 207, 208, 209, 232

Nguyen, Viet Thanh, 255n4

Nixon, Richard M., 35

nostalgia, 43, 92–93, 114, 120, 121, 128

nuclear weapons: testing, 19–24; on U.S. bases, 45, 49, 65

Oedipal configurations, 100, 101, 129
Of Different Races (Magkaibang lahi), xiii–xvi, xvii, xviii–xx, xxiii, xxix
Olongapo . . . The Great American Dream (Exit Subic), 70–71, 82–91, 99, 103–4, 253n5, 254n28
Once a Moth (Minsa'y isang gamugamo), 33, 34, 39–52, 55, 62, 63, 66, 254n21, 260n48
Orapronobis, 184, 263n18
O'Regan, Tom, xxx, 262n8
Orientalism, tropes of, 172, 175, 176, 187
Ortega, Kenny (*Michael Jackson's This Is It*) (film, U.S.), 238
Overbey, David, 171
overkill factor, 22

Pablo, Crisaldo (*Bathhouse*), 172
parental substitution fantasy, 76–77, 82, 85–86, 93, 99, 102, 103. *See also* family romance fantasy
parents, xxviii, 71, 87; first-generation immigrant, 137, 139–50, 153, 155, 156, 166–67. *See also* fathers, American; homeland: parental; mothers, Filipino
patriarchy, xvi, 93, 146; alternatives to, 104, 239; colonial, 58, 97, 98; failures of, 24–27, 141, 159, 163, 164; Filipino, 86, 88, 221; nationalist, 9, 108, 127, 133, 239; rejection of, 100, 101–2, 140–41, 143; renewal of, 95, 128–29, 130, 147–48; women's relationship to, 108, 119–20, 135, 229
patriotism, 119, 160–61, 165
Pearl S. Buck Foundation, 73

People Power Revolution of 1986, 64, 103, 110–23, 133, 182, 183, 187, 197
peripheral corruption scenario, 231, 233
periphery, xxx, 201; metropole and, 205–6, 214, 229–30, 231, 232–33. *See also* bases, U.S. military: life on periphery of
Peters, John Durham, 121
Phil-American Boy (Batang PX), 70, 91–102, 252n4
Philippine–American relations: films about, xix–xx, xxiii, 7, 78; future of, 73–74, 79–82; postcolonial, xv–xviii, 31–32, 35, 70, 80, 90, 155; transformation of, 97, 98; U.S. military bases' effects on, 37, 42, 60–65; war on terror and, 158, 160, 164, 165
Philippine–American War, 8, 250n60
Philippines: American films made in, 3–32; constitution of 1987, 64, 65, 264n35; culture of, 63, 138, 142–43, 149, 161, 167, 238; dependence on U.S., xvi–xviii, 34, 38, 77–78, 98; Filipino Americans as outsiders in, 150–57; history of, 138, 167; laws of, 229; political repression in, 121, 182, 184, 251n71, 251n73, 263n17; sovereignty of, 34, 35, 36, 39–42, 60–65. *See also* cinema, Philippine; homeland; middle class: Filipino; nation-state, Philippine; People Power Revolution of 1986
Philippines 2000 program, 97–98
Phone Booth, 158
Pichel, Manuel, 268n60

politicians, Filipino, 61–64
politico-voyeuristic curiosity, 175, 180
politics, 241n7, 245n21; cultural, 138, 148, 154, 159, 216, 258n9; gay, 173, 183, 188–90, 192, 194, 196–97; gender, 109, 123, 188, 192, 197, 229, 256n10; of identity, 164–65; of modernity, 46, 52, 249n41; nationalist, 109, 123; of pornography, 180–88, 196, 197; sexual, 188, 190. *See also* agitprop films; biopolitics; thanatopolitics
pornography: politics of, 180–88, 196, 197; Third-World, 175–76, 262n11. See also *John Wayne Bobbit Uncut*
Portes, Gil (*'Merika*), 107, 108, 109–23, 124, 126, 129, 132, 133, 137, 256n11
postcolonialism, 70, 82; culture of, xix, xxvii; decolonization and, 103–4, 242n27; Filipino American perspective on, 31–32, 138; films of, xx–xxi, 241n8, 244n1; future of, 71–74; subjectivities of, 81–82, 127. *See also* ex-colonized, the; ex-colonizers
postnationalism, 89, 103–4. *See also* nationalism/nationalists, Philippine
poverty, 49, 184, 186, 187, 196. *See also* slums, Philippine; Third World: squalor of
Pratt, Mary Louise, 241n3, 267n40
Private Show, 185
prostitution: children resulting from, 83, 84, 92; child/teenage, 161, 180; female, xiv, 178, 181, 190; male, 172–92; as path to immigration, 53, 57, 85–86; on periphery of U.S. military bases, 53, 61, 62; poverty as cause of, 187; violence related to, 55, 57–58. *See also* sex workers
Pulido, Rod (*The Flip Side*), 135, 136, 137, 150–57, 158, 161, 166, 167
PX, 33, 34, 52–60, 62, 63

queer, use of term, 188, 264n40. *See also* homosexuality
Quintos, Rory: *Dubai*, 131, 235–36, 237; *I Need You*, 132
Quito, Gil, 256n13

race/racism, issues of, 133, 138, 140–41, 151, 159–60, 165. *See also* Amerasians; children: mixed-race; Filipino Americans; minorities; self, the: racialized
Ramos, Fidel, 97–98, 100
rape: in films, 61, 65–66, 67, 178, 228; marital, 224; by U.S. Marine, 35–36, 237
redemption, 70–74; by American fathers, 75–76, 81, 98, 103; in *Hellow, Soldier*, 74–82; in *Olongapo . . . The Great American Dream*, 82–91
repatriation, xix, 109, 110–23, 127, 128–32, 133, 236
Republic of the Philippines (RP). *See* Philippines
repudiation. *See* fathers, American: repudiation of; homeland: repudiation of; mothers, Filipino: repudiation of
Restivo, Angelo, xxx, 176, 262n12
revenge, 50, 52, 72–73, 194. *See also* taking it on the face

Reyes, Emmanuel, 90, 219, 254n28, 256n11, 263n18
Reyes, Jose Javier: *Hopefully, Once More*, 257n28; *Phil-American Boy*, 70, 91–102, 104, 252n4
Robertson, Roland, xxiv
Rofel, Lisa, 214
rogue states, 28, 30, 165
Romero, Eddie, 3, 5–6, 7, 28, 245n19; *Beast of Blood*, 7, 27–31; *Black Mama, White Mama*, 4, 5; *Cavalry Command*, 4, 8; *Mad Doctor of Blood Island*, 7, 24–27; *Walls of Hell*, 5
Roño, Chito: *Is it a Sin to Worship You?*, 199–201, 203, 205, 207–19, 220, 231, 232, 233; *Olongapo . . . The Great American Dream*, 70–71, 82–91, 99, 103–4, 253n5, 254n28; *Private Show*, 185
Rose, Jacqueline, xxi–xxii, 261n56
RP–U.S. mutual defense treaty, 37, 42

Sa kuko ng agila. See *In the Claws of an Eagle*
Salonga, Lea, 110, 124, 128, 130
Sana maulit muli (film). See *Hopefully, Once More*
Sana maulit muli (theme song), 130, 257n34
Santiago, Cirio H., 3, 4, 6, 250n57
Sartre, Jean-Paul, xxiv, 59
schlock films, 3, 9. See also Blood Island (Isla de Sangre) films
Schmitt, Carl, 37, 248n14
Schumacher, Joel, *Phone Booth*, 158
science fiction horror films, xviii, 3–32, 33, 239, 247n47
Scott, James, xxvii
secret wars. See cold war: U.S. tactics of
self, the, 36, 93, 147, 239; Filipino American, 135–36, 157, 158; racialized, 127, 138, 151, 157, 164, 165
self-loathing, Filipino American, 158–67
self-sufficiency, fantasy of, 97, 100
September 11, 2001, attacks, aftermath of, 160–61, 164, 165
Service (*Serbis*), 172
servicemen, U.S. See bases, U.S. military
sexploitation films, 4
sex tourists, 175
sexuality: female, 108–9, 119, 126; identity of, 190, 214, 264n40. See also eroticism
sexual relations, xiv, 26, 30, 226, 269n64; deprivation of, 12, 13, 14
sex workers, 177–80, 181, 184, 185, 187, 193. See also prostitution
Sheehan, Harry, 180
Shen nu. See *Goddess*
Sherzer, Dina, 244n1
Shimakawa, Karen, 159
Shohat, Ella, 242n23
Sibak. See *Midnight Dancers*
slums, Philippine, 75, 76, 77, 82, 103, 197. See also Third World; squalor of
Smith, Daniel, 65, 67
Smith, Kevin (*Clerks*), 150
social conditions, films commenting on, 175, 180–88, 194, 195–96, 202
social engineering, 10, 14, 16, 17, 19
social justice, 113, 263n29
Solito, Auraes (*The Blossoming of Maximo Oliveros*), 196
Sontag, Susan, 247n47

Southeast Asia. *See* Asia, U.S. presence in
South Korea, xxix–xxx
sovereign exception, American, 36–52, 65–66, 67. *See also* exceptionalism, American
sovereignty, 248n14, 248n21, 251n65; Philippine, 34, 35, 36, 39–42, 60–65
Soviet Union, cinema in, 46, 250n43
spectatorship. *See* audiences, domestic; foreign markets, Philippine films made for; United States: Philippine films made for
specularization, 214, 216
Spivak, Gayatri, xxiii, 137, 156, 242n27
spousal abuse, 219, 222, 224–31, 268n60
Stackha. See *Strike*
state, the, xxi, 37–38, 98, 164, 184, 187, 237
Stoler, Ann Laura, 72, 86, 94, 95, 100
Strand Releasing, 192, 265n51
Strike (*Stackha*), 46, 250n43
Subic Bay naval base, 35–36, 49, 52–60
subjectivities: critical, 138, 166; formation of, 146; imperial, 12, 93; minority, 159–60; postcolonial, 81–82, 88, 89, 127; split, 121–23
subjugation, themes of, 13, 17, 138
Sundance Film Festival, Philippine films shown at, 150, 196
superficiality, 214, 216

Tadiar, Neferti, xxi–xxii
Taiwan, films from, xxviii–xxix
taking it on the face, 211, 213–14, 216, 219, 232
Tan, Raymond, 64
Tarantino, Quentin, 3, 4, 6
Tatlo, dalawa, isa. See *Three, Two, One*
Taylor, Charles, 258n9
telenovelas, 238
television, Philippine films made for, 4
Terror is a Man, 7, 9–18, 19, 246n37
terrorism/terrorists. *See* Marcos, Ferdinand: reign of terror; Muslims: terrorist activities of; war on terror
thanatopolitics, 46, 50, 52, 53, 58, 250n63
Third World, 164, 167; challenge to the metropole, 229–30; cinema in, 200, 240; cultural production of, 180, 205–6, 238; exhibitionism in, 174, 183–84; First World's relationship with, 208, 231, 232–33; Hollywood remakes in, 214, 219; kitsch of, 87, 140, 177; pornography in, 175–76, 181, 189; squalor of, 74, 161, 165, 175, 194, 196, 262n11; West's relationship with, xxv, 30, 66, 98; women in, 221–22, 229–31. *See also* slums, Philippine
This Is the Way It Was . . . How Is It Today?, 5
Three, Two, One (*Tatlo, dalawa, isa*), 70. See also *Hellow, Soldier*
Thriller (music video), 238
thriller films, 33, 52, 53, 58, 158
Tolentino, Rolando, 138, 175, 263n17
Tomlinson, John, xxiv, 208, 220, 269n69

toro (sex shows), 185
Torok, Maria, 261n56
Toronto Film Festival, Philippine films shown at, 173
transculturation, xix, 214, 241n3, 267n40
transgenerational haunting, 53, 159, 261n56
translation. *See* cultural translation; expedient translation
transmutation. *See* complex transmutations
transnationalism, xxiv, 89, 149, 167, 180–88, 269n67. *See also* cinema, Philippine: transnational; culture(s): transnational; feminism: transnational
trapos (kitchen rags), 62. *See also* politicians, Filipino
true crime films, 219, 221, 224
Twilight Dancers, 195

United States, xxix, 202; anticommunist containment, 19, 28, 34, 251n73; benevolence of, xiii, xxix, 33, 34, 41, 42, 43, 65–66, 67; cold war tactics of, xxviii, 22, 28, 30–31, 37, 42; culture of, 7–8, 136, 149, 151, 237–38; Filipino Americans as outsiders in, 109, 140, 151, 165; Filipino images of, xix, 107; free trade policies of, 98, 204; immigration policies, 73, 136; militarism of, xxiii, 66, 116, 251n73; Philippine films made for, 3–32, 171–97, 199; Philippine films made in, xviii, 135–67; Philippines' dependence on, xvi–xviii, 34, 38, 77–78, 98; racism in, 133, 138, 151, 159–60, 165; repressed history of imperial activities, 3, 7–8, 9, 31–32, 245n21. *See also* American dream; bases, U.S. military; fantasies, American; middle class: American; multiculturalism: American; Philippine–American relations; sovereign exception, American

vampire films, 4
Velez, Vivian, 207, 211, 213, 214, 215
Vera, Noel, 128
video, Philippine films made for, 196
vigilante groups, 182, 184
Villavicencio, Raquel, 219
violence: cycles of, 55, 57; of decolonization, 58; of empire, 12, 23, 32, 33, 35, 41, 59; military, 42, 186, 251n73, 263n18; of neocolonialism, xxvii; related to prostitution, 178. *See also* rape; spousal abuse; war on terror
visibility, 172, 173, 197
Visiting Forces Agreement (VFA), 35–36
visuality, 172, 187, 262n12
Vizconde Massacre Story, The: God Help Us!, 219
voyeurism, 187, 196. *See also* politico-voyeuristic curiosity
Vrechek, Frank, 88, 89, 253n5

Walls of Hell, The, 5
war films, xxiii, 4, 5, 8
war on terror, 66, 158, 160–61, 164, 165
Waugh, Thomas, 183

West, the: culture of, 205; gay politics in, 190; immigration to, 236, 237; imperialist role of, 32; mobility in, 131; Philippine films made for, 171–97; repudiation of, xxiv–xxv, 89, 101, 162; Third World's relationship to, xxv, 240, 262n11. *See also* First World; United States

whiteness, 145, 151, 174; desire for, 69–70, 74, 75–76, 79, 85–86, 103. *See also* fathers, American

woman's films, 4, 108, 119, 121, 123, 126, 128–29

women, 192, 251n71, 256n10; gutsy, 29, 30, 32; liberation of, 108, 123–33, 229–31; mobilization of, 119–20, 121; Philippine subordination of, 119–20, 123, 132; Third World exploitation of, 221–22. *See also* feminine, the; feminism; migrant women

Wood, Leonard, 73
Wood, Robin, 9, 23, 32
Worcester, Dean, 17
World Bank, 267n37
World War II: Bataan death march, 42–43, 154–55, 249n29, 260n48; devastation of Philippines during, xvi–xvii, 38, 77–78; films of, xxiii, 4, 5, 8; Japanese American internment, 160; lack of benefits for Filipino veterans, 154, 237
Wu, Yonggang (*Goddess*), 251n71

Xing, Jun, 167

Yang, Edward (*A Brighter Summer Day*), xxviii–xxix
Yúdice, George, 204
yuppies, 207–9, 210, 216–17

Zulueta, Dawn, 207, 211, 213

JOSÉ B. CAPINO is assistant professor of English and cinema studies and affiliate in gender and women's studies at the University of Illinois at Urbana–Champaign.